Old Testament Theology in Outline

OLD TESTAMENT
THEOLOGY
IN
OUTLINE

WITHDRAWN

by

Walther Zimmerli

Translated by David E. Green

T. & T. CLARK LTD
36 GEORGE STREET, EDINBURGH

*To the University of Strassburg,
with which I am now associated as a
Docteur de l'Université de Strasbourg h. c.,
I gratefully dedicate this book.*

The German original of this book was published under
the title *Grundriss der alttestamentlichen Theologie* by
Kohlhammer Verlag, Stuttgart.

Abbreviations

ANET	*Ancient Near Eastern Texts Relating to the Old Testament.* Edited by J. B. Pritchard. Princeton: Princeton University Press, 1950.
*AOT*²	*Altorientalische Texte.* 2d ed. Edited by Hugo Gressmann. Berlin: Walter de Gruyter, 1926.
ARM	*Archives royales de Mari.* Paris: Imprimerie nationale, 1950ff.
HO	*Handbuch der Orientalistik.* Edited by Bertold Spuler. Leiden: Brill, 1948ff.
KAI	*Kanaanäische und aramäische Inschriften.* Edited by Herbert Donner and Wolfgang Röllig. Wiesbaden: Harrassowitz, 1968–71.
MT	masoretic text
pi	piel
TGI	*Textbuch zur Geschichte Israels.* Edited by Kurt Galling. Tübingen: Mohr, 1950.

Contents

Preface

Any "Old Testament theology in outline" must do two things. It must deal with the most important narrative complexes of the Old Testament. At the same time, it must lead readers to bring together in their own minds the diverse statements the Old Testament makes about God, who wishes to be known not as a manifold God but as the one Yahweh. The limited compass of an "outline" imposes an unpleasant burden on both purposes. It is necessary to be selective. No selection will gain universal approval. Certain things must be emphasized when one thinks one has found a statement of essential points. This emphasis unavoidably presupposes a certain overall understanding of the Old Testament not shared by all. The present "outline," which the author would like to see followed by a more exhaustive presentation of Old Testament theology as a whole, presupposes that in Old Testament prophecy the confrontation between Yahweh and his people Israel achieves its radical depths, revealing not only the fundamental nature of the God of Israel, to whom the Old Testament bears witness even where the explicit term "God of Israel" recedes into the background, but also revealing the fundamental nature of humanity's encounter with this God.

It is not the purpose of this "outline" to talk "about" the Old Testament, but to bring to the fore what the Old Testament itself has to say. It is therefore crucially important that those who use this book keep an open Old Testament handy, read for themselves the texts under discussion, compare the texts (cited very selectively) originating elsewhere in the ancient Near East, and if possible make use of a Hebrew lexicon as well. In order to introduce the reader unacquainted with Hebrew to the Hebrew conceptuality in its Hebrew dress, the (unvocalized) Hebrew words have also been cited in transliteration. As a rule, only the consonants of the Hebrew roots themselves are given. Proper names follow the Revised Standard Version Bible.

The bibliographies presented a problem, since completeness was totally out of the question. I decided to cite works in the following four categories: (1) Certain classic monographs that must be taken into account by anyone concerned to understand what the Old Testament says (such as those of Gunkel, Mowinckel, Noth, von Rad, etc.). (2) Articles and monographs in which more extensive bibliographies give the reader access to more complete information. Among works in this category, the first volume of the *Theologisches Handwörterbuch zum Alten Testament (THAT)* and the first four fascicles of the *Theologisches Wörterbuch zum Alten Testament (ThWAT,* vol. 1, cols. 1–512) were available to me before completion of the manuscript. (3) More specialized articles or monographs mentioned in the text. (4) A few articles and monographs containing a fuller discussion of statements that often could only be stated thetically within the limited compass of an "outline," without a detailed analysis of other views. At the end of each section, works are cited in the order they are mentioned in the text. Reasons of space also precluded explicit reference at every point to the more recent presentations of the theology of the Old Testament, as well as citations of the standard commentaries. The informed reader will probably realize how much the present outline owes to them, and above all how much it is the outgrowth of constant dialogue, in both agreement and disagreement, with Gerhard von Rad's *Old Testament Theology,* from which much has been learned with gratitude.

The reader is presumed to be familiar with the problems dealt with in introductory studies and in the history of Israel, since these disciplines are dealt with in other volumes of the series in which this work was originally published.

The distinction of Deuteronomy (found in the book by the same name), the deuteronomist (found in the Deuteronomistic History), and the more general deuteronomistic literature, representing a broader intellectual milieu, is a thorny problem. They have been distinguished according to the author's best judgment, albeit not to his complete satisfaction.

I dedicate this summary outline in gratitude to the University of Strassburg, whose Old Testament scholar Edmond Jacob has given us a more detailed presentation of the *Thèmes essentiels d'une Théologie de l'Ancien Testament.* The association I have always had with Strassburg through my mother has been vitalized by their academic recognition.

I wish to thank Dr. Christian Jeremias for his assistance in reading the proofs and Siegmund Böhmer for preparing the index of passages.

Göttingen, end of July 1972   W. ZIMMERLI

The text of the first edition has been reviewed once more; a few changes have been made, and some additional bibliographical references have been added. Besides some minor additions, a passage has been added on the theology of the Chronicler (p. 182). The chapter dealing with Old Testament apocalypticism (§22) has been almost totally rewritten.

Göttingen, beginning of March 1975   W. ZIMMERLI

Purpose and Scope

Any "Old Testament theology" has the task of presenting what the Old Testament says about God as a coherent whole.

The collection of documents constituting the Old Testament was not preserved and handed down as the fortuitous literary heritage of ancient Israel. It was assembled as a canon ("rule"). The term "law," occasionally found in the New Testament as a designation for the Old Testament as a whole, derives from the Hebrew word *tôrâ* (תורה), best translated "instruction." The Hebrew canon exhibits three rings of growth. The innermost, the Torah in the narrow sense (Genesis to Deuteronomy), was accorded the greatest honor when read in the synagogue. The second, the "Prophets" (the narrative books from Joshua through 2 Kings, the books of the literary prophets Isaiah, Jeremiah, and Ezekiel, and the Book of the Twelve), was read as historical exposition of the Torah. The third, to which the colorless term "Writings" was applied, finally came to include materials of many different types (Psalms, Proverbs, Job, the five "Festival Scrolls," the apocalyptic book of Daniel, and the late double narrative of the Chronicler: Ezra—Nehemiah and Chronicles).

Somewhat earlier, the Greek-speaking Jews of Egypt brought together in their Greek Bible, the so-called Septuagint (LXX), a canon more extensive than the Hebrew canon. This larger collection of Scriptures was then taken over by the Vulgate; in 1546, by decree of the Council of Trent, it was defined as the form of the Old Testament sanctioned by the Catholic Church. The churches of the Reformation, under the influence of humanism but also for reasons of theological content, went back to the Hebrew canon. Some of the additional documents of the "Apocrypha" were appended by Luther to his translation of the Bible as "books not thought equal with the Holy Scriptures and yet useful and good to read."

The following presentation of Old Testament theology is based on the Hebrew-Aramaic canon.

Approach

The Old Testament comprises a set of documents that came into being over a period of almost a thousand years. During this period Israel, from whose world the documents contained in the Old Testament derive, underwent many changes. Nomadic beginnings give way to settled life in Canaan. Herdsmen become farmers and also infiltrate earlier urban cultures. A loose association of the groups constituting Israel in the period before there was any state develops into a state, first as a single kingdom, then as two. The latter are destroyed by the blows of the great powers, first the Assyrians and then the Neo-Babylonians. The people lose their identity as a separate state; a major portion of the intellectual leadership lives in distant exile in Mesopotamia. Then a new entity, something like an ecclesiastical state, consolidates itself around Jerusalem, first under Persian, then under Macedonian-Greek hegemony.

The change in sociological structures produced changes in liturgical life, resulting finally in the elimination of a multiplicity of sanctuaries and focusing on Jerusalem. And of course, alongside of this, the exile forced the establishment of places of worship in distant lands. Modern scholarship has revealed how this historical movement has its inward aspect in the faith of Israel. Religious traditions in new situations find new interpretations. According to the law of challenge and response, a new historical challenge brings about a novel formulation of the response.

A presentation of Old Testament theology cannot close its eyes to all this movement and change, the more so in that it is characteristic of the faith of the Old Testament not to live with its back turned to the world and to history, turning inward to guard its arcanum, but rather to relate closely to the world and the course of events and engage in dialogue with whatever it encounters in history.

On the other hand, this raises the question of whether the "coherent whole" of what the Old Testament says about God, which it is the task of an Old Testament theology to present, consists merely in the continuity of history, that is, the ongoing stream of historical sequence.

The Old Testament itself makes a different claim: it firmly maintains its faith in the sameness of the God it knows by the name of Yahweh. Throughout all changes, it maintains that this God Yahweh takes an active interest in his people Israel. In the face of all vexation and anguish, when "the right hand of the Most High" seems to have lost its power (Ps. 77:11), the devout person takes refuge in this confession and "remembers" the former works of Yahweh (Ps. 77:12). Here, in Yahweh himself, who has made himself known in his deeds of bygone days, this faith believes it can find the true and authentic continuity on which it can rely.

Thus it is advisable to turn our attention first to this central focus, where alone we find the inner continuity acknowledged by the faith of Israel itself. But a second point must be added at once. This faith knows that Yahweh was not the God of Israel from the beginning of the world. In the account of how the world began, Israel does not yet appear in the great table of nations displayed in Genesis 10. Not until Genesis 12, with the beginning of the story of Abraham, and in the "fathers" descended from him, do we begin to hear distant echoes of the promise of the history of Israel. According to Genesis 32:29 (35:10), the name "Israel" is given first to the patriarch Jacob. With the beginning of the book of Exodus we encounter Israel as a people.

This striking phenomenon goes hand in hand with another. As early as Genesis 2:4*b*, that is, in the context of the story of how the world began, the earliest source stratum, J, speaks quite artlessly of Yahweh as creator of the world. But the two other narrative strands, E and P, on the other hand, know that the name "Yahweh" was first revealed to Moses, when he was commissioned to lead Israel out of Egypt. This obviously preserves the correct recollection that there can be no talk of the Yahweh of the Old Testament until he reveals himself as the God of Israel and accomplishes the deliverance of Israel from Egypt.

From this perspective, too, it is advisable to take as our point of departure that focal point where the faith of the Old Testament specifically confesses the God of Israel under the name of Yahweh. It will be clearly evident that this "focal point" does not present an "image" of God to be understood statically. The God who is invoked by the name "Yahweh" repeatedly demonstrates his freedom by dashing to pieces all the "images" in which humanity would confine him. This takes place not only in Exodus 3:14, in the account of how the divine name is revealed to Moses, but to an equal degree in the great prophets, or, in the realm of wisdom, in Ecclesiastes and Job.

Zimmerli, Walther. "Alttestamentliche Traditionsgeschichte und Theologie." In *Probleme biblischer Theologie* (Festschrift Gerhard von Rad), pp. 632–647. Edited by Hans Walter Wolff. Munich: Kaiser, 1971. Reprinted in his *Studien zur alttestamentlichen Theologie und Prophetie*, pp.

9–26. Theologische Bücherei, vol. 51. Munich: Kaiser, 1974.—Smend, Rudolf. *Die Mitte des Alten Testaments.* Theologische Studien, vol. 101. Zurich: EVZ, 1970.—Hasel, G. F. "The Problem of the Center in the Old Testament Theology Debate." *Zeitschrift für die Alttestamentliche Wissenschaft* 86 (1974):65–82.—Zimmerli, Walther. "Zum Problem der 'Mitte des Alten Testamentes.' " *Evangelische Theologie* 35 (1975):97–118.

I. Fundamentals

"I am Yahweh, your God, who brought you out of the land of Egypt, the house of servitude. You shall have no other gods beside me." (Exod. 20:2–3; Deut. 5:6–7)

At the beginning of the great revelation to Israel at Sinai, the mountain of God, stands the proclamation of the Decalogue, introduced with full solemnity by the words quoted above. The God who here appears in the storm makes himself known through his name, recalling at the same time his act of delivering Israel from servitude. On the basis of this act his people may and shall know him.

The recollection of this deliverance and the subsequent journey to Canaan under the guidance of God, which re-echoes in later summaries and creed-like statements, constituted the nucleus of what is today the monstrously expanded first portion of the canon, the Pentateuch. It is therefore advisable in the fundamental exposition of this introductory section to take as our point of departure Yahweh (§1), the God of Israel since Egypt (§2). We shall then turn our attention to the discussion of the God of the fathers (§3), which precedes this nucleus, and of the creator of the world (§4), proclaimed in the primal history. We shall conclude by treating the theologoumena of election (§5) and covenant (§6), which describe in more detail the relationship between Yahweh and Israel.

§1 The Revealed Name

The faith of the Old Testament knows its God by the name of Yahweh. This pronunciation of the tetragrammaton (יהוה), which is no longer recorded in the masoretic vocalization, can be shown to be highly probable on the basis of evidence from the church fathers.

The passages that deliberately avoid speaking of Yahweh by name can as a rule be understood on the basis of specific considerations. E and P do not speak of Yahweh before the time of Moses because of a specific view of the history of revelation, which will be discussed below. The elimination of the name of Yahweh from the so-called Elohistic psalter (Psalms 42—83) is the result of editorial revision probably based on a dread of pronouncing the holy name of

God. In Judaism, this tendency later resulted in a total avoidance of pronouncing the tetragrammaton. This tendency appears also to have been at work in the book of Esther. In the book of Job, the name of Yahweh is avoided in the discourses of chapters 3—37 because the discussion is between non-Israelites; it is replaced by the more general terms אֱלוֹהַּ *ĕlôah* or שַׁדַּי *šaddai*. The introductions to the speeches of God and the framework narrative in chapters 1—2 and 42 use the name of Yahweh without hesitation. Elsewhere, too, as in the Joseph story, the name of Yahweh is not placed in the mouth of non-Israelites. In Ecclesiastes, the name is probably avoided because the wise man in question prefers to distance himself from God (see below, pp. 161–163). In the book of Daniel, too, the final chapters show clearly that the Lord referred to as "God of Heaven" or "the Most High God" or simply as "God" is none other than he who is called by the name of Yahweh. The prayer in Daniel 9 uses the name "Yahweh" quite naturally.

For the audience of the Old Testament, a "name" is more than a randomly selected label. Those who are named are vulnerable; they can be invoked by means of their name. Two questions arise in this context:

1. How does the faith of the Old Testament come by its knowledge of the name of its God? The Old Testament can be heard to give various answers:

a) J uses the name "Yahweh" without hesitation even in the primal history and the patriarchal narratives.

In the context of J, the statement in Genesis 4:26 stands out: in the days of Enosh, who represents the third human generation, people began to call on the name of Yahweh. Since the name "Enosh," like "Adam," can simply mean "man," it is possible there was an earlier version according to which Yahweh was called upon in the generation of the very first man. According to Horst, the present text can be understood on the basis of the distinction common in comparative religion between the high god present from the beginning (i. e., the creator) and the god that people call upon in the cult of the historical present. The special contribution of the Old Testament would then be the statement that the creator and the god called upon in worship are the same Yahweh.

b) E and P take a different approach. Each in its own way represents a specific view of how the name of Yahweh was revealed. According to both, this takes place in the time of Moses, the initial period of Israel's history as already mentioned. According to E, it is at the mountain of God that Moses learns to invoke God by name; in the earlier narratives the general term אֱלֹהִים *ĕlôhîm*, "God," was used, which could also be applied to non-Israelite deities. When Moses is commanded to lead his enslaved people out of Egypt, he asks the name of the God under whom this is to happen; the name of Yahweh is communicated to him in a veiled way that will be considered in more detail below (Exod. 3:1, 4b, 6, 9–15).

c) P, whose peculiar organization of God's history with Israel will be discussed in more detail later (see below, pp. 55–57), exhibits a process by which the name of God is revealed in three stages. Like E, P uses the general term אֱלֹהִים *ĕlôhîm* at the outset when referring to the acts of God in the primordial era. According to Genesis 17:1, however, God reveals himself to Abraham, the earliest of the patriarchs of Israel, under the name שַׁדַּי אֵל *ēl* šaddai (see below, p. 41). Then, according to Exodus 6:2ff., he encounters Moses with equal spontaneity, introducing himself of his own accord under his name Yahweh, while referring explicitly to Genesis 17: "I am Yahweh. To Abraham, Isaac, and Jacob I appeared under the name שׁדּי אל *ēl šaddai,* but in my name Yahweh I was not made known to them." This passage expresses most emphatically the sponaneity and novelty of the revelation of the name Yahweh. The name by which Israel may call upon its God does not simply lie ready to hand for people to use. Neither, as in E, is it given in response to a human question; it is the free gift of the God who sends his people their deliverer, thereby forging a bond between himself and them (Exod. 6:7).

2. Does the name of Yahweh, which Israel calls upon, reveal something of the nature of this God?

To answer this question, we must distinguish two directions of inquiry. (a) Quite apart from the statements made by the Old Testament texts themselves, we can inquire whether philological investigation can give us any information about the original meaning of the name "Yahweh." But of course an answer in these terms need by no means have any relevance for the faith of the Old Testament. The name might have taken shape in a totally different context. This does not hold true in the same way, however, if (b) we ask whether the Old Testament context itself says anything about the meaning of the name. With such a statement, whatever its original philological accuracy may be, we are in any case dealing with an actual statement of the Old Testament that is significant for an Old Testament theology.

a) There is no lack of suggestions about what the name "Yahweh" originally meant.

Philological investigation must first deal with the question of whether we should take as our point of departure the long form "Yahweh," an abbreviated form "Yahu" as found in many names (יְשַׁעְיָהוּ *yša'yāhû;* ירמיהו *yirm'yāhû;* יהויקים *y'hôyāqîm,* etc.), or the monosyllabic form "Yah," as found, for instance, in the acclamation "Hallelujah" (הללו יה *hal'lû yâ*). Driver claimed that he could interpret the form "Yah" as a shout of ecstatic excitement, which then turned into a divine name and, in association with the deliverance from Egypt, became the long form with the meaning "he who is" or "he who calls into being." Eerdmans derives the name from a disyllabic form, in which he hears what was originally an onomatopoetic imitation of thunder. There are good reasons to consider the long form original; it probably represents an imperfect form of a verb הוה *hwh.* But is this root related to the Arabic verb meaning "blow," which would suggest the name of a storm god, or to the verb meaning "fall," which would suggest a god of lightning and hail? Or should we take הוה *hwh* as equivalent to היה *hyh* and interpret it as "he is" or "he shows himself efficacious" or "he calls into being"? And are we then to follow Cross in thinking of an abbreviated form of the more complete יהוה צבאות *yahweh ṣ'bā'ôt,* "he who calls the (heavenly) hosts into being" (see below, p. 75)? It is unlikely that we are dealing with a noun form having the meaning "being."

b) We come next to the actual statements of the Old Testament itself. When Moses asks the name of the God who sends him to Israel, he is given, according to Exodus 3:14, the answer: אֶהְיֶה אֲשֶׁר אֶהְיֶה *ehyeh ăšer ehyeh* ("I am who I am . . . and so you shall say to the Israelites, 'I am [אֶהְיֶה*ehyeh*] has sent me to you' "). Here the name "Yahweh" is unequivocally interpreted on the basis of the verb הָיָה *hyh* (= הָוָה *hwh*).

This passage, therefore, has provided the basis for most attempts to interpret the name in a way consonant with the faith of the Old Testament. The Septuagint led the way with its translation *egō eimi ho ón*, "I am the one who is," transforming the verbal expression into a nominal participle and, following Greek example, finding an ontological concept of being in Exodus 3:14. It was probably sensed, however, how inappropriate this concept was within the framework of Old Testament thought. Scholars have therefore gone on to ask whether הָיָה *hyh* might not be better taken to mean "be efficacious" (Ratschow), "be there, be present" (Vriezen), "be with someone" (Preuss).

But the name "Yahweh" is here not meant to be understood on the basis of the isolated verb הָיָה *hyh*, but rather on the basis of the figure of speech "I am who I am." This form may be compared to the lordly statement of Exodus 33:19: "To whom I am gracious I am gracious, and to whom I show mercy I show mercy." In this figure of speech resounds the sovereign freedom of Yahweh, who, even at the moment he reveals himself in his name, refuses simply to put himself at the disposal of humanity or to allow humanity to comprehend him. We must also take into account God's refusal to impart his name to Jacob in Genesis 32:30: "Why do you ask about my name?" According to the statement of Exodus 3:14, at the very point where Yahweh reveals his true name so that people can call him by it, he remains free, and can be properly understood only in the freedom with which he introduces himself.

This knowledge, which also lies behind God's free revelation of his name in Exodus 6:2 (P), coming not in response to any human question, was given further expression in certain characteristic Priestly turns of phrase. In the laws of the Holiness Code in Leviticus 18ff., the legislation is underlined by copious use of the appended phrase "I am Yahweh" or "I am Yahweh, your God." Here, in the context of proclamation of the law, this formulaic phrase of self-introduction maintains the majesty of him who issues the law, who encounters people as their Lord. It is possible to ask, even if a definitive answer cannot be given, whether there were occasions in the liturgical life of Israel when this free self-introduction of Yahweh in his name was publicly spoken (by the priests?). The preamble to the Decalogue with its אֱלֹהֶיךָ יְהוָה אָנֹכִי *ánōkî yahweh ĕlōhêkā* may also support this suggestion.

In a different way this element entered into the prophetical formulation of the so-called "proof-saying" (*Erweiswort*), found repeatedly in the book of Ezekiel but apparently originating in earlier pre-literary prophecy and its messages from God in the context of the Yahweh war (1 Kings 20:13, 28). Here a statement of what Yahweh will do with or for his people (expanded by the addition of a motivation or stated without any motivation at all) can be concluded with the formula: "And you [he, they] will know that I am Yahweh." This formula declares the announced action of Yahweh to be the place where people will know—and acknowledge—Yahweh as he introduces himself. Yahweh declares himself in what he does. This rhetorical form is also found in Joel and the late exilic Deutero-Isaiah (see Isa. 49:22–26). See also below, pp. 207, 229.

This freedom of Yahweh means he is never simply an "object," even in his name which he graciously reveals—the third commandment of the Decalogue seeks to protect the freedom implicit in Yahweh's name in a very specific way against "religious" abuse. And this freedom of Yahweh must be taken account of in all other statements about the faith of the Old Testament. In the only passage where the Old Testament itself attempts to provide an explanation of the name "Yahweh," it refuses to "explain" the name in a way that would confine it within the cage of a definition. It seeks to express the fact that we can speak of Yahweh only in attentive acknowledgment of the way he demonstrates his nature (in his acts and his commandments).

Baumgärtel, Friedrich. *Elohim ausserhalb des Pentateuch.* Beiträge zur Wissenschaft vom Alten Testament, vol. 19. Leipzig: Hinrichs, 1914.—Horst, Friedrich. "Die Notiz vom Anfang des Jahwekultes in Gen. 4,26." In *Libertas Christiana* (Festschrift Friedrich Delekat), pp. 68–74. Edited by Walter Matthias. Munich: Kaiser, 1957.—Mayer, Rudolf. "Der Gottesname Jahwe im Lichte der neuesten Forschung." *Biblische Zeitschrift* 2 (1958):26–53.—Eissfeldt, Otto. "Jahwe." In *Die Religion in Geschichte und Gegenwart,* 3d ed., vol. 3, cols. 515–516. Tübingen: Mohr, 1957–65. Includes bibliography to 1959.—Jenni, Ernst. "Jahwe." In *Theologisches Handwörterbuch zum Alten Testament,* vol. 1, cols. 701–707. Edited by Ernst Jenni and Claus Westermann. Munich: Kaiser, 1971.—Ratschow, Carl Heinz. *Werden und Wirken.* Beihefte zur Zeitschrift für die Âlttestamentliche Wissenschaft, vol. 70. Berlin: Töpelmann, 1941.—Preuss, Horst Dietrich." ' . . . ich will mit dir sein.' " *Zeitschrift für die Alttestamentliche Wissenschaft* 80 (1968): 139–173.—Cross, Frank Moore. "Yahweh and the God of the Patriarchs." *Harvard Theological Review* 55 (1962):225–259.—Zimmerli, Walther. "Ich bin Jahwe." In *Geschichte und Altes Testament* (Festschrift Albrecht Alt), pp. 179–209. Tübingen: Mohr, 1953. Reprinted in his *Gottes Offenbarung,* 2d ed., pp. 11–40. Theologische Bücherei, vol. 19. Munich: Kaiser, 1969. —Idem. *Erkenntnis Gottes nach dem Buche Ezechiel.* Abhandlungen zur Theologie des Alten und Neuen Testaments, vol. 27. Zurich: Zwingli, 1954. Reprinted in his *Gottes Offenbarung,* pp. 41–119. —Idem. "Das Wort des göttlichen Selbsterweises (Erweiswort), eine prophetische Gattung." In *Mélanges bibliques rédigés en l'honneur de André Robert,* pp. 154–164. Travaux de l'institut catholique de Paris, vol. 4. Paris: Bloud & Gay, 1957. Reprinted in his *Gottes Offenbarung,* pp. 120–132. —Elliger, Karl. "Ich bin der Herr—euer Gott." In *Theologie als Glaubenswagnis* (Festschrift K. Heim), pp. 9–34. Hamburg: Furche, 1954. Reprinted in his *Kleine Schriften zum Alten Testament,* pp. 211–231. Theologische Bücherei, vol. 32. Munich: Kaiser, 1966.

§2 Yahweh, God of Israel since Egypt

In Hosea 13:4 we hear the words: "I, Yahweh, am your God since the land of Egypt. You do not know any god except for me, or any savior except for me." This statement corresponds in content with the beginning of the Decalogue (Exod. 20:2-3); like the latter passage, it says two things. First, where Yahweh presents himself to the faith of the Old Testament, he does so as the God of Israel, who will not tolerate any other god. And even more clearly than the beginning of the Decalogue it underlines the fact that this "God of Israel" is a relationship that has existed from the beginning of time, in the sense, for instance, that the Babylonian god Shamash was the sun god by definition. Yahweh is the God of Israel by reason of certain historical events associated with the name of Egypt (to which the preamble to the Decalogue adds: "the house of servitude").

This phrase points to the events recorded in the book of Exodus, in which the people of Israel first makes its appearance. Their forebears, as Exodus 1:11 maintains with historical accuracy, were compelled to perform forced labor for the building of the provision cities Pithom and Ramses during the reign of Ramses II (1290-1224 B.C.). Moses, who bears an Egyptian name, led them forth at the command of Yahweh. At the Sea of Reeds they escaped miraculously from the pursuing Egyptians, whose king had refused to let them go. This event is recorded in the earliest hymn preserved in the Old Testament, the Song of Miriam. "Sing to Yahweh, for highly exalted is he; horse and rider he cast into the sea." (Exod. 15:21) What Israel experienced was no piece of chance good fortune such as might be recounted dispassionately. In this experience Israel recognized and confessed Yahweh, who refuses to be worshiped alongside others. The glorification of this initial experience of the exodus also appears in the observation that there is no other event in the entire history of Israel so surrounded by a plethora of miraculous interventions on the part of Yahweh as the event of the deliverance from Egypt. Again and again the description of the exodus makes mention of the "signs and wonders" performed by Yahweh for his people, "with mighty hand and outstretched arm." Then the road leads out into the desert, toward the land that is to be given to Israel. The Old Testament returns again and again to creed-like mentions (von Rad) of this event, in detailed summaries of Yahweh's history with Israel as well as in succinct formulas like the preamble to the Decalogue. When the farmer brings his offering to the sanctuary, he speaks in his prescribed prayer of what Yahweh did for his fathers (Deut. 26:5-10). When a father tries to make the commandments meaningful to his son, he tells of this event (Deut. 6:20ff.). According to Joshua 24, it was spoken of when Israel assembled at Shechem. The poetry of the cult recounts the exodus immediately after speaking of Yahweh's acts at creation (Ps. 136). Commandments in the Holiness Code can be underlined by reference to it (Lev. 22:32-33; 25:55). Even the prophet Ezekiel, narrating the story of Israel's sins, with the two kingdoms personified in two girls with bedouin names, says in Ezekiel 23 that they come from Egypt, where they became Yahweh's own. Cf. also Ezekiel 20; Isaiah 51:9–10.

Alongside such passages, there are a few that state that Yahweh "found Israel in the desert" (Deut. 32:10; Hos. 9:10; cf. Bach). This can hardly refer to a different story of Israel's origins; these passages must be interpreted in the same light. In Ezekiel 16, the motif of the foundling has been incorporated into the story of Jerusalem's beginnings, a story organized very differently.

The student of comparative religion who presses further will find that many questions remain open. First, it is unlikely that the ancestors of all "Israel" (in the later sense of the term) took part in the exodus from Egypt. We are probably dealing only with a small group from one part of the later Israel, roughly the "house of Joseph." But the confession celebrated in the Song of Miriam subsequently captivated all Israel, including Jerusalem, whose own traditions must be discussed later. Other early traditions were in part simply forgotten, in part, with suitable changes, incorporated into this "creed" and subordinated to it. It has been suggested that Joshua 24 preserves a reminiscence of the religious alliance between, on the one hand, the tribes already in the land, to which the name "Israel" may have been attached (cf. the "Israel Stele" of Merneptah, *TGI*[2], pp. 39–40), and, on the other, the group that brought the confession of Yahweh with them from Egypt. This possibility cannot be excluded. It is clear in any case that the name "Yahweh, the God of Israel," based on an earlier אל אלהי ישראל *ēl ĕlōhê yiśrā'ēl*, subsequently had a special association with the altar at Shechem (Gen. 33:20; Josh. 8:30).

Religio-historical investigation suggests likewise that Yahweh was previously worshiped by this name by Midianite groups at the mountain of God out in the desert. Jethro, the priest of Midian, may have played some role in transmitting this faith to Israel (Exod. 18). But even if the divine name "Yahweh" and the mountain of God, which Israel likewise considered sacred at the outset because of its association with Yahweh, trace their origins back to the desert (the Sinai tradition will be discussed in §6), this god only became the God of Israel, of whom the Old Testament speaks, in the celebration of the initial act of deliverance of those brought out of Egypt. No reminiscence of Yahweh on the part of "Israel" goes back beyond this event. For a discussion of the patriarchal narratives, into which the name of Yahweh was later interpolated, see below, §3.

Linguistically, the creed-like statement of the deliverance from Egypt exhibits a twofold form. If we may follow Wijngaards, the use of the term "bring out, lead out" (הוציא *hôṣî'*) in connection with Egypt refers primarily to the act of deliverance, whereas the use of the verb "bring up, lead up" (העלה *he'ĕlâ*) already presupposes the occupation of Canaan and envisages Yahweh's leadership of Israel along their historical road with him.

We must now consider the significance of this fundamental confessional statement for the faith attested by the Old Testament.

1. In the first place, it is quite clear that the Old Testament, however much it thinks of Yahweh as majestic and free, knows this God from the very outset as the God who wants to involve himself with Israel. In the Old Testament we never come across any attempt to inquire into the nature of Yahweh *per se*. This could be observed even in the only passage that reflected on the significance of the name "Yahweh." How the God of Israel acts with respect to his people, with respect to the individual Israelite, and later, as the horizon of religious thought expands in head-on encounter with other forms of religious belief, with respect to all of creation and the nations dominates the Old Testament statements.

2. At the beginning of the exodus story, on which the faith of the Old Testament never ceases to reflect, stands the great deliverance from the house of servitude. It is not really accurate to turn this event into an "exodus principle," which in turn produces a "principle of hope" (Bloch). What is really central is not the fact of the "exodus," which would lead to new forms of "going out" into the future, but the encounter with the God who has pity on those who are enslaved. We often hear the Old Testament speak of the God who hears the crying of the oppressed and sends them their deliverer; this image becomes a category by which subsequent experiences in the history of Israel can be understood (the judges, Saul, David). Therefore even Ezekiel and above all Deutero-Isaiah can paint deliverance from the terrible distress of the exile in the glowing colors of a new exodus, in which the events of the first exodus out of Egypt return antitypically. In Trito-Isaiah we can observe how the images of exodus and roads in the desert begin to form part of the stock language of religious discourse (see below, p. 226).

3. Having seen that in the "exodus" we are dealing with an act of mercy on the part of the God who has pity on his people and delivers them, we must go on at once to say that the help Israel experiences sets it on a course on which God continues to be with it. The theme of "guidance in the desert" (Noth) is intimately associated with the theme of "exodus." From the very beginning, Yahweh was known to Israel as the "shepherd of Israel," who accompanies it. Victor Maag has justifiably placed great emphasis on this heritage of Israel from its nomadic past. But a sociological reference to "the nomadic heritage" will not in itself suffice for a theological understanding. We must go on to state that when Israel proclaims "Yahweh, your God since Egypt," as an element of its faith, it is also keeping alive the knowledge of the God who remains with Israel on its journey. Neither is this knowledge abrogated by all the later theologoumena about the presence of Yahweh in specific places (see below, §9). This knowledge makes it possible for Israel not to lose its God in all its subsequent "departures," when it is snatched out of the "rest" to which God brings it in the land (Deut. 12:9–10), and to survive with the guidance of the "shepherd of Israel." Israel remains preeminently a people of hope.

4. In the confession of "Yahweh, the God of Israel since Egypt," Israel's faith receives an intimate association with a historical event. An initial historical deliverance, experienced by those escaping from Egypt, resounds in the earliest extant hymn of Israel. It has recently been accurately pointed out (Albrektson) that it is quite inappropriate to set up a contrast between Israel, with its sense of history, and the nature religions of the surrounding world, without any historical ties. The world of Assyria and Babylonia is also familiar with the intervention of the gods in the course of history and dependence on divine aid in historical crises. But it remains undeniable that Israel's basing

of its faith on that early act of deliverance, in which it knew that a single Lord was at work, not a multiplicity of powers, established a particularly intimate relationship between its faith and its historical experiences.

Having said this, we must still avoid the mistaken assumption that for Israel history as such became the revelatory word of Yahweh. Such an understanding of history as a phenomenon in its own right, to be taken as an independent quantity in God's revelation, is alien to the Old Testament. By the same token, an isolated fact of history is not as such simply a proclamation of Yahweh. Vast stretches of Israel's historical experience that come to light in the Old Testament remain silent, having nothing new to say. But then it can happen that messengers speaking for Yahweh appear unexpectedly in the context of exciting events, proclaiming the historical events to be Yahweh's call to decision. Here we recognize very clearly that "history" by no means simply proclaims Yahweh in its course of events; in the very midst of the historical disaster that is accompanied by the message of the prophets, it is especially urgent that Yahweh's word be heard. See below, §20 and §21.

Thus we must also remember in retrospect that the "deliverance from Egypt" was also accompanied by Yahweh's word. The preponderance of evidence still supports the assumption that Moses, the man with the Egyptian name, did in fact lead Israel out of Egypt "in the name of Yahweh" and thus, however we may go on to define the "office" of Moses more precisely, determined the subsequent "representation" (Noth) of the acts of Yahweh in Israel.

5. In this event Yahweh declared himself for the faith of Israel. In what took place he made himself known as the deliverer of that company, which then handed on its confession to all "Israel" living at a later date in Canaan as the twelve tribes. Starting with this confession, he is the "God of Israel." Not because Israel chose him voluntarily or because he has a "primary relationship" with Israel, but simply because by a free act he delivered those who dwelt in the house of servitude in Egypt—therefore he is their God. What the self-introduction formula sought to express in its own way is defined in terms of this historical self-statement of Yahweh and given concrete meaning. Whatever those who dwelt in Egypt may previously have known of Yahweh, under this new event his name was either forgotten or subsequently incorporated into this "initial knowledge": he who is invoked in the name "Yahweh" made himself known as the God of those brought up out of the house of servitude in Egypt and became the "God of Israel" through an expansion of the circle of those confessing him in the land of Canaan. Only when this self-statement of Yahweh is recognized is the phrase "Yahweh, God of Israel since Egypt" properly understood.

6. This makes a final point clear. The event that bears significance for the beginning of "Israel's" faith in Yahweh has from the outset a political

dimension. The beginning does not consist in the illumination of a single individual who then assembles other individuals around him, like Buddha, but in the deliverance experienced by a cohesive group. This political dimension, relating to a people defined in secular terms, will subsequently remain a hallmark of Yahwism. The individual is not forgotten and individual responsibility is increasingly stressed as time goes on, but it remains clear even in the late statements of the book of Daniel that individuals are not isolated from the people of Yahweh as a whole, nor can they take refuge in a special relationship with their God such as might remove them from the concrete events of the "secular" world. On the special problems posed by "wisdom," see below, §18.

The relationship of Yahweh to his people can find expression in various formulas. He is "the rock of Israel" (2 Sam. 23:3); Israel is his "possession" (סְגֻלָּה s°gullâ, נַחֲלָה naḥalâ), or simply "his people." He "acquired" his people (קָנָה qnh, Ps. 74:2). For a discussion of Yahweh as "creator of Israel" and its "king," see below, §4; on "the mighty one of Israel," see below, §3.

Two complexes of images used to describe this relationship deserve to be singled out. Not frequently but in a few important passages Israel is termed Yahweh's son. Hosea 11:1 links this image with the exodus confession: "Out of Egypt I called my son." Exodus 4:22 terms Israel the firstborn son of Yahweh. More frequently we find personification in the plural: "I have brought up sons. . . ." (Isa. 1:2 and other passages) This image combines a statement of origin (a son is irreversibly descended from his father) with a reference to the bond of love (Ps. 103:13). In a few passages the image of a mother can be used as a metaphor of comfort and devotion (Isa. 49:15; 66:13).

The bond of love is expressed even more emphatically in the image of marriage, which appears with various emphases from Hosea through Jeremiah and Ezekiel down to Deutero-Isaiah. In the patriarchal perspective of the Old Testament, this image combines the notion of God's free choice with that of unwavering love.

Von Rad, Gerhard. *Das formgeschichtliche Problem des Hexateuch.* Beiträge zur Wissenschaft vom Alten und Neuen Testament, series 4, vol. 26 (vol. 78 of the whole series). Stuttgart: Kohlhammer, 1938. Reprinted in his *Gesammelte Studien zum Alten Testament,* pp. 9–86. Theologische Bücherei, vol. 8. Munich: Kaiser, 1958. English: "The Form-Critical Problem of the Hexateuch." In his *The Problem of the Hexateuch and Other Essays,* pp. 1–78. Translated by E. W. Trueman Dicken. New York: McGraw-Hill, 1966.—Herrmann, Siegfried. *Israels Aufenthalt in Ägypten.* Stuttgarter Bibelstudien, vol. 40. Stuttgart: Katholisches Bibelwerk, 1970. English: *Israel in Egypt.* Translated by M. Kohl. Studies in Biblical Theology, 2d series, vol. 27. Naperville, Ill.: Allenson, 1973.—Noth, Martin. *Überlieferungsgeschichte des Pentateuch.* Stuttgart: Kohlhammer, 1948. English: *History of Pentateuchal Traditions.* Translated by B. W. Anderson. Englewood Cliffs, N.J.: Prentice-Hall, 1971.—Bach, Robert. "Die Erwählung Israels in der Wüste." Ph.D. dissertation, Bonn, 1951.—Steuernagel, Carl. "Jahwe, der Gott Israels." In *Studien zur semitischen Philologie und Religionsgeschichte* (Festschrift Julius Wellhausen), pp. 329–349. Edited by Karl Marti. Beihefte zur Zeitschrift für die Alttestamentliche Wissenschaft, vol. 27. Giessen: Töpelmann, 1914.—Wijngaards, Joanne. "הוֹצִיא and הֶעֱלָה. A Twofold Approach to the Exodus." *Vetus Testamentum* 15 (1965):91–102.—Bloch, Ernst. *Das Prinzip Hoffnung.* His Gesamtausgabe, vol. 5. Frankfurt: Suhrkamp, 1959. For a discussion of Bloch's views, see: Zimmerli, Walther. *Der Mensch und seine Hoffnung im Alten Testament,* pp. 163–178. Kleine Vandenhoeck-Reihe, vol. 272 S. Göttingen: Vandenhoeck & Ruprecht, 1968. English: *Man and His Hope in the Old Testament,* pp. 151–165. Studies in Biblical Theology, 2d series, vol. 20. Naperville, Ill.: Allenson, 1971. See also: Kraus, Hans-Joachim. "Das Thema 'Exodus.' " *Evangelische Theologie* 31 (1971):608–623.—Maag, Victor. "Der Hirt Israels." *Schweizer Theologische*

Umschau 28 (1958):2–28.—Idem. "Das Gottesverständnis des Alten Testaments." *Nederlands Theologisch Tijdschrift* 21 (1966/67):161–207.—Albrektson, Bertil. *History and the Gods.* Coniectanea Biblica; Old Testament series, vol. 1. Lund: Gleerup, 1967.—Noth, Martin. "Die Vergegenwärtigung des Alten Testaments in der Verkündigung." *Evangelische Theologie* 12 (1952/53):6–17. Reprinted in his *Gesammelte Studien zum Alten Testament,* vol. 2, pp. 86–98. Theologische Bücherei, vol. 39. Munich: Kaiser, 1969.—Zimmerli, Walther. *Die Weltlichkeit des Alten Testaments.* Kleine Vandenhoeck-Reihe, vol. 327 S. Göttingen: Vandenhoeck & Ruprecht, 1971.—Hempel, Johannes. *Gott und Mensch im Alten Testament.* 2d ed. Beiträge zur Wissenschaft vom Alten und Neuen Testament, 3d series, vol. 2. Stuttgart: Kohlhammer, 1936.—Lohfink, Norbert. "Beobachtungen zur Geschichte des Ausdrucks יהוה עַם." In *Probleme biblischer Theologie* (Festschrift Gerhard von Rad), pp. 275–305 (with bibliography to 1970). Edited by Hans Walter Wolff. Munich: Kaiser, 1971.

§3 Yahweh, God of the Fathers: The Promise

According to the account of the Pentateuch, the history of Yahweh with the people of Israel begins with the events described in the book of Exodus. Now this narrative is preceded by a narrative beginning in Genesis 12, in which, although the people of Israel does not yet exist, its ancestors are mentioned, one of whom, Jacob, is even renamed "Israel" according to Genesis 32:28 (J); 35:10 (P). These ancestors, too, come in contact with the God who will later be invoked by the name "Yahweh" in Israel. Indeed, it is impossible to miss the fact that in the events narrated the account fully intends to speak of the roots of Israel's life as the people of Yahweh. Galling has pointed out the peculiarity of this double beginning of the history of Yahweh with his people and believes it necessary to conclude that we are dealing with a double tradition of Israel's election. Therefore we must investigate the particular significance of this "prehistory" for what the Old Testament says about God.

We have already noted in §1 that, in contrast to the unanimity with which the God of Israel is called Yahweh from the time of Moses on, there is a peculiar lack of agreement among the three major strands of the patriarchal narrative in how they refer to God. While J speaks unhesitatingly of "Yahweh" from the very beginning, in Genesis 17:1, the actual beginning of God's history with Abraham (in 11:27, 28*b*, 31–32; 12:4*b*, 5; 13:6, 11*b*–12*a;* 16:1*a*, 3, 15 P makes brief statements without any mention of God), P provides a solemn self-introduction of God to the ancestor of Israel: "I am שַׁדָּי אֵל *ēl šaddai.*" This statement is then explicitly referred to in Exodus 6:3. As a rule, E simply uses the general term "God" (אֱלֹהִים *ĕlōhîm*). But in the scene at the mountain of God in which Moses asks God's name and the name "Yahweh" is revealed, a fuller form of appellation may be heard at the beginning, likewise with the solemnity of a self-introduction. God appears before Moses with the words: "I am the God of your father, the God of Abraham, the God of Isaac, and the God of Jacob," whereupon

Moses covers his face in awe (Exod. 3:6). In this appellation the connecting link with the patriarchal narratives of Genesis is unmistakably forged. But Alt has gone beyond this obvious point, and shown with great probability that, from the perspective of comparative religion, in this "God of the fathers" we are dealing with a form of faith deriving from the ancestors of Israel, who as yet did not know the name "Yahweh."

Alt cites a plethora of comparative material, which, to be sure, is a good thousand years later. In Nabatean inscriptions deriving from groups on the point of establishing a sedentary way of life and already inscribing some of their monuments in Greek, we find a sizable number of divine appellatives of the "god of the fathers" type, in which the general term for god is combined with a human name ("the god of . . ."). On the basis of this analogy, Alt believes he can conclude that there were three patriarchal deities: a "God of Abraham"; a "God of Isaac," who, according to Genesis 31:42, 53 bore the special cultic appellation פחד יצחק *paḥad yiṣḥāq*, "Fear of Isaac," or, according to Albright's translation, "Kinsman of Isaac"; and a "God of Jacob," who according to Genesis 49:24 (Isa. 49:26; 60:16; Ps. 132:2, 5) may have borne the fuller cultic appellation אביר יעקב *ăbîr yaʿăqōb*, "Mighty One of Jacob." Seebass adds a fourth, the "God of Israel." Diverging from Alt, others (Andersen, Cross), on the basis of Assyrian and Amorite analogies, consider it necessary to see a more general designation in the term "god of the fathers"; for example, the term was not necessarily associated with the name of a person, but was originally attached to a god known by name.

In the present context, within the framework of "theology," we must inquire what the accounts in Genesis of how God acted with and toward the patriarchs contribute to "what the Old Testament has to say about God." This is not the place to test the historicity of the individual elements that are significant for the prehistory of Israel in the patriarchs. That is the job of a "history of Israel." Neither, however, is this the place to work out the pre-Mosaic form of religion we may presume to be represented in the "God of the fathers." That would be the task of a history of Israel's religion. The patriarchal narratives of Genesis are themselves uniformly persuaded that it was of course Yahweh who was at work in the acts of God with the patriarchs, albeit, according to E and P, under the cover of a different name in a peculiar preliminary stage.

Having said this, however, we already have the essential assertion of these patriarchal narratives in view. They may all be brought under the rubric of "promise," a promise that precedes the history of Israel and prepares the way for it.

In line with the secular nature of what the Old Testament has to say about God, the term "promise" in this context does not refer to something inward or spiritual. The promise is concerned in the first place with those very material possessions that will make the people into a nation. The patriarch is promised that he will have descendants and through these descendants multiply to become a nation. Genesis 12:2 goes on to state that the patriarch will thus receive a great name, that is, honor in the Gentile world. Genesis

17:16 contains a similar notion in the promise that in this nation kings will be among the descendants of the patriarch's wife. To the promise of increase to become a nation is joined a second: the promise of the land that God will give his people. In J this land is promised first in vague terms to Abraham, who is to set out from his homeland (12:1); somewhat later, when he is in Canaan, it is made more specific (12:7; 13:14–15).

These two great promises, which were probably already contained in the earlier patriarchal tradition, are more closely defined by J and P, in their individual ways, by an additional emphasis. In 12:2–3 (J), it is the great saying about the "blessing" that Abraham is to receive—which in fact he is to be for the broad expanse of the Gentile world, but also in this primal history of the Yahwist painted in the somber tones of an ever more terrible curse. In P, the third element is the promise that the God who appears to Abraham wishes to be the God of Abraham and his descendants (Gen. 17:7–8). One gets the impression that a prefiguration can be found here of the sacred service for which Moses prepares the sacred tent or tabernacle (Exod. 25—31; 35—40) into which Yahweh descends with his shining glory (Exod. 40:34–38).

This promise—its delayed fulfillment and the perils lying in its way, the errors and obedience of those who are its agents—constitutes the subsequent subject matter of the patriarchal history recounted by the various narrative strands, each with its particular emphases. The stratum P, deriving from the worship of Israel, focuses on God's great decree; E stresses to a much greater degree how the fear of God (see below, pp. 145–146) exhibited by the agent of the promise is put to the test; in J, failure and obedience reveal how truly human the patriarchs of Israel are. In Genesis 15:6, which is hard to assign to a particular source, the word "belief" or "faith" appears in this context (see below, pp. 146–147).

But what is the real point of this strange "preliminary" phase of promise and expectation leading up to the actual time of Yahweh, the God of Israel since Egypt? Are we dealing merely with a solution to the narrative problem of how to incorporate the earlier reminiscences of the preliminary era before Yahweh, the era of the "patriarchal God" (replaced in P by an era of שׁדּי אל *ēl šaddai*)?

The following points may be made in response to the question of the theological relevance of the account depicting this era of promise:

1. The story of the patriarchs is unmistakably meant to answer the question of how Israel, the people of Yahweh, came into being. Genesis 12:1–3 has been termed the "etiology of Israel." The question of origins is also raised in the nations surrounding Israel. The Babylonian creation epic answers the question of how Babylon came to be by recounting how its heavenly prototype is constructed at the creation of the world (*AOT*[2], p.

123). Egyptian belief tells how the kingdom of heaven came to earth. Even Greek mythology reports that Athens owed its origin to the demigod Theseus. It is against this background that the story of Israel's origins in the patriarchal narratives found in Genesis 12—50 should be viewed. Unlike analogous accounts from elsewhere in the Near East, this story does not connect Israel through any mythological association with the beginnings of the world. In the primal history of Genesis 1—11 there is no mention of Israel. Israel does not even figure in the great table of nations in Genesis 10, which illustrates the genealogy of the nations of the world. It is in the midst of the history of these nations, already set in motion, that God calls the ancestor of Israel and grants him the promise of a future nation dwelling in its own land.

A mythological point of origin has here been replaced by the account of a call that comes to Israel's ancestor within the course of human history. Mythical derivation from a divine beginning has here been replaced by a specific event, a "promise." This puts Israel squarely in a history moving toward a fulfillment, but a history in which even its beginnings have a part.

2. But this point of departure makes it possible to call particular attention to the pilgrimage and expectation of the patriarchs. The nomadic nature of life in response to the call of Yahweh, one component of which is also represented in the deliverance from Egypt, is given special emphasis in the story of the patriarchs, who are on their way to an expected destination. It is no accident that Genesis 15:7 looks back on the departure of Abraham from his homeland in words that echo the terminology of the exodus: "I am Yahweh, who brought you up from Ur of the Chaldeans. . . ." In Genesis 20:13, E even puts in the mouth of Abraham the dangerously harsh expression "lead astray" (probably in the sense of "led into immediate uncertainty") to describe God's call to Abraham. But the expression stands here in the context of a story that shows how God's hand protects the man led into uncertainty.

3. "Promise" means also that the history in which Israel is guided by the "shepherd of Israel" is preceded by a pledge. The history of God's people —in its dimension as a people—begins, we are here given to understand, as a promise fulfilled: the experience of Israel in the deliverance from Egypt and the occupation of Canaan. Because of the promise these events take on the nature of words addressed personally to Israel. The experience of Israel at the exodus from Egypt and the occupation of Canaan is not a historical coincidence or a momentary divine caprice, but something announced long before.

4. This, however, implies an awareness that Yahweh is faithful, that he does not forget his promise but does what he promises. In what took place under Moses, at the beginnings of the nation, God's faithfulness is already evident—so says the faith of the Old Testament.

This in turn raises the question whether the promise does not come to a halt once Israel has become a nation and taken possession of the land. This is suggested at first glance by several statements within the context of the Deuteronomistic History, which stress that Yahweh has fulfilled all his promises (Josh. 21:45; 23:14; 1 Kings 8:56). But anyone who continues to follow the Deuteronomistic History into the period of the post-Solomonic monarchy will discover that in this period there reappears in full force the tension that moves from prediction to fulfillment of the word. The promise made to David by Nathan runs through the entire monarchy. Again and again Yahweh remains faithful, preserving the house of David from the destruction it deserves by way of judgment "for the sake of his servant David." Following the fall of Judah, the second book of Kings ends with the account of how Jehoiachin accedes to the kingship after a long period of captivity at Babylon; it has been suggested that in this conclusion we can still hear the author asking whether God's promise for David cannot finally be extended beyond the catastrophe of 587. For a discussion of this point, see below, pp. 179–180.

Above all, the prophets who make their appearance time and time again throughout the books of Kings to announce disaster, only to have their predictions fulfilled by the course of history, are somber witnesses to the reality of the God, here depicted in negative tones, who moves through history with his word and honors the commitments he has made.

This aspect of Yahweh's nature attains its extreme limit in the phenomenon of the great literary prophets, in whom both aspects of God's word are combined while the full tension between them is preserved. Prediction of disaster to come does not remain an empty word. But neither does the promise of a new beginning in freedom—beyond the catastrophe—remain an empty word, even though the promises far surpass the reality of their fulfillment after the exile, more and more calling the faith of Israel to hope for a fulfillment yet to come—an expectation given a final increment in what is shown to the apocalyptist Daniel (see below, §§21–22).

Thus it is clear that "promise," a note struck so unmistakably whenever Yahweh, the God of the fathers, is spoken of, does not remain an element limited to the early history of Israel, but reappears unexpectedly even when Israel has temporarily come to a halt, setting the nation once more on its pilgrimage and upholding it as it travels. The Old Testament people of Yahweh thus becomes in a very special sense a people of hope.

The Old Testament terminology of "fulfillment" includes not only the piel form מלא *millē'*, "make full, fulfill" (1 Kings 8:15, 24), which might support the misconception that God's pledge can be made good the way a debt is paid, so that an end is put to the matter, but also such terms as the verb הקים *hēqîm*, "set up, cause to stand." (e. g., Isa. 44:26) Such terminology makes it incomparably clearer that what Yahweh promises "stands" (Isa. 40:8) and that in the word thus made historical reality he who makes the promise remains fully present.

Galling, Kurt. *Die Erwählungstraditionen Israels.* Beihefte zur Zeitschrift für die Alttestamentliche Wissenschaft, vol. 48. Giessen: Töpelmann, 1928.—Alt, Albrecht. *Der Gott der Väter.* Beiträge zur Wissenschaft vom Alten und Neuen Testament, 3d series, vol. 12. Stuttgart: Kohlhammer, 1929. Reprinted in his *Kleine Schriften zur Geschichte des Volkes Israel,* vol. 1, pp. 1–78. Munich: Beck, 1953. English: "The God of the Fathers." In his *Essays on Old Testament History and Religion,* pp. 1–78. Translated by R. A. Wilson. Oxford: Blackwell, 1966.—Clements, Ronald. " אברהם." In *Theologisches Wörterbuch zum Alten Testament,* vol. 1, cols. 53–62 (with bibliography). Edited by G. J. Botterweck and Helmer Ringgren. Stuttgart: Kohlhammer, 1973. English: "אברהם *'abhrāhām.*" In *Theological Dictionary of the Old Testament,* vol. 1, pp. 52–58. Translated by J. T. Willis. Grand Rapids, Mich.: Eerdmans, 1974.—Seebass, Horst. *Der Erzvater Israel.* Beihefte zur Zeitschrift für die Alttestamentliche Wissenschaft, vol. 98. Berlin: Töpelmann, 1966.—Andersen, K. T. "Der Gott meines Vaters." *Studia Theologica* 16 (1962):170–188.— Cross, Frank Moore. "Jahweh and the God of the Patriarchs." *Harvard Theological Review* 55 (1962):225–299. Also his *Canaanite Myth and Hebrew Epic,* pp. 3–12. Cambridge, Mass.: Harvard University Press, 1973.—Wolff, Hans Walter. "Zur Thematik der elohistischen Fragmente im Pentateuch." *Evangelische Theologie* 29 (1969):59–72. English: "The Elohistic Fragments in the Pentateuch." *Interpretation* 26 (1972):158–173. Reprinted in *The Vitality of Old Testament Traditions,* pp. 67–82. Edited by Walter Brueggemann. Atlanta: John Knox, 1975.—Zimmerli, Walther. "Verheissung und Erfüllung." *Evangelische Theologie* 12 (1952/53):34–59.—Idem. *Der Mensch und seine Hoffnung im Alten Testament.* Kleine Vandenhoeck-Reihe, vol. 272 S. Göttingen: Vandenhoeck & Ruprecht, 1968. English: *Man and His Hope in the Old Testament.* Studies in Biblical Theology, 2d series, vol. 20. Naperville, Ill.: Allenson, 1971.

§4   Yahweh, Creator and King

1. It may seem surprising that the section dealing with Yahweh as creator of the world was not placed at the beginning. In the creed of the Christian faith the first article speaks of the creator, and "creation" must in any case be taken as coming at the beginning, standing among the *principia mundi.* But it is hardly possible to overlook the fact that in what the Old Testament has to say the "deliverance of Israel from Egypt," an event in the midst of history, furnishes the primary orientation. With this as the starting point, however, Israel comes to speak ever more clearly of the creator, a confession it was called upon to make in its encounter with the fully developed creation myths of its Canaanite environment. In like manner, the introductory "I believe in God, the Father" in the first article of the Christian creed, which precedes the confession of the "creator of heaven and earth," cannot be understood without the second article.

In Canaan Israel encountered a firmly formulated belief in creation; this can be observed most clearly in the Melchizedek episode of Genesis 14:18–20. Abraham, returning from his campaign against the kings of the east, meets Melchizedek, the king of Salem (according to Ps. 76:3 to be identified with Zion/Jerusalem), who is called a priest of עֶלְיוֹן אֵל *ēl ʿelyôn,* "the Most High God/El." To this term for God, verse 19 adds the epithet "creator of heaven and earth." It is significant that Abraham's oath in verse 22, which did not attain its present form until after the interpolation of the Melchizedek episode, speaks of "Yahweh, God Most High, creator (קנה *qnh*) of heaven and earth." The phrase "El Most High" still points clearly to a polytheistic environment in which the creator is the highest in the circle of the gods (see below, p. 41); in view of this challenge, however, it is clear for the faith of the Old Testament that "El Most High" can be none other than Yahweh, alongside whom, as becomes increasingly clear afterward, there is no room for any other god.

Everything the Old Testament has to say about the deliverance from Egypt is remarkably uniform and unambiguous. In contrast, what the Old Testament says about Yahweh as creator is more varied, and formulated in terms of different cosmologies; this is a sign of the secondary development of this matter.

2. In the account of J (Gen. 2:4*b*-25), which admittedly does not contain any elaborate creation narrative but is content merely to sketch the beginnings of Yahweh's history with the world and humanity, the world is pictured as an arid tract of land. A stream of water from the ground which waters the arid desert makes it possible for Yahweh to plant an exquisite garden and form animals, and later, the man, out of moist clay. The goal of creation is the man, to whom Yahweh gives his beautiful garden as a dwelling place, for whom he creates the animals, and finally forms the woman from the skeleton of the man himself, because "it is not good for man to be alone." In other words, concern for man's welfare stands at the beginning of Yahweh's activity. Unlike the Babylonian Atrahasis epic, for example, where man is thought of as nothing more than a supplier of the gods' table, the whole account of J is dominated by Yahweh's concern for man. The privilege of naming the animals clearly singles the man out from the other creatures (2:20; cf. also 2:23; according to 2 Kings 23:34 and 24:17, the giving of names is the act of a sovereign).

With regard to the terminology of J, we may say that here, as in later accounts, there appears no term for "world" in the sense of a coherent whole brought into being by creation; the thematic superscription in 2:4*b* speaks of "earth and heaven." Yahweh's acts are summarized by the simple verb עָשָׂה ('*śh*. In the account that follows, Yahweh like a potter (יָצַר *yṣr*) forms humans and animals (vss. 7, 19) from the ground (vs. 7). In the case of the man, it is explicitly stated that Yahweh blew the breath of life (נִשְׁמַת חַיִּים *nišmat ḥayyîm*) into his nostrils; cf. Ecclesiastes 12:7 (רוּחַ *rûaḥ*). Animals also possess the breath of life (רוּחַ *rûaḥ*), as Ecclesiastes 3:21 states, although the latter passage (in contrast to the assumption in Eccles. 12:7) raises the critical question of whether at death the breath of both humans and animals does not equally go "down" (into the earth; cf. Ps. 139:15). In Genesis 2:8, Yahweh "plants" (נָטַע *nṭ'*) the garden of paradise and causes trees to sprout (vs. 9; hiphil of צָמַח *ṣmḥ*) from the earth. From a rib taken from man Yahweh "builds" (כָּנָה *bnh*) woman (2:22). In the entire account, terms from the realms of handicraft and gardening are used just as they are in the realm of human endeavor.

3. No primal history belonging to E can be recognized. In Genesis 1:1—2:4*a*, however, P furnishes an extensively elaborated account of creation exhibiting a marked cosmological interest. The cosmology is based on the annual flooding of an alluvial plain.

The watery or muddy primordial chaos is depicted three times. The closest religio-historical parallel is found in the description of chaos given by the Phoenician Sanchuniaton. It is characterized as תֹהוּ וָבֹהוּ *tōhû wābōhû* (LXX *aóratos kaì akataskeúastos*), two terms whose etymology is unclear. It is described as darkness lying over the primordial deep (תְּהוֹם *t^ehôm*). In the "wind of God" that is upon the waters scholars have likewise claimed to find a formless primordial element (a divine gale; Sanchuniaton's *pneûma*). All of this is depicted, however, without any trace of an independent power that might stand in the way of the creator. Whatever mythical power may originally have resided in the individual elements, they have here become mere material for the creator to work with. At God's command, everything takes shape, starting with the foundations of the cosmos (the firmament of heaven, the earth, the sea, the stars). But the first thing created by God is "light"; this prefatory element gives all the other elements a characteristic orientation, one which probably cannot be understood without a certain interpretative emphasis. The impassioned desire to demythologize the cosmic elements shows itself not only in the sequence that places the earth's flora before the astral entities, which rank highest in the Babylonian environment of P, but above all in the avoidance of the words "sun" (שֶׁמֶשׁ *šemeš*) and "moon" (יָרֵחַ *yārêaḥ*), which obviously have mythological connotations. These powers of heaven are strikingly instrumentalized; the author speaks merely of the greater and lesser "luminaries" (מָאוֹר *mā'ôr*).

After the structure of the world is established, it is peopled with plants, fish, and birds, and finally with land animals and man, who signifies the culmination and goal of God's creative work.

All this activity is compressed within the framework of six days of labor; it leads up to the real goal, the seventh day, on which God rests from all his work. The term "Sabbath" does not occur. Neither is any Sabbath commandment formulated, but this resting on God's part obviously lays the groundwork for the Sabbath, which will later be given to Israel as a commandment that also has the nature of a gracious gift (see below, pp. 125–126). According to 2:3, this day is blessed and hallowed. The structure of this passage, leading up to the day of rest, betrays Priestly ideology and sensibility. Creation is associated with reverence for God—a reverence that will take on liturgical form in Israel.

This account of creation bears the unmistakable stamp of theological reflection, far surpassing that of the Yahwistic account. The formal stylization in terms of six days of labor is not simple; both the third day and the sixth had to accommodate two acts. That the structure leads up to the day of rest makes it possible to link the creation narrative clearly with the history of Israel. In Israel, which observes the Sabbath, God receives the honor that the course of history has been leading up to since the beginning of the world. At the same time, the assignment of all the works of creation to the peremptory word of God, which calls the elements of the world into being without opposition, clearly eliminates the possibility of any secondary power that might be looked for in the structure of the universe alongside the one God of Israel. Psalm 33:9 summarizes this aspect of creation briefly by saying, "He spoke and it took place; he commanded and it stood there." Psalm 148:5 says, "He commanded and they were created." This account certainly recognizes that there are powers within the created world. In the case of the heavenly bodies, for instance, there is no hesitation about saying that they exercise "rule." It is not, however, a rule that binds the conscience; they merely "rule over the day and over the night," by "separating the light from the darkness." (Gen. 1:18) Likewise when the plants are created we see that "the earth" is commanded "to put forth vegetation"; thereupon "the earth brought forth vegetation." (vss. 11–12) Here we still find echoes of the notion of "mother earth." Like the rule of the heavenly bodies, however, the work of the earth is subordinated to the clear command of God, who remains fully sovereign, creating through his own command.

When we examine the terminology of this account, we can discern behind the present text an earlier stage of redaction in which, as in J, God was spoken of as "making" (עשׂה *ʿśh;* 1:7, 16). This stage also spoke of the "separation" (הבדיל *hibdîl*) of the regions of the world (1:4, 7). This earlier account has had superimposed upon it the "word" account, in which the introductory phrase "and God said" is usually followed by a command in the jussive. In the case of the great cosmic orders, there is furthermore an explicit act of naming, in which God himself as sovereign gives the day and night, the firmament, the earth, and the sea their names (1:5, 8, 10; cf. 2:19, 23). The P account, too, does not have any term for "world." In contrast to J, P uses the sequence "heaven and earth" (1:1; 2:1, 4*a*).

Especially characteristic of Genesis 1 is the use of the verb ברא *br'*, which appears to be a term uniquely reserved for the process of creation, having no analogy in the sphere of human action. In Old Testament usage, this verb exhibits two peculiarities. (a) Only God can be its subject. To speak of human artistic "creation" using this word would sound blasphemous within the Old Testament. (b) When this verb is used, there is never any mention of a material from which something "is created"—in contrast to all human activity. This word is used in 1:1 for God's "creation" of the world as a whole, as well as in 1:21 for the creation of the great sea monsters (is the point here, too, to avoid ascribing any independent mythological power to the beasts of the "sea"?), in 1:27 for the creation of man, and once again at the conclusion in 2:3*b*, 4*a*. It is not yet possible in Genesis 1 to speak of creation *ex nihilo*, the first clear formulation of which is not found until 2 Maccabees 7:28. But the peculiarities of ברא *br'* and the absolute formulation of 1:3 and 1:14 are moving in this direction.

The account of the creation of man as the second work of the sixth day demands special attention. The blessing given him, according to which he is to be fruitful and multiply, still links him initially with the creatures of the sea and the birds of the heavens (1:22). In 8:17 the same blessing is pronounced upon the land animals. Probably the only reason the latter are not so blessed in Genesis 1 is that a double blessing would have overloaded the work of the sixth day. For a discussion of the "blessing," see below, pp. 68–69. More significant is the fact that the creation of man is explicitly preceded by an act of deliberation on the part of God, according to which man is to be created "after the image of God." The double expression in 1:26 בצלמנו כדמותנו *b̠ṣalmēnû kidmûtēnû* (5:3 exhibits the reverse sequence: בדמותו כצלמו *bidmûtô kṣalmô*) combines the concrete term צלם *ṣelem*, referring to a physical likeness, with the abstract form דמות *d̠mût*, which means "similarity." It is a familiar fact that in the ancient Near East the king was called the "image" of the deity. But even the Egyptian Instruction of Meri-kare can state quite generally that men are "his likenesses, gone forth from his members" (*AOT*[2], p. 35).

This raises the question of what it means to say in the context of the Old Testament that man is made in the image of God. We may state at the outset that the Old Testament knows nothing of any later loss of this status. No detailed story of man's fall is to be found in P (see below, p. 173). On the contrary, the present form of the primal history, already expanded by the addition of J's account of the fall, says explicitly in Genesis 5:3, using the same terminology, that Adam's son Seth was begotten in the "image and likeness" of Adam. Thus all the many theological speculations about man's being only partially in the likeness of God at this time are rendered nugatory.

On the other hand, it can be observed that the statement in Genesis 1 is made subject to certain clear limitations. In the first place, God's preliminary deliberations are surprisingly cast in the first person plural. The Babylonian accounts of how humanity was created spoke of a council of the gods, in which the plan was made. Usually P shows no hesitation in recasting the material he borrows; so in this passage his dependence on a form of speech that is fundamentally alien to his theology probably reveals a deliberate avoidance of the first person singular ("I will make man after my image") in God's preliminary deliberations. That man is made in the image of God does not mean that he resembles the God in his uniqueness (the God who from Exod. 6:2 appears bearing the name of Yahweh). This is elegantly demonstrated by Psalm 8, which expresses the same situation. In this psalm, the name "Yahweh" is used without hesitation from the beginning; verse 6, however, which speaks of humanity's exalted status in similar terms but using different words, surprises the reader by its avoidance of the name "Yahweh": "You made him little less than God (אלהים *ĕlōhîm*)." Humanity is very close to the sphere of the "divine beings," which includes the messengers of God. Therefore the LXX is quite correct in translating "God" here as *ángeloi*. The addition of the more abstract term דמות *dĕmût*, "likeness," "similarity" to the dangerously concrete צלם *ṣelem* probably represents an additional safeguard. An element of distance from the uniqueness of God can probably also be observed in the way Genesis 1:27 continues the narrative: "And God created man after his image, after the image of God he created him, man and wife he created them." Since the inclusion of Yahweh in the bipolarity of sexuality is alien to the Old Testament throughout, the remark that humans are created in this bipolarity from the beginning clearly sets humanity apart from the uniqueness of God.

One can ask to what extent the term צלם *ṣelem* implies similarity of form. Any notion of God as having an animal form is alien to the Old Testament. But whoever might therefore conclude that the Old Testament conceives Yahweh and his environment "anthropomorphically" (cf., for example, Ezek. 1:26) would completely miss the particular emphasis of Genesis 1. This chapter does not speak of God as having human form, but of humans as having the form of God. Humans, the author is seeking to say, can be understood only in terms of this point of origin. They are not self-sufficient beings, but derive from God. In Genesis 1, as in Psalm 8, there is added a clear explanation of what it means for humans to have the honor of being made in the image of God. "Let them rule over the fish of the sea, the birds of the heavens, and domestic animals, over all wild animals and everything that creeps upon the earth." This passage refers to the special mandate given to humans: they are to take the lower forms of animal life into their service. God puts humanity into a position of partial sovereignty. In § 18 I will discuss how humans live "before God," in obedience to this mandate.

This sovereignty of the final created being resembles the power of the earth to bring forth vegetation and the power of the heavenly bodies to control the calendar: it is bestowed by the creator within the framework of his creation. It is therefore a power for which account must be rendered from time to time; it never makes humanity the ultimate sovereign. Genesis 1 points to this creator, who always stands over against his creatures, who are to live "before him." With almost monotonous regularity, we are told at each act of creation that "God saw that it was good." The point is not to glorify and stabilize the empirical world with all its unrighteousness and injustice (*pace* E. Bloch). How questionable this world really is will be discussed later (§19). What is suggested is probably that God wishes to be honored even above the good things that come from his hand.

4. Deutero-Isaiah furnishes a fertile field for statements about the creator. For this prophet, who lived in the late exilic period and preached imminent deliverance, creation is one of the great evidences of Yahweh, proving the worthlessness of the gods and the true sovereignty of Yahweh for all eyes to see.

The colorful rhetoric of Deutero-Isaiah combines the vocabulary of J and P. Yahweh created (ברא *br'*; 40:26, 28; 42:5) the stars, the ends of the earth, and the heavens; he formed (יצר *yṣr*; 45:18) the earth like a potter; he made (עשׂה *'śh*; 44:24; 45:12, 18) all things. More vivid expressions are also used: Yahweh stretched out (נטה *nṭh*; 40:22; 42:5) the heavens, hammered down (רקע *rq'*; 42:5; 44:24) the earth, "called" (קרא *qr'*; 40:26) the stars, and led forth (הוציא *hôṣî'*; 40:26) the host of them by number.

Deutero-Isaiah also exhibits a more radical invasion of new realms by creation terminology:

a) Genesis 1 had shown how Yahweh's intervention brought order into a primal chaos of darkness, banishing the darkness by means of the light he created and assigning it a fixed place in the "night." Isaiah 45:7 radicalizes this statement to its ultimate extreme, when Yahweh describes himself as follows: "I make (יצר *yṣr*) light and create (ברא *br'*) darkness, I author prosperity (עשׂה *'śh*) and create (ברא *br'*) trouble—I, Yahweh, do (עשׂה *'śh*) all this." Nothing in the created world lies outside his creative realm. Of course even this passage does not intend to sanction an evil world as God's world. But despite all the conflict with Yahweh's declared beneficence, there is a position being maintained: over the powers of darkness there is no other recourse to which humans can turn.

b) It is further characteristic of Deutero-Isaiah that "creation" does not remain just a cosmological term referring to the material world from its beginning, but is intimately associated with Yahweh's intervention in the history of Israel. This association is expressed with particular emphasis in the invocation of the mighty arm of Yahweh in 51:9–10, where protological and cosmological elements combine with the soteriological statement of Israel's historical credo. The mythological story of the slaying of the chaos monster, found in the Babylonian creation epic, is used to depict Yahweh's initial act: "Awake, awake, put on your strength, O arm of Yahweh, awake as you did long ago, in days gone by. Was it not you who hacked Rahab in pieces and ran the dragon through? Was it not you who dried up the sea, the waters of the great abyss, and made the ocean depths a path for the redeemed?" The Babylonian myth tells how the creator god chopped the chaos monster into pieces, from which he formed heaven and earth (*AOT*[2], p. 120). Here that primordial act, with a smooth transition, is made transparent to the dividing of the waters of the Sea of Reeds (Exod. 14), which let the Israelites pass through and destroyed the pursuing Egyptians. It would be impossible to state more emphatically that the God who created the world is none other than the God who brought Israel out of Egypt. Psalm 136 deals with roughly the same theme.

c) A further point, however, must be made immediately: this creator God is not the distant God of a long-past act of deliverance. He is present as creator in the present moment of Israel and in the salvation that will come to pass. Not only do we hear in 44:24, for example, that Yahweh is the redeemer and creator of Israel; 45:8 (cf. 41:20; 48:7) goes on to state that Yahweh will "create" (ברא *br'*) salvation. Here the category of creation becomes all-encompassing, referring to Yahweh's work at the beginning of the world, at the historical beginning of Israel, and in the present that lies open to the future, to which a message of salvation, bearing eschatological overtones, is addressed.

5. In language and imagery, Deutero-Isaiah exhibits a close affinity to the Psalms. There, too, we find a series of statements about the creator.

Quite like Genesis 1:26–28, Psalm 8 likens the majesty of God's creation, with emphasis on the heavens and the stars as the work of his hands, to the astonishing grandeur of humans, to whom sovereignty has been given over the lower creatures. Psalm 19:2–7 describes the works of God, the heavens (his handiwork) together with day and night, as proclaiming the glory of God (כבוד אל *k'bôd 'ēl*). Their sound is heard, without speech or language, to the ends of the earth. The sun in its course through the heavens is all but personified, being compared to a bridegroom emerging from his chamber; scholars have found here material based on the mythology of the sun god, especially when the hymns to the sun found elsewhere in the ancient Near East are cited for comparison. It is characteristic, however, that in both Psalms and Genesis 1 the sun has become a created object in the heavens, which can only help proclaim the glory of God in its brightness. The second half of the hymn in the present book of Psalms sings the praises of Yahweh's revealed law, insisting that the term "God" (אל *'ēl*) can refer only to Yahweh.

Psalm 104, a beautiful psalm of creation, extols the wonders of the world, in which Yahweh's rebuke appointed the waters their place (vss. 6–9), and its inhabitants, all of whom receive their nourishment from God. In many passages this psalm exhibits a striking similarity to Akh-en-Aton's Hymn to the Sun (*AOT*², pp. 15–18). Once again, however, it is characteristic that it is not the sun with its life-giving powers that is extolled, but Yahweh, who wraps himself in a robe of light and spreads out the heavens like a tent (vs. 2), and ordains the course of the moon and the sun (vs. 19).

Psalm 139 is unique: in it (vss. 13–16) a single individual gives thanks to Yahweh for his creation (קנה *qnh*). Mythological references to the battle with the chaos monster at the beginning of the world, after the fashion of Isaiah 51:9–10, are also found in Psalm 74:13–14 (15–16) and 89:10–11 (12–13).

Yahweh's creative work is also extolled in the context of his royal sovereignty (Ps. 95:4–5; 96:5). This theme will be discussed shortly.

6. Wisdom literature constitutes a final realm in which statements about creation take on a distinctive shape. It will be seen in §18, which discusses wisdom, that wisdom ideology is controlled by the perspective of creation. Therefore we also hear of creation in the corpus of wisdom literature. In Genesis 1, the primary theme was God's efficacious word; in Genesis 2, it was his merciful condescension toward man, associated in Deutero-Isaiah with the reference to God's salvific will toward his people; wisdom discourse emphasizes that God performed his act of creation "in wisdom." This emphasis is not far removed from the insistent statements in Genesis 1 that God's work was good. The assertion that God created the world wisely is fully developed in the speeches of God from the book of Job, where Job, having challenged God, is asked whether he was present at the creation of each of God's creatures (38:4ff.). From questions about Job's participation in the events of the world's beginning, the discourse passes imperceptibly to a description of the astonishing natural phenomena of the present, leading up to the detailed descriptions of the hippopotamus and crocodile. Confronted with these wonders, Job must confess that he can only keep silence and admit the inappropriateness of his statements and questions.

The statements in the collection found in Proverbs 1—9, where wisdom is personified, move in another direction. Proverbs 3:19 states: "Through wisdom Yahweh founded the earth, by understanding he set the heavens in their place." This notion becomes totally personified in 8:22ff., where we read how Yahweh created wisdom at the very beginning, as the first of his works, and how she was present as his darling at creation and played in his presence. In this image we seem to hear echoes of Egyptian thought; the goddess Maat, the embodiment of order in the world of humans and nature, plays before the creator god and is his delight (Kayatz). Once again, it is characteristic how this image is transformed in the Old Testament. There is no suggestion of any deity present alongside the creator. She is instead the first of all the works created (קנה *qnh*) by Yahweh. It is as such a creature, made by Yahweh and deriving all her life from him, that she is present at the works of the beginning. Not as a second being alongside Yahweh, but as one of his creatures, having all that she is from him alone, is she present at God's creation. Yahweh speaks the word; she has nothing to add. Her mention serves to bring out more fully that side of God's creative act that reveals itself to the wondering gaze confronted with the mystery of creation. "The heavens declare the glory of God," as Psalm 19:2 puts it.

At this point we can raise the question whether such talk of the works of creation leads to a second mode of revelation. In discussing this question, we must note at the outset that in this realm, too, Israel names no other name than that of Yahweh, the name through which its God had revealed himself in historical encounter. The works of creation reveal more fully the glory of Yahweh. The talk of creation in the accounts of the primal history such as those in Deutero-Isaiah shows also that in the creator Israel knows no other Lord than the Lord who demonstrates his love for humanity in the works of the creation. Whether this knowledge derives directly from the phenomena of nature and the course of the universe or was introduced into the world by Israel's specific knowledge of its God will require further examination in the context of our discussion of Israel's wisdom literature (see below, §18).

7. In some of the Psalms creation is mentioned in the context of Yahweh's kingship. The title "king," which expresses Yahweh's sovereign power, requires closer examination.

Earlier scholars were of the opinion that the use of the term "king" for Yahweh should be understood as a counterpart to the royal Psalms, which have the earthly king in view (see below, pp. 90–93). According to this theory, Israel began to address its God as king and sing his praises after analogy with its own king. Mowinckel has sought to deal with the problem from the contrary angle. According to him, the enthronement of Yahweh was celebrated annually in Israel on the occasion of the New Year's festival. In the Psalms containing the phrase יהוהמלך (yahweh mālak), to be translated "Yahweh has become king" (Ps. 93:1; 96:10, etc.), we have the acclamation celebrating Yahweh's repeated accession at the beginning of a new annual cycle. In the ritual of this festival, the celebration which renews the forces of the annual cycle, Mowinckel finds the myths of creation and the battle with the chaos monster, the battle of the gods and the battle of the nations, the exodus and Yahweh's judgment, and the determination of destinies, associated with the proclamation of deliverance from disaster. Babylonian parallels appear to have suggested this interpretation to him. Engnell, the most prominent representative of the Uppsala School, has gone beyond Mowinckel, proposing the associated hypothesis of a specific ritual for the earthly king, whose abasement to death and restoration to life played a significant role (the myth of Tammuz).

In opposition to this theory, Maag has insisted that in Israel's notion of the kingship of God there is preserved a feature of its nomadic heritage, which thinks of Yahweh as a companion on the way and leads not to a static ritual but to faith in a God who goes along with his people. Grammatically it has become clear that the phrase יהוהמלך (yahweh mālak) should not be understood as meaning "Yahweh has become king" in the context of a new enthronement, but should be translated as "Yahweh [and none other] is king." This kingship, however, declares not only his sovereignty over Israel, but his universal sovereignty, encompassing all creation; above all, it looks forward to Yahweh's coming in judgment. In this sense, Gunkel already proposed speaking of "eschatological enthronement hymns."

Speaking of the origin of such royal terminology as applied to Yahweh, Alt hypothesizes that Israel borrowed the Canaanite notion of a pantheon and claimed for Yahweh the kingship among the inhabitants of heaven, the rest of whom were demoted to the rank of angels.

The kingship of Yahweh, which we first encounter in Isaiah 6:5—a text that can be dated with certainty in the second half of the eighth century— is by nature universal, as the hymn of the seraphim in 6:3 shows: "All the earth is full of his glory." Praise of the glory (כבוד *kābôd*) of king Yahweh also dominates Psalm 29 (vss. 1, 2, 3, 9), which, like the Babylonian *amatu* hymns, depicts the force of Yahweh's voice (the thunder). Here, too, in the very first verse, the whole realm of the gods (בני אלים *bᵉnê ēlîm*) is addressed. Psalm 93 still suggests some of the hostile power of the chaotic abyss. Cf. also Psalms 47, 96, and 98. Psalm 95 shows that praise of God's kingship could be embellished with material drawn more specifically from Israelite traditions: it concludes with an exhortation that holds the obdurate generation of the wilderness before the eyes of the congregation. The same is true of Psalm 99, which is constructed on the basis of the Trisagion (Isa. 6:3), sung upon Zion (Ps. 99:2), at the site of the ark (99:5; cf. below, pp. 75–76), and in its third strophe mentions Moses, Aaron, and Samuel.

8. When the faith of Israel applied the title "king" to Yahweh, it assigned to him the place occupied in the Canaanite pantheon by El, the highest god, as the Ugaritic texts reveal. We also note the striking phenomenon that in the Old Testament the name "El" has been transferred to Yahweh without hestitation, whereas the younger figure of Baal met with violent rejection— especially after the time of Elijah and Hosea. That this hostility was not always present is attested with sufficient clarity by the name "Bealiah" ("Yahweh is Baal") in 1 Chronicles 12:6. In Psalm 29, verse 3*aβ* reveals that in Canaan worldwide "glory" (כבוד *kābôd*) was ascribed to El. Psalm 19:2 leads to the same conclusion. The assembly of the gods is referred to as עדת אל *ᵃdat ēl* in Psalm 82:1. Cross goes even further, hypothesizing "that JHWH originated as an El-figure who separated from the old god when Israel's God broke away from his polytheistic environment"; religio-historical considerations make this suggestion hardly tenable.

Besides El, the lord of the gods, Canaan also knew local forms of El, more closely defined by an added epithet. As a rule, Israel identified these local El-figures also with Yahweh.

a) "El Most High" of Jerusalem has already been mentioned in the context of Genesis 14:18–20. Later the term עליון *ᵉlyôn* (which just possibly may at one time have been an independent divine name) can appear by itself as an epithet or substitute for Yahweh. In Psalm 82:6, the gods brought to judgment on account of their unrighteousness are called "sons of the Most High." The term "Most High" could be applied to Yahweh without any difficulty.

b) According to Genesis 21:33, Yahweh received the epithet אל עולם *ēl ʿôlām*, "El Everlasting," at Beersheba. This attribution, too, could not have made any difficulties for Yahwism.

c) P uses אל שדי *ēl šaddai* as a special designation for Yahweh in the patriarchal period (see above, p. 18). The interpretation of the name is uncertain; it may have meant "El of the Mountain." The Hebrew ear probably heard an echo of שדד *šdd,* "destroy." This probably explains Jerome's rendering *"omnipotens,"* which in turn led to the common translation "almighty." Unfortunately it is no longer possible to determine the original locus of this form of El.

d) In Genesis 16:13, אל ראי *ēl rŏ'î* is referred to as the deity of Beer-lahai-roi and is used as an epithet for Yahweh. The meaning of the name remains obscure.

e) According to Genesis 33:20, אל אלהי ישראל *ēl ĕlōhê yiśrā'ēl,* "El the God of Israel," was called upon at Shechem and later identified with Yahweh. This form has been sufficiently discussed above, p. 23.

f) In Genesis 35:7 (E), אל בית אל *ēl bêt ēl,* "God of Bethel," appears as a place name; in 31:13 (E) it appears as a divine name in the context of God's appearance to Jacob at Bethel. Eissfeldt has shown that "Bethel" was used as a divine name elsewhere in the ancient Near East. W. H. Schmidt, on the other hand, points out how uncertain the Genesis tradition is.

g) In Judges 9:46, אל ברית *ēl bᵉrît,* "El of the Covenant," refers to a god at Shechem not yet identified with Yahweh, who can probably be identified with the violently rejected בעל ברית *ba'al bᵉrît,* "Covenant Baal," of Judges 8:33 and 9:4.

This last example shows that Yahwism did not simply eliminate the notion of alien deities, however much it considered Yahweh alone the only divinity for Israel. Israel knows nothing of any theoretical monotheism. It takes for granted that there are other gods among the other nations. How the faith of the Old Testament came to terms with this problem is shown, for example, by Deuteronomy 32:8–9: "When the Most High gave the nations their inheritance, when he dispersed humanity, he laid down the boundaries of the nations according to the number of the sons of God" (LXX; MT reads בני ישראל *bᵉnê yiśrā'ēl,* "sons of Israel"). Deuteronomy 4:19–20 takes a different position, cautioning against worship of the heavenly bodies, "which Yahweh your God assigned for the worship of the various nations under heaven; but you are the people whom Yahweh brought out of Egypt, from the smelting-furnace." In the book of Daniel we find the notion that every nation has its angel (Dan. 10:13, 20–21; 12:1). Israel's angel is Michael, whose name expresses ("Who is like God [El]?") the incomparability of Yahweh (= El) (Labuschagne).

All-out polemic against other gods, calling them nothings, if not simply denying their existence, is found in Deutero-Isaiah, at a time when the exile had dispersed Israel among the foreign nations. Psalm 82 takes a different approach, telling how the gods are brought to judgment on account of their unrighteousness and asserting that they will die like men.

All this discussion clearly illustrates how unspeculative the faith of the Old Testament is. It does not enter the lists on behalf of a purified image of the universe and the gods; at first it leaves the phenomenon of alien gods alone, but deprives them of all their power and vigorously denies any claim they may have upon Israel. In Deutero-Isaiah, at the very time of Israel's utmost humiliation, we see how foreigners come to Israel and confess: "God is among you and there is no other." (45:14) Here, too, we find expressed the expectation that one day every knee shall bend before Yahweh and every tongue swear by him (45:23). For a discussion of this theme, see below, p. 220.

Schmidt, Werner H. *Die Schöpfungsgeschichte der Priesterschrift.* 3d ed. Wissenschaftliche Monographien zum Alten und Neuen Testament, vol. 17. Neukirchen: Neukirchener Verlag, 1973.— Eissfeldt, Otto. *Taautos und Sanchunjaton.* Sitzungsberichte der Deutschen Akademie der Wissenschaften zu Berlin; Klasse für Sprachen, Literatur und Kunst, 1952, no. 1. Berlin: Akademie-Verlag, 1952.—Gunkel, Hermann. *Schöpfung und Chaos in Urzeit und Endzeit.* 1895. Reprint. Göttingen: Vandenhoeck & Ruprecht, 1921.—Westermann, Claus. *Genesis.* Biblischer Kommentar, vol. 1, pp. 203–204. Neukirchen: Neukirchener Verlag, 1966. Includes bibliography on the image of God.—Von Rad, Gerhard. "Das theologische Problem des alttestamentlichen Schöpfungsglaubens." In *Internationale Tagung alttestamentlicher Forscher, Göttingen, 1935. Werden und Wesen des Alten Testaments,* pp. 138–147. Edited by Paul Volz, Friedrich Stummer, and Johannes Hempel. Beihefte zur Zeitschrift für die Alttestamentliche Wissenschaft, vol. 66. Berlin: Töpelmann, 1936. Reprinted in his *Gesammelte Studien zum Alten Testament,* pp. 136–147. Theologische Bücherei, vol. 8. Munich: Kaiser, 1958. English: "The Theological Problem of the Old Testament Doctrine of Creation." In his *The Problem of the Hexateuch and Other Essays,* pp. 131–143. Translated by E. W. Trueman Dicken. New York: McGraw-Hill, 1966.—Rendtorff, Rolf. "Die theologische Stellung des Schöpfungsglaubens bei Deuterojesaia." *Zeitschrift für Theologie und Kirche* 51 (1954): 3–13. Reprinted in his *Gesammelte Studien zum Alten Testament,* pp. 209–212. Theologische Bücherei, vol. 57. Munich: Kaiser, 1975.—Bauer-Kayatz, Christa. *Studien zu Prov 1—9.* Wissenschaftliche Monographien zum Alten und Neuen Testament, vol. 22. Neukirchen: Neukirchener Verlag, 1966.—Mowinckel, Sigmund. *Psalmenstudien. II: Das Thronbesteigungsfest Jahwäs und der Ursprung der Eschatologie.* 1922. Reprint. Amsterdam: Schippers, 1961.—Engnell, Ivan. *Studies in Divine Kingship in the Ancient Near East.* 2d ed. Oxford: Blackwell, 1967.—Maag, Victor. "Malkût Jhwh." In International Organization for the Study of the Old Testament. *Congress Volume, 1959,* pp. 129–153. Supplements to Vetus Testamentum, vol. 7. Leiden: Brill, 1960.—Alt, Albrecht. "Gedanken über das Königtum Jahwes." In his *Kleine Schriften zur Geschichte des Volkes Israel,* vol. 1, pp. 345–357. Munich: Beck, 1953.— Cross, Frank Moore. "אֵל." In *Theologisches Wörterbuch zum Alten Testament,* vol. 1, cols. 259–279 (with bibliography). Edited by G. J. Botterweck and Helmer Ringgren. Stuttgart: Kohlhammer, 1973. English: "אֵל *ēl.*" In *Theological Dictionary of the Old Testament,* vol. 1, pp. 242–261. Translated by J. T. Willis. Grand Rapids, Mich.: Eerdmans, 1974.—Eissfeldt, Otto. "Der Gott Bethel." *Archiv für Religionswissenschaft* 38 (1930):1–30. Reprinted in his *Kleine Schriften,* vol. 1, pp. 206–233. Tübingen: Mohr, 1962.—Schmidt, Werner H. "אֵל *ēl* Gott." In *Theologisches Handwörterbuch zum Alten Testament,* vol. 1, cols. 142–149. Edited by Ernst Jenni and Claus Westermann. Munich: Kaiser, 1971.—Labuschagne, C. J. *The Incomparability of Yahweh in the Old Testament.* Pretoria Oriental Series, vol. 5. Leiden: Brill, 1966.

§5 The Election of Israel

As creator and king Yahweh makes himself known in the full extent of his universal dominion and revelation. The extent of Yahweh's power raises the question of how his special relationship to Israel is to be understood. Reflection on this problem has already been noted in Deuteronomy 32:8–9, where Israel is termed Yahweh's "portion" (חלק *ḥēleq*) and the "lot of his inheritance" (חבל נחלתו *ḥebel naḥălātô*). Deuteronomy 4:20 speaks of Yahweh's "taking" (לקח *lqḥ*) Israel.

The fully thought-out formulation of this circumstance uses the verb "elect." The very nature of the case suggests that this formulation does not appear at the beginning in Israel's theology, but comes to prevail when someone, looking at the vast possibilities open to Yahweh as creator of the world, reflects on the mystery of why Yahweh should concern himself in such a special way with Israel. It turns out, in fact, that, after several statements whose terminology is less precise, the theology of election first takes on its full significance in the period of Deuteronomy, where it is developed with great emphasis.

The terminology of election is almost totally uniform. Unlike בוא *br'*, the verb בחר *bḥr* that is used in this context is not applied to Yahweh alone. Alongside the 99 passages in which Yahweh is the subject of the verb "elect" stand 68 with human beings as the subject, with both religious and secular meaning. Three additional passages are corrupt. The verbal adjective בחיר *bāḥîr* occurs 13 times; in the 12 original passages, Yahweh is meant as the subject of the election. It must be noted that there is no abstract noun meaning "election," like the Akkadian *itûtu*. The formulation is predominantly verbal. Closely related to בחר *bḥr* is the use of ידע *yd'* with מן *min*, "to know especially out of a multitude," found as early as Amos 3:2. This "knowledge" is not to be understood as being purely intellectual. It includes the full force of "recognize" and "accept" (see below, pp. 144–145). Verbs of distinguishing (הבדיל *hibdîl*, as in Lev. 20:24, 26), seizing, and calling (החזיק *heḥĕzîq* and קרא *qr'* alongside בחר *bḥr* in Isa. 41:9) depict the process of separation but do not contain the full force of "selection."

In the human realm, "selection" is a decision of the will, preceded, if carried out correctly, by reflection. Lot "selects" (Gen. 13:11) the best share of the land after carefully considered examination; in 1 Samuel 17:40, David selects the best stone for his sling in the same way. In this context, what is selected is something of particular value. The noun בחור *baḥûr* refers to a valiant young fighter; the niphal participle נבחר *nibḥār* can practically become a term for something precious, something of special value. True selection also presupposes a multiplicity of given possibilities. When there is only one possibility, it is impossible to speak seriously of "selection." In Amos 3:2, for example, we see the Lord of the nations, who has many possibilities open to him, but decides: "You alone have I known among all the nations of the world." Such selection marks the starting point of Israel's history and makes Israel the people of Yahweh. We see this in the recapitulation of Israel's earliest history in Ezekiel 20:5, the only passage in Ezekiel where the theology of election appears. It begins with the statement from the mouth of Yahweh: "On the day that I chose Israel, with uplifted hand I bound myself by oath. . . ."

When Yahweh is said to "choose," what is expressed is the free sovereignty of the Lord, who is answerable for his choice to nothing that he chooses. Now since human choice as a rule implies previous reflection, it is reasonable to ask in the case of Yahweh what could have occasioned his election of Israel and no other nation. At this point, however, we find a striking reticence on the part of the Old Testament. The idea that Israel is especially precious, which might be suggested by the use of נבחר *nibḥar*, is never brought forward. The introductory discourses of Deuteronomy go out of their way to make the contrary point. Israel is the "least of all the nations." (7:7) Yahweh drives out before Israel nations that are "greater and more powerful." (4:38) Later passages can go even further and speak of Israel's moral worthlessness and stubbornness (9:4–6; 10:14–16). As a positive motivation for the deliverance of Israel from Egypt, in which the association between Yahweh and Israel becomes historically manifest, we find only one reason: a reference to Yahweh's love of the patriarchs and his faithfulness to his promise: "Because Yahweh loved you and because he stood by his oath to your forefathers, therefore he brought you out with his strong hand." (7:8) An irrational, free decision of love as early as the time of the patriarchs, which cannot be examined further, stands behind Yahweh's election.

In this context it must also be considered what the sense of this divine election meant for the elect. In the first place, Israel is set apart with special honors. It is Yahweh's special possession. "Yahweh has chosen Jacob to be his own, and Israel as his special treasure" (סגלה *sgullâ;* Ps. 135:4). This special distinction can also be described by means of the term "holy," which essentially does not refer to any ethical qualification, but to being set apart as the special possession of Yahweh. "You are a people holy to Yahweh your God; Yahweh your God chose you out of all nations on earth to be his special possession." (Deut. 7:6 = 14:2) Most momentous are the words of Exodus 19:5–6, a passage that is probably "protodeuteronomic" (*pace* Wildberger). Here we read: "And now, if you will listen to me and keep my covenant, then out of all people you shall become my special possession; for the whole earth is mine. You shall be to me a kingdom of priests and a holy nation." The conditional element introduced by the demand to keep the "covenant," will be discussed more fully in §6. The significant point is that here Israel is described not only as Yahweh's special possession and a holy people, but as a "kingdom of priests." It has been suggested that this phrase reflects the designation of someone set apart for priestly service of mediation. This feature is strongly underlined by Deutero-Isaiah, who likes to refer to Yahweh's elect as the "servant" of Yahweh. "Hear now, Jacob my servant, hear me, my chosen Israel. . . . Have no fear, Jacob my servant, Jeshurun whom I have chosen." (44:1–2) This is said in a context that expresses with particular clarity how Yahweh's own people are to be open to receive outsiders who

would join Israel (cf. 44:3–5). At the same time, however, the obligation to
have nothing to do with pagan practices can be heavily stressed. The warning
against having dealings with the people of Canaan is a particular theme of
the deuteronomistic writings. This sense of being distinct from the other
nations is much older, however, as the words of Balaam in Numbers 23:9
show with all the clarity one could wish; the seer says: "Behold a people that
dwells alone, that has not made itself one with the nations [Gentiles]." The
undoubtedly ancient idiom, "We do not do such things in Israel" (2 Sam.
13:12), directed against the Canaanites and the designation of sexual sins
above all as "an outrage in Israel" (Gen. 34:7) presupposes this sense of
distinctiveness. The postexilic period, with Ezra's passionate campaign to
dissolve mixed marriages, placed one-sided emphasis on this distinctiveness
and came to conclusions that had a severe impact on the people. In this period
the somber antithesis of rejection (מאס m's) of those not chosen can also be
stated in blunt terms with respect to Edom: "I love Jacob, but I hate Esau."
(Mal. 1:2–3)

As a rule, however, there is a stronger sense of responsibility on the part
of the elect. Israel, the chosen nation, is not a passive privileged object; it is
always called to act obediently as subject. The "dialogical" nature of election
is made especially clear by the possibility of speaking of a "choice" on the
part of people. Joshua, for example, demands of the people assembled at
Shechem: "If it does not please you to worship Yahweh, choose today whom
you will worship." When the populace decides in favor of Yahweh, he states
explicitly: "You are witnesses against yourselves that you have chosen Yahweh and will worship him." (Josh. 24:15, 22) Cf. also Judges 5:8 (?); 10:14;
Isaiah 41:24. In Psalm 119:173, the object of the "choice" is the commandments of God.

The notion of Israel as Yahweh's own people is not the only context in
which God is said to choose. Even the predeuteronomistic period spoke of
the selection of the king, using terminology (found elsewhere in the ancient
Near East as well) expressing divine election. Israel's use of the term reveals
a double sense: Israel has a sense of choosing its own kings, and also knows
that Yahweh chooses the king. For the first, cf., for example, 1 Samuel 8:18;
12:13; for the second, in the same context, the words of Samuel in 1 Samuel
10:24: "Look at the man [i. e. Saul] whom Yahweh has chosen." The two
ideas appear remarkably and uniquely intertwined in 2 Samuel 16:18, in the
early narrative recounting the court history of David, when Hushai says to
Absalom, who is suspicious of his loyalty, "I mean to attach myself to the man
chosen by Yahweh, by this people, and by all the men of Israel; and with him
I will remain." The royal law of Deuteronomy, on the contrary, draws a
sharper distinction, stating in 17:15: "Appoint (שׂים śîm) over you the king
whom Yahweh your God will choose (בחר bḥr)." In this context the election
of David and his house deserves special mention (see below, pp. 88–89).

Here too we find the notion of election combined once again with the title "servant" (Ps. 78:70; 89:20–21; vs. 4 uses the nouns בחיר *bāḥîr* and עבד *'ebed* in parallel). Chronicles no longer speaks of the election of Israel, but lays great emphasis on the election of the Davidic dynasty (1 Chron. 28:4–6, 10). In verse 6, election terminology is linked with the title "son": "I have chosen him [Solomon] to be a son to me and I will be a father to him."

It is also possible to speak of Yahweh's election of the priestly house (1 Sam. 2:28, the priesthood of Eli; Deut. 18:5; 21:5, that of Levi; cf. also Num. 16:5, 7; 17:20 and 1 Chron. 15:2; 2 Chron. 29:11). Psalm 105:26 speaks in parallel of Moses, the servant (עבד *'ebed*) of Yahweh, and Aaron, whom he chose (בחר *bḥr*).

Uniquely deuteronomic is the statement that Yahweh has chosen a site in order to place his name there or cause his name to dwell there (Deut. 12:5, 11, and *passim*). This terminology may be based on earlier usage, in which the deity himself rather than his worshipers determines the site of his altar. What is uniquely deuteronomic is the associated theology of the name of God (see below, p. 78), as well as the inclusion of this selection of the worship-place in the context of the election of God's people. For it is quite clear that here the point is not the uniqueness of a sacred site in itself. The election of Israel shades off into the particular selection of the place. The internal logic of Deuteronomy's statements runs: one God, one people chosen by this God, one single place within the territory of this people chosen by God so that his people may call upon his name there.

It may appear striking that the pre-exilic prophets almost never speak of the election (בחר *bḥr*) of Israel. The only mention of this notion in the early exilic prophet Ezekiel (20:5), like the statement using ידע *yd'* in Amos 3:2, shows how critical the prophets are of all self-satisfied claims on the part of Israel to be a "chosen people," making their silence on this point easy to understand. Even with reference to their own persons, they never—with one exception—speak of being "chosen" for their office. Only Jeremiah 1:5 comes close to this notion, once more using the verb ידע *yd'*, when Yahweh says to the prophet at the moment of his call: "Before I formed you in the womb I knew you. Before you were born I consecrated you, I appointed you a prophet to the nations." For those who proclaim judgment, their duty is so urgent that they do not stop to reflect on their own office. For Jeremiah, a prophet who suffers from being unable to escape from his calling, knowledge of having been "known" (= "chosen") long in advance of any act of his own will is a source of great distress. His reaction casts a clear light on the anteriority of election, which removes it from human control. Of the servant of Yahweh in Deutero-Isaiah, designated in 42:1 by the parallel terms "servant" (עבד *'ebed*) and "chosen one" (בחיר *bāḥîr*), I shall speak later (pp. 221–224).

In Exodus 19:5, a condition is imposed on the dignity Israel enjoys as

Yahweh's chosen possession; in the midst of the Sinai events, we read: "If you listen to my voice and keep my covenant, then you shall be my special possession." To this special emphasis of the accounts of what took place at Sinai we must now turn our attention.

Rowley, Harold Henry. *The Biblical Doctrine of Election.* Louisa Curtis Lectures, 1948. London: Lutterworth, 1950.—Vriezen, Theodorus Christiaan. *Die Erwählung Israels nach dem Alten Testament.* Abhandlungen zur Theologie des Alten und Neuen Testaments, vol. 24. Zurich: Zwingli, 1953.—Idem. *De Verkiezing van Israel volgens het Oude Testament.* 1974.—Wildberger, Hans. *Jahwes Eigentumsvolk.* Abhandlungen zur Theologie des Alten und Neuen Testaments, vol. 37. Zurich: Zwingli, 1959.—Idem. "בחר *bḥr* erwählen." In *Theologisches Handwörterbuch zum Alten Testament,* vol. 1, cols. 275–300. Edited by Ernst Jenni and Claus Westermann. Munich: Kaiser, 1971. Bergman, Jan; Ringgren, Helmer; and Seebass, Horst. "בחר" In *Theologisches Wörterbuch zum Alten Testament,* vol. 1, cols. 592–608 (with bibliography). Edited by G. J. Botterweck and Helmer Ringgren. Stuttgart: Kohlhammer, 1973. English: "בחר *bāḥar.*" In *Theological Dictionary of the Old Testament,* vol. 2, pp. 73–87. Translated by J. T. Willis. Grand Rapids, Mich.: Eerdmans, 1974.

§6 Yahweh, God of Sinai: Covenant and Commandment

Of the great complexes making up the Pentateuch, one has not yet been discussed. After their departure from Egypt, the people experience in the desert a temporary halt at Mount Sinai. The description of what takes place there has been expanded enormously. To the accompaniment of terrifying fire and earthquake, Yahweh appears upon the mountain (Exod. 19), proclaims the Ten Commandments to the people (20:1–17), and imparts other commandments to Moses, sent up the mountain by the terrified populace as their representative (20:22—23:33). Recorded in a book, according to Exodus 24:7, they constitute the "Covenant Code," the basis for a covenant ceremony at the foot of the mountain. This is followed by an ascent of the mountain on the part of a sizable delegation, where they behold the "God of Israel" and join in a meal. From this point to Numbers 10:10 there follows a plethora of Priestly directives, interrupted only in Exodus 32—34 by the narrative of how the Israelites sinned with the image of the golden bull and the consequences of their sin. Then the people break camp and prepare to go on. Once again, however, the narrative is interrupted, this time just before entry into the land of Canaan. A discursive address delivered by Moses shades off once more in Deuteronomy into the events that took place at the mountain of God, now called Horeb; in Deuteronomy 12—26 we find once more a corpus of commandments.

Theophany, covenant, and commandments constitute the primary theological accents of this major complex. The phenomenon of the divine presence, which here takes on the form of an actual theophany, will be discussed in §9. But the theologoumena of covenant and commandment must be discussed within the framework of the Part devoted to "fundamentals."

The word "covenant" is not a completely satisfactory rendering of the Hebrew בְּרִית *b'rît*, translated by the LXX as *diathḗkē*, by the Vulgate Psalter (Psalterium Gallicanum) and some other passages from the Vulgate as *testamentum*, but by the vast majority of other passages as *foedus* (135 times) or *pactum* (96 times). Etymological approaches have proposed various definitions: on the basis of Genesis 15:9ff. and Jeremiah 34:18, it has been associated with an Arabic root meaning "cut (apart)"; with the Akkadian *birītu*, meaning "bond" (a "binding" contract); with the Akkadian *birīt*, "between," meaning "mediation"; and with the Hebrew בָּרָה *brh*, "eat," meaning "meal." Referring to Isaiah 28:15, 18, where חֹזֶה / חָזוּת *hōzěh/hāzût* are used in parallel to בְּרִית *b'rît*, and to 1 Samuel 17:8, where we find the hapaxlegomenon בָּרָה *brh*, "see, search out, select," Kutsch suggests a basic meaning "that which is noted, stipulation, obligation." This sense can refer to an obligation imposed on another, an obligation accepted, or even a mutual obligation. In this case, however, there is a sense in which two parties are joined (Pedersen), and the term "covenant" can properly be retained (on this point I differ from Kutsch). The purpose of the covenant is to establish שָׁלוֹם *šālôm*, "peace, well-being, wholeness." The common idiom כָּרַת בְּרִית *krt b'rît*, to "cut" a בְּרִית *b'rît*, is often associated with the ritual mentioned above, in which sacrificial animals are cut apart to reinforce the obligation. Following Pedersen and others, Kutsch takes כָּרַת *krt* to mean "fix, determine," and כָּרַת בְּרִית *krt b'rît* to mean "define an obligation."

The word בְּרִית *b'rît*, too, is not limited to theological use. The obligation it expresses can also be a matter of agreement between two human beings and can be reinforced by oath (אָלָה *ālâ*). According to Genesis 26:26–33, for example, Abimelech comes to Isaac to make a treaty with him that will strengthen the שָׁלוֹם *šālôm* between them (vs. 29). "So Isaac gave a feast and they ate and drank. The next morning they arose early and exchanged oaths (שָׁבַע *šb'*). Then Isaac bade them farewell, and they parted from him in peace (בְּשָׁלוֹם *b'šālôm*)." (vss. 30–31) According to Genesis 31:43–54, something similar takes place between Jacob and Laban; according to the version of E, the feast does not take place until after the oaths are sworn. There is no mention of any feast associated with the covenant made between Israel and the Gibeonites (Josh. 9), but the obligation appears to be primarily upon Israel. Here, too, it guarantees the Gibeonites safety. In like fashion, in the covenant between David and Jonathan the latter is the one who gives (1 Sam. 18:3–4).

Begrich attempted to understand the meaning of בְּרִית *b'rît* from within, primarily by studying terminology and phraseology. He came to the conclusion that in the earlier period of Israel's history a בְּרִית *b'rît* was thought of as a gift, in which one party gives close friendship to the other. According to him, the idiom כָּרַת בְּרִית ל *krt b'rît l* suggests this understanding, while (עִם, בֵּין וּבֵין) כָּרַת בְּרִית אֶת *krt b'rît et* ('*im, bên ûbên*) points to the infiltration of contract or treaty ideology under Canaanite influence.

The next step was the analysis of texts from elsewhere in the ancient Near East to illuminate the meaning of the "covenant." Noth, for example, pointed out a Mari text in which the sovereign undertakes to mediate between hostile tribes. The sacrifice of an ass, which marks acceptance of the covenant, plays a role in the ceremony. Most recently, however, much more attention has been given to the treaty formularies of Hittite sovereigns in their so-called suzerainty treaties with their vassals. Many of these have been preserved and studied. Mendenhall was the first to analyze them, in a study that was programmatically concise, but not carefully worked out. Baltzer next tried to use the texts, published as early as 1923 by Weidner and Friedrich and analyzed more precisely from the legal perspective by Korošec, to illuminate the Old Testament covenant form. He finds six fundamental elements in these treaties: (1) a preamble giving the name and titles of the sovereign; (2) a historical introduction that recounts the antecedent history leading up to the treaty; (3) a statement of substance or general clause, summarizing the purpose of the individual stipulations that follow; (4) the individual stipulations, which constitute the actual body of the treaty; (5) the invocation of the gods as witnesses; (6) curses for disobedience and blessings for adherence to the sovereign. In some cases it is also stated that a copy of the treaty is laid "before" or "at the feet of" the principal deities of the lands in question. We also find the requirement that the text of the treaty be regularly read in public, in the presence of the vassal.

The debate that followed upon this presentation has been summarized soberly and critically by D. J. McCarthy. Three major considerations have been advanced that seem to warn against too close comparison between these treaty formularies and the earlier statements about Yahweh's covenant with Israel: (1) The "missing link." It has not been shown how this treaty form, primarily employed by the sovereign of Asia Minor in the period before 1200, came within the purview of early Israel, semi-nomads invading the settled regions from the desert. (2) The adoption of a formulary that is fully comprehensible in the realm of human politics to describe the relationship between Yahweh and Israel or the appropriate group of Israel's ancestors (but see below, p. 53) raises unsolved problems. (3) Nowhere in the Old Testament do we find the fully developed Hittite formulary complete. The points of contact are limited to individual elements in each instance. It is therefore just as well not to associate the Old Testament theological בְּרִית *b'rit* too closely with the highly organized Hittite treaty texts.

1. Discussion of the Old Testament theological statements about the "covenant" must not overlook the fact that it is most fully attested in the deuteronomic and deuteronomistic literature. Perlitt has worked out the details impressively. According to him, the original framework of Deuteronomy spoke of the "covenant" in the context of the patriarchs. Yahweh made a "sworn covenant" with Israel's forefathers (7:9, 12*b*). In other words, "covenant" stands for the promise Yahweh offers his people whom he has "chosen." The substance of the promise is possession of the land (see below, §8). In addition, however, especially in the later strata of Deuteronomy (e. g., 5:2 with its appended proclamation of the Decalogue), the influence of the menacing events at the close of the seventh century makes itself felt in a growing tendency to associate the "covenant" with the proclamation of the commandments at Horeb (the term used by Deuteronomy for the Sinai material in Exod. 19ff.). In this latter context, the "covenant" emphasizes the imperative aspect of the divine will.

The so-called "covenant formula" should probably also be mentioned in the context of this discussion of the "covenant." It is a two-sided idiom that expresses quite explicitly the mutual relationship between Yahweh and Israel.

Smend was the first to point out that, although the two phrases "Yahweh, the God of Israel" and "Israel, the people of Yahweh" occur very early, it is not until the deuteronomic and postdeuteronomic period that we find them both combined in a double formula, which comes dangerously close to involving Yahweh in a contractual relationship with equal obligations on both parties. In this context Deuteronomy 26:16–19 is important, because the rare hiphil of אמר *'mr* is used for the statement of each half of the formula by each of the parties involved. Lohfink differs with this view.

Gerhard von Rad claimed even earlier to find the steps in the conclusion of the covenant reflected in the outline of Deuteronomy, which exhibits four sections: (1) introductory parenesis with historical content (1—11); (2) statement of the law (12:1—26:15); (3) covenant ceremony (26:16–19); (4) blessings and curses (27—30). If these observations are correct, this would be the closest approximation to the form of the Hittite treaty formularies.

A peculiarity of Deuteronomy, found only in the concluding sections (28/29), is its mention of a covenant in Moab, i. e. a covenant entered into by Israel at the end of its period of wandering in the desert immediately before entering the promised land. Perlitt is probably right in finding here not an early tradition but merely a particular interpretation of what is said in Deuteronomy 5:2–3. Speaking to the generation that is about to enter the promised land after forty years of wandering in the desert, Moses emphasizes: "Yahweh our God made a covenant with us at Horeb. It was not with our forefathers that Yahweh made this covenant, but with us, all of us who are alive and are here this day." The purpose of this passage is to actualize the Horeb covenant, not denying the historical transaction that took place between Yahweh and the generation that stood at Horeb, but emphasizing that what took place there is an immediate presence for the following generation. The reinterpretation of this statement so as to make it refer to an actual covenant ceremony in the land of Moab historicizes this actualization of the covenant in a way not anticipated by Deuteronomy 5:2–3.

2. Having examined the extensive deuteronomic and deuteronomistic covenant theology, we can look both back and ahead, asking whether this talk of a covenant also has a place in the earlier documents of the Old Testament and how it influenced the postdeuteronomic theological models. Deuteronomy shows that two questions are actually involved: Does earlier tradition know anything of a covenant between Yahweh and the patriarchs (Abraham)? Does earlier tradition know anything of a covenant between Yahweh and the people of Israel before the time of Josiah?

If we turn first to the patriarchal tradition before P, we must speak of Genesis 15, where verse 18 states in recapitulation that Yahweh made a covenant with Abraham. This covenant seals Yahweh's promise to give to Abraham's descendants the land "from the River of Egypt [the Nile] to the Great River [the Euphrates]." This promise is reinforced by the ceremony, depicted in unusual detail, of cutting up sacrificial animals and making those undertaking the obligation pass between the bloody pieces. In the secular realm, this ceremony is attested by Jeremiah 34:18–19, as well as an eighth-century treaty between Barga'ya, king of KTK, and Mati'el, king of Arpad (*KAI,* i. 222. A 40). The latter contains the statement: "Just as this calf is cut apart, so shall Mati'el be cut apart and his great ones be cut apart!" This statement shows that in this ceremony we are dealing with a hypothetical curse upon oneself. In Genesis 15, therefore, a ritual originally belonging to the secular realm has been adopted to refer to the covenant relationship between God and humanity. The audacity of this borrowing is fully sensed. Abraham, who receives the divine promise, can perceive what is happening only under the protective cover of a deep sleep; Yahweh takes upon himself the ceremony of passing between the pieces of the dismembered animals and (hardly thought through to its logical conclusion!) the hypothetical self-curse, passing between the pieces in the form of fire ("a smoking brazier and a flaming torch"; vs. 17).

It is not certain what source this passage belongs to. It can hardly have been a part of J in its original form, since it interrupts the clear sequence of chapters 12, 13, 18. The interpolation in verses 13–16, at least, can probably be assigned to E. Probably, however, we are dealing with a predeuteronomic tradition, just as distinct from the precise notions of Deuteronomy and the deuteronomistic corpus as from the later P. This conclusion allows us to state that talk of a covenant promise made by Yahweh to the patriarchs did not originate with Deuteronomy, but represents an earlier tradition. The substance of this promise, in which Yahweh appears quite unilaterally as the God who freely makes this promise to Israel's descendants, is the land: Yahweh promises to give it to Israel in terms of the hypothetical self-curse of an oath, even though the word "swear" does not appear here. Here the covenant promise occurs in the context of the great promise to Israel's forefathers (§3).

The deuteronomic use of the term "Horeb covenant," too, as we would expect from the explicitly restorative nature of the deuteronomic movement, has historical antecedents in early tradition. At this point I must discuss the Sinai narrative complex.

This discussion is particularly difficult because there is still no consensus with respect to the assignment of particular sections to the sources strata; this means in turn that there is no agreement over the precise definition of the individual statements in this complex, which has been subject to extensive expansion and revision. The contribution of P can be clearly distinguished in Exodus 19:1a, 2a; 24:15b—31:18a; 35—40. In the remainder of the complex, however, the various voices are simply indistinguishable. Here we shall try to make out at least some of the theological accents that make themselves heard. Cf. the attempted analysis in *Festschrift Eichrodt.*

Exodus 19:5 speaks of the "covenant." This verse occurs in the context of an interpolation (vss. 3b–8) that, as already mentioned, could well be called "protodeuteronomic" on account of its terminology, which takes on significance, for example in Deuteronomy. The great titles of dignity that the chosen people will receive (see above, p. 45) are conditional upon their first "observing my covenant." Here the term בְּרִית *bĕrît* refers to the commandments imposed by Yahweh.

The interpolation anticipates the subsequent narrative of Yahweh's mighty theophany and its appended declaration of the law in the Decalogue (addressed to all the people) and the Covenant Code (addressed to Moses to transmit to the people). Exodus 24 develops the response of the people to this statement of the law. It is divided into two distinct acts. A central scene (vss. 9–11) tells how Moses, Aaron, Nadab, Abihu, and seventy of the elders of Israel go up the mountain to see the "God of Israel" in his glory ("under his feet was, as it were, a pavement of sapphire, clear blue as the very heavens") and feast before him. It has been suggested that here we have a narrative from E. As in Numbers 11:16–17, 24b–30 (E), the seventy elders are representatives of Israel. They are deemed worthy to behold God upon the mountain, "and God did not stretch forth his hand against the nobles of Israel." What, however, is the significance of the feast that is held in the presence of God? It is reminiscent of the scenes in Genesis 26:26–33 and 31:43–54 where the feast has a fixed place within the framework of a covenant ceremony in which specific agreements are made. In these latter instances it is a feast enjoyed by the two human parties. In Exodus 24:9–11, a transformation has taken place that from a distance recalls the transformation of Genesis 15 when compared with Jeremiah 34. In both passages it is equally unthinkable that God and humans should meet on an equal footing in the covenant ceremony. Here we are told that Yahweh is present in all his glory, but only the human participants celebrate the feast. It is not unlikely, however, that here, too, we are dealing with a festal meal to confirm the covenant.

Now, however, we come to the question of what is agreed to in this covenant. In the present context the Decalogue comes next, but its insertion here is clearly secondary. The next element is the legislation of the Covenant Code, but it, too, looks suspiciously like a secondary interpolation between Exodus 20:21 and 24:9. Did a shorter corpus of legislation once occupy this position, later to be replaced by the fuller Covenant Code? It is clear in any case that in the present text of 24:3–8, which describes a scene at the foot of the mountain, the feast in the presence of the God of Israel is to be preceded by the prior acceptance on the part of the people of the law God has given. Here the ceremony of covenant-making is expressly reported, in which Israel is further represented by twelve masseboth by Moses and the young men who offer sacrifice. The blood ritually sprinkled upon the altar and the people establishes a bond between Yahweh and his people. The statement in 24:8*b*, "This is the blood of the covenant which Yahweh has made with you on the terms of all these commandments," explicitly establishes the significance of the blood in the context of the covenant. The whole ceremony takes place on the terms of the "commandments" (literally "words") that Yahweh has spoken to Moses and Moses has recorded in a book.

The statements in Exodus 24 have obviously been brought together through a lengthy and complex process of transmission. When we seek to judge their theological import, two points become clear: through its representatives, Israel has been graciously vouchsafed a close encounter with the "God of Israel" that is totally unique. But the solidarity between Israel and its God is based on an unequivocal appeal to concrete obedience to the commandments of Yahweh. Perlitt has stated: "It is not because these laws were proclaimed by Moses that Sinai was holy ground; rather, it was because Sinai was holy ground that the laws were associated with it" (194). This hypothesis, which assigns the earliest association between the covenant and the law to the deuteronomic period, overestimates the ability of the restorative deuteronomic movement to create traditions.

The "covenant" is spoken of once more in Exodus 34. In its present position, this chapter represents a second statement of the law and a second conveyance to Moses of the stone tablets on which Yahweh's commandments are written, after Moses' destruction of the first tablets on account of the sin committed by the people with the image of the golden calf. It has been suggested that in this chapter with its supplementary details and insertions we have the J parallel to the account of Exodus 24 with its insertions. This hypothesis cannot simply be rejected out of hand. Here it is no longer the entire people who are vouchsafed the presence of God through their seventy representatives, but Moses alone. He is told that Yahweh is making a covenant (vs. 10). In verses 12, 15–16, an interpolation by a deuteronomic hand contrasts this covenant with the prohibition against making any covenant with the inhabitants of the land promised by Yahweh or entering into marriage with them. The original text in verses 27–28 asserts that the covenant was made with Moses on the terms of Yahweh's commandments ("words"), which are (later?) explicitly called the "Ten Commandments" ("Ten Words"). In verse 27 a secondary hand, correctly interpreting the intent of the passage, has added to the phrase "[covenant] with you" (addressed to Moses) the phrase "covenant with Israel." The ark of Yahweh in which the law-tablets of the covenant were to be placed subsequently came to be called the "ark of the covenant." This point will be discussed later in another context (see below, pp. 78–79).

Different as the account in Exodus 34 is, it agrees with the narrative of Exodus 24 in stating that the covenant of Yahweh with Israel was made on the terms of the divine law.

The account of Joshua's assembly at Shechem (Josh. 24) also exhibits an association between covenant and law. In its present form, the account appears in a deuteronomic dress that cannot be missed. The possibility must be entertained seriously, however, that behind the present stylized account a genuine reminiscence has been preserved of an act of decision in early Israel. It is striking that Joshua does not simply call upon the people to obey Yahweh, as Moses does in Deuteronomy, but offers those he addresses the freedom to choose among Yahweh, the gods of their forefathers, or the gods of Canaan, while he and his house have already chosen. It is impossible to silence the question of whether this account does not preserve a reminiscence of the occasion when those coming from Egypt called on the tribes already in Canaan to join in accepting "Yahweh, God since Egypt." It is historically likely (Noth) that this should take place at Shechem, which must have occupied a special place in Israel until the division of the kingdoms and where, according to Genesis 33:20, "El, God of Israel" was worshiped in the patriarchal period. If this hypothesis is true, we have here a reminiscence of the occasion when the "people of Yahweh" became identical with "Israel."

But if the people of Yahweh used the term ברית *brît* to describe their relationship with Yahweh even in the context of the events that took place at the mountain of God in the desert, the possibility cannot be eliminated that this crucial expansion of the people of Yahweh to include all "Israel" took place once more under the rubric of a "covenant," to which the stone set up at Shechem was a "witness" (Josh. 24:26*b*).

What has been said rejects the view that covenant and law were fundamentally separate concepts (Gerstenberger). For at Shechem, Joshua 24:25 states that besides calling on the people to make a decision Joshua drew up for them חֹק וּמִשְׁפָּט *ḥōq ûmišpāṭ* ("a statute and an ordinance"); the same is said of Moses in the striking (secondary?) statement about what took place at Marah (Exod. 15:25). The undoubtedly ancient element of tradition concerning two stones with ordinances inscribed on them is nowhere particularly associated with Shechem. Other passages, however, contain brief statements, strangely out of place and intrusive, about events involving the law in the vicinity of Shechem (Josh. 8:32, 34; Deut. 27:11ff.; cf. also the act of renunciation in Gen. 35:4, which Alt considers secondary but was probably incorporated early in the period of the monarchy into the combined ritual of the "pilgrimage from Bethel to Shechem" [see below, p. 116]). Alt has also suggested that the requirement of Deuteronomy 31:10–11 that the deuteronomic law be read every seven years in the Year of Remission (שְׁמִטָּה *šᵉmiṭṭâ*) at the Feast of Booths is based on an early custom of proclaiming God's law anew at the beginning of every seven-year cycle, at the festival marking the new Israelite year. The old idioms "we do not do such things in Israel" (2 Sam. 13:12) and "an outrage in Israel" (Gen. 34:7 and elsewhere) show, as was mentioned above (p. 46), that Israel drew a clear distinction between itself and its Canaanite environment, especially in the realm of sexual conduct. The association of this distinction with the name "Israel" suggests that we are dealing not merely with ancient nomadic customs but with ordinances laid down by the "God of Israel," in which Israel defined itself as the people of Yahweh.

The "silence" of the great predeuteronomic prophets with respect to the covenant (Perlitt), to which Hosea constitutes an exception, can be explained on the basis of their specific situation, which also explains their "silence" on the subject of רוּחַ *rûaḥ* ("spirit"; see below, pp. 101–102) and, by and large, on the subject of "election" (see above, p. 47).

3. The בְּרִית *bᵉrît* category also played a significant role in the postdeuteronomic period. In the Priestly material it serves to structure the historical account of both Israel and the world. Wellhausen's initial designation of P as *liber quattuor foederum* ("Book of the Four Covenants"; Q), it is true, has proved untenable. The four phases of history within which P structures its narrative are not all introduced by a covenant. There is no covenant involved in the process of creation, recounted in Genesis 1:1—2:4*a*, which constitutes

the actual first stage. On the other hand, the post-Deluge world in which all
the creatures preserved in Noah's ark, together with Noah and his family,
increase and multiply, is marked by an explicit בְּרִית *bĕrît* that God "set up"
(הקים את [בין ובין]) *hēķîm et* [*bên ûbên*]; Gen. 9:9, 11) or "gave"
(נתן בין ובין *ntn bên ûbên;* Gen. 9:12). The substance of this covenant is
God's promise never again to subject the world to a deluge. This promise
is guaranteed by a sign. God's (war-) bow hung up in the clouds is to remind
him of his promise if his wrath should ever again burst forth in a storm. This
"covenant" is a pure promise of God's beneficence toward the entire world,
given unconditionally. It is striking that the "Noachian laws" recorded in
9:1–7 precede the promise of the covenant totally independent of it, and
have no conditional significance for the "covenant."

According to Genesis 17, another בְּרִית *bĕrît* serves to set one individual,
Abraham, apart from the rest of humanity. In him is pronounced the promise
of the future Israel. God first introduces himself under the new name
אֵל שַׁדַּי *ēl šaddai* (see above, p. 41). Next follows a general demand to live
in God's presence. Then God gives a "covenant" (נתן בין ובין *ntn bên ûbên,*
vs. 2; simple בריתי|אתך *bĕrîtî ittāk,* vs. 4; הקים בין ובין *hēķîm bên ûbên,* vs. 7;
הקים את *hēķîm et,* vss. 19, 21). The threefold promise that constitutes the
substance of this "covenant" has already been discussed (see above, p. 28).
Once again we are dealing initially with a pure promise, as was the case with
J's version of the covenant with Abraham in Genesis 15 (the substance of
which, however, consisted only of the promise of territory). This "covenant," too, is also associated with a sign, which, however, occupies in events
as a whole a very different position from the sign in Genesis 9. Abraham and
his descendants are required to undergo circumcision (see below, pp. 131–
133), which is termed both a "sign" (אות *ôt*) and a בְּרִית *bĕrît* to be observed
(שמר *šmr*), under penalty of being cut off from the people if uncircumcised.
Despite this requirement, it is not possible to speak of a conditionally given
covenant, since the punishment affects only the disobedient individual; the
covenant as a whole remains intact. Abram, who receives the promise, is
renamed Abraham ("father of a host of nations"; 17:5); his wife Sarai is
renamed Sarah ("princess"; vs. 15); the transforming power of the covenant
is thus once more stated quite unconditionally. The fourth phase of history
as narrated by P, sharply delineated by the final revelation of the name of
Yahweh (see above, pp. 18–19), begins with the call and sending of Moses
(Exod. 6:2ff.). Here it is striking that, in contrast to the predeuteronomic and
deuteronomic account, nothing is said about any בְּרִית *bĕrît.* Some traces still
plainly suggest that such may have been the case in an earlier phase. In
Exodus 31:17, for example, the Sabbath, Yahweh's gift to Israel, is, like the
rainbow in Genesis 9, a "sign between me and the Israelites." Like circumcision in Genesis 17, it is here termed a בְּרִית *bĕrît* ("commandment"), observ-

ance of which is strictly enjoined, although nothing is said about the "setting up" or "giving" of a ברית *bᵊrît* between Yahweh and Israel. That the Priestly tradition formerly spoke of a covenant in the Mosaic period is revealed in the final chapter of the Holiness Code, where the instrument of God's vengeance is termed חרב נקמת נקם ברית *ḥereb nōḳemet nᵊḳam bᵊrît,* "the sword that carries out the covenant punishment." (Lev. 26:25) P's elimination of any explicit covenant made in the Mosaic period has as its consequence the fact that the age of Israel becomes exclusively the age in which the promise to Abraham is fulfilled. This notion is probably based on a conscious theological reflection that is understandable from the perspective of the postexilic period. In the pre-exilic period, Israel foundered on the law that was associated with the "covenant" of the Mosaic period. P no longer looks upon the age of Israel's national history, which begins with Moses, as an age characterized by the covenant defined in the law. This age, too, is dominated by the promise given to Abraham.

Thus we may see how the "covenant" concept served throughout the history of Israel to express certain ideas about how a particular epoch fit into the history of the people of God. The talk of a covenant established between Yahweh and Israel can take on various emphases. On Daniel, see below, p. 236.

4. It must also be noted, however, that the term ברית *bᵊrît* can be applied to particular realms within the people of Yahweh. In a later context we shall have to discuss the figures through which Yahweh exerts his influence on his people Israel: the king, the priest, the prophet, the wise man (§10). When Yahweh establishes an enduring kingship with the house of David, we hear of a "covenant" with David. In 2 Samuel 23:5, the so-called "last words of David" speak of the "eternal covenant" that Yahweh made with David. Cf. also Psalm 89:4, 29; Jeremiah 33:20–22. The substance of this "covenant" is God's gracious promise to preserve the house of David.

Something analogous also applies to the priesthood of the house of Aaron. The fidelity displayed by the priest Phineas when Israel sins with Midianite women is responded to by Yahweh with the promise of an "eternal priestly covenant" (ברית כהנת עולם *bᵊrît kᵊhunnat 'ôlām;* Num. 25:13). Numbers 18:19 is unique in speaking of a perpetual covenant of salt. Is it possible that salt played a role in the covenant ceremony (Lev. 2:13)? A covenant with Levi is alluded to in Malachi's invective (2:4, 5, 8). Malachi 2:5 once more gives full expression to the substance of the ברית *bᵊrît:* "The covenant with him meant life and prosperity (שלום *šālôm*)."

It is clear at the same time that "covenant" is a form of fidelity to which permanence is promised. The charismatics who receive individual calls, the prophets and the wise men, are never said to have a ברית *bᵊrît* with Yahweh.

Weinfeld, Moshe. "ברית" In *Theologisches Wörterbuch zum Alten Testament*, vol. 1, cols. 781–808 (with bibliography). Edited by G. J. Botterweck and Helmer Ringgren. Stuttgart: Kohlhammer, 1973. English: "ברית *bᵉrîth.*" In *Theological Dictionary of the Old Testament*, vol. 2, pp. 253–279. Translated by J. T. Willis. Grand Rapids, Mich.: Eerdmans, 1974.—Kutsch, Ernst. "ברית *bᵉrît* Verpflichtung.*" In *Theologisches Handwörterbuch zum Alten Testament*, vol. 1, cols. 339–352. Edited by Ernst Jenni and Claus Westermann. Munich: Kaiser, 1971.—Idem. "Sehen und Bestimmen; die Etymologie von ברית." In *Archäologie und Altes Testament* (Festschrift Kurt Galling), pp. 165–178. Edited by Arnulf Kuschke and Ernst Kutsch. Tübingen: Mohr, 1970. —Pedersen, Johannes. *Der Eid bei den Semiten.* Studien zur Geschichte und Kultur des islamischen Orients, vol. 3. Strassburg: Trübner, 1914.—Begrich, Joachim. "Berit." *Zeitschrift für die Alttestamentliche Wissenschaft* 60 (1944): 1–11. Reprinted in his *Gesammelte Studien zum Alten Testament,* pp. 55–66. Theologische Bücherei, vol. 21. Munich: Kaiser, 1964.—Noth, Martin. "Das alttestamentliche Bundschliessen im Lichte eines Mari-textes." *Annuaire de l'Institut de Philologie et d'Histoire Orientales et Slaves* 13 (1953):433–444. Reprinted in his *Gesammelte Studien zum Alten Testament,* pp. 142–154. Theologische Bücherei, vol. 6. Munich: Kaiser, 1957. English: "Old Testament Covenant-Making in the Light of a Text from Mari." In his *The Laws in the Pentateuch and Other Studies,* pp. 108–117. Translated by D. R. Ap-Thomas. Edinburgh: Oliver & Boyd, 1966.—Mendenhall, George E. "Law and Covenant in Israel and the Ancient Near East." *Biblical Archaeologist* 17 (1954):26–46, 49–76. Reprinted separately under the same title, Pittsburgh: Biblical Colloquium, 1955.—Baltzer, Klaus. *Das Bundesformular.* Wissenschaftliche Monographien zum Alten und Neuen Testament, vol. 4. Neukirchen: Neukirchener Verlag, 1960. English: *The Covenant Formulary.* Translated by David E. Green. Philadelphia: Fortress, 1971.—McCarthy, Dennis J. *Der Gottesbund im Alten Testament.* 2d ed. Stuttgarter Bibelstudien, vol. 13. Stuttgart: Katholisches Bibelwerk, 1967. English: *Old Testament Covenant: a Survey of Current Opinions.* Growing Points in Theology. Richmond: John Knox, 1972.— Perlitt, Lothar. *Bundestheologie im Alten Testament.* Wissenschaftliche Monographien zum Alten und Neuen Testament, vol. 36. Neukirchen: Neukirchener Verlag, 1969.—Smend, Rudolf. *Die Bundesformel.* Theologische Studien, vol. 68. Zurich: EVZ, 1963.—Lohfink, Norbert. "Dt. 26,17–19 und die 'Bundesformel.' " *Zeitschrift für katholische Theologie* 91 (1969):517–553.— Von Rad, Gerhard. *Das formgeschichtliche Problem des Hexateuch.* Beiträge zur Wissenschaft vom Alten und Neuen Testament, 4th series, vol. 26. Stuttgart: Kohlhammer, 1938. (Especially section 5, "Das Formproblem beim Dtn.") Reprinted in his *Gesammelte Studien zum Alten Testament,* pp. 9–86, esp. 33–41. Theologische Bücherei, vol. 8. Munich: Kaiser, 1958. English: "The Form-Critical Problem of the Hexateuch." In his *The Problem of the Hexateuch and Other Essays,* pp. 1–78, esp. 26–32. Translated by E. W. Trueman Dicken. New York: McGraw-Hill, 1966.—Lohfink, Norbert. *Die Landverheissung als Eid: eine Studie zu Gen 15.* Stuttgarter Bibelstudien, vol. 28. Stuttgart: Katholisches Bibelwerk, 1967.—Zimmerli, Walther. "Erwägungen zum 'Bund'; die Aussagen über die Jahwe-ברית in Ex 19—34." In *Wort, Gebot, Glaube* (Festschrift Walther Eichrodt), pp. 171–190. Edited by Hans Joachim Stoebe. Arbeiten zur Theologie des Alten und Neuen Testaments, vol. 59. Zurich: Zwingli, 1970.—Vriezen, Theodorus Christiaan. "The Exegesis of Exodus 24, 9–11." *Oudtestamentische Studiën* 17 (1972):100–133. —Noth, Martin. *Das System der zwölf Stämme Israels.* Beiträge zur Wissenschaft vom Alten und Neuen Testament, 4th series, vol. 1. 1930. Reprint. Darmstadt: Wissenschaftliche Buchgesellschaft, 1966.—Gerstenberger, Erhard. "Covenant and Commandment." *Journal of Biblical Literature* 84 (1965):38–51.—Alt, Albrecht. *Die Ursprünge des israelitischen Rechts.* Berichte über die Verhandlungen der Sächsischen Akademie der Wissenschaften zu Leipzig; Philologisch-historische Klasse, vol. 86, part 1. Leipzig: Hirzel, 1934. Reprinted in his *Kleine Schriften zur Geschichte des Volkes Israel,* vol. 1, pp. 278–332. Munich: Beck, 1953. English: "The Origins of Israelite Law." In his *Essays on Old Testament History and Religion,* pp. 79–132. Translated by R. A. Wilson. Oxford: Blackwell, 1966.—Zimmerli, Walther. "Sinaibund und Abrahambund." *Theologische Zeitschrift* 16 (1960):268–280. Reprinted in his *Gottes Offenbarung,* 2d ed., pp. 205–216. Theologische Bücherei, vol. 19. Munich: Kaiser, 1969.

II. The Gifts Bestowed by Yahweh

It was made clear at the outset that the faith of the Old Testament knows Yahweh only as the God who bestows his favor on his world. At the very dawn of Israel's history as a people, in the exodus from Egypt, Yahweh spoke his "Yes" to Israel. How Israel continued to experience this "Yes" to its life in specific gifts will be the subject of our second section.

In our discussion of Yahweh's gifts, however, we must never lose sight of the fact, already noted in our discussion of the election of Israel and even more markedly in our treatment of the "covenant," that every gift to Israel is also a summons to a "calling," every benefit an obligation demanding a response. Therefore what is said in Part II cannot be understood without reference to what will be said in Part III under the rubric of "Yahweh's Commandment."

§7 War and Victory

It is not in a concealed spiritual experience but in concrete historical deliverance that Israel heard the "Yes" of its God to its life and responded with the earliest extant hymn (Exod. 15:21): "Sing to Yahweh, for he is highly exalted; horse and rider he hurls into the sea." After this it was in the wars that threatened its very existence that Israel saw the principal field for God's intervention. The name "Yahweh is my banner" given to an altar and the ancient battle cry "Hand on the banner of Yahweh [?], Yahweh is at war with Amalek from generation to generation" (Exod. 17:15–16) probably go back to early battles between the people of Yahweh coming out of Egypt and their desert foes. In Saul's holy war (1 Sam. 15) and even in the exhortation that concludes the laws of Deuteronomy in the narrow sense (Deut. 25:17–19), in a period when there was certainly no basis in reality for a war against Amalek, we can still sense in the concluding "Do not forget!" something of the ardor of the ancient appeal to the banner of Yahweh. In the fragment of a victory hymn following the battle near Gibeon (Josh. 10:12–13), as well as in the Song of Deborah, which has been preserved in its entirety, concluding with the wish after the defeat of the Canaanite cities in the plain of Jezreel, "So perish all your enemies, O Yahweh; but let all who love you be like the sun rising in strength" (Judg. 5:31), the presence of Yahweh upon the battlefield of Israel can be felt as strongly as in the undoubtedly ancient battle cry of the Midianite war, "For Yahweh and for Gideon" (Judg. 7:18; expressed even more sharply in the variant in 7:20: "A sword for Yahweh and for Gideon"). A direct account of Yahweh's personal intervention in a battle can still be found in the early campaigns of David against the Philistines, when David is told: "As soon as you hear a rustling sound in the treetops, then act at once; for Yahweh will have gone out before you to defeat the Philistine army." (2 Sam. 5:24) Amos, too, sees a fundamental act of deliverance by Yahweh in the destruction of the Amorites before Israel (Amos 2:9).

In his study on the "holy war," Gerhard von Rad has worked out the particular stylization that is peculiar to the "Yahweh war" (to use the preferable term taken from the title of the "Book of the Wars of Yahweh" [Num. 21:14]) in the witness of Israel, a stylization that marks it as a sacral sphere. A trumpet is sounded to call up the army. The bloody pieces of a dismembered animal constitute a particularly solemn summons (1 Sam. 11:7; cf. Judg. 19:29). The people assembled in the camp, the "militia of Yahweh," are subject to strict sacral regulations; they are a consecrated militia (1 Sam. 21:5-6). Before battle sacrifice is offered. An oracle is sought. The mouth of a man of God pronounces a promise, phrased in the perfect tense: "Yahweh has given the enemy into your hand." In battle Yahweh goes before his people; the enemy is seized by panic. The תרועה *t'rû'â,* a loud shout (the term can also refer to a shout of rejoicing in worship), begins the battle. The ban ends it. These are the stylized elements; there is no account of any battle that preserves them all, but they can be discerned in a synopsis of the individual accounts. A Yahweh war is never an imperialistic war of conquest; it always secures the rights guaranteed to Israel by Yahweh. The fact that the wars involved in the occupation of Canaan can be described in the same stylized terms as the Yahweh war reveals that they pertain to the territory guaranteed to Israel by Yahweh. The wars fought by David to create his empire, by contrast, are no longer represented as Yahweh wars. Associated with the notion of the Yahweh war is the understanding of Yahweh's aid in his wars in "legal" terms. Yahweh's victories are called צדקות יהוה *ṣidḳôt yahweh,* "righteous acts of Yahweh" (Judg. 5:11; 1 Sam. 12:7). They are particular demonstrations that Yahweh is "righteous" or "just" toward his people, thereby establishing their righteousness. For a discussion of צדקה *ṣ'dāḳâ,* see below, pp. 142-144. The use of the term "judge" for the military deliverers of Israel in the period before the monarchy may also be understood in this light; cf. for example Judges 3:10.

Von Rad links the Yahweh war as a cultic institution with the institution of the early Israelite amphictyony postulated by Noth; Smend finds its historical roots (with great likelihood) not in an institution, but in the "event" of the exodus. Stolz goes even further in his criticism, arguing (p. 198) that the Yahweh war in the early period of Israel's history was not a "continuous empirical context." Weippert seeks to weaken von Rad's hypothesis by showing that individual elements of the holy war are also found in Assyria.

On the basis of a totally different understanding of the original relationship between El and Yahweh (see above, p. 41), Cross and Miller have attempted to understand the bellicose nature of Yahweh as deriving from an antecedent belief in Baal or El.

Yahweh manifests his affirmation of Israel historically in his wars; he can therefore be described as a warrior. "Yahweh is a warrior," we read in Exodus 15:3. The entrance liturgy in Psalm 24 announces the king of glory as he comes through the gates: "It is Yahweh, strong and mighty, Yahweh mighty in battle." An extreme metaphor in Isaiah 63:1ff. describes Yahweh as coming from Edom in garments drenched with blood. The sword of Yahweh also takes on an independent existence. It is unresting in the struggle against the Philistines (Jer. 47:6); it is sated in the battle with the Egyptians (Jer. 46:10); it is described as drunk on blood in the battle with Edom (Isa. 34:5–6). In a different context, we encounter military imagery where the worshiper expresses confidence in Yahweh as a shield (Ps. 3:4; also Gen. 15:1) or prays that he will take up shield and buckler and hasten to help (Ps. 35:2). Contrariwise, Job feels in his incomprehensible sufferings how the arrows of the Almighty find their mark in him (6:4).

If Yahweh is Israel's leader in battle, what is the role of the people? Initially the faith of Israel did not make light of the human role (Seeligmann, Schmidt). The Song of Deborah recounts in detail the part played by specific individuals in the victory. Judges 5:23 goes so far as to reproach Meroz, which refused to take part, by using the remarkable expression: "They did not come to the aid of Yahweh." Always, however, the glory remains Yahweh's. The Old Testament, whose stories are full of men of war, never developed any kind of hero worship. The heroic age of the valiant warriors, familiar to Israel through stories from elsewhere in the ancient Near East, took on here a basically different emphasis. According to Genesis 6:1–4, the birth of the semidivine heroes of the primordial age was a cause of the great Deluge. The figure of Nimrod in Genesis 10:8–12 belongs to pre-Abrahamic humanity, whose history in J culminates with the story of the Tower of Babel. Cf. also Ezekiel 32:27. Victory remains always a gift of Yahweh. It is probably no coincidence that human "victory" is expressed by a passive form— "receive help" (נוֹשַׁע *nôšaʿ*).

Subsequently the expression of God's part in human victories takes different forms.

1. Some accounts state that a divine spirit grips a man and gives him the power to triumph in battle (see below, §10b, c).

2. We read how Yahweh governs the course of events through his instructions placed in the mouth of a priest or prophet who makes inquiry of God. The casting of lots can also play a role in this inquiry (cf. Num. 27:21; Judg. 1:1; 1 Sam. 23:2; 30:8; also 1 Sam. 14:37; 28:6). Dreams can contain messages from God (Judg. 7:13–14; cf. 1 Sam. 28:6, 15).

3. It is Yahweh who sends terror upon the enemy (Exod. 23:27–28; Deut. 7:20, 23; Josh. 24:12), so that their hearts fail (Josh. 2:11) and they are put to rout (Judg. 4:15).

4. In addition, the Old Testament accounts repeatedly speak of miracles. Yahweh has the forces of nature at his disposal: the tempest in the battle fought by Deborah (Judg. 5:20–21), the hailstones that fall upon the fleeing

Canaanites (Josh. 10:11), the thunder that puts the Philistines to flight (1 Sam. 7:10). Later legends do not shrink from recording the most impossible events. In a single night the destroying angel slays 185,000 men in the camp of Sennacherib (2 Kings 19:35).

Alongside these references to direct intervention on the part of Yahweh, we find a tendency to represent the human agents of victory in the most humble possible terms. According to Judges 6:15, Gideon is the youngest of his father's household, which is the least in the tribe of Manasseh. He collects an army of 32,000, of which Yahweh says: "The people with you are more than I need to deliver Midian into their hands: Israel will claim the glory for themselves and say that it is their own strength that has given them the victory." (Judg. 7:2) And so their number is reduced, first to 10,000 and finally to 300. Saul, who is to conquer the Philistines, must be fetched from among the baggage where he is bashfully hiding. David, too, according to 1 Samuel 16 is smaller than his brothers. Jonathan formulates the sense of humility in Yahwism on the occasion of his daring attack upon the Philistine outpost: "It is an easy matter for Yahweh to help (לְהוֹשִׁיעַ *hôšia‘*), whether we be few or many." (1 Sam. 14:6) In consequence, human armor comes to be looked on with suspicion. When David, armed merely with a sling, attacks the heavily armed Philistine, the later version of the story of Goliath, which has undergone theological reflection, has him say: "You have come against me with sword and spear and dagger, but I have come against you in the name of Yahweh of hosts, the God of the army of Israel." (1 Sam. 17:45) Again and again Israel is admonished not to be afraid, even when it is outwardly at a disadvantage. To the Israelites at the Sea of Reeds, pursued by the Egyptians, Moses says (J): "Yahweh will fight for you, so hold your peace." (Exod. 14:14) This is also the tone of the war speech that the priest addresses to the assembled army according to Deuteronomy 20:1ff.: "Do not lose heart, or be afraid, or give way to panic in the face of them; for Yahweh your God will go with you to fight your enemy for you and give you the victory." These are almost exactly the words spoken by Isaiah in his exhortation during the Syro-Ephraimite war (Isa. 7:4). In Isaiah the battle against false confidence in alliances and armaments also reaches its high point, with echoes in Psalms 20:8; 146:3; and Zechariah 4:6. According to von Rad, the demand that Israel "believe" or "have faith" is rooted in the ideology of the Yahweh war and refers to the attitude that springs from knowledge of Yahweh as the giver of victory. This may also be the context of the expectation that Yahweh will destroy all the weapons of war, which we encounter at the threshold of a hope for universal peace (Bach). Cf. Psalm 46:9–10; Isaiah 2:4; 9:4; Zechariah 9:10.

One further point must be made. From the very outset Israel repeatedly experienced the "yes" of its God when he gave the Israelites victory over their enemies; the entire Old Testament, nevertheless, is permeated by the knowledge that Yahweh is always free to give Israel victory or to deny it, according to his holy will. Yahweh is never merely a "victory God of Israel."

When the Israelites making their way through the desert hear the report of their spies, at first they are hestitant and refuse to enter the land of Canaan; then, after Yahweh has sent them back into the desert, they venture battle without his authorization and are defeated (Num. 13—14). In 14:44, a statement has been added (secondarily?) that Moses and the ark of the covenant did not leave the camp, indicating that Yahweh did not take part in this war. During the Philistine war (1 Sam. 4), following an initial defeat, Israel attempts to gain a victory by bringing the sacred palladium of Yahweh, the ark, into camp. Once again Yahweh denies Israel victory and allows the ark, which Israel believed to indicate the presence of "Yahweh of hosts" (see below, pp. 75–76), to fall into the hands of the Philistines. Of course 1 Samuel 5—6 makes it clear that capture of the ark did not make the Philistines in turn possessors of the victory given by Yahweh.

In his freedom, Yahweh has the power to grant victory to Israel's enemies. According to 1 Kings 19:15; 2 Kings 8:12–13, Hazael of Damascus, who afflicts Israel terribly, is called by the prophet of Yahweh. The Syrian Naaman receives his victories from the hand of Yahweh (2 Kings 5:1). According to 2 Kings 15:37; Isaiah 9:11, Yahweh unleashes Rezin of Damascus against Israel. Above all, however, this freedom of the holy God is proclaimed by the great prophets, according to whom the mighty Assyrian is an instrument in Yahweh's hand to punish his people—albeit an instrument that Yahweh himself calls to account when it arrogantly claims to be the final master. According to Jeremiah 25:9; 27:6; 43:10, Nebuchadnezzar, the destroyer of Jerusalem, is the servant of Yahweh. For a discussion of Cyrus, see below, pp. 218–219.

Throughout the course of Old Testament history, it becomes increasingly clear that the "yes" of Yahweh to his people cannot be measured by the victory or defeat of Israel as a political entity. Of all the prophets, Isaiah developed most fully the idea that God's counsel is an unfathomable mystery. But in Deutero-Isaiah, too, in the confession of the "God who hides himself" (45:15), we hear the note of wonder at the mystery.

In apocalyptic literature we find the supreme expression of the notion that Yahweh's final victory, in which he conclusively demonstrates his solidarity with his people, does not need any military assistance on the part of the people of Yahweh. Ezekiel 38—39 already depicts how the army of Gog, the prince of Meshech and Tubal, is mysteriously defeated by Yahweh himself. In Zechariah 2:1–4, four mysterious smiths strike down the horns that embody the powers of the world in their totality. According to Daniel 2, a stone not hurled by any human hand destroys the image that represents the

kingdoms of the world. Here faith relies entirely on what Yahweh alone does
to bring life to his people.

Von Rad, Gerhard. *Der Heilige Krieg im alten Israel.* Zurich: Zwingli, 1951.—Lohfink, Norbert.
"Beobachtungen zur Geschichte des Ausdrucks יהוה עם." In *Probleme biblischer Theologie*
(Festschrift Gerhard von Rad), pp. 275–305 (with bibliography). Edited by Hans Walter Wolff.
Munich: Kaiser, 1971.—Smend, Rudolf. *Jahwekrieg und Stämmebund.* Forschungen zur Religion
und Literatur des Alten und Neuen Testaments, vol. 84. Göttingen: Vandenhoeck & Ruprecht,
1963. English: *Yahweh War & Tribal Confederation.* Translated by M. G. Rogers. Nashville:
Abingdon, 1970.—Stolz, Fritz. *Jahwes und Israels Kriege.* Abhandlungen zur Theologie des Alten
und Neuen Testaments, vol. 60. Zurich: Theologischer Verlag, 1972.—Weippert, Manfred.
" 'Heiliger Krieg' in Israel und Assyrien: Kritische Anmerkungen zu Gerhard von Rads Konzept des 'Heiligen Krieges im alten Israel.' " *Zeitschrift für die Alttestamentliche Wissenschaft* 84
(1972):460–493.—Cross, Frank Moore. "The Divine Warrior in Israel's Early Cult." In *Biblical
Motifs: Origins and Transformations,* pp. 11–30. Edited by Alexander Altmann. Philip W. Lown
Institute of Advanced Judaic Studies, Brandeis University; Studies and Texts, vol. 3. Cambridge,
Mass.: Harvard University Press, 1966.—Miller, Patrick D. *The Divine Warrior in Early Israel.*
Harvard Semitic Monographs, vol. 5. Cambridge, Mass.: Harvard University Press, 1973.—
Fredriksson, Henning. *Jahwe als Krieger.* Lund: Gleerup, 1945. —Seeligmann, Isaac Leo.
"Menschliches Heldentum und göttliche Hilfe." *Theologische Zeitschrift* 19 (1963):385–411.—
Schmidt, Ludwig. *Menschlicher Erfolg und Jahwes Initiative.* Wissenschaftliche Monographien zum
Alten und Neuen Testament, vol. 38. Neukirchen: Neukirchener Verlag, 1970.—Bach, Robert. " '. . . der Bogen zerbricht, Spiesse zerschlägt und Wagen mit Feuer verbrennt.' " In
Probleme biblischer Theologie (Festschrift Gerhard von Rad), pp. 13–26. Edited by Hans Walter
Wolff. Munich: Kaiser, 1971.—Stamm, Johann Jakob, and Bietenhard, Hans. *Der Weltfriede im
Alten und Neuen Testament.* Zurich: Zwingli, 1959.—Schmid, Hans Heinrich. *šalôm: Frieden im
Alten Orient und im Alten Testament.* Stuttgarter Bibelstudien, vol. 51. Stuttgart: KBW Verlag,
1971.

§8 The Land and Its Blessings

1. Israel's confession of the God who brought them out of Egypt did not
remain in isolation. It was understood at the same time as a confession of the
God who also brought Israel into the land of Canaan. The farmer's prayer
in Deuteronomy 26:5–10 gives classic expression to this belief.

Therefore Israel never developed any sense of being autochthonous in
Canaan. It always thought of its land as being a gift from the hand of the God
who delivered Israel from captivity and gave the Israelites freedom from
their oppressors.

As Herrmann has shown, the promise of the land is formulated in two
distinct ways:

a) In the account of the call of Moses, it is closely associated in the mouth
of Yahweh with the promise of the exodus: "I have seen the misery of my
people in Egypt. I have heard their outcry against their oppressors. . . . I have
come down to rescue them from the hand of the Egyptians, and to bring them
up out of that country into a fine, broad land, a land flowing with milk and
honey." (Exod. 3:7–8 [J?])

b) The promise of the land to the patriarchs, to which the expression "flowing with milk and honey" is alien, derives from different traditio-historical roots. The land was already promised to Abraham, whom God brought out of Mesopotamia—in fact, God brought him into this land, promised him by oath (Gen. 50:24; Deut. 1:8, 35, and *passim*) in the "covenant" (Gen. 15:18).

It is also striking that the Old Testament recounts two "occupations" of the land—a first, remarkably provisional, in which the patriarchs look forward in hope to the day when the land will really be totally given to their descendants, and a second occupation by what is now the people of Israel. The P stratum framed the theological conception for the first phase by speaking of the "land of sojourning" or "land of temporary citizenship" (ארץ מגורים *ereṣ mᵉgûrîm*).

These two ways of speaking about the promised land define the unique relationship of the Old Testament faith to the land. Israel does not dwell in a land to which the changes and chances of history just happen to have brought it, but in a land destined for it by Yahweh's decision even before there was an Israel. In this sense it is possible to speak of the land as a "primary datum" for Israel (Buber). One must always remember, however, that this "primary relationship" is something quite different from the primary relationship between "blood and soil," which presupposes an initial relationship that cannot be examined further. The relationship between Israel and its land rests on a decision made by Yahweh, which can never be separated from his holy will as expressed in the various stages of belief in the "covenant." In certain sections of the introductory discourses of Deuteronomy, for example, possession of the land is made frankly conditional upon keeping God's commandments (Deut. 11:8; cf. also Exod. 20:12; 1 Chron. 28:8). The whole message of the prophets in their age, the experience of the exile and its survival, rest on this foundation. Without an awareness of this unique relationship to the land, it is impossible to understand the course of Israel's history down to the present—including the phenomenon of an apparently quite secular Zionism.

The statements about the land found in the Old Testament therefore comprise two components: (1) a sense that possession of the land is a gift, never simply an obvious fact; and (2) a sense that this is a very special benefit, not definable simply in terms of material value, but always associated with the status of Israel as the "people of Yahweh," and therefore impossible to esteem too highly.

This high esteem may be observed in Deuteronomy 8:7–9; 11:10–15, where the words of Moses depict the promised land in the most glowing colors, and, in the latter passage, contrast it with Egypt. If you have had the opportunity to compare with your own eyes the actual possibilities offered by the fertile valley of the Nile with those offered by the sterile mountain landscape of Palestine, you will see at once how much this land, the pledge of divine favor, is here viewed in the light of a faith in divine splendor and a glory that far transcends reality. There are also certain stereotyped formulas used to express this feeling. In the phrase "a land flowing with milk and honey" (וּדְבָשׁ הָלָב זָבַת אֶרֶץ *ereṣ zābat hālāb ûd̲baš*), Usener has claimed to find a reference to the food of the gods in paradise, an equivalent to the Greek nectar and ambrosia. It is more likely, however, that this probably ancient formula preserves a semi-nomadic ideal of food in profusion. Jeremiah 3:19 speaks of the "pleasant land," the "patrimony fairer than that of any nation" (גּוֹיִם|צִבְאוֹת צְבִי נַחֲלַת *naḥălat ṣ̌bî ṣibʾôt gôyîm*). The term "fair" (צְבִי *ṣ̌bî*) recurs in Ezekiel 20:6; and in Daniel 8:9; 11:16, 41, 45 it becomes a standard way of referring to the land in apocalyptic language. The designation of the land in Deuteronomy 12:9 as a place of "rest" for Israel likewise transcends empirical reality. When the Nile and Euphrates appear in descriptions as the limits of its boundaries (Gen. 15:18; cf. Exod. 23:31), we may find a reference to the age of David, when for a brief moment Israel's sphere of influence was in fact that great. But in the retention of this description we can recognize once again the element of glorification of the promised land. Taking this as its point of departure, Ezekiel 20:6 places the description given by the spies in Numbers 13—14 directly in the mouth of Yahweh: Yahweh himself spied out the land for his people.

The double nature of the land is reflected in still other Old Testament terminology. Gerhard von Rad has pointed out that the term "heritage" or "patrimony" (נַחֲלָה *naḥălā*), which initially designates the defined property of a clan or tribe, is extended in deuteronomic usage to refer to the "patrimony of Israel" (יִשְׂרָאֵל נַחֲלַת *naḥălat yiśrāʾēl*), a term that expresses Israel's right to occupy this land as its own defined property. But the land is also spoken of as the "patrimony of Yahweh," an expression that makes the land a holy land, Yahweh's personal property. This terminology should probably be interpreted against the background of the cult. The alien land to which Israel is deported in the exile stands in contrast as an "unclean land" (Amos 7:17; cf. Ezek. 4:13). In this land that belongs to Yahweh Israel dwells as a tenant. In this context the Israelites can be called "aliens and settlers" in Yahweh's land (Lev. 25:23), a phrase that shatters any proprietary notions that might be harbored by a nation thinking in terms of "blood and soil."

It is immediately obvious that such a sense of the land will have consequences in the way the land is apportioned and subsequently administered. "Gift" and "commandment" in this context, too, represent two sides of the same coin. Joshua 14ff. tells how Joshua apportioned the land to the tribes by casting lots "before Yahweh." (18:10) The peculiar second apportionment of the land according to the scheme of Ezekiel 48 takes account of Yahweh's ownership of the entire land by setting aside in the midst of the land, alongside the portions of the twelve tribes, a thirteenth portion designated a "holy reserve." Upon it the Temple will stand, and there those who serve the Temple will receive their portions, together with the prince of Israel. A law intended to prevent gradual undermining of the divine apportionment is found in Numbers 36, an appendix that regulates the inheritance of daughters. Within the framework of the regulations laid down in the book of Ezekiel, Ezekiel 46:16ff. likewise attempts to prevent the breakdown of order with reference, say, to the property of the prince. Knowledge that possession of the land is a benefit entailing certain responsibilities toward God, so that land cannot simply be treated as "commercial property," probably lies behind the reaction of Naboth to Ahab, who wishes to purchase his patrimony (1 Kings 21:3). And Isaiah (5:8) and Micah (2:1ff.) above all will protest vehemently against real estate profiteering.

In view of all that has been said, it is not surprising that in the discourses of the prophets that look forward to an age of salvation following God's judgment the land retains an important place (Hos. 2:17; Jer. 32:15; Ezek. 36:28ff.; 37:25).

2. The "land" is the place where agriculture is carried on. But the farmers must rely on other gifts than the gift of victory discussed in §7 and the apportionment of the land already discussed here. They need more than casual "help," like that experienced in the Yahweh war; they need the regular alternation of rain and sun, the gifts of fertile soil, the rain from heaven, and the slow but constant growth of crops and livestock.

A preliminary religio-historical comment must be made in this context. In contrast to the gift of historical deliverance and victory, these gifts do not involve Israel with something that is Yahweh's own property as they occupy the land. Instead, Israel, with little advance preparation through its faith in Yahweh, finds a land that has much to say about the powers of fertility and the blessings of rain from heaven. Canaan is familiar with the forces of fertility as divine powers. As the texts from Ugarit have confirmed, Baal is a crucial figure of the pantheon in this context (Kapelrud). Faith in Baal is also intimately associated with the agricultural practices through which the farmer seeks to guarantee the blessings of this power and its feminine counterparts. The ritual of the sacred marriage, of the dying and reviving vegetation represented in the sacred drama, is important in this regard (Hvidberg). By observing these rituals farmers guarantee divine blessing on their land; at the same time they secure human fertility, the blessing of children, and health.

The encounter of Israel with these Canaanite beliefs and rituals could have taken three possible courses.

1. Israel could worship the God who had proved to be the guide of its history since the time of the exodus as being specially associated with the historical realm, alongside the world of Baal, associated with fertility and prosperity. Life in the land would then be assigned to the various powers according to the principle of division of labor.

2. Israel could identify Yahweh with the existing local powers, just as it rediscovered Yahweh in the "God of the fathers" and applied the predicates and sovereignty of "El Most High" to Yahweh.

3. Israel could embark on a hostile campaign in which Baal and the realm of belief associated with him, together with the ritual honoring him, would be rejected or else incorporated only with crucial changes.

In the Old Testament we can make out traces of all three possibilities; as a rule, history does not move exclusively in a single direction. The name Bealiah (1 Chron. 12:6), already mentioned above (p. 41), betrays, as does the polemic of Hosea, that Yahweh could sometimes simply be called "baal" ("lord," "proprietor"). In the polemic of Elijah we can see, albeit in the context of a foreign influence emanating from Tyre, the worship of the Tyrian Baal, how a cult of Baal (prophets of Baal in 1 Kings 18) ranks itself openly alongside Yahwism, whereas in the polemic of Hosea and Jeremiah we are led to think in terms of syncretism involving both Baal and Yahweh. In the course of these bitter disputes, however, the third of the options mentioned above proved itself to be the only legitimate possibility for Yahwism: Yahweh alone can bestow the blessings of the heavens and the fertility of the earth. The name of Baal is subsequently outlawed and the ritual associated with him is adopted by the peasants of Israel only after crucial transformation. This will be seen clearly in our discussion of the agricultural festivals of Israel (see below, pp. 126ff.). This same process can be observed in all the areas associated with growth and prosperity. The form of the sacred marriage, with its corresponding ritual involving sacral prostitutes at the sanctuaries, is outlawed and eliminated, as is belief in a dying and rising god of vegetation and such associated rituals as the lament for Tammuz (Ezek. 8).

Israel receives the blessings of the soil and fecundity solely from the hand of Yahweh, by whom all the powers of fertility and increase are restricted to the created realm (§4) and cease to possess any power independent of him. The farmer's prayer in Deuteronomy 26:5–10, already mentioned several times, is an especially impressive piece of liturgical evidence for the way even the farmers, bearing to the sanctuary a basket filled with the produce of their land, give thanks to the God who gave them the land after bringing them out of Egypt.

Thus the great words of Moses' blessing upon Joseph (Deut. 33:13ff.), "the most precious things from the heaven above [?] and from the deep that lurks below [i. e., the rain and springs of water], the most precious things ripened by the sun and produced by the months, the best things from the ancient mountains and the most precious things of the everlasting hills, the most precious things of earth," derive from the blessing of Yahweh and "the favor of him who dwells in the burning bush." (Exod. 3:2) Instead of using the term "precious," the parallel passage in Jacob's blessing upon Joseph in Genesis 49:25–26 speaks of "blessings," referring to him who bestows them as שׁדׄי אׅל ēl šaddai (?), while "help" comes from the "God of your father" (אׇבׅיךָ אׅל ēl ābîkā). Jeremiah polemicizes against those who are ungrateful to Yahweh, who do not say, "Let us fear Yahweh our God, who gives us the rains of autumn, and spring showers in their turn, who brings us unfailingly fixed seasons of harvest" (5:24); cf. also Hosea 2:10ff. Above all, however, the blessings that flow from Yahweh are elaborated most fully in the concluding corpora of the great legal codes in H (the Holiness Code) and Deuteronomy. Here we also find expressed once more the circumstance already mentioned with respect to the gift of the land: this blessing, too, cannot be received by the people apart from Yahweh's will as expressed in his law; it is clearly conditional upon obedience. "If you listen to the voice of Yahweh . . . , you will be blessed in the city and you will be blessed in your fields. Blessed will be the fruit of your body and the fruit of your land, the offspring of your cattle and the increase of your sheep. Blessed will be your basket and your kneading trough. . . . Yahweh will offer his blessing, that he may be with you in your storehouses and in all that you undertake. . . . Yahweh will open for you his rich treasury, the heavens, that he may give to your land rain in its season, and that he may bless all the work of your hands." The corresponding curse threatens withdrawal of all these blessings (Deut. 28; cf. Lev. 26:3ff.). The passage cited refers to the "increase" (or "ewes") by means of the Hebrew phrase עַשְׁתְּרֹת צֹאנֶךָ *'aštrōt ṣō'n'kā;* the original association with the Canaanite goddess Astarte can hardly be overlooked. In the present text, however, this association has been totally forgotten. The blessing of fertility is solely the gift of Yahweh.

When the gifts of heaven fail to come, we see how Israel on its days of penitence cries out to Yahweh, imploring him to look with favor upon Israel once more (Jer. 14; Joel 2:12ff.; cf. 1 Kings 8:35–36). When drought comes, we see how Israel seeks to discover what sin could have brought about such punishment at the hands of Yahweh (2 Sam. 21); we hear the prophet's straightforward statement that neither dew nor rain will fall on account of the sin of Ahab and Jezebel (1 Kings 17:1; cf. also Hag. 1:6ff.; 2:15ff.).

According to J (Gen. 12:2–3), the history of Israel stands first under the sign of an unconditional blessing, which promises to Abraham that he will increase to become a nation and become an agent of blessing for all the families of the earth, and second under conditionally stated promises of the immediate blessings of nature—but the promises even in this area call on Israel to obey the bestower of the blessings.

In any case, however, the blessing remains the free gift of the Lord, who does not himself participate in the alternation of day and night, drought and heat, life and death, but holds them all freely in his hands.

Herrmann, Siegfried. *Die prophetischen Heilserwartungen im Alten Testament.* Beiträge zur Wissenschaft vom Alten and Neuen Testament, 5th series, vol. 5. Stuttgart: Kohlhammer, 1965.—Buber, Martin. *Israel und Palästina.* Erasmus-Bibliothek. Zurich: Artemis, 1950. English: *Israel and Palestine.* Translated by Stanley Godman. New York: Farrar, Straus and Young, 1952.—Usener, Hermann. "'Milch und Honig.'" *Rheinisches Museum für Philologie* new series 57 (1902):177–195.—Von Rad, Gerhard. "Verheissenes Land und Jahwes Land im Hexateuch." *Zeitschrift des Deutschen Palästinavereins* 66 (1943):191–204. Reprinted in his *Gesammelte Studien zum Alten Testament,* pp. 87–100. Theologische Bücherei, vol. 8. Munich: Kaiser, 1958. English: "The Promised Land and Yahweh's Land in the Hexateuch." In his *The Problem of the Hexateuch and Other Essays,* pp. 79–93. Translated by E. W. Trueman Dicken. New York: McGraw-Hill, 1966.—Kapelrud, Arvid. *Baal in the Ras Shamra Texts.* Copenhagen: Gad, 1952.—Kühlewein, Johannes. "בַּעַל *ba'al* Besitzer." In *Theologisches Handwörterbuch zum Alten Testament,* vol. 1, cols. 327–333. Edited by Ernst Jenni and Claus Westermann. Munich: Kaiser, 1971.—Mulder, M. J. "בַּעַל." In *Theologisches Wörterbuch zum Alten Testament,* vol. 1, cols. 706–727 (with bibliography). Edited by G. J. Botterweck and Helmer Ringgren. Stuttgart: Kohlhammer, 1973. English: "בַּעַל *ba'al.*" In *Theological Dictionary of the Old Testament,* vol. 2, pp. 181–200. Translated by J. T. Willis. Grand Rapids, Mich.: Eerdmans, 1974.—Hvidberg, Flemming. *Weeping and Laughter in the Old Testament.* Leiden: Brill, 1962.—Westermann, Claus. *Der Segen in der Bibel und im Handeln der Kirche.* Munich: Kaiser, 1968.—Keller, Carl; and Wehmeier, Gerhard. "בּרך *brk* pi. segnen." In *Theologisches Handwörterbuch zum Alten Testament,* vol. 1, cols. 353–376. Edited by Ernst Jenni and Claus Westermann. Munich: Kaiser, 1971.—Scharbert, Josef. "בְּרָכָה בּרך." In *Theologisches Wörterbuch zum Alten Testament,* vol. 1, cols. 808–841 (with bibliography). Edited by G. J. Botterweck and Helmer Ringgren. Stuttgart: Kohlhammer, 1973. English: "בּרך *brk;* בְּרָכָה *b'rākhāh.*" In *Theological Dictionary of the Old Testament,* vol. 2, pp. 279–308. Translated by J. T. Willis. Grand Rapids, Mich.: Eerdmans, 1974.

§9 The Gift of God's Presence

The Old Testament has more to say about Yahweh than that he reveals himself to his people in guiding them and bestowing his blessings. It speaks also under various circumstances of Yahweh's gift of his personal presence to his people or their representatives. This presence takes on various forms in the course of Israel's long history and is expressed by means of various theologoumena.

1. A summons into God's presence already marks the initial event of the exodus: "Let my people go in order to worship me," is Yahweh's command, as Moses monotonously insists over and over again to Pharaoh (Exod. 7:26; 8:16; 9:1, 13; 10:3 [J]). Israel wishes to go three days' journey into the desert for a festal sacrifice to Yahweh, its God (3:18; 5:3; cf. 5:8; 8:22–24). Nothing more is said of this "feast of Yahweh" (10:9) in the remainder of the narrative. At most, an echo of it may be made out behind Exodus 32. Instead there follows in Exodus 19, much further from Egypt according to the introductory statement of P (19:1), the account of the mighty theophany at Sinai, the mountain of God, in which Yahweh comes to his people directly. Jeremias has shown that the Sinai theophany has played a crucial role in the development of the Old Testament theophany genre, even if its literary expression in Exodus 19 did not exert a direct influence. According to him, the *Sitz im Leben* of the theophany description is initially in the Israelite victory hymn. It then takes on independent status and finds use in other contexts.

The nature of Yahweh's presence at the mountain of God varies in detail in the different accounts. According to the account of the call of Moses (J?), Moses encounters Yahweh in the mysterious phenomenon of a burning bush that is not consumed by the fire. Cf. also Deuteronomy 33:16: "he who dwells in the burning bush" (סנה שכני *šōkenî senê*). He is commanded: "Come no nearer; take off your sandals, for the place where you are standing is holy ground." (Exod. 3:5) Thus Yahweh appears as a blazing fire, albeit fire of a special kind. What is here depicted in miniature in terms of a thorn-bush in a particular holy place becomes a stupendous event in Exodus 19, when the people brought forth from Egypt encounter Yahweh at the mountain of God. J, to whom Exodus 19:18 can probably be assigned, tells how Yahweh comes down upon the mountain of God in fire. The mountain smokes like a smelter's furnace. It has been suggested that observation of a volcanic eruption may have furnished the colors in which this description is painted. E, whose description is found in 19:16, speaks instead of peals of thunder, flashes of lightning, and dense smoke, suggesting a severe thunderstorm. When the verse goes on to speak of a loud trumpet blast (vs. 13b: sounds of the ram's horn), it is likely that features of the liturgical ceremony surrounding the proclamation of the Decalogue at a later date have been interwoven (Ps. 81, esp. vs. 4). The account of P (Exod. 24:15b–18a), which is the most sharply delimited, speaks of a cloud covering the mountain as the effulgent glory of Yahweh descends upon Mount Sinai. The cloud covers the effulgence to protect humans from its consuming fire. For six days the cloud rests upon the mountain, until on the seventh day Moses is summoned to go up the mountain. According to 19:14–15 (J?), Moses decrees a period of three days of preparation for the people (washing their clothes) before the day of Yahweh's coming. Whereas J goes on to speak of the barrier placed around the area of the holy mountain, which neither human nor beast may enter, E (vs. 13b) seems initially to assume that the people are to go up the mountain. The meal of the seventy (plus four) representatives of the people upon the mountain (24:9–11; cf. above, p. 52) is best associated with this narrative strand. The (volcanic?) fire shining out of the dark clouds is mentioned also in the recapitulation of the event in Deuteronomy 4:11; 5:23. All these accounts, with their diverse emphases in detail, share a common reference to the consuming majesty of the one who vouchsafes his presence to his people (on Exod. 33, see below, pp. 73ff.).

Belief in the association of Yahweh with the mountain of God (called Sinai in J and P, Horeb in E and Deuteronomy, a difference so far unexplained) should be understood as a heritage from the early period of the tribes. The mountain of God has been located in both what is today the Sinai peninsula and in northwest Arabia, where there were still active volcanoes in historical times. Presumably various tribes from the surrounding region worshiped their god there under the name "Yahweh." The mountain was a pilgrimage site for these groups, which have been identified as Kenites or Midianites. But this worship of Yahweh at the mountain of God did not become part of the Old Testament faith until it was connected with belief in Yahweh's historical deliverance of those who were enslaved in Egypt. For Israel, the God who appears in his majesty at Sinai/Horeb is the God who is confessed to have led Israel out of Egypt into liberty. This deliverance laid the foundation for the special relationship between Yahweh and those he delivered. The theophany at the mountain of God then became a component of the covenant ceremony; the covenant meal, according to Exodus 24:9–11, was eaten by the representatives of the people in the presence of Yahweh, and the acceptance of the covenant's obligations took place, according to 24:3–8, at the foot of the mountain. According to P, the events surrounding the theophany at Sinai then became the locus of the decree governing Israel's worship "in the presence of Yahweh," a decree making Israel indeed the "people of Yahweh."

In this new setting, belief in "the lord of Sinai" (the phrase זה סיני *zēh sînai* in Judg. 5:5; Ps. 68:8 appears to attest this title for Yahweh) continued to influence the twelve tribes in the land of Canaan. According to Judges 5:4–5, Yahweh appears from the south for a historical act of deliverance in the plain of Jezreel, where he does battle from heaven with the enemies of Israel. Deuteronomy 33:2 also speaks of Yahweh as coming from Sinai, and goes on in verse 3 (?) to speak of his love for his people. This image still echoes in the psalm of Habakkuk (3:3). In 1 Kings 19, Elijah, the fanatic devotee of Yahweh, flees in his distress to Horeb, the mountain of God, where he learns to encounter Yahweh neither in storm, nor in earthquake, nor in fire, but in a soft whispering voice. Noth has suggested that the itinerary of a "pilgrimage to Sinai" has been incorporated into Numbers 33.

2. After the Israelites settled in Canaan, they had new experiences of Yahweh's presence in their own land to set alongside this faith in Yahweh's appearance at the mountain of God, far off in the desert. Some time after the

occupation, we find the complex picture of a series of major local sanctuaries scattered throughout the land, to which the Israelites traveled at specific seasons of the year to "behold the face of Yahweh" (cf. 1 Sam. 1). All males are to make this pilgrimage three times a year (Exod. 23:17; 34:23; Deut. 16:16). As Nötscher has demonstrated in detail, the expression "to behold the face of Yahweh" derives from Israel's polytheistic environment, where the image of the deity was viewed and worshiped in each sanctuary. A later age, which found this idiom embarrassing for Yahwism, revocalized the text so that the masoretic text now reads that everyone is "to appear [literally 'be seen'] before the face of Yahweh." The basis for this belief in Yahweh's presence at the sacred site within the boundaries of the land itself can be seen in the law governing altars in Exodus 20:24. In this law's earliest form, Yahweh commands that an altar of earth be made, and promises: "Wherever I cause my name to be remembered, I will come to you and bless you." This statement assumes openly that Yahweh will make known where in the land he wishes to see his name invoked. An actual instance of this can be seen in 1 Samuel 14:33–35: after winning a battle, Saul has a great stone rolled up, alongside which the people can slaughter the livestock they have captured according to the proper ritual. "Then Saul built an altar to Yahweh, and this was the first altar to Yahweh that he built." Is it coincidence that a victory of Israel over the Philistines is the occasion for the building of an altar at which Yahweh was believed to be present? According to 1 Samuel 7:12, the legendary account of the victory over the Philistines following Samuel's prayer results in the setting up of the Stone of Help (אֶבֶן הָעֵזֶר *eben hā'ēzer*) although there is no explicit mention of any sacrifice.

Other passages illustrate how the sanctuary legends of the sacred places of Canaan are redated to the patriarchal period. This redating reflects the accurate reminiscence that we are dealing with ancient local sanctuaries, originally pre-Yahwistic. For example, according to the narrative in Genesis 28:10–12, 17–18, 20, 22 (E), Jacob sets up the stone that lay under his head when he had his amazing vision of the heavenly ladder on which "messengers of God" were ascending and descending and pours oil upon it. Genesis 35:7 adds the statement that he built an altar. According to Genesis 28:17, the setting up of the stone is preceded by the terrified exclamation: "How fearsome [= holy] is this place! This is no other than the house of God [thus explaining the name 'Beth-El'], this is the gate of heaven." The J parallel says more directly: "Truly Yahweh is in this place, and I did not know it." In 35:7 an explanation is appended for the building of the altar and the naming of the place: "It was there that God had revealed himself to him when he was running away from his brother." The early history of this sanctuary legend is clearly polytheistic; the messengers of God were probably deities origi-nally.

There are similar episodes from the story of Abraham. Yahweh appears to Abraham at Shechem (Gen. 12:7), Bethel (12:8; 13:4, 14–17), and Mamre near Hebron (13:18; 18:1ff.) at the site of an altar. In all these instances we see clearly that a man does not build an altar in order to insure the presence of God by his own act, but because he knows that the presence of God is vouchsafed to him. Cf. also the Penuel story in Genesis 32:23–33. In this gift of his presence Yahweh still remains free, making his presence known to his people according to his own free decision.

3. Exodus 33 betrays intensive speculation on the question of whether Yahweh, who was once sought out by his people at the mountain of God, continued along with them, and how this might have taken place. Various answers are suggested. To the people who have just sinned by worshiping the golden bull, Yahweh says: "If I journey in your company for even a moment, I will annihilate you." (33:5) Somewhat later we hear the question in the mouth of Moses, "You have not told me whom you will send with me," to which Yahweh replies, "My countenance (פָּנַי *pānai*) will go with you, and I will bring you to rest." Moses at once takes up this idea: "If your countenance does not go with us, do not send us up from here." (vss. 12ff.) Here the "countenance of Yahweh" appears as an independent entity. Although verses 16–17 seem to state once more that Yahweh himself will go along, the meaning is probably that Yahweh's consuming holiness, which would annihilate the sinful people, is in a sense "mediated" in his countenance (but cf. also 33:20). In his countenance, which is frequently mentioned without this particular emphasis (it is an impressive element, for example, in the Aaronitic blessing in Num. 6:24–26), Yahweh promises his presence to his people in a form that does not cost them their lives. On certain Carthaginian steles the female deity Tinnit is referred to as פֶּן בַּעַל *pn b'l* (*KAI* 78.2; 79.1, 10/11; and elsewhere). Here the gracious countenance of the deity takes on independent form in a female figure. It is characteristic of the Old Testament idiom that in the "countenance of Yahweh" none other is present than Yahweh himself.

The statement in Exodus 33:2, which clearly derives from another hand, reveals a different notion in an analogous context. Here Yahweh says: "I will send my messenger (מַלְאָכ *mal'āk*) before you." Alongside passages like the incident at Bethel, which speak of a multitude of "messengers," others, like the present passage, speak of "the messenger of Yahweh." Elsewhere it is striking how talk of the messenger can pass directly to talk of Yahweh himself. According to Genesis 16, when Hagar runs away from the house of Abraham, she is met in the desert by the messenger of Yahweh who comes to give her a promise. Verse 13 concludes the episode with the statement: "She called the name of Yahweh, who had been speaking with her, *ēl rŏ'î.*" In Genesis 31:13, the "messenger" of God who appears to Jacob when he is in a foreign land says: "I am the God who appeared to you at Bethel." In like fashion, according to Genesis 22:15ff., the "messenger of Yahweh" calls to Abraham from heaven and says: "By my own self I swear, says Yahweh . . ."; once more the messenger is probably none other than Yahweh himself. Once again, there are parallels in other religions: in Greek religion, for example, Hermes is understood as the messenger of Zeus; in other words, the high god holds converse with humans through his messenger, whom he sends to them (cf. Acts 14:12). In Israel the "messenger" who speaks to people is none other than Yahweh himself, whom no one, as he says to Moses, can see and survive (Exod. 33:20). In Exodus 23:21 Yahweh identifies himself with his messenger by saying: "My name is in him."

4. According to the accounts of the Mosaic period, Yahweh's presence with the people as they journeyed was particularly associated with two cultic objects. Exodus 33:7–11 speaks of the "tent" that Moses pitches outside the camp. The possibility cannot be ruled out that the full phrase אהל מועד *ōhel mô'ēd,* probably best translated "tent of meeting (between Yahweh and Moses)," has been inserted secondarily into the earlier texts from P, where the tent stands in the midst of the camp. Joshua, who is not a priest, stands guard in the tent. The presence of God descends upon it in a cloud when Moses goes out to it for some purpose. "Yahweh would speak to Moses face to face, as a man speaks with his friend." In Numbers 12:8, in a different context, Yahweh himself says of Moses: "Mouth to mouth I speak with him. . . . He sees the very form of Yahweh." According to Numbers 11:16–17, 24–25, Yahweh speaks with Moses and places a portion of Moses' spirit upon the seventy elders of the people who are assembled round about the tent. The purpose of all this is to maintain Yahweh's direct presence with his people and their true representative, even after they depart from Sinai. At the same time, however, it expresses Yahweh's freedom: he is not bound to one fixed place, but appears from time to time in an encounter with people. These statements stand in curious tension with the scene, likewise recounted in Exodus 33, where Yahweh refuses to allow Moses to see his countenance: "My countenance you may not see, for no mortal man may see me and live." (33:20; cf. also Isa. 6:5) Here the sense of the consuming majesty of Yahweh, the annihilating *deus nudus,* clashes openly with Israel's confession that in Moses open access to the present God has been vouchsafed. The cult associated with the tent, which will be described by P, is not mentioned in any of these early accounts.

After the occupation, little is heard of the tent of God. Its association with Shiloh (Josh. 18:1; 19:51; 1 Sam. 2:22) seems to be as much a later fiction as its association with Gibeon (1 Chron. 16:39; 21:29; 2 Chron. 1:3; 5:5) and Jerusalem (1 Kings 8:4). The "tent of Yahweh" of the Davidic period (1 Kings 1:39; 2:28–34) in which the ark is housed must not be identified with the "tent" of the Mosaic period in which Moses receives messages from God. Yahweh's "journeying in tent and tabernacle" (2 Sam. 7:6), which characterizes the pre-Davidic period of Israel, probably refers to a similar shelter for the ark in earlier times; it can hardly be interpreted as meaning that the ark was kept in the "tent of meeting."

5. In P the "tent of meeting" has been robbed of its independent significance and has become the place where the ark of Yahweh is kept. It is impossible to avoid the suspicion that Exodus 33:1–6 was once followed by an early account of how the ark was made out of jewelry cast aside by the Israelites, and that this account fell victim to the more circumstantial description in Exodus 25:10–22/37:1–9 when P was incorporated. On the use of discarded jewelry to make cult objects, cf. Exodus 35:22 (P) and Judges 8:24ff. Outside of the Priestly accounts of the Mosaic period, the ark is mentioned only in Numbers 10:35–36, the ritual accompanying its being picked up and set down (which probably derives from the ark processions [Ps. 24:7–10]), and in Numbers 14:44. It plays an important role in the accounts of the crossing of the Jordan and the conquest of Jericho in Joshua 3—4 and 6 as a sign of the mighty presence of Yahweh, before whom the waters of the Jordan part and the walls of Jericho collapse. Kraus and Wijngaards claim to have found here an echo of a regular ark procession at Gilgal. But the Jerusalem "cult legend" of the ark of God (הָאֱלֹהִים אֲרוֹן ’ărôn hā’ĕlōhîm) is found in 1 Samuel 4—6 and 2 Samuel 6, which trace its progress from its resting place at Shiloh through its temporary exile in Philistine territory and its return to Beth-shemesh and Kiriath-jearim down to its transfer to Jerusalem by David.

The word "ark" (אֲרוֹן ’ărôn), which is used for a coffin in Genesis 50:26 and for a money chest in the Temple in 2 Kings 12:10–11, probably referred initially to a container in which something is kept. There is no hint of this meaning in the cult legend of the ark, but the terrifying holiness of this object, at which Yahweh is present with his awesome power, is emphasized. The Philistine god Dagon is toppled from his pedestal as the ark stands before him. The people of Beth-shemesh, as well as the well-meaning Uzzah, who merely seeks to steady the ark, are struck down. On the other hand, the freedom of the one present with the ark is shown by Israel's failure to gain a victory even by bringing the ark into the camp of its army. In 2 Samuel 6:11, by contrast, we see how Yahweh blesses Obed-edom, in whose house the ark is kept.

The name "Yahweh of hosts" (צְבָאוֹת יהוה yahweh ṣĕbā’ôt) is associated with the ark, probably as far back as when it was at Shiloh. However the term "hosts" is interpreted (a heavenly army, the earthly army of Israel, or an originally independent word meaning "power"; cf. also above, p. 19), it refers to the "mighty one" whose name is pronounced over the ark (2 Sam.

6:2), expressing his claim to ownership. With this designation is associated the title "he who is throned on the cherubim" (הכרובים ישב *yōšēb hakkrûbîm*), which may at one time have been independent. According to Psalm 99:1 (18:11), this phrase refers to the cherubim as figures who bear Yahweh up, not the cherubim in the Jerusalem Temple who spread their wings protectively over the ark (1 Kings 8:7).

The precise mode of Yahweh's presence with his ark is a matter of controversy. Some have conceived the ark as Yahweh's throne, pointing out Greek analogies in which empty thrones were worshiped as the thrones of certain gods. Jeremiah 3:16–17 seems to support such an interpretation. But there are also passages that picture the ark as Yahweh's footstool (Ps. 99:5; 132:7–8). Isaiah 6 also appears to suggest the image of Yahweh sitting high up on a throne in the heavens with his feet in the Temple, which is filled with the edges of his flowing robes, resting on the ark as on a footstool. Ezekiel 43:7 combines the two conceptions: Yahweh calls the Holy of Holies (albeit with no mention of the ark) the "place of my throne, the place where I set my feet." However Yahweh's presence with the ark is pictured, its description as a "chest" remains puzzling: it is natural to ask what the chest contained. Gressman proposed two divine images, but his suggestion has not been accepted. Later tradition (Deuteronomy and P) mentions the two tablets of the law (Exod. 40:20; 1 Kings 8:9), Aaron's staff (Num. 17:25), and a jar containing manna (Exod. 16:33–34) as being contained in the ark. Does this preserve an earlier tradition about the contents of the ark?

6. David's transfer of the ark to Jerusalem was of crucial significance for the notion of Yahweh's presence. The ancient, pre-Israelite sanctuary legend of Jerusalem can still be discerned behind 2 Samuel 24 and even more clearly behind 1 Chronicles 21. According to 1 Chronicles 21:16, David, who is to be punished for taking a census of the nation, is met at the threshing-floor of Ornan (Arauna) the Jebusite by "the angel of Yahweh standing between earth and heaven, with his sword drawn in his hand and stretched out over Jerusalem." But by building an altar at this site David is able to avert the plague that is raging among the people. It has been suggested that we can see here an early story about the appearance of a deity at the site of the altar, and presumably also the site of the later Temple built by Solomon. But this local legend later took a back seat to the more momentous statements made about Jerusalem. The name "Zion," which originally may have referred to the height overlooking the city, on which the sanctuary came to be located, became the primary designation of Jerusalem, and it was glorified as the city of God. The transfer of the ark to Zion, coupled with the strong belief in Yahweh, the Lord of Israel, and in particular Lord in the wars of Yahweh, led to an especially intensive adoption of Canaanite idioms in Jerusalem, where, reinterpreted, they became the building blocks for the "Zion tradi-

tion" (Jeremias). Above all, these elements helped give a universal dimension to the belief in Yahweh, who dwells on Zion (Isa. 8:18). Now Yahweh is said to have his dwelling place at the source of the rivers that water the world (Ps. 46:5; cf. Ezek. 47:1–12), as the Canaanites had said of El. Zion becomes the world mountain, Zaphon (צָפוֹן *ṣāpôn*) in the north, which was referred to at Ugarit as the dwelling place of Baal (Ps. 48:3). Even the term "city of God" is probably based on a Canaanite model. Under the influence of the ark theology of יהוה צבאות *yahweh ṣ'bā'ôt*, however, these notions are brought together and related to the idea of Yahweh's victory in his wars. Strangely exaggerated statements are formulated about the attack launched by the nations against the city of God and its impregnability. In the Yahweh wars of Israel, Yahweh was described as being superior to his enemies, and their weapons were destroyed. Now Zion becomes the site where Yahweh destroys the weapons of the attacking nations. In the Zion psalms (Pss. 46, 48, and 76) and in the words of Isaiah that move within the realm of this Zion tradition, the faith in the impregnability of the city of God, within which Yahweh is present, finds its boldest expression. Here the way is paved for those final words about the church of God, against which the very gates of hell shall not prevail (Matt. 16:18).

The name "Zion" is not found in Ezekiel. He speaks instead of the "lofty mountain of Israel" on which Yahweh will be duly honored and where he is present in the midst of his people (20:40; 40—48). Here the very terminology completes the assimilation of the Zion tradition and the Israel tradition.

7. The deuteronomic movement gave a new form to the belief in Yahweh's presence in Jerusalem. The legal sections of Deuteronomy contain a requirement that the cult be centralized; this centralization is described programmatically in Deuteronomy 12, at the beginning of the legal material. It is a matter of debate whether these passages from the very beginning meant Jerusalem to be the single cultic site of the one God Yahweh (Deut. 6:4). In view of the possibility that the nucleus of Deuteronomy might have originated in the Northern Kingdom, it has been suggested that at one time Shechem or some other site was thought of as the sacral focus of the old tribal league. With the shift to Judah, the only possible site to which the lawgiver could refer was Jerusalem, which had harbored the ark since the time of David. This is clearly the case in all deuteronomic thought. In this context, belief in the presence of Yahweh among his people undergoes a reinterpretation that makes the theological basis for this belief stand out in bold relief.

In Deuteronomy Moses calls the place that Israel is supposed to seek out as the true place where God is present the "place which Yahweh your God will choose out of all your tribes, that he may establish his name there" (12:5) or the "place which Yahweh your God will choose as a dwelling for his

name." (12:11) The first point to note is the use of the "election" category
for this place—the same category used to explain the special status of the
people of Yahweh in the eyes of their God Yahweh. This eliminates any
notion of an intrinsic holiness in the place itself, as expressed elsewhere by
use of the category "navel of the world" (used in Judg. 9:37 to refer to a
place near Shechem, and in Ezek. 38:12 to refer to the entire land in which
Israel dwells). The place of Yahweh's presence is the place Yahweh freely
chooses. Ezekiel 5:5 combines the idea of the center found in the *omphalos*
("navel") image with the decree of Yahweh by formulating Jerusalem's
status as follows: "This is Jerusalem—I have set it in the midst of the nations."

    There is also a second element: the presence of Yahweh is expressed in
the new theologoumenon of the chosen place as the presence of the divine
"name." It was stated at the outset that a "name" is not merely an arbitrary
label, but comprehends within itself the nature of that which it names. It is
also clear that the "name" is the aspect of an entity that can be addressed or
invoked. The one addressed is met in the name; invocation of the name
"touches" the addressee. Now it can be observed once more that elsewhere
in the ancient Near East, as we have already discussed with respect to the
פנים *pānîm* and the מלאך *mal'āk,* the aspect of the deity that is present or at
least accessible to human invocation can take on separate existence in the
form of an independent deity. The Eshmunezer inscription from Sidon (early
5th century B.C.) tells how King Eshmunezer built a temple at Sidon for
Astarte, the "name of Baal" (שם בעל *šm b'l*) (*KAI* 14.18). In sharp contrast
to this usage, Deuteronomy speaks of the absolute unity of the invoked God.
It is not another, mediating god who is present in the "name of Yahweh,"
but Yahweh himself, and he alone. One can ask whether the deuteronomic
theologoumenon of the "name" is not meant to express the free activity of
Yahweh as well as his ability to be invoked in human prayer. Isaiah 30:27,
for example, speaks of the active power of Yahweh's "name": "See, the name
of Yahweh comes from afar, his anger blazing." In Deuteronomy itself this
aspect of the name is not especially brought out. Deuteronomy does, however, underscore with particular emphasis how Israel can come to the place
where the name of Yahweh dwells, and there rejoice in the presence of its
God, bring him offerings to express its rejoicing, and celebrate a feast in his
presence.

    It is illuminating to see what happens in this context to that ancient cultic
object the ark, from which the notion of Yahweh's presence in his holy city
Jerusalem took its start. The introductory discourses of Deuteronomy refer
(in chapter 10) once more to the ark (whereas the tent of meeting is not
mentioned). Now, however, the ark is stripped of all its numinous character;
it has become simply a container for the "law" in the form of the two tablets
given to Moses at the mountain of God. The entire structure of

Deuteronomy is planned to call Israel to hear God's instruction; the ark, too, is now understood exclusively in terms of the words of divine instruction it contains. This perspective explains the designation of the ark as the "ark of the covenant" (ארון הברית *ărôn habb^erît*), a term that then found its way into other passages. In this context, the word ברית *b^erît* refers to the requirements of the covenant, which are formulated in the law.

8. Following our examination of the deuteronomic approach, we must now consider the form that belief in Yahweh's presence takes in P. It was mentioned in §3 that the organizing principle of P's narrative is the expectation of Yahweh's coming in the midst of his community. In Genesis 17:7 even the promise to Abraham is given a special emphasis with reference to the community of Yahweh; the promise is concretely realized by the setting up of the sacred tent in the midst of the camp (Exod. 35ff.). In the description of the sacred focus of the people camped at the mountain of God, whose designation as a "community" (עדה *'ēdâ*) should probably be connected with the אהל מועד *ōhel mô'ēd*, here located in the midst of the camp (Rost), the twin elements of tent and ark are indissolubly linked. We may note that the tent no longer has any independent significance as a place of meeting between Yahweh and his people or their representatives. The ark, too, for which Exodus 25/37 provides a precise description, complete with dimensions, material, and decoration, quite likely basically accurate for the ancient ark, has undergone significant revision in the light of belief in Yahweh's presence. According to Exodus 25:17, there is a cover (כפרת *kappōret*) over the ark, and verses 21–22 state explicitly that Yahweh would station himself there to meet Moses and speak with him "from above the cover, between the two cherubim over the ark of witness." In his designation of the ark, P replaces the "ברית *b^erît*" of Deuteronomy with "עדות *'ēdût,*" meaning "witness" or "testimony"; here, too, the notion of Yahweh's "ordinance" is probably in mind. About the origin of this new element, the כפרת *kappōret,* which now becomes the specific site of the divine presence, nothing can be said. It is dubious that it has any connection with כפר *kpr,* "propitiate," as the LXX translation *hilastērion* presupposes. But the other element of the Sinai tradition that was likewise already associated with the tent of meeting reappears here: the cloud that hides the effulgence of Yahweh. After the holy tent is pitched and furnished, according to Exodus 40:34–35, the cloud covers the tent of meeting and the glory of Yahweh fills the tent so that even Moses cannot enter. According to 40:36–37, the lifting and descending of the cloud gives the signal each time Israel is to break and make camp. Other passages in P speak of Yahweh's actual appearances in the form of the cloud and the "glory" (כבוד *kābôd*). Although Exodus 29:45–46 states that Yahweh will dwell (שכן *škn*) in the midst of his people, this "dwelling" should not be misconstrued as a static presence. Yahweh preserves his freedom to

come and go. This freedom is also fully expressed by the priestly prophet Ezekiel, who experiences the presence of Yahweh's glory in distant exile (Ezek. 1:1–3:15) and sees in a vision the glory of Yahweh departing from the Temple and then returning (8—11; 43:1ff.).

The word "כבוד *kābôd,*" which is firmly anchored in the Priestly phrase "glory of Yahweh" (כבוד יהוה *kᵉbôd yahweh*), means primarily "that which is heavy, weighty"; by extension, it means "that which lends dignity." It was already applied to the awesomeness of a theophany in pre-Israelite usage, as Psalm 29 can illustrate, extolling Yahweh as אל הכבוד *ēl hakkābôd.* It glorifies meteorological phenomena as effects of the "voice of Yahweh," and concludes with the statement: "In his palace all cry out, כבוד *kābôd.*'" According to Psalm 19:1, the heavens extol the כבוד אל *kᵉbôd ēl,* and the vault (of heaven) proclaims his handiwork. Cf. also the hymn of the seraphim in Isaiah 6:3.

Then, however, the notion becomes increasingly concrete and comes to refer to the actual mode of Yahweh's presence. According to Exodus 33:18ff., Moses demands to see the כבוד *kābôd* of Yahweh. In the subsequent conversation, in which Yahweh refuses Moses' request, "פנים *pānîm*" replaces "כבוד *kābôd*" without further explanation. Yahweh concedes only this much to Moses: "When my *kābôd* passes by, I will put you in a crevice of the rock and cover you with my hand until I have passed by. Then I will take away my hand, and you shall see my back—but my countenance (פנים *pānîm*) shall not be seen." This understanding accounts for P's speaking of the כבוד יהוה *kᵉbôd yahweh* as the actual form taken by the presence of Yahweh, in which he repeatedly appears to his people throughout the desert period (Exod. 16:10; Lev. 9:6, 23; Num. 14:10; 17:7; 20:6). Numbers 17:7; 20:6 (14:10?) also explicitly speak of the אהל מועד *ōhel mô'ēd* as the place where Yahweh appears. But this feature has also found its way (secondarily?) into the account of the dedication of the Temple, in association with the moment when the ark is brought into the Temple (1 Kings 8:10–11). A unique description going into greater detail is found in Ezekiel 1 (10). Here Yahweh's throne is associated with the theophany. Four creatures bearing the throne are described in detail. The introduction of wheels alongside the winged animals, which suggest a throne chariot, probably represents a second phase. The "chariot" is later mentioned without comment: 1 Chronicles 28:18; Ecclesiasticus 49:8; cf. also the LXX of Ezekiel 43:3. The notion of the "stool for Yahweh's feet" associated with the ark is incorporated into the phrase "the place where I set my feet" in Ezekiel 43:7 (in parallel to "the place of my throne"), which describes the place where the effulgent glory of God is present.

Thus we see that the faith of the Old Testament uses a great variety of forms to indicate its belief in the God of Israel, who is present from time to time in the midst of his people, bringing blessing and judgment.

Jeremias, Jörg. *Theophanie.* Wissenschaftliche Monographien zum Alten und Neuen Testament, vol. 10. Neukirchen: Neukirchener Verlag, 1965.—Noth, Martin. "Der Wallfahrtsweg zum Sinai (4. Mose 33)." *Palästina-Jahrbuch* 36 (1940):5–28. Reprinted in his *Aufsätze zur biblischen Landes- und Altertumskunde,* vol. 1, pp. 55–74. Neukirchen: Neukirchener Verlag, 1971.— Nötscher, Friedrich. *Das Angesicht Gottes schauen nach biblischer und babylonischer Auffassung.* 1924. 2d ed. Darmstadt: Wissenschaftliche Buchgesellschaft, 1969.—Görg, Manfred. *Das Zelt der Begegnung.* Bonner biblische Beiträge, vol. 27. Bonn: Hanstein, 1967.—Koch, Klaus. "אֹהֶל ʾhl." In *Theologisches Wörterbuch zum Alten Testament,* vol. 1, cols. 128–141 (with bibliography). Edited by G. J. Botterweck and Helmer Ringgren. Stuttgart: Kohlhammer, 1973. English: "אֹהֶל ʾōhel; אָהַל ʾāhal." In *Theological Dictionary of the Old Testament,* vol. 1, pp. 118–130. Translated by J. T. Willis. Grand Rapids, Mich.: Eerdmans, 1974.—Zobel, Hans-Jürgen. "אָרוֹן." *Ibid.,* cols. 391–404. English: "אָרוֹן ʾᵃrôn." *Ibid.,* pp. 363–374.—Kraus, Hans-Joachim. "Gilgal—ein Beitrag zur Kultusgeschichte Israels." *Vetus Testamentum* 1 (1951):181–199.— Wijngaards, Joanne. *The Dramatization of Salvific History in the Deuteronomic Schools.* Oudtestamentische Studiën, vol. 16. Leiden: Brill, 1969.—Von Rad, Gerhard. "Zelt und Lade." *Neue kirchliche Zeitschrift* 42 (1931):476–498. Reprinted in his *Gesammelte Studien zum Alten Testament,* pp. 109–129. Theologische Bücherei, vol. 8. Munich: Kaiser, 1958. English: "The Tent and the Ark." In his *The Problem of the Hexateuch and Other Essays,* pp. 103–124. Translated by E. W. Trueman Dicken. New York: McGraw-Hill, 1966.—Maier, Johann. *Das altisraelitische Ladeheiligtum.* Beihefte zur Zeitschrift für die Alttestamentliche Wissenschaft, vol. 93. Berlin: Töpelmann, 1965.—Eissfeldt, Otto. "Jahwe Zebaoth." *Miscellanea Academica Berolinensia* 2/2 (1950):128–150. Reprinted in his *Kleine Schriften,* vol. 3, pp. 103–123. Tübingen: Mohr, 1966. —Schreiner, Josef. *Sion-Jerusalem, Jahwes Königssitz.* Studien zum Alten und Neuen Testament, vol. 7. Munich: Kösel, 1963.—Jeremias, Jörg. "Lade und Zion." In *Probleme biblischer Theologie* (Festschrift Gerhard von Rad), pp. 183–198. Edited by Hans Walter Wolff. Munich: Kaiser, 1971.—Rost, Leonhard. *Die Vorstufen von Kirche und Synagoge.* Beiträge zur Wissenschaft vom Alten und Neuen Testament, 4th series, vol. 24. 1938. 2d ed. Darmstadt: Wissenschaftliche Buchgesellschaft, 1967.—Westermann, Claus. "Die Herrlichkeit Gottes in der Priesterschrift." In *Wort, Gebot, Glaube* (Festschrift Walther Eichrodt), pp. 227–249 (with bibliography). Edited by Hans Joachim Stoebe. Arbeiten zur Theologie des Alten und Neuen Testaments, vol. 59. Zurich: Zwingli, 1970. Reprinted in his *Forschung am Alten Testament,* pp. 115–137. Theologische Bücherei, vol. 55. Munich: Kaiser, 1974.

§10 Charismata of Leadership and Instruction

The gifts that Yahweh gives to Israel include the gift of a succession of men charged with the task of leadership and instruction. The Old Testament contains a wealth of reflection upon these men and the specific charisma that is theirs.

Within the framework of a theology of the Old Testament, it is not appropriate to describe the sociological structure of Israelite "society" and trace its historical development. It is our task instead to depict the way the faith of the Old Testament recognizes and describes Yahweh's work in these individuals or groups.

a) Moses and Joshua

At the beginning of Israel's history as a nation stands Moses, a man with an Egyptian name who is charged with the task of leading Israel out of Egypt in the name of Yahweh and bringing them to the promised land. Tradition shows how Israel's faith reflected on the "office" of this man, singled out by his God to be the instrument of a fundamental act of liberation, without ultimately being able to assign him to a specific category. This attempt to categorize Moses is also reflected in recent Mosaic scholarship (Smend, Osswald). Following the account of Moses' call, in which according to both E and P the name of Yahweh was first revealed to Moses, we are told that he is given the power to work miracles (Exod. 4). This power, with varying emphases in the different source documents, is made use of in the events that lead up to the exodus. Moses' staff plays a special role in this context. We then see how a later period seeks to understand Moses after the example of a prophet (Perlitt), especially in Deuteronomy 18 (see below, pp. 104–105). In this context the possibility can also be considered that Moses may have been invested with the spirit of God. But Numbers 11 comes to the realization that Moses must have possessed the spirit of God to a degree that surpasses measure. A mere portion of the spirit that rests on Moses suffices to enable seventy elders to prophesy (11:25). Then we come once more to the statements, already spoken of, in Exodus 33:11 and Numbers 12:8, statements sharply distinguishing Moses from anything having to do with "prophecy" and associating him directly with the presence of Yahweh in a manner unique to him. The enigma of Moses' person is also illustrated by his description in one passage as blazing with anger in his zeal for Yahweh (Exod. 32:26–29) and in another as the most humble man on earth (Num. 12:3). The "obituary" of Moses in Deuteronomy 34:10–12 emphasizes that Moses transcends all the usual categories of the charismatic, even though he resists accepting his divine mandate (Exod. 4:10ff.), groans under the enormous burden (Num. 11:11–12), and is finally revealed in his full distress as suffering God's wrath "for the sake of Israel." (Deut. 1:37; 3:26)

Joshua, the leader of Israel during the occupation of Canaan as described in the book of Joshua, stands totally in the shadow of Moses: he merely finishes what Moses began. Using the language and conceptual milieu of P, Numbers 27:12–23 describes how Moses places his hands upon Joshua in the presence of the priest Eleazar, thus transferring to Joshua some of his "authority" (הוד hôd). According to Deuteronomy 31:14–15, Joshua is appointed in the "tent of meeting," upon which Yahweh himself descends in the pillar of cloud. In Deuteronomy 3:21–22, 28 it is Moses alone who gives Joshua his mandate. Joshua 1 describes expansively how Yahweh inspires Joshua with courage to carry out his mandate and promises him help. Thus he appears as a military leader, the trustee of Yahweh at the apportionment of the land, and a preacher exhorting the people to genuine obedience to Yahweh (Josh. 23—24). Within the context of the Old Testament he never became the specific prototype of any priestly or even prophetic authority.

Beek's suggestion that he even owes his name to the "deliverer" figure he is supposed to represent (מוֹשִׁיעַ *môšia'*) is unlikely.

Smend, Rudolf. *Das Mosebild von Heinrich Ewald bis Martin Noth.* Beiträge zur Geschichte der biblischen Exegese, vol. 3. Tübingen: Mohr, 1959.—Osswald, Eva. *Das Bild des Mose.* Theologische Arbeiten, vol. 18. Berlin: Evangelische Verlagsanstalt, 1962.—Perlitt, Lothar. "Mose als Prophet." *Evangelische Theologie* 31 (1971):588–608.—Alt, Albrecht. "Josua." In Internationale Tagung alttestamentlicher Forscher, Göttingen, 1935. *Werden und Wesen des Alten Testaments,* pp. 13–29. Edited by Paul Volz, Friedrich Stummer, and Johannes Hempel. Beihefte zur Zeitschrift für die Alttestamentliche Wissenschaft, vol. 66. Berlin: Töpelmann, 1936. Reprinted in his *Kleine Schriften zur Geschichte des Volkes Israel,* vol. 1, pp. 176–192. Munich: Beck, 1953.—Beek, Martinus Adrianus. "Josua und Retterideal." In *Near Eastern Studies in Honor of William Foxwell Albright,* pp. 35–42. Edited by Hans Goedicke. Baltimore: Johns Hopkins, 1971.

b) Judge and Nazirite

The book of Judges tells the stories of the so-called "judges." Here we must distinguish the perspective of the deuteronomistic framework from that of the sections deriving from earlier sources.

1. The first thing to strike the reader's eye is the picture of the judges presented by the framework, whose internal structure as worked out by Richter in his analyses of the book we must pass over. The groundwork is laid by the thematic exposition in Judges 2:6ff., which outlines a specific course of events that is to take place repeatedly. According to this picture, after the death of Joshua and the elders of all Israel who survive him, Israel commits apostasy, worshiping Baals and Astartes. Yahweh thereupon delivers the Israelites into the hands of their enemies, who press their attack vigorously. But Israel repents and cries out to Yahweh, whereupon Yahweh sends a deliverer and gives Israel rest from its oppressors—a rest that lasts as long as the judge lives. Then the process begins all over again.

In this deuteronomistic perspective on history (see below, §20), a very specific picture is drawn of the "judges," characterized by three features:

a. There is no line of succession among the judges. Each appears anew as a helper sent by Yahweh. The series of judges is discontinuous; they are not linked by any fixed historical succession.

b. The appearance of the judges is not the consequence of any human excellence; they are sent solely on Yahweh's initiative, as he takes pity on his tortured people who have returned to him in their distress. It is not "heroes" who are celebrated in the figures of these judges, but instruments of Yahweh, who sees the suffering of his people: "They delivered them from the hand of their oppressors." (2:16) In the "deliverer" (מוֹשִׁיעַ *môšia'*) Israel learns once more that Yahweh wants his relationship to Israel to be that of a helper.

c. At the same time, however, the judges and their appearance are connected with Yahweh's righteous will. A judge appears when the people repent and return to Yahweh. And during their lifetime they "judge" his nation, in other words, they see that the people are obedient to the righteous will of Yahweh. Only when the judge is dead does the nation fall back into disobedience.

The unique way in which these "judge" figures are presented makes two unmistakable points. On the one hand, the judges are pictured as being sent unexpectedly by Yahweh; they hold no prior "office." Their discontinuity is meant to express the freedom exercised by Yahweh in demonstrating his help. On the other hand, however, an attempt is made to perceive once more a "law" in the way they appear: the principle of Yahweh's faithfulness and mercy toward Israel, which are inseparable from his righteous will. This will takes on concrete form here in the command to worship him alone. Thus the deuteronomistic framework seeks to represent in the judges the principle of Yahweh's free grace, bound to no law, which is never separable from his righteous will.

2. The sections from the earlier sources that are set within the deuteronomistic framework do not yet exhibit this strict stylization. Two distinct elements have been joined together in the deuteronomistic book of Judges: (a) A short early book of Judges that mentions only real judges, concerned with the legal system of Israel; military exploits of liberation are not ascribed to them. Only the story of Jephthah transcends the horizon of these judicial figures. (b) Accounts of deliverers from the period before Israel was a state; according to Richter, these had already been collected in a "Book of Deliverers" before being incorporated into the deuteronomistic work. None of these "deliverers" is ever associated with all Israel, although at times, as in the battle fought by Deborah, they can unite several tribes in military alliance.

The figure of Othniel is hard to define. According to 3:7–11, the spirit of Yahweh comes upon him, he takes the field, and defeats Israel's oppressor Cushan-rishathaim (Moor of double wickedness?). The audacious action of Ehud (3:12–30) is recounted in totally secular terms. He slays Eglon, Israel's Moabite oppressor, in his own palace and then summons the Israelites to battle. He appears to be associated with the tribe of Benjamin alone. In the case of Shamgar (3:31), there is some doubt whether we are even dealing with a figure from Israel. On the other hand, the freeing of the tribes that had infiltrated the plain of Jezreel from the oppression of the Canaanite cities, as recorded in prose in Judges 4 and in the Song of Deborah in Judges 5, bears the stamp of a Yahweh war. Seven tribes, inflamed by the hymns of the "prophetess" (4:4) Deborah, come together to do battle with their tormentors under the leadership of Barak, from the tribe of Naphtali; Yahweh comes to the aid of his people from Sinai, sending a storm. The Song of Deborah gives thanks to Yahweh that the people of Israel and their leaders showed their willingness to venture this battle. Jael, a Kenite woman who had been dwelling in the vicinity with her tribe, is singled out for special acclaim, having slain Sisera, the leader of the enemy, in her tent. The fullest account is the story of Gideon, who freed Israel from the incursions of roving bands of Midianites. At the beginning of the account he receives his call from a messenger of Yahweh. The gift of the power to lead in battle is described in a striking idiom: "The spirit of Yahweh clothed (לבשׁ/*lbš*) Gideon." Gideon appears subsequently to have held a position of leadership within a small region, although according to 8:22–23 he expressly refuses (royal) sovereignty over Israel. The story of Abimelech, whatever its original position, reveals once more the destruction of such a move. Structurally, the rise of the mercenary leader Jephthah to be "head and leader" (וְקָצִין רֹאשׁ *rō'š uᵉḳāṣîn*) in Gilead (11:11) anticipates the later course of David's rise. In his case, too, however, it is the spirit of Yahweh that is said to be what really enables this mercenary leader to free the Gileadites from the Ammonites (11:29). And this is emphatically the case with the stories about Samson, which are loosely tacked on like an appendix to the book. They are even preceded by an infancy narrative in which the "messenger of Yahweh" predicts the birth of Samson. The mighty deeds of Samson, directed against increasing Philistine pressure, are understood in 13:25; 14:6, 19; 15:14 as being due to the spirit that fills him. According to 13:25, the "spirit of Yahweh" begins to "drive" (פָּעַם *pᵉ'm*) Samson. According to the other passages, it actually seizes him (צָלַח *ṣlḥ*).

Apart from 5:8*a,* which is textually quite insecure, the apostasy and return of Israel play no part in these early deliverer stories, nor does the judicial activity of the judge. Everywhere we find instead the element of charismatic spontaneity. Wherever there is theological reflection, the notion of the divine spirit (רוּחַ *rûaḥ*) appears. This spirit is understood as the power from Yahweh that comes over each judge, "drives" them, "clothes" them like a garment, and gives them the power to perform spontaneous deeds to help his people. Here the notion of God's free intervention dominates the accounts without any systematic interpretation of history. But in his freedom Yahweh sends "helpers" to Israel. Here, too, just as in the central element of the framework narratives, we cannot miss the point that Yahweh is once more acclaimed as the God who sees the distress of his people and delivers them from it, as in the exodus from Egypt.

3. According to Judges 13:5, 7, Samson is a Nazirite (נָזִיר *nāzîr*). The Old Testament exhibits two different forms of this phenomenon. In Numbers 6 we find a law governing the Nazirites. It regulates an oath freely taken for a specific period. The Nazirite abstains from wine and cutting his hair. He avoids any uncleanness through contact with the dead. The end of his period under vows is celebrated with a solemn sacrifice (cf. Acts 18:18; 21:23ff.). These Nazirites take vows of their own free will for a specific period. Samson, on the other hand, is a Nazirite because he is called by God. His abstinence from wine and refusal to cut his hair are thought of as lifelong obligations. Amos 2:11–12 clearly attests that such a vocation, like prophecy, is thought of as Yahweh's beneficent gift to his people. The idea of a special election and consecration is also found in the reference to Joseph in the blessings of Jacob and Moses, where Joseph is singled out as a "Nazirite among his brothers." The term is also used in Leviticus 25:5, 11 for the vine left unpruned in the sabbatical and jubilee year.

A Nazirite is accordingly a man consecrated to Yahweh in a special way; in the story of Samson, he is thought of as a bearer of a divine charisma who takes his place among the "deliverers" of Israel.

Grether, Oskar. "Die Bezeichnung 'Richter' für die charismatischen Helden der vorstaatlichen Zeit." *Zeitschrift für die Alttestamentliche Wissenschaft* 57 (1939):110–121.—Richter, Wolfgang. *Traditionsgeschichtliche Untersuchungen zum Richterbuch.* Bonner biblische Beiträge, vol. 18. Bonn: Hanstein, 1963.—Idem. *Die Bearbeitungen des "Retterbuches" in der deuteronomischen Epoche.* Bonner biblische Beiträge, vol. 21. Bonn: Hanstein, 1964.

c) The King

Anyone reading the accounts of how the monarchy came into being in Israel (1 Sam. 8—12) will find two different verdicts on this institution. When Samuel laments the people's desire to have a king, Yahweh answers in 1 Samuel 8: "They have not rejected you, it is I whom they have rejected, I whom they will not have to be their king." (1 Sam. 8:7) This means that human kingship is contrary to the kingship of Yahweh. This is also the reason given by Gideon in Judges 8:22–23 when he refuses royal office. In 1 Samuel 9:16, by contrast, Yahweh's command to Samuel to anoint Saul "prince" (נָגִיד *nāgîd*) over Yahweh's people Israel is connected with the statement: "He shall deliver my people from the Philistines, for I have seen the sufferings [?] of my people and their cry has reached my ears." According to this account, the anointed leader is a gracious gift from Yahweh, sent by Yahweh himself to help his oppressed people.

The two lights in which the monarchy appears in Israel demonstrate with particular clarity that this "office" was not simply a natural outgrowth of genuine tendencies within Yahwism. At this very point we can see clearly that it came into being in response to the "challenge" of the surrounding world: in some way the monarchy represents an assimilation to this world, in others a distinction from it. While the Israelite monarchy was taking concrete form, elsewhere in the ancient Near East kingship had long been a unique institution, invested with religious significance.

Ancient Egypt exercised its influence on Palestine through its Canaanite vassal princes in the early period of the New Kingdom, and then, in the Solomonic period, directly on the royal court at Jerusalem, as the marriage of Solomon with an Egyptian princess (1 Kings 3:1) reveals. In Egypt the pharaoh was simply called "the god." He is also the "son of god." On the wall of the temple at Luxor we can see how the god Amon-Re has intercourse with the queen mother to beget the king (Brunner). The official royal style, the so-called royal protocol, which is determined at the accession of each king, consists of five parts, the first of which comprises the terms "Horus, golden Horus." As such the king has ritual significance: he is the mediator between heaven and earth, on whom the prosperity and fertility of the land depend. This can be seen especially clearly at the Sed festival, a jubilee celebration whose elaborate ritual is designed to renew the king's power totally.

In the great kingdoms of Mesopotamia the New Year's festival, lasting eleven days, was the most prodigious ritual act, in which the kingship and the prosperity of the land were linked. Here, however, features suggesting deification of the king lose significance after the Sumerian period. The king was viewed as a mortal being, but the kingship was of heavenly origin, the king a figure of divine election. As such he had to "grasp the hands of Marduk" at Babylon at the beginning of each year. During the New Year's festival he had certain functions to fulfill, albeit much more limited than those in the Egyptian royal ritual. He played a role in the sacred marriage of the gods, which guaranteed the fertility of the new year, and in the great procession to the site of the celebration, the *bīt akītu*. Here the king had more to do than merely give the sign for the great procession of the gods to begin. Sennacherib, as he had depicted on the copper doors of the *bīt akītu* at Asshur, himself stood in the chariot of the god Asshur.

At the beginning of its monarchy, Israel initially goes its own way. The kingship of Saul still appears as something not far different from what the deliverers in the book of Judges do. 1 Samuel 11 depicts how the "spirit of God" seizes Saul as, returning from the field, he hears of the disgrace King Nahash of the Ammonites is threatening to inflict on the inhabitants of Jabesh-gilead. With the bloody pieces of his oxen and the threat that the oxen of anyone who refuses to follow him in battle will be treated likewise Saul calls Israel to arms. The fear of Yahweh falls upon the people, so that men follow Saul and break the siege of Jabesh. Then the people who have seen how "Yahweh has won such a victory [תשועה *tšû'â*, literally 'deliverance'] in Israel" (11:13) go to the sanctuary at Gilgal where sacrifice is offered and Saul is made king "in the presence of Yahweh." The following points are significant: As in the case of the "deliverers" in the book of Judges, it is the spirit of God (רוח אלהים *rûaḥ ĕlōhîm*)—the element of divine spontaneity— that arouses the "deliverer." It is "fear of Yahweh" (פחד יהוה *paḥad yahweh*) that makes the men of Israel willing to join Saul's army (cf. Judg. 5:2) so that the victory can be won. This spontaneous act of divine help for Israel, in which the "deliverer" was revealed, is followed by a novel element, the acclamation of the deliverer by Israel's army. The deliverer in whom Yahweh has declared himself is made king in the presence of Yahweh at the sanctuary.

In the context of the earlier, pro-kingship tradition, this story of the deliverer-king is preceded by another account, telling how God "makes known" his elect. Just as in the patriarchal narratives the divine promise of what is to come preceded the actual history of Israel, so here Samuel, the man of God, announces Yahweh's decision to deliver Israel and his choice of the deliverer by anointing the unsuspecting peasant lad Saul, who is looking for his father's asses, to be נגיד *nāgîd*. The etymology of the term has not yet been explained satisfactorily; it may mean "one who is proclaimed" or "one who steps to the fore." Richter, Schmidt and others find in it a title originally used for Israel's military leaders before the monarchy. General considerations argue for this view, but it remains difficult to explain why the title does not appear in any of the pre-monarchic deliverer stories. It is unlikely that this title was already associated with the act of anointing in the pre-monarchic period (Richter).

Among the great kingdoms of the ancient Near East, the ritual of anointing (חשׁמ *mšḥ*) is definitely attested only among the Hittites. There is also letter 51 of the Amarna letters (Knudt-zon), in which a fifteenth-century Egyptian vassal prince, Addu-Nirari of Nuhašše, writes to Pharaoh Thutmoses IV, saying that the pharaoh's grandfather (Thutmoses III) "made [Addu-Nirari's] grandfather king in Nuhašše and poured oil upon his head" and declared: "Let no one overthrow [?] him whom the King of Egypt has made king and upon whose head he has poured oil." The anointing, which is not repeated for each of the king's successors, is therefore a kind of "warrant" issued by a sovereign (Kutsch). Thus, anointing by a prophet probably means that the one anointed receives his "warrant" through the power of Yahweh. That the "anointed of Yahweh" receives a kind of taboo status among the people in consequence of Yahweh's claim upon him is shown by 1 Samuel 24:7, 11; 26:9, 23. Later the term "anointed of Yahweh" becomes a more general title of the king. In Isaiah 45:1, the Gentile Cyrus, king of Persia, who is empowered by Yahweh to deliver Israel from exile, is called the חישׁמ *māšîaḥ* of Yahweh.

The second king of Israel, David, came by his kingship differently from Saul. Like the mercenary leader Jephthah in the book of Judges, he worked his way slowly and deliberately to the top by means of his military proficiency. It is characteristic, however, that Old Testament tradition also begins its account of this king, who was subsequently to be of immeasurably greater importance for the faith of Israel, with a story of how Samuel anointed the unsuspecting shepherd boy David. Thus the Old Testament confesses its belief that this king, too, who is described in 1 Samuel 16 as the youngest and least prepossessing of his family, was singled out to serve Yahweh's people Israel by Yahweh's free decision even before he had done a single proficient deed. Here, too, 16:13 states that the gift of the spirit of Yahweh, an act of divine intervention, marked the beginning of the rise of this unknown man. In his case, too, the anointing as king by his tribe of Judah at Hebron, like his recognition and anointing by the elders of Israel (the northern tribes) "in the presence of Yahweh" at Hebron, achieved by dint of laborious negotiations (2 Sam. 5:3), introduces the element of acclamation. The people recognize him as the גיד *nāgîd* (5:2) designated by Yahweh, thus responding to Yahweh's initiative. Designation by the man of God, the gift of the spirit, a string of military victories, acclamation by the people, and anointing as king: this, according to the account of David's rise in its present final form, is the course of events by which his kingship, too, should be understood. We can still see how the story of David's rise (1 Sam. 16—2 Sam. 5) seeks to reveal the face of Yahweh, the God of Israel, whom Israel has known since the exodus from Egypt, behind all that takes place. In the fight with Goliath, David intervenes on behalf of the "army of the living God" (1 Sam. 17:26, 36), which is being defied by the uncircumcised Philistine. He fights "Yahweh's battles" (1 Sam. 18:17; 25:28). Through him Yahweh wins a "great deliverance" for Israel (19:5). In 2 Samuel 3:18, the words of Abner are cited as an oracle from Yahweh: "By the hand of my servant David I will deliver my people Israel from the Philistines and from all their enemies." This leads to the acclamation of David by the elders of

Israel, who likewise cite an oracle from Yahweh: "And Yahweh said to you, 'You shall be shepherd of my people Israel and shall be prince (נגיד *nāgîd*) over Israel.' " (2 Sam. 5:2) At this very point, where the individual stages in David's rise are still so clear and everything seems to develop along normal political lines, it is particularly impressive how the Old Testament tradition places the same accent on this event, outwardly so different, as on the way Saul came to be Israel's first king.

The rise of the third king of Israel, Solomon, followed yet another course. The narrative of the court history of David, a sober presentation without any attempts to make anyone a hero, does not suppress the fact that Solomon was born of a marriage that grew out of adultery and murder. It does not suppress the intrigues within the court of the aging David that brought about the succession of Solomon at David's directive and his anointing at Gihon by Zadok the priest. Nevertheless the terse statement "Yahweh loved [Solomon]" and the additional remark that Nathan "for Yahweh's sake" gave the name Jedidiah, i. e. "beloved of Yahweh," to the child entrusted to his care (2 Sam. 12:24–25) maintain the mystery that through all these twists and turns the hand of Yahweh governed the decision. Thus Solomon's kingship, too, rests ultimately on a decision made by Yahweh, although we are left totally in the dark about its inner motivation. We shall return to the detail that here for the first time a son succeeds his father.

Alt has shown that the form of free election of the king, in which the people acclaim as king the man marked for the office by his charisma, continued to be fundamentally preserved in the Northern Kingdom.

For the Northern Kingdom, too, there is no lack of accounts of how designation by a prophet precedes the king's accession. 1 Kings 11:29ff. describes the designation of Jeroboam I. According to 1 Kings 14:14, the same prophet, Ahijah of Shiloh, proclaims a new king in the context of a judgment oracle; this king appears in the person of Baasha (cf. also the words of the prophet Jehu in 1 Kings 16:1–4). The designation of a new ruler by a disciple of the prophet Elisha is recorded in 2 Kings 9:1ff. There were also occasional instances when a son would succeed his father. The succession of Omri by Ahab may be explained by the fact that in Ahab a man stood ready who was qualified for the office. In the case of the five generations of the house of Jehu, on the other hand, the explanation is the general exhaustion of the land on account of the wars with the Syrians. As soon as there was a political recovery under Jeroboam II, the old principle of free succession comes to the fore once again. After a brief "interim," Jeroboam's son Zechariah is replaced by a new man, as had already happened in the cases of two kings' sons, Nadab (1 Kings 15:25ff.) and Elah (1 Kings 16:8ff.). Characteristically, the new king is once again a military leader. In Hosea's lament of Yahweh, "They make kings, but not by my will; they set up officers, but without my knowledge" (8:4), there is expressed not only the disintegration of this means of election, which is now simply based on power, but also the prophet's knowledge that the true choice of kings in Israel should be based on the question of what Yahweh decides. Very nicely formulated, as was mentioned earlier, is the "law governing the king" in Deuteronomy 17:14ff., which presupposes the situation in the Northern Kingdom. The correct manner of choosing the king is put thus: "You shall appoint (שׂים *śîm*) as king the man whom Yahweh your God will choose (בחר *bḥr*)." The "choice" is up to Yahweh. Israel "appoints" its king in light of this choice, whether it is known through the words of a prophet or through alert notice of a man who is attested by Yahweh in his deeds. The law governing the king in Deuteronomy 17 is also quite in the spirit of Israel's faith in forbidding the king, probably on the basis of previous bad experiences, to acquire many wives, much armament, or great quantities of silver and gold for himself. All of these would distract his heart and his confidence from relying on Yahweh alone. The king is forbidden to sell men to Egypt (as mercenaries or slaves) in order to increase his military might. Such an act would reverse the initial act of *Heilsgeschichte* with its exodus out of Egypt. And a later addition enjoins the king particularly to write down the (deuteronomic) law and read it regularly. In these ordinances, which assume an affirmative stance toward the kingship, we already hear unmistakable echoes of a criticism that distrusts an increasingly autocratic kingship, which would displace Yahweh from his rights as king over Israel. Concrete experiences of this sort explain the hostile attitude toward the kingship mentioned at the outset. It must not be overlooked, however, that even this hostile account maintains that Yahweh chooses (בחר *bḥr*) Saul to be king (by lot), whereupon his acclamation by the people follows (1 Sam. 10:24).

The monarchy in the Southern Kingdom, Judah, took a different course. With an amazing continuity the family of David maintained its position, even in its weak representatives, throughout the four centuries that the monarchy existed in Jerusalem. In seeking historical explanations, one must give full weight to David's success in making an unassailable "private force" for himself in Jerusalem, which, according to 2 Samuel 5:6ff., was taken by these mercenaries and then made by him into the "city of David." Omri later tried to do something similar in the Northern Kingdom by founding Samaria (1 Kings 16:24), albeit without succeeding in giving his family the long-term stability the Davidic dynasty had in Jerusalem (2 Kings 9—10). Considerations of power politics do not therefore alone suffice to explain the historical vitality of the house of David. Its roots go deeper. It is a striking peculiarity of the Davidic narrative in its present form that not only does a prophetic oracle at the beginning call him to a kingship like that of Saul, but in the middle of his reign a second prophet comes to him with a new oracle. However the literary structure of 2 Samuel 7 is analyzed, the chapter records a promise by Nathan the prophet to David that Yahweh would make his house endure. This promise is associated with a rejection of David's plan to build a house (i. e., a temple) for Yahweh in Jerusalem. "You shall not build me a house—I will build you a house."

This promise to the house of David explains why subsequently no prophet ever appeared in Judah promising the royal office to anyone. According to 1 Kings 1, Solomon is anointed by Zadok the priest, not by Nathan the prophet (whose mention in 1:34 is not original; cf. 1:39). The acceptance of Nathan's promise in "Israelite" Judah is further illustrated by the fact that when there was conflict over succession to the throne in the city of Jerusalem, the realm of the private power of the Davidic dynasty, it was the upper class from the countryside of Judah that intervened to set matters in order again (cf. 2 Kings 21:24; 23:30). Particularly characteristic are the differing reactions of the city and the countryside when Queen Athaliah is deposed (2 Kings 11:20).

With the establishment of the Davidic dynasty a new element, familiar to Canaan but previously unknown in Israel, is associated with the monarchy. At this point the gates are thrown open to the adoption of foreign rituals associated with the king.

There is much evidence to support the hypothesis that, in the figure of his second priest Zadok, David accepted a representative of the ancient Jerusalem tradition into priestly service before the ark of Yahweh; Zadok now appears alongside Abiathar, of the house of Eli. This Jerusalem tradition is the locus of the figure of Melchizedek, that earlier priest-king of Jerusalem who, according to Genesis 14:18–20, came out to meet Abraham, blessed him, and received tithes from him.

The psalter contains a series of royal psalms, including two that allude to the ceremonies on the day the Jerusalem king of the house of David acceded to the throne. In Psalm 110 two oracles are quoted that were recited over the young king on this occasion. The first, 110:1, accords the king coregency with Yahweh. 1 Kings 2:19 shows that this coregency in the realm of earthly politics was expressed in court ceremonial by the placing of a throne at the king's right hand. Thus the oracle in Psalm 110:1 says: "Sit at my right hand, until I make your enemies the footstool under your feet." The second oracle is a promise made under oath: "You are a priest for ever after the manner of Melchizedek," to which is added the promise that Yahweh will destroy the enemies of the king. In Psalm 2, written in the style of the rulers of the great kingdoms, an initial oracle guarantees security against the raging of the nations: "I have enthroned my king on Zion my holy mountain." In a second oracle, which has been considered analogous to the Egyptian royal protocol, the young king is told: "You are my son; this day I have begotten you." (Ps. 2:7) Here we find the designation of the king as God's son that is common in Egypt, albeit with a characteristic modification. In contrast to the temple wall at Luxor, this oracle does not fix the begetting in the period before the birth of the king, but rather on "this day," the day of his accession. This change turns the statement into an act of adoption. It is not an act of physical begetting but rather the divine declaration on the day of the king's accession that makes the king the "son of God." Despite the different basis of the kingship in Northern Israel, elements of the royal ritual were probably not absent from the court. According to the information we find in Psalm 45, a wedding hymn and the only royal psalm that can be definitely traced to the Northern Kingdom, royal ideology went even a step further in the north: verse 7 states that the king was actually referred to as "God" (אלהים *ĕlōhîm*, not "Yahweh"). That the custom of exalted throne-names was not unknown in Jerusalem is shown by the "messianic" passage Isaiah 9:5–6, where the "birth" of the child should probably be understood in the sense of Psalm 2, in a context where we hear the throne names "Wonderful Counselor, Divine Hero, Eternal Father, Prince of Peace." The use of the term "god" and the promise of peace (= prosperity) are recognizable borrowings from Israel's environment. But the term "Wonderful Counselor" exhibits genuinely Isaianic vocabulary (see below, p. 195).

Psalm 72 is revealing in its linking of a righteous kingship (as in Ps. 101 also) and the universal sovereignty of the king with the notion of prosperity in the natural world under his rule. "May there be abundance of corn in the land, growing in plenty to the tops of the hills." (vs. 16) In the messianic passage Isaiah 11:1ff., verses 6–8 depict in paradisal colors how peace will grow in power until it extends even to the animal world. In the first half of the same passage, there is a striking elaboration of Israelite belief in the gift of the spirit to the king. We no longer hear of the dynamic power that incited Saul, hot with anger, to perform a daring deed, but of the charisma of the wisdom (cf. also 2 Sam. 14:17–20) and righteousness of the ruler from the stock of Jesse. Even without the exaggerations of the courtly style, however, the king is still looked upon as the responsible figure among the people of Yahweh, in need of Yahweh's help and afterwards grateful for the help that has been given (Pss. 20—21).

All this raises the question of whether it is possible to justify theologically the adoption of the sonorous phrases of the courtly style, matured in the soil of the great Near Eastern monarchies. For the faith of the Old

Testament, its justification is the continual appearance of the sovereignty of
Yahweh, the Lord of the whole world, behind the sovereignty of the descendants of David, the minor Palestinian dodecarch. The conclusion of
Psalm 2, for example, which is part of the accession ceremony of the earthly
king, speaks directly only of the sovereignty of Yahweh. The king of Israel
makes the domain of Yahweh visible on earth. This notion is expressed most
audaciously in the narrative sections of Chronicles, which in the late period
seek to describe the nature of the Davidic monarchy according to God's
promises. In recording the words of Nathan to David from 2 Samuel 7:16,
1 Chronicles 17:14 formulates Yahweh's promise concerning David's descendants so that it reads: "I will set him over my house and my kingdom
forever." 1 Chronicles 28:5 states that Solomon "sits upon the throne of
Yahweh's sovereignty"; cf. also 1 Chronicles 29:23; 2 Chronicles 9:8. This
is the result of his "being chosen to be a son," as 1 Chronicles 28:6 states
plainly. Yahweh's cause on earth is maintained by his son whom he has
chosen. Here the kingship of Yahweh is linked in exciting fashion with the
rule of the "son of David."

Alongside belief in the divine election of the descendant of David, we
find at an early date belief in the divine election of Zion, discussed in §9 as
the place chosen by Yahweh for his presence. Psalm 132 makes the double
election especially clear. Kraus even concludes on the basis of this psalm that
there was a "royal Zion festival," combining the two elections in a single
observance. In the context of historical narrative, 1 Kings 11:13 speaks of
the partial preservation of the house of Solomon despite God's judgment
"for the sake of my servant David and for the sake of Jerusalem, my chosen
city."

As some passages already cited have made clear, these exalted statements about the king from the house of David contain the seeds of a unique
development. The discrepancy between the exalted promise of the kingship
and the disappointing reality of the actual monarchy, coupled with a faith in
the God who governs history, necessarily put expectations off into the future.
The promise to the house of David thus becomes the seedbed of messianic
expectations. Psalm 89 illustrates the attempt to puzzle out Yahweh's purpose in his covenant with his anointed. That the "covenant" category could
be used to describe the promise to the house of David has already been
mentioned; see above, p. 57. This expectation of the coming son of David
who will bring righteousness and justice, but also peace, is expressed particularly clearly in the "messianic" prophecies of the first Isaiah. But it is also
found in the secondary additions Amos 9:11–12 and Hosea 3:5, as well as
in Jeremiah 23:5–6 and Ezekiel 34:23–24; 37:24. Zechariah 9:9–10 attests
its survival in the postexilic period, following the collapse of the glowing
hopes placed in the Davidic Zerubbabel upon his return to Jerusalem, re-

flected in Haggai 2:20ff. and Zechariah 4. The outcry for the "son of David" that we hear in the New Testament reveals that this expectation (which is far from universal in the prophetic literature; see below, p. 220) was also alive in Israel at the beginning of the Christian era. It looks forward to the royal descendant of David in whom deliverance and righteousness will be concretely embodied upon earth on the throne of God's sovereignty, so that the earthly monarchy will no longer be at odds with the kingdom of God.

Alt, Albrecht. *Die Staatenbildung der Israeliten in Palästina.* Leipzig: Edelmann, 1930. Reprinted in his *Kleine Schriften zur Geschichte des Volkes Israel,* vol. 2, pp. 1–65. Munich: Beck, 1953.— Bernhardt, Karl-Heinz. *Das Problem der altorientalischen Königsideologie im Alten Testament.* Supplements to Vetus Testamentum, vol. 8. Leiden: Brill, 1961.—Brunner, Hellmut. *Die Geburt des Gottkönigs.* Ägyptologische Abhandlungen, vol. 10. Wiesbaden: Harrassowitz, 1964.—Frankfort, Henri. *Kingship and the Gods.* 2d ed. Oriental Institute Essay. Chicago: University of Chicago Press, 1955.—Johnson, Aubrey Rodway. *Sacral Kingship in Ancient Israel.* 2d ed. Cardiff: Wales University Press, 1967.—Hooke, Samuel Henry, ed. *Myth, Ritual and Kingship.* Oxford: Clarendon, 1958.—Richter, Wolfgang. "Die *nāgīd*-Formel." *Biblische Zeitschrift* new series 9 (1965): 71–84.—Schmidt, Ludwig. *Menschlicher Erfolg und Jahwes Initiative.* Wissenschaftliche Monographien zum Alten und Neuen Testament, vol. 38. Neukirchen: Neukirchener Verlag, 1970.—Kutsch, Ernst. *Salbung als Rechtsakt im Alten Testament und im Alten Orient.* Beihefte zur Zeitschrift für die Alttestamentliche Wissenschaft, vol. 87. Berlin: Töpelmann, 1963.—Rost, Leonhard. *Die Überlieferung von der Thronnachfolge Davids.* Beiträge zur Wissenschaft vom Alten und Neuen Testament, 3d series, vol. 6. Stuttgart: Kohlhammer, 1926.—Von Rad, Gerhard. "Das judäische Königsritual." *Theologische Literaturzeitung* 72 (1947):211–216. Reprinted in his *Gesammelte Studien zum Alten Testament,* pp. 205–213. Theologische Bücherei, vol. 8. Munich: Kaiser, 1958. English: "The Royal Ritual in Judah." In his *The Problem of the Hexateuch and Other Essays,* pp. 222–231. Translated by E. W. Trueman Dicken. New York: McGraw-Hill, 1966. —Idem. "Erwägungen zu den Königspsalmen." *Zeitschrift für die Alttestamentliche Wissenschaft* 58 (1940/41): 216–222.—Kraus, Hans-Joachim. *Die Königsherrschaft Gottes im Alten Testament.* Beiträge zur historischen Theologie, vol. 13. Tübingen: Mohr, 1951.—Mowinckel, Sigmund Olaf. *He That Cometh.* New York: Abingdon, 1956.

d) Priest

According to Jeremiah 18:18, Jeremiah predicted in his pronouncement of judgment that *"tôrāh"* ("guidance" or "instruction") would depart from the priest, דבר *dābār* (the word of Yahweh) from the prophet, and עצה *'ēṣâ* (wise counsel) from the wise man. This prophecy speaks of three groups within Israel and their charismata that are important for the survival of the nation: priests, prophets, and wise men, who deal with torah, the word, and counsel.

We shall discuss the priest first. If one turns to the Old Testament to inquire about the origin of the priesthood, there seems initially to be an unambiguous answer. According to P in Exodus 28, in the context of Yahweh's instructions for setting up and outfitting the "tent of meeting," Yahweh decrees that Moses shall make priests of his brother Aaron and the latter's four sons and produce the individual priestly vestments for their "investiture." Exodus 29 gives instructions for the consecration of the priests. Exodus 39—40 and Leviticus 8 tell how Moses carries out Yahweh's decree, and Leviticus 9 describes Aaron's first sacrifice. We also find in Numbers 3—4 ordinances for the Levites, who are to serve alongside the priests, assisting them in their holy work.

Upon closer examination, however, this clear answer becomes remarkably complex. There is no mention of the priestly figure of Aaron or of his sons in the legal code of Deuteronomy. Instead, Deuteronomy 18:1–8, which regulates the priesthood in the people of God, speaks of the tribe of Levi: "It was he whom Yahweh your God chose from all your tribes to attend on Yahweh and to minister in the name of Yahweh, both he and his sons for all time." This may be compared with the somewhat earlier account in Exodus 32, where Aaron, in the absence of Moses, makes the image of the golden bull at the mountain of God and decrees a festival, obviously exercising a priestly function. But when Moses comes down from the mountain, sees what is happening, and in rage smashes the tablets containing the law of God, the Levites assemble around him in response to his summons to those who are still faithful and they inflict a terrible judgment on the apostate. Aaron remains apart in a strange kind of twilight. After these events, Moses says to the Levites: "Fill your hand today for Yahweh." (vs. 29) This technical term, which is also found at Mari (*ARM*, ii. 13, 17), refers primarily to the "allotment of certain income for performance of a certain office"; then it comes to mean installation in an office. According to this narrative, which is hostile to Aaron, the Levites are the true priests of Yahweh. Unlike the later genealogies, this account does not think of Aaron as a member of the tribe of Levi. The Levi section in the blessing of Moses (Deut. 33:8–11) has the same purpose, basing the special privileges of Levi in the worship of Yahweh on an act of fidelity, which echoes Exodus 32:25–29 but takes place at Massah and Meribah. Closer to P but still independent is the priestly ordinance in the great concluding vision of the book of Ezekiel (44:6ff.), in which the name "Aaron" does not appear, and the priests are instead called "sons of Zadok." They are contrasted to the Levites, who failed Yahweh in the great crisis of the pre-exilic period and are therefore condemned to menial service. The prophecy of a man of God against the sinful house of Eli in 1 Samuel 2:27–36 is probably connected with the Zadokite strand; he prophesies to the priestly family at Shiloh that there will be a "priest who will be faithful," who will do what is in Yahweh's heart and serve throughout his lifetime before the anointed of Yahweh. This prophecy probably refers to Zadok, the priest, presumably of Jebusite Canaanite background, whom David set alongside Abiathar, the descendant of Eli. Solomon's further exile of Abiathar to Anathoth (1 Kings 2:26–27) and recognition of Zadok as the only true priest of Jerusalem probably represents the carrying out of this threat.

The few important passages just discussed suggest radical changes in the early history of the priesthood, which was eventually reduced to uniformity in terms of a genealogical sequence: Levi—Aaron—Zadok. This early history is far from being clearly understood. We are undoub - edly dealing with very diverse roots out of which the priesthood of Israel grew. At the originall·ᵧ Canaanite sanctuaries we should probably think in terms of non-Israelite priestly families. Doeṣ Aaron belong initially in this category as ancestor of the priests of Bethel, who then performed their function before the image of the golden bull? In all likelihood Zadok belongs in this category. On the other hand, Moses' blessing on Levi (Deut. 33:8–11), which mentions the desert sites Massah and Meribah, points to the early pre-Canaanite history of the Israelite tribes. In the pre-monarchic period, we find individual Levites, who are subject to the "Levitical rule" (Gunneweg) of owning no real property, in Judges 17—18 and 19—21. Judges 17—18 shows that people tried to recruit such Levites for priestly service. But the deuteronomic requirement that all priests should be "Levitical priests" did not carry the day. The centralization of the cult in Jerusalem under Josiah led to the predominace of the Zadokite priesthood at Jerusalem. 2 Kings 23:9 proves that the priests from the sanctuaries of the countryside were unable to maintain their equal right to offer sacrifice as Deuteronomy 18:6–8 had required, at least for the Levites among them. The draft of a law governing priests and Levites in Ezekiel 44:6ff., which is not from the hand of Ezekiel, illustrates the severe tension existing between the two groups toward the close of the exilic period, which led to a distinct defamation of the Levites, who were assigned to menial tasks in the sanctuary. The small number of Levites willing to return to Jerusalem at the time of Zerubbabel (Ezra 2:40=Neh. 7:43) and even of Ezra (Ezra 8:15ff.) illustrates this situation quite clearly. The settlement found in Numbers 3 obviously represents a compromise that the Levites were able to accept: as a punishment they no longer perform their services in the sanctuary, but they have a much nobler position, representing the ransomed firstborn of the people. The Korah narrative in Numbers 16 suggests tensions be- tween the aspirations of the Korahites, who, according to the superscriptions of Psalms 42, 44—49, 84—85, 87—88 and 2 Chronicles 20:19 represent a group of Temple singers, and the full-fledged priests embodied in Aaron. The high priest, on the other hand, an office that becomes fully developed in the postexilic period, adopts in his official regalia as described by P insignia of the vanished king (turban, a "rosette" on the turban, breastpiece; cf. Noth).

It is easy for the priesthood to appear as something static and official in contrast to the free charismatic words of the prophets. Jeremiah 18:18 repre- sents a different view: it juxtaposes the torah of the priests directly with the prophetic "word" as a gift bestowed by Yahweh, but a gift that he can also refuse to give. The work of the priests is also a charisma given by Yahweh, which makes it possible for Israel and the individual Israelite to have "life" in the presence of God. In the following discussion I shall survey the work of the priesthood.

　　1. The blessing on Levi in Deuteronomy 33:8 begins with a petition to Yahweh: "Give [?] to Levi your Thummim (תמים *tummîm*) and your Urim (אורים *ûrîm*) to the man of your favor." This hendiadys refers to the sacred oracle that is particularly entrusted to the priest. The exact significance of the terms is unclear. Is "Urim" to be associated with אור *ôr*, "light" (Luther: "light and right"), or with the root ארר *'rr*, "curse," in contrast to its opposite "Thummim," derived from תמם *tmm*, "be whole, intact"? What is clear is that we must be dealing with a form of lot-casting (using arrows or marked stones?) to obtain a "yes" or "no" answer to a question. The use of the oracle is vividly described in 1 Samuel 14:40ff. (with additions from the LXX). The priest in charge of the oracle is present in the camp in order to

answer any decisions that may arise by this means of inquiring into God's will. 1 Samuel 28:6 mentions three means of obtaining an oracle from God, all of which fail to give Saul an answer: dreams, Urim, and prophets. Once again the inclusion of this priestly means of obtaining an oracle, between oracles furnished through dreams or the words of prophets, shows that the casting of sacred lots is by no means merely a matter of neutral technical manipulation: it is a place where Yahweh speaks in his freedom. Ezra 2:63 (= Neh. 7:65) also shows that the casting of lots is not merely a technique that anyone can master. After the return of a group from exile, the question whether families that have lost proof of their genealogy are of priestly origin is set aside by the governor "until there should be a priest able to consult the Urim and the Thummim." According to Exodus 28:15–30, the high-priestly vestments of Aaron as described by P include an elaborately deco-rated breastpiece, bearing twelve gems engraved with the names of the tribes, which contains the Urim and Thummim.

According to Exodus 28, these vestments also include the ephod, which in accounts of the period of Saul and David has a function strikingly similar to that of the Urim and Thummim; cf., for instance, 1 Samuel 14:18 (LXX) or 1 Samuel 23:9; 30:8, where David obtains an oracle by means of the ephod worn by the priest. In the regalia of Aaron, where it likewise repre-sents an article of clothing, it is distinct from the breastpiece. Its interpreta-tion is made difficult by the fact that in Judges 8:24ff. (Gideon's ephod) the item in question appears to be an image of the deity. This raises the question whether we should think in terms of two different forms of the priestly ephod or of a vestment appropriate for a god, giving its name later to a divine image (Elliger; for a different view, see Friedrich).

The priestly use of lots and ephod to answer concrete questions in historical situations demanding a "yes" or "no" decision comes strikingly close in structure to the prophetic oracle in 1 Samuel 22:5. That priests and prophets (seers) are closely associated in the early period will be stressed below (pp. 99–100) from a different perspective. The priest, too, in what Deuteronomy 33:8 describes as his primary office, is a preserver of Yahweh's freedom, which no human decision can command. It is revealing in this connection that in the postexilic period, when the priesthood took on added significance in the person of the "high priest" after the elimination of the monarchy, the result was not what analogies from the field of comparative religion might lead one to expect. There was no elaborate development of the oracular system such as would have made the priest the powerful manipulator of divine decisions. As long as the sacred lot is employed in the Old Testament, it is limited to questions that can be answered with a simple "yes" or "no." Ezra 2:63 seems to suggest that the postexilic period believed it no longer had the authority to make use of this form of inquiry.

2. The priestly function of imparting torah is explained in greater detail in Ezekiel 44:23: "They shall give my people instruction (torah) to distinguish the sacred from the profane, and show them the difference between clean and unclean" (cf. also Ezek. 22:26). Haggai 2:11ff. furnishes a vivid example of such torah instruction. Because the Old Testament believes that Yahweh enters into the human realm quite realistically and concretely, there are fearsome places (Gen. 28:17*a*) that are "holy" (קָדוֹשׁ *qādôš*) (Exod. 3:5; Josh. 5:15) as well as those that are "profane" (חֹל *ḥōl*); in every realm down to the foods people eat, some things are permitted, "clean" (טָהוֹר *tāhôr*), others forbidden, alien to God, "unclean" (טָמֵא *tāmē'*). The priest is the expert protector of these distinctions, who instructs people, for example, in the "rules that ensure life" (Ezek. 33:15) to be observed by anyone who enters the holy place. The so-called "entrance toroth" or "entrance liturgies" (Ps. 15; 24:3–5; cf. Isa. 33:14*b*–16) show how wide-ranging such instruction can be. The realm in which the priests give instruction includes not only the symptoms of contagious leprosy (Lev. 13), which to us seem to belong in the realm of medicine, the distinction between permitted and prohibited foods (Deut. 14:3ff.), and the proper way to offer sacrifice (Lev. 1ff.), but also proper ethical and liturgical conduct. This will be the subject of Part III. Such expertise in torah is acquired only through true fear of Yahweh's holiness. It is a terrible rebuke to say: "Her priests profaned the sanctuary and did violence to the torah." (Zeph. 3:4)

3. The third element mentioned in Moses' blessing on Levi (Deut. 33:10*b*) is usually the first thing associated with the priestly office: sacrifice. "They place incense before your nose and burnt offerings upon your altar." Expertise in the ordinances governing sacred things necessarily gave the priest a special competence in the proper way of offering sacrifice. Judges 17—18 shows that it was considered a particular stroke of good fortune to get a Levite as a "father and priest" (17:10) at a "house of God" (17:5); cf. also verse 13. Thus according to the narrative in Judges 17—18, undoubtedly intended as a polemical caricature, the passing Danites make off not only with Micah's image but also with his priest, whom they make the priest of their tribal sanctuary in Dan. In 18:30 we can still make out the fact that the priesthood in Dan derives from Moses.

Sacrifice holds a primary place in the liturgical ordinances of P. With the distinction between priests and Levites in Ezekiel 44:6ff. and P, sacrifice is reserved to the priests, while the Levites merely perform menial assistance. Cf. also the Levitical singers and doorkeepers in 1 Chronicles 25—26. The offering of sacrifice by someone who is not a priest, attested in the early period, later becomes impossible. The functions of the "priest" are also eliminated from the royal office, although in Psalm 110 these are still accorded the young king upon his accession, after the model of the priest-king

Melchizedek. 1 Kings 8:62ff. proves that Solomon offered sacrifice at the
dedication of the Temple, and the list of officials in 2 Samuel 8:18 names
David's sons as priests; the postexilic period must consider this sacrilege.
2 Chronicles 26:16 ascribes the leprosy of King Uzziah to his sacrilege in
offering incense. For a discussion of the various types of sacrifice, see
below, §17.

4. In this context it is appropriate to mention that the liturgical blessing
of the people became increasingly the privilege and function of the priest.
According to 1 Kings 8:55, King Solomon blesses the people assembled for
worship, just as according to Genesis 14:19–20 the priest-king Melchizedek
blessed Abraham. Deuteronomy 10:8 decrees that the tribe of Levi is to carry
the ark of the covenant of Yahweh, to attend on Yahweh and minister to him,
and to give the blessing in his name. The carrying of the ark by the Levites,
which P elaborates in great detail in Numbers 4, is transformed into menial
service by the theory developed in 1 Chronicles 23:25ff. at the time when
the ark comes to rest in the Temple. By contrast, P makes the blessing of the
community the special privilege reserved to the high priest Aaron and his
sons. As Numbers 6:27 expresses it, they put the name of Yahweh upon the
Israelites when they recite the words of the Aaronic blessing in Numbers
6:22ff.

5. It is less easy to determine the part played by the priest in judicial
cases. The present text of Deuteronomy 17:8ff. speaks of judge and priest
together as being empowered to resolve lawsuits. Ezekiel 44:24 also ordains
that the priests are to sit in judgment when there are disputes. According to
the evidence of Exodus 22:7–8, the sanctuary becomes involved in the legal
process only to clear up crimes that would otherwise go unexplained.
Deuteronomy 31:9ff. and 27:14ff. speak of solemn legal proclamations before the assembled community in which the Levites play an important role.
But the full involvement of the priests in legal transactions is probably best
ascribed to the period when Israel ceased to be an independent state.

Our survey of what the Old Testament says about the priestly office
indicates that it experienced many fluctuations in the course of history. With
increasing clarity, however, Israel came to look upon the priesthood as a
special office set apart by God to protect the boundaries at the place of the
divine presence, to teach the people proper conduct with respect to the
sacred realm, and to mediate the blessing promised from this realm. In the
postexilic period there is added the office of mediator of atonement, seen in
its most concentrated form in the ceremonial of the high priest on the great
Day of Atonement (Lev. 16). For a discussion of the Day of Atonement, see
below, p. 129. The traditional ancient "Levitical rule" prohibiting possession
of real estate, which sets Levi apart from the material blessings given the
other tribes, is now interpreted to mean that in the share of the sacrifices

reserved for the Levites Yahweh has made himself the special "heritage" of the tribe of Levi, which he has set apart (Deut. 10:9; 18:2; Ezek. 44:28; Num. 18:20). The meditative sublimation of the Levitical statement "God is my portion" in the piety of the psalms (Pss. 16:5–6; 73:26) has been impressively expounded by Gerhard von Rad.

Cody, Aelred. *A History of Old Testament Priesthood.* Analecta Biblica, vol. 35. Rome: Pontifical Biblical Institute, 1969.—Gunneweg, Antonius H. J. *Leviten und Priester.* Forschungen zur Religion und Literatur des Alten und Neuen Testaments, vol. 89. Göttingen: Vandenhoeck & Ruprecht, 1965.—Noth, Martin. *Amt und Berufung im Alten Testament.* Bonner akademische Reden, vol. 19. Bonn: Hanstein, 1958. Reprinted in his *Gesammelte Studien zum Alten Testament,* 2d ed., pp. 309–333. Theologische Bücherei, vol. 6. Munich: Kaiser, 1960. English: "Office and Vocation in the Old Testament." In his *The Laws in the Pentateuch and Other Studies,* pp. 229–249. Translated by D. R. Ap-Thomas. Edinburgh: Oliver & Boyd, 1966.—Zimmerli, Walther. "Erstgeborene und Leviten." In *Near Eastern Studies in Honor of William Foxwell Albright,* pp. 459–469. Edited by Hans Goedicke. Baltimore: Johns Hopkins, 1971. Reprinted in his *Studien zur alttestamentlichen Theologie und Prophetie,* pp. 235–246. Theologische Bücherei, vol. 51. Munich: Kaiser, 1974.—Begrich, Joachim. "Die priesterliche Tora." In Internationale Tagung alttestamentlicher Forscher, Göttingen, 1935. *Werden und Wesen des Alten Testaments,* pp. 63–88. Edited by Paul Volz, Friedrich Stummer, and Johannes Hempel. Beihefte zur Zeitschrift für die Alttestamentliche Wissenschaft, vol. 66. Berlin: Töpelmann, 1936. Reprinted in his *Gesammelte Studien zum Alten Testament,* pp. 232–260. Theologische Bücherei, vol. 21. Munich: Kaiser, 1964.—Elliger, Karl. "Ephod und Choschen." *Vetus Testamentum* 8 (1958): 19–35. Also in *Festschrift Friedrich Baumgärtel zum 70. Geburtstag,* pp. 9–23. Edited by Johannes Herrmann. Erlanger Forschungen, series A, vol. 10. Erlangen: Universitätsbund, 1959.—Friedrich, Ingolf. *Ephod und Choschen im Lichte des Alten Orients* (with bibliography). Wiener Beiträge zur Theologie, vol. 20. Vienna: Herder, 1968.

e) Prophet

When Jeremiah speaks in 18:18 about the departure of the charismata from the people of Yahweh, he mentions second the "word" (דבר *dābār*) of the prophet. Amos 2:11 also ranks the prophets with the (charismatic) Nazirites as outstanding gifts given by Yahweh to his people (and afterwards disdained by them). Cf. also Jeremiah 7:25 and similar passages. We shall now speak of the prophets from this perspective, as the gift of Yahweh to his people, and inquire how Yahweh encounters his people in this gift. The special content found in the preaching of the writing prophets will be examined in §21.

The phenomenon of prophecy takes many forms. 1 Samuel 9:9 shows that the Old Testament itself demonstrates its awareness of this variety through the terminology it employs. "In days gone by, when a man wished to consult God, he would say, 'Let us go to the seer (ראה *rō'ēh*).' For what is nowadays called a prophet (נביא *nābî'*) used to be called a seer." Thus the early period considers one form of the "man of God" (this general term can be used to cover the various phenomena) to be the figure of the "seer," called either ראה *rō'ēh* or חזה *ḥōzēh*. The latter term is also frequently applied to the prophets in Chronicles. Alongside these stands the term נביא *nābî'*, which is formally comparable to the ancient titles נגיד *nāgîd* and נשיא *nāsî'*. The question is open whether the term should be understood in the passive sense,

"one who is called," or the active, "one who calls, one who speaks." There were individual
prophets to whom one might go, like Samuel for example (1 Sam. 9), to find out where some
runaway asses might be found; and there was the collective phenomenon of the "company of
prophets." (1 Sam. 10:5, 10) These prophets/seers can be connected with sanctuaries. From
the prophetess Miriam who begins the victory hymn (Exod. 15:20–21), from the unrestrained
music played by the company of prophets in 1 Samuel 10 and the statement in 2 Kings 3:15
that the hand of Yahweh comes upon Elisha while music is being played, we arrive without
intermediate stages at the music of the Temple singers, referred to in 1 Chronicles 25:1–2 with
the niphal of the verb נבא nb'. The mention of intercession as a special office of the prophets
also leads toward the liturgical realm (Jer. 14—15 and von Rad; Macholz takes a different view).
But it simply will not do to claim all prophecy as "cult prophecy," even the great figures of the
writing prophets. Cf. the sensible discussion by Johnson.

The Old Testament itself is aware that the phenomenon of prophecy is not limited to Israel
and the people of Yahweh. Alongside the seer Balaam, who is sent for from afar to curse Israel
(Num. 22—24), we find the multitude of the prophets of Baal with whom Elijah has to contend
on Mount Carmel (1 Kings 18). As we have already seen from a different perspective on p. 96,
the use of the term kâhin for the early Arabian seer suggests that seers and priests (כהן
kōhēn) spring from roots that are not far apart. In the account of Wen-Amon's travels (AOT²,
p. 72), we encounter the figure of an ecstatic "prophet" in ancient Byblos. The Aramaic ZKR
inscription (around 800 B.C.; KAI, 202 A 12) speaks of עדדן 'ddn, "counters," and חזין ḥzyn,
"seers," through whom the Baal of heaven provides answers. Above all, however, the recently
discovered Mari letters have brought to our attention a form of prophecy containing elements
of both the seer and the ecstatic, with some individuals associated with the cult and others not
(Ellermeier).

Unlike the (Jerusalem) kingship and priesthood, but like the office of the
deliverer/judge and the Nazirite, the office of the prophet is not hereditary
among the individual prophets (the situation differs in the case of the Temple
singers). A man is called to be a prophet. 1 Kings 19:19–20 recounts how
Elijah called Elisha to be his disciple and thus to be a prophet by throwing
his prophet's cloak over him. According to this account the call to be a
disciple appears to come from the master who is already a prophet. The
observation that there were "prophetic schools," suggested above all by the
Elisha narratives in 2 Kings 4 and 6 (but cf. 1 Sam. 19:18ff.), makes it seem
not impossible that prophets were "called" in this manner. But even in the
case of Elisha, it is in fact Yahweh who is to be understood as issuing the call.
According to 1 Kings 19:16, Yahweh commanded Elijah to anoint Elisha to
be a prophet. Since this command is subsequently carried out in a very
different manner, and since the only other mention of "anointing" a prophet
is found in Isaiah 61:1, we should probably think in terms of a metaphorical
use of the term. It is significant, however, that the call derives from a decision
made by Yahweh. 2 Kings 2:9–10 adds that the special gift to Elisha of a
double portion of the spirit of Elijah is once more the decision of God, not
of Elijah himself. We find explicit reference to Yahweh's call as early as the
case of Samuel (1 Sam. 3), but also in the great later prophets (Isa. 6;
Jer. 1; Ezek. 1:1—3:15; Isa. 40:6–8). Amos 7:14–15, too, however it is to
be interpreted, refers to Yahweh's call. In view of this resolution to ground
the prophet's call in the decision made by Yahweh, it is reasonable to expect

the prophets to speak of being "chosen" by Yahweh for their office. As was already mentioned, Jeremiah 1:5 contains a statement along these lines: "Before I formed you in the womb I knew (ידע *yd'*) you, before you were born I consecrated you [i. e., set you apart as my very own], I appointed you a prophet to the nations." In view of this passage, it is striking that Deuteronomy, which is generally so lavish with election terminology, never speaks of the election (בחר *bḥr*) of the prophet in its law governing prophecy (see below). Not until Isaiah 42:1, if the figure of the "servant of Yahweh" spoken of there is to be thought of as a prophet, do we find mention of the בחיר *bāḥîr*. In the minds of the prophets themselves it is clearly other categories that play a role when they speak of their relationship to Yahweh.

Before the writing prophets, the primary category is the "spirit," רוח *rûaḥ*, already encountered in the figures of the deliverer/judge and the king. In the "spirit of Yahweh" we find no trace of an idealistically interpreted intellectual "brilliance" possessed by the prophet. Here, as in the case of the deliverer/judge and the king, the term "spirit of Yahweh" (or "spirit of God") refers to a dynamistic phenomenon emanating from Yahweh that seizes the prophet and impels him to do things that would be impossible in rational everyday life. According to 1 Samuel 10:6, 10, the spirit of Yahweh, which is inciting the prophets to rush down from the hills under the stimulus of their music, also takes possession of the young Saul, so that he, too, falls into prophetic ecstasy. According to 1 Samuel 19:20ff., it is the "spirit of God" among the prophets who are Samuel's disciples that seizes first Saul's messenger and then Saul himself, so that he strips off his clothes and finally falls exhausted. Both stories purport to explain the traditional question, "Is Saul also among the prophets?" which still reflects 'something of people's astonishment at finding Saul in this unaccustomed company of the prophets. According to 2 Kings 2:16, the members of the prophetic school at Jericho consider it possible after the ascension of Elijah that the "spirit of Yahweh" might have seized him and removed him to one of the mountains or valleys.

The dynamistic component is even more marked in the idiom of the "hand of Yahweh," which means the same thing. After the judgment on Mount Carmel, the hand of Yahweh seizes Elijah so that he can run alongside the chariot of Ahab all the way to Jezreel (1 Kings 18:46). According to 2 Kings 3:15–16, the hand of Yahweh comes upon Elisha as music is being played for him, enabling him to give an oracle in a difficult military situation. Roberts points out that elsewhere in the ancient Near East the symptoms of illness are associated with being touched by the "hand of the deity."

It is striking that the earlier writing prophets avoid all mention of the prophetic spirit. In Hosea 9:7 we once hear the people refer to Hosea as a "man of the spirit" (איש הרוח *'îš hārûaḥ*) in their polemic against him. In Micah 3:8, the meter indicates that Micah's claim to be filled with the spirit of Yahweh is a later addition. Only in Ezekiel, with an effect that is remarkably archaic, do we hear the terminology common among the early prophets: the spirit "lifts" the prophet (נשׂא *nś'*; 3:12, 14; 8:3, and elsewhere), "carries" him away (לקח *lķḥ*; 3:14), "falls" upon him (נפל *npl*; 11:5), or "transports" him (הביא *hēbî'*; 8:3; 11:1, 24*a*; 43:5). The silence of the earlier writing prophets on the subject of the spirit is probably to be understood in the light of Hosea 9:7 (and 2 Kings 9:11) as a deliberate dissociation from bizarre works of the spirit. Another part of the explanation may be that these prophets are so directly constrained by the message of Yahweh that they simply do not reflect on the notion of a mediating spirit. Isaiah 8:11 speaks of the "strong hand of Yahweh" and Jeremiah 15:17 (in one of Jeremiah's confessions) of the constant pressure of God's hand.

The old designation of the man of God as a "seer" reveals that visions played a role in the prophetic experience of God. This element, which can shade off into dreams, is present from the vision of Balaam through Elisha (vision of distant events; 2 Kings 5:26) down to the great prophets (Isa. 6; Amos 7:1ff.; Jer. 4:23–26; 24). Jeremiah is extremely critical of dreams as vehicles of divine revelation (Jer. 23:25–28). The visionary element is very marked in Ezekiel (1:1—3:15; 8—11; 37:1–14; 40—48) and the cycle of seven night visions (later increased to eight by the addition of 3:1–7) in Zechariah.

Even in early prophecy, but above all in the classic writing prophets, a dominant position is held by the "word of Yahweh" (דבר יהוה *d*bar *yahweh*), which is received through an audition. Within the formulaic material in which the messages of the prophets are embedded, messenger formulas and oracle formulas are especially prominent. Messenger formulas have their original *Sitz im Leben* in the dispatch of a messenger; this is also the *Sitz im Leben* of the letter formulary, which is conceived primarily not as a direct communication from the sender to the receiver, but as a "memorandum" for the messenger who carries it. For example, a letter from the governor Kibridagan to King Zimrilim of Mari begins: "To my lord [i. e., Zimrilim] say: Thus says Kibridagan . . ." (Ellermeier, 29). In this formula the messenger is first addressed and entrusted with a message. Now the prophet also appears in the guise of a messenger. If the emphasis in the phrase כה אמר יהוה *kōh āmar yahweh* is still on the past event ("thus spoke Yahweh"), this way of introducing prophetic discourse would hark back to the moment when the messenger received his message, with which he now comes before the people. In other words, it is not a mystical union with Yahweh that enables the prophet to speak his message in the first person as the very word of Yahweh, but the relationship of a messenger to the one who sends him, a relationship that puts words in his mouth. This is also the basis on which we should interpret the oracle formula "the word of Yahweh" (נאם יהוה *n*'*ūm yahweh*), which may be an ancient seer formula (Num. 24:3). Alongside the notion of a message received directly from the one Lord, however, the prophets also speak of receiving a message from Yahweh's heavenly council. 1 Kings 22:19–22 describes this council, from which intially a רוח *rûaḥ* (here an evil spirit) is sent to the prophets. The same notion probably lies behind the plural form in Isaiah 6:8, repeated in Amos 3:7 and Jeremiah 23:22 with explicit use of the term סוֹד *sôd*, "confidential discussion," "circle of confidants."

The messenger role accounts for the real legitimation of the prophet in his commission (Ezek. 2:3). The most dangerous attack upon a prophet is to say: "Yahweh has not sent you." (Jer. 28:15)

When he is commissioned with a message, the prophet receives a "word" (דָּבָר *dābār*). Jeremiah 18:18 speaks of the "word" as the attribute of the prophet. The lack of a word means the end of his service as messenger. "Word" and "vision" can actually be identified, as in Isaiah 2:1: "The word that Isaiah saw . . ." (cf. 1:1). Thus the lack of a vision also means the end of the prophet's service as a messenger (Mic. 3:6–7). Our discussion of the prophetic word includes the following points:

1. It is characteristic of the great prophets that they know nothing of an amorphous glossolalia that has to be interpreted. At most some of the shapeless raw material of speech might be found in the two nonsense conglomerations of Isaiah 8:1, which, however, are given a very clear interpretation with respect to a specific situation. In all other instances the prophetic word is repeatedly clear and rational. Jeremiah looks with profound suspicion on all self-important secondary phenomena that produce an aura of vagueness and mystery (23:25–26, 31).

2. The second characteristic of the "word" spoken by the great writing prophets is its clear reference to the historical situation of Israel. In the context of the situation foreign nations can also be addressed. Oracles to foreign nations can even take on a degree of independence. But the focus of the prophets' message remains the destiny of Israel, to which the prophet speaks as Yahweh's messenger. His message refers quite concretely to specific historical situations. The prophets do not outline programs or even, like Muhammad, shape political structures and exercise sovereignty within them. They remain messengers, kept tightly in check and dispatched in particular situations. This holds true even for Ezekiel 18, where many have erroneously claimed to find a timeless doctrine; see below, p. 213.

3. If, however, we were to conclude that the prophets deal *only* with the prophetic "word," the spoken message, this "only" would be inaccurate. The prophets also know a "word" that creates reality, that indeed in itself anticipates reality. For the prophet, the "word" is not only the expression of a thought or idea: it is an event. This dynamic character is brought out in the formula frequently used to introduce the words of the prophets: "And the word of Yahweh came to me. . . ." Isaiah 9:7 speaks of the word that "falls upon Israel." Grether expounds this idiom with the audacious image of a "bomb with a time fuse." Jeremiah likens the word to a fire and to the hammer that splinters rock (23:29). The word that comes in the preaching

of the prophets creates reality. The nature of the prophetic message as an event that anticipates what will happen is especially clear in the prophetic "signs" (to use a term borrowed from Old Testament usage, e. g. Ezek. 4:3; 24:24, in preference to "symbolic actions"). Ahijah of Shiloh tears up his cloak and gives ten of the twelve pieces to Jeroboam (1 Kings 11:30–31). Elisha commands the king of Israel to shoot an arrow toward the east and then to strike the ground with his remaining arrows (2 Kings 13:14ff.). Hosea marries a prostitute and gives their three children significant names (Hos. 1). Isaiah goes about naked for three years (Isa. 20). Jeremiah shatters a jar at the Potsherd Gate (Jer. 19:1ff.). After the death of his wife, Ezekiel sits still and omits all the rites of mourning (Ezek. 24:15ff.). Zechariah makes a crown out of the gold donated by the returnees and places it on the head of Zerubbabel (according to the original text of Zech. 6:9ff.). These are not merely didactically intended illustrations of the message they accompany, but are themselves part of the coming event that is announced in the word (Fohrer).

In a reflection encompassing the whole of history this character of the divine word is expressed in the framework to the collection of Deutero-Isaiah's discourses. In 40:6–8, all the transitoriness of people and their history is set in contrast to the word of Yahweh, which is set apart from the realm of the transitory and "endures" (יָקוּם *yāqûm*). In 55:10–11, the effectual power of this word is likened to the fertilizing power of the rain and snow. Like them, it will not return until it has effected its purpose.

4. Even in the classic prophets we can still see how the prophet is approached for oracles and intercession, and how he practices intercession where this is not forbidden. But the real characteristic of the great prophets is the spontaneity with which they act on the basis of Yahweh's own freedom. In their declarations, which often contradict the expectations and venerable traditions of their people, the prophets are the most impressive voices proclaiming the God Yahweh, who comes to his people, but also addresses himself in his own freedom to this people in his words and actions and remains present in his "I, I" (Hos. 5:14; Isa. 43:25).

Within the context of legislation for the people of God as they enter the promised land, Deuteronomy 18:9–22 formulates a "law governing prophets." This raises the question of how the element among the people of God that most actively embodies the spontaneity of Yahweh's appearance can be governed by a "law." Closer examination shows that, after an introductory exhortation to Israel, the discussion of the prophet takes on the form of a promise, thus severing any connection with the legislative framework.

The introductory exhortation first surveys the various ways the surrounding nations seek to determine the will of the deity and find out what the future holds: soothsaying, augury, magic, necromancy, etc. All of these are strictly forbidden to Israel. The people of Yahweh—and here the law turns into a promise—will always be given a prophet by their God. The promise must be understood in this iterative sense; it does not refer, as Acts 3:22–23 and 7:37 assume, to a single future figure who will bring salvation. In this context Moses is considered the prototype of the prophet (§10a). Yahweh will raise up a prophet like him from time to time among his people. The fundamental event at the mountain of God becomes the etiology of the prophet. Because Israel could not bear to hear God speak directly from the fire at the mountain of God, Yahweh chose Moses to be his mediator. In like fashion, a prophet will rise up again and again as mediator of God's will. In line with the entire context of Deuteronomy, this will is understood primarily as a command. But the element of announcing what Yahweh is about to do is not lacking when the question is finally asked how the true prophet can be identified, and the answer is given that the true prophet can be recognized through the fulfillment of his predictions.

There are four items of note in this singular deuteronomic law governing prophecy:

1. Deuteronomy 18 presupposes that the prophetic word belongs irrevocably to the people of Yahweh. Yahweh will never leave his people without this word.

2. The nature of prophecy is maintained in purity by a refusal to set it within the limits of any type of office guaranteed by human invention. There is no line of succession, no pedigree that can guarantee Israel prophecy. It is guaranteed solely by the promise of Yahweh, who will never leave his people without his direct instruction.

3. Although the purpose of the deuteronomic law is to proclaim a divine will transcending temporal limitations, the prophet is not divorced from his association with a specific moment in history. He speaks to his age.

4. What is new and unique, however, is the notion of a permanent succession of prophets within which Yahweh raises up each new member. This guarantee is meant to combine the faithfulness of Yahweh with his freedom. In John 14:18, as Christ is about to depart from his disciples, he expresses the same assurance in a metaphor: "I will not leave you orphans."

But there is also another voice heard in the Old Testament, speaking in an age when there are few if any prophets, which looks forward to a final fulfillment of prophecy. Malachi 3:23–24 speaks of the prophet Elijah who will arise just before the day of Yahweh. In a different fashion Joel looks forward to the fulfillment of the desire already heard in the story of Moses (Num. 11:29): when Joshua is upset because the spirit has fallen upon men who did not do as Moses commanded, Moses expresses the heartfelt wish, "Would to God that all the people of Yahweh were prophets, that Yahweh would confer his spirit upon them all!" Joel 3:1ff. looks forward to the day when all the people will share in the prophetic spirit of Yahweh. Sharing in the gift of the prophet is here replaced by the expectation of a final total fulfillment of what Yahweh wishes to give his people in his prophets.

At the conclusion of the deuteronomic law governing prophecy a question is touched on that becomes increasingly vital in the great writing prophets. In the chaotic age of Jeremiah, just before the fall of Judah, totally contrary prophetic statements confront each other in Jerusalem. How is true prophecy to be distinguished from false prophecy, God's gift from human seduction? 1 Kings 22:19ff. alarmingly locates this problem within Yahweh himself: when he wants to bring Ahab to judgment, he sends forth a lying spirit to counterfeit the word of his prophets, so that the king, deluded, rushes to destruction. Ezekiel 14:9 and Isaiah 6:9–10 touch on the same idea. Deuteronomy 18 proposes the strangely feeble criterion of whether what the prophet predicts actually comes to pass, which can only be known after the event. This way of dealing with the problem, which is also found in Jeremiah 28:8–9, seeks in any case to maintain the principle that the true word of Yahweh is effectual. But it does not provide an "objective" possibility for evaluating the prophetic word when it is spoken. Deuteronomy 13:2ff. presupposes that even a false prophet can perform signs and wonders, thus lending his words the dimension of an event. But if he preaches apostasy and worship of other gods, he is to be handed over to judgment as a false prophet despite all these deeds of power. In another passage (Jer. 23:14; 29:23) the subjective obedience of the prophet to Yahweh's command is weighed: a prophet who commits adultery cannot be a true prophet of Yahweh. Here we see a further instance of the impossibility of separating the gift of Yahweh's word from his commands. Approaching the question from a different perspective, Jeremiah 23:14, 22 takes the position that a prophet who reassures the godless in their wickedness cannot have been sent by Yahweh. And we have already mentioned the deep mistrust on Jeremiah's part of all prophecy that seeks to build itself up through external incidentals: the mysterious assurance, thrice repeated, "I have had a dream, a dream, a dream" (Jer. 23:25–26 [?]); the dire whisper of God's name (23:31); but also the theft of God's word from other prophets (23:30).

Fundamentally, however, none of these are criteria that allow an "objective" decision in a critical situation like that recorded in Jeremiah 28. When Hananiah breaks the yoke that Jeremiah was using to proclaim submission to Nebuchadnezzar as the will of Yahweh, he apparently performs a sign that is clear to everyone. Jeremiah, confronted with the openly contradictory word of the other prophet, goes off in silence. He has no "objective" criterion by which to judge. He must wait until the effectual word comes to him once more from Yahweh. When this happens, however, he confronts Hananiah and predicts his death; Hananiah does in fact die a few months later. A similar situation can be seen in Jeremiah 42:1ff. The people are in a desperate situation following the murder of Gedaliah. Fearing the vengeance of the Babylonians, they seek an oracle from Jeremiah that will free them to take flight to Egypt. Jeremiah had undoubtedly made up his own mind early on, but he must wait ten days in this critical situation until the word of Yahweh comes once more. Once again we see that Jeremiah does not have any superior cr::érion at his disposal by which the word of God can be judged. With everything hanging in the balance, all that can happen is for Yahweh himself to send his word once more to his prophet. Despite all the provisional criteria that can be cited, in the final analysis it is only Yahweh himself who can say what is the "word of Yahweh." 1 Corinthians 2:11 speaks in the same vein when it says that only the spirit of God can say what is within God.

Thus the message of the prophets brings us unexpectedly back once more to the mystery of the God of Israel, whose name is "I am who I am" (§1).

Hölscher, Gustav. *Die Profeten.* Leipzig: Hinrichs, 1914.—Duhm, Bernhard. *Israels Propheten.* 2d ed. Lebensfragen, vol. 26. Tübingen: Mohr, 1922.—Lindblom, Johannes. *Prophecy in Ancient Israel.* Oxford: Blackwell, 1962.—Johnson, Aubrey Rodway. *The Cultic Prophet in Ancient Israel.* 1944. 2d ed. Cardiff: University of Wales Press, 1962.—Von Rad, Gerhard. "Die falschen Propheten." *Zeitschrift für die Alttestamentliche Literatur* 51 (1933):109–120.—Macholz, Georg Christian. "Jeremia in der Kontinuität der Prophetie." In *Probleme biblischer Theologie* (Festschrift Gerhard von Rad), pp. 306–334. Edited by Hans Walter Wolff. Munich: Kaiser, 1971.—Ellermeier, Friedrich. *Prophetie in Mari und Israel.* Herzberg: Jungfer, 1968.—Roberts, Jimmy Jack McBee. "The Hand of Yahweh." *Vetus Testamentum* 21 (1971):306–334.—Grether, Oskar. *Name und Wort Gottes im Alten Testament.* Beihefte für Zeitschrift für die Alttestamentliche Wissenschaft, vol. 64. Giessen: Töpelmann, 1934.—Westermann, Claus. *Grundformen prophetischer Rede.* Beiträge zur evangelischen Theologie, vol. 31. Munich: Kaiser, 1960. English: *Basic Forms of Prophetic Speech.* Translated by H. C. White. Philadelphia: Westminster, 1967.—Zimmerli, Walther. "Der Prophet im Alten Testament und im Islam." *Evangelisches Missionsmagazin* 87 (1943):137-146, 168–179. Reprinted in his *Studien zur alttestamentlichen Theologie und Prophetie,* pp. 284–310. Theologische Bücherei, vol. 51. Munich: Kaiser, 1974. —Fohrer, Georg. *Die symbolischen Handlungen der Propheten.* 2d ed. Abhandlungen zur Theologie des Alten und Neuen Testaments, vol. 25. Zurich: Zwingli, 1968.—Quell, Gottfried. *Wahre und falsche Propheten.* Beiträge zur Förderung christlicher Theologie, vol. 46, pt. 1. Gütersloh: Bertelsmann, 1952.

f) Wise Man

Alongside the priest and the prophet who are threatened with loss of their charisma, Jeremiah 18:18 cites a third figure, the "wise man" (חכם *ḥākām*), who will lose the charisma of "counsel" or "advice" (עצה *ēṣâ*). In a differently structured list of three groups within the populace, Jeremiah 9:22 warns the wise man against boasting of his wisdom (חכמה *ḥokmâ*), just as the warrior should not boast of his might or the rich man of his wealth.

Other passages show that the term "wise man" here refers to political counselors in the government. The parallelism with the "scribes" (ספרים *sōp̄rîm*) in Jeremiah 8:8-9 shows that they are also involved in the torah of Yahweh, which Josiah made the law of the land (2 Kings 23:1-3). The term "scribe" (ספר *sōp̄ēr*) appears in the lists of David's and Solomon's officials (2 Sam. 8:17; 1 Kings 4:3) as a designation for one of the highest state offices. The key passage in the story of Absalom's revolt shows not only how critical "counsel" can be in determining the fate of the land (2 Sam. 17:14), but also how Yahweh joins in saying the crucial word in the deliberations of the secret royal council. Cf. Proverbs 19:21.

That "wisdom" in this context is a gift of God is exemplified in the story of King Solomon, who then becomes the archetype of the wise man, so that subsequently wisdom literature is ascribed to him whenever possible (Proverbs, Ecclesiastes, Wisdom). At the outset of the account of his reign, 1 Kings 3 tells how the young king offers sacrifice at Gibeon; Yahweh thereupon promises to fulfill one request (cf. also Ps. 2:8a), and Solomon asks not for power but for wisdom to judge rightly. Yahweh's favorable response begins: "Behold, I grant your request. Behold, I give you a heart so wise and so understanding that there has been none like you before your time nor will be after you." (1 Kings 3:12) Later, 3:16–28 gives an example of "Solomonic judgment"; 5:9–14 describes the accomplishments of Solomon's wisdom; and 10:1–13 tells how the Queen of Sheba, having tested this wisdom personally, leaves full of admiration for Solomon. The purpose of these passages, as 5:9 repeats thematically, is to describe the gift given by Yahweh. At the same time, 5:10 recognizes quite artlessly that there is also wisdom outside of Israel, in Egypt and among the peoples of the East. The association of wisdom with the royal charisma of the רוח rûaḥ in Isaiah 11:2 is distinctly unusual.

These few citations show that in the Old Testament the "wise man" is not the "philosopher" or theoretician speculating on people and the world. With all its mastery of artistically expressed proverbs and songs, wisdom remains eminently practical and devoted to successful living. This is why חכמה ḥokmâ can also be said to be found in craftsmanship. Isaiah 40:20 describes the construction of an idol by a "wise craftsman (חרש חכם ḥārāš ḥākām)." King Hiram of Tyre promises to send Solomon the artisan Huram-Abi to help him in his building projects, to work in Israel "together with your wise men [= artisans] and the wise men of my lord David, your father." (2 Chron. 2:12–13) Here again foreign wisdom is acknowledged quite unaffectedly. In the context of describing how Aaron's vestments were made, Exodus 28:3 (P) says that Yahweh put the "spirit of wisdom" into the hearts of all the חכמי לב ḥakmê lēb (cf. also 35:10; 36:1–2, 4, 8; referring to women, 35:25). Here again we find the notion of the "spirit" (רוח rûaḥ) that confirms the divine charisma. And again, as Isaiah 28:23ff. shows with its cryptic metaphor of the ploughman who knows when to plant and when to harvest, right conduct is described as being based on the wonderful counsel (עצה 'ēṣâ) of God.

On the role of wisdom in determining how people live in the presence of God, see the discussion and bibliography in §18.

III. Yahweh's Commandment

In Part II I have considered those things that Israel, in its unfolding history, experienced as Yahweh's gifts. This approach was to a degree one-sided. Now we must turn our attention to what the faith of the Old Testament has to say about what God requires. It must be emphasized once more that this is not a second, additional element, over and above what God gives. In the association between Yahweh and Israel, which Israel recognizes as Yahweh's gracious gift, and in all the gifts that derive from this association, there is always a summons, a requirement on God's side. Every gift implies an element of duty. But in the duty required and in the instruction on proper conduct, the faith of the Old Testament sees repeatedly God's gracious guidance through the ambiguity of human life. Psalm 119 is a prodigious hymn in praise of this instruction, which is a "lamp to the feet" and a "light to the path." (vs. 105)

The following pages will discuss the concrete form taken by this divine instruction in the law and its commandments.

§11 The Location, Terminology, and Nature of the Commandments

I have discussed in §6 how Israel, according to the account of the Pentateuch, encountered its God at the mountain of God immediately after its deliverance from Egypt. Here the freedom vouchsafed the people of Yahweh in the exodus is confirmed in a "covenant" with Yahweh. The very use of the "covenant" category shows clearly how close together are Yahweh's promise of salvation and the people's promises of obedience.

A wealth of scholarship has demonstrated how many strata there are in the corpus of divine ordinances associated with the Sinai narrative and how many different historical stages it reflects. In the midst of all this variety, however, it is impossible to miss the fundamental principle maintained throughout: anything that is to have the status of a divine ordinance, at whatever period in Israel's history, must be grounded in that initial event when Israel was summoned into the presence of its God. Deuteronomy was not the first document to enshrine this view. Except for the divine regulations proclaimed, according to P, in the covenants with Noah and Adam, only the material incorporated into the concluding vision in Ezekiel 40—48 and the ordinance of David governing the singing in the Temple found in the Chronicler's history represent significant complexes of legal material placed in a different setting. Minor elements like the "law governing the king" cited by Samuel (1 Sam. 8:11–17) and David's ordinance governing division of booty (1 Sam. 30:24–25) need not be taken seriously into account.

1. In a late phase of redaction, the Decalogue in Exodus 20:2–17 was deliberately placed at the beginning of the commandments proclaimed by Yahweh at the mountain of God. In the preamble, Yahweh speaks in the first person, establishing that the legislation given in his name is his own. All "responsibility" in Israel, this emphatic "I" at the beginning of the legislation means to say, must be a "response" to this one God, whose initial act of deliverance is recalled in Yahweh's introduction of himself.

Exodus 34:28 refers to the Ten Commandments as a group with the strikingly simple phrase "the Ten Words" (עשרת הדברים *ʿăśeret haddᵉbārîm*). The group of ten commandments may have been assembled for catechetical purposes, so that they could be counted off on the fingers. Formally, such a decalogue can be contrasted with the dodecalogue of twelve curses found in Deuteronomy 27:15–26 (one for each of the twelve tribes of Israel?). Psalms 50 and 81 probably suggest that the Decalogue was proclaimed in liturgical ceremonies as a summary of God's will. The eight prohibitions and two commandments in Exodus 20 have unmistakably been brought together with the intent of covering as many of the important areas of life as possible. The more disorganized series in Ezekiel 18:5–9 seems to reveal a similar outline of subject matter. Comparison of the Decalogue in Exodus 20:2–17 with that in Deuteronomy 5:6–21 gives an insight into two stages of interpretation and thus into the ongoing process of transmission out of which the Decalogue must have arisen. Formally, it is noteworthy that only the first two commandments (Exod. 20:2–6/Deut. 5:6–10) are given as having been spoken by Yahweh in the first person, clearly singling out these two commandments for special significance. They will be discussed individually in §12 and §13.

The theological background of the Decalogue in its present form, including the interpretive expansions of the brief commandments, can be seen in the remarkable tension between Yahweh's two descriptions of himself that frame the first two commandments. In the preamble (Exod. 20:2/Deut. 5:6), Yahweh introduces himself as the God of Israel, who, in an act of mercy, led the Israelites out of slavery in Egypt. This stands in contrast to a second self-characterization in Exodus 20:5b–6/Deuteronomy 5:9b–10 in which Yahweh says: "I, Yahweh your God, am a jealous God. I punish the children for the sins of the fathers to the third and fourth generations of those who hate me. But I keep faith with thousands among those who love me and keep my commandments." Exodus 34:14 states the same thing even more bluntly immediately after the first commandment (prohibiting worship of other gods): "Yahweh, Jealous (קנא *kannāʾ*) is his name, a jealous God (אל קנא *ēl kannāʾ*) is he." Cf. also Deuteronomy 4:24: "Yahweh your God is a

devouring fire, a jealous God"; Deuteronomy 6:15; and, in the form
קַנּוֹא אֵל *ēl ḳannô'*, Joshua 24:19, where Joshua states: "You cannot worship
Yahweh, for he is a holy God (קְדֹשִׁים אֱלֹהִים *ēlôhîm qdōšîm*), a jealous God
(קַנּוֹא אֵל *ēl ḳannô'*)." Nahum 1:2 makes the same point with reference to
Yahweh's enemies: "Yahweh is a jealous God (קַנּוֹא אֵל *ēl ḳannô'*) and an
avenger, an avenger is Yahweh and quick to anger (חֵמָה בַּעַל *ba'al ḥēmâ*),
Yahweh is an avenger against his adversaries." The statement in the Decalogue about vengeance on the third and fourth generations did not originally
mean a series of punishments extending from one generation to the next, but
a devastating blow that would annihilate a family in all its branches (Rost;
cf. "great-grandmother, grandmother, mother, and child assembled in a
single room . . ."). Such is the harshness of God's vengeance on those who
do not keep his commandments. The clause about "keeping faith with thousands" is not formally parallel; it was probably added in a later stage. This
exuberant addition is meant to indicate that God's benevolence far ex-
ceeds his wrath and reveals God's true desires. Nahum 1:3*a* represents a
similar addition to 1:2. But in Yahweh's wrath against those who "hate"
him, i. e. are not prepared to obey his commandments, there glimmers
the sinister possibility that Yahweh's commandments can have their deadly
side.

The promise of long life in the land, in return for obedience to the
commandment to honor one's parents, leads into the realm of specifically
deuteronomic ideas, which will be discussed later.

2. The Covenant Code begins with an introductory formula in Exodus
20:22 and concludes in 23:20–33 with a prospect of the entry into Canaan.
It does not exhibit the formal organization of the Decalogue. We find instead
a major extension of Yahweh's will, which includes many different subjects.

Exodus 21:1 stands as a superscription to a complex of casuistic law extending, with sporadic
interruption by other forms, to 22:16; in form and subject matter it resembles the legal corpora
of Mesopotamia and the Hittites. The superscription refers to the individual laws as
מִשְׁפָּטִים *mišpāṭîm*. These comprise a protasis in highly developed style that formulates a given
set of legal circumstances and an apodosis that gives the appropriate decisions for both civil and
criminal cases. With these are associated laws governing capital offences, which were probably
at one time combined into series (21:12, 15–17; 22:18, 19 [?]), as well as apodictic commandments and prohibitions governing human conduct (above all the protection of the weak),
administration of justice, and worship. In contrast to the מִשְׁפָּטִים *mišpāṭîm*, these have no specific
designation. The suggestion that we have such a term in חֹק *ḥōḳ*, "statute," is unlikely
(Hentschke). In Exodus 15:25 (Moses at Marah), Joshua 24:25 (Joshua at Shechem), 1 Samuel
30:25 (David during the war with the Amalekites) we read that a וּמִשְׁפָּט חֹק *ḥōḳ ûmišpāṭ* was
decreed. None of these passages, especially the last, can refer to two different forms of law. The
Covenant Code therefore attests Yahweh's wide-ranging claim over quite diverse areas of life
and law, but does not provide any more profound theological penetration of its legal materials
apart from the scattered accretions containing motivating clauses, in which Yahweh is said to
be especially attentive to the weak (Exod. 22:22, 26) and Israel's former alien status in Egypt
is recalled (22:20; 23:9).

3. Deuteronomy is a different matter. It purports to be a discourse delivered by Moses immediately before Israel crosses the Jordan, impressing on Israel the commandments of Yahweh made known to Moses at the mountain of God. Much of its subject matter follows the Covenant Code. But especially in the first half of the legal corpus proper and in the preliminary introductory discourses it exhibits infinitely more theological reflection.

In the terminology, we find once more the term "law" (מִשְׁפָּט *mišpāṭ*) already noted in the Covenant Code. In 5:28; 6:1; 7:11 it is coupled with "ordinance" (חֹק *ḥōk*) and "commandment" (מצוה *miṣwâ*); the latter term is clearly associated with the root that means "command" or "order." That the law can actually be referred to by means of the word "covenant" (ברית *bərît*) was already mentioned in §6. A less common term for Yahweh's commandments found also in Deuteronomy is "admonition" (עֵדוּת *'ēdût*). New in Deuteronomy is the use of "instruction" (תורה *tôrâ*) as a summary term. What had been a term for an individual instruction, called "torah" above all in the priestly realm, has here become a comprehensive term for the (deuteronomic) law in its entirety, to which the people must decide to hearken obediently.

The introductory discourses of Deuteronomy make it clear, furthermore, that the multiplicity of individual commandments is meant to inculcate a proper overall attitude in Israel. To this attitude of love for Yahweh and proper fear of him we shall return in §16.

Deuteronomy switches the entire proclamation of the law from the beginning of the desert period to its end. This change has profound internal significance. It associates God's law intimately with his gift of the land. Possession of land means rest after the long period of wandering (12:9-10); it means a blessing, it means life. At the threshold of this life the law is heard. In this context its two aspects can be recognized. The law with its good and wise ordinances is part of the great blessing intended by Yahweh for his people. "What great nation has a god close at hand as Yahweh our God is close to us whenever we call to him? What great nation is there whose statutes and laws are just, as is all this law (תורה *tôrâ*) which I am setting before you today?" (4:7-8) At the same time, however, this law calls on people to decide rightly. "I offer you the choice of life or death, blessing or curse: choose life." (30:19) Even the scholar who feels compelled to assign the two aspects to the different situations of Israel before and during the exile (Perlitt) cannot fail to recognize this tension in Deuteronomy as it now stands.

Texts of treaties from the ancient Near East conclude with blessings on those who observe the treaty and curses on those who ignore it. Deuteronomy follows this model. Josiah's terror upon hearing the contents of the book that is brought to him (2 Kings 22) suggests that the "book of the law" he had before him was already cast in this form. Deuteronomy 27

—28 describe the blessings and curses associated with obedience and disobedience.

In this context an idea is suggested that perhaps attains full expression only in the exilic additions to the book: the notion that Israel's disobedience to the torah of Yahweh could forfeit possession of the land. In many passages the admonitions have an almost conjuring air, suggesting that the life that the law is intended to provide (Lev. 18:5; Ezek. 20:11, 21) might also be forfeit. At the same time, Deuteronomy emphasizes that the law and obedience to it are not unattainably distant. In its original context, Deuteronomy 30:11-14, which Paul cites in Romans 10:6–8 to illustrate the gospel, speaks of the "commandment" (מצוה *miṣwâ*). This commandment is not far off, so that one would have to go up to heaven to obtain it. It is not beyond the sea, so that one would have to bring it thence. "The word is very near to you, upon your lips and in your heart ready to be kept."

4. The authors of the Priestly legislation speak in a different manner. In the Holiness Code (Lev. 17—26) they have incorporated a complex that itself comprises distinct sections but must have been brought together as a unit before being included in the present structure of P.

Here we do not find the inclusive term תורה *tôrâ*. We usually hear instead of חקות *ḥuḳḳôt* and משפטים *mišpāṭîm* from Yahweh (18:4, etc.), and less frequently of מצות *miṣwôt*, "commandments" (22:31, etc.). The "covenant" is mentioned in 26:15; 18:30 uses the very general term משמרת *mišmeret;* and and 26:46 the plural תורת *tôrôt*.

This collection of laws also leads up to alternative perspectives on the future: the gracious gift of all life has to offer if obedience is chosen, ruin and loss of everything if disobedience is chosen. The words "blessing" and "curse" are not used, but substantially they represent the choice. Some of the statements in Leviticus 26 also clearly assume the experience of the exile. The possibility of repentance, return to Yahweh, and his renewed favor is fully described in 26:40ff., a later addition.

Within the nucleus of the legal materials in H, however, other elements emerge (Lev. 18—20). The framework of chapter 18 (vss. 24–30, as well as 20:22) considers the former inhabitants of the land and comes to the conclusion that the land spewed them out because they were unclean. This example is held up before Israel as a warning. Here we see how the perspective of cultic purity or "holiness" takes a dominant position. Here, in this legislation shifted back to Sinai, there is no trace of a people standing on the threshold of a land to be occupied by crossing the Jordan. There is instead a striking emphasis on Yahweh's pronouncing of his name to underline his commandments. When Yahweh's specific demands are made known to the people, who are called to be holy, we repeatedly hear the phrase "I am Yahweh" (אני יהוה *ănî yahweh*), in which Yahweh speaks his name to his people and expects them to keep his commandments in recognition of his name. Along-side the terse mention of Yahweh's name without further addition (Elliger's "sovereignty formula") we find the expression "I am Yahweh your God" (Elliger's "allegiance formula"). There is no reference here to the totality of God's law, evoking fear and love, as in Deuteronomy. Here the immediate emergence of the Holy One in his holy name is intended to move Yahweh's people to obey his commands.

5. P then goes in detail into the cultic regulations surrounding the tent of meeting, sacrifice, and ritual purity. All of these regulations, down to the proper organization of the camp and the correct marching order, are set down on the basis of faith in Yahweh's presence in the midst of his people. They are therefore not "laws," valid quite apart from Yahweh's gracious gift of his presence, but regulations intended to uphold the proper way of treating this gracious gift. In this context it can also be stated that improper familiarity with holy things can lead to mortal peril (cf. Lev. 10). But the community of Israel as a whole is vouchsafed this presence of Yahweh. Occupation of the land has been totally lost sight of. In the terminology we find a frequent use of the word "admonition" (עדות *ēdût*) for Yahweh's law. The ark containing the tables of the law is called ארון העדות *ărôn hāʿēdût;* the tent of meeting can also be called אהל העדות *ōhel hāʿēdût* or משכן העדות *miškan hāʿēdût.* The use of the term פרכת העדות *pārōket hāʿēdût* for the veil hiding the ark is already found in Leviticus 24:3 (Holiness Code).

6. Here it is also appropriate to cite the scheme outlined in Ezekiel 40—48, which antedates the final form of P. There is no mention of any law given at Sinai, of Moses as legislator, or of Aaron his brother as high priest. The liturgical life of the community is regulated within the context of the proclamation of God's eschatological presence in the new sanctuary seen by the prophet in his divine vision. This explains the close relationship to the legislation of P. The major difference is that here, in the post-Ezekiel concluding section, we find a new distribution of the land, meant to do full justice to the presence of Yahweh in the land and striving to honor the Holy One who dwells in the midst of the land by distributing it properly.

7. In a unique passage Chronicles accounts for David's new organization of music in the Temple. There is no mention here of any divine revelation bidding David to impose this organization. Instead, the theory is propounded that in this undertaking David is not fundamentally laying down a new law but merely adapting the previously promulgated law of Yahweh to a new situation. According to P (Num. 4; cf. also Deut. 10:8), the Levites were entrusted with the task of carrying the sanctuary while the Israelites were traveling through the desert. When the people and the ark of Yahweh came to a final halt, this service lapsed. David, already mentioned in Amos 6:5 as the great musician, thereupon undertook his great adaptation of the Levites

to the worship of the Temple: since they would be "out of work" after the ark was brought into the temple he had planned, he gave them a new "job" in honor of the Holy One. Only in this limited sense is David described as the author of new sacred ordinances governing the people of Yahweh. Thus even Chronicles with its apparently innovative basis for the law reveals once more how everything that is right and proper within the people of Yahweh must ultimately be grounded in the "law of Moses." In fact, Chronicles refers especially often to the torah of Moses.

A survey of the world of Old Testament law reveals the many different perspectives from which God's commandments could be viewed with the passage of time, and the extensive domain within which Israel considered itself subject to the imperatives of its God.

We must now turn our attention to the particular aspects of the divine imperative in Yahweh's law.

Alt, Albrecht. *Die Ursprünge des israelitischen Rechts.* Berichte über die Verhandlungen der Sächsischen Akademie der Wissenschaften zu Leipzig; Philologisch-historische Klasse, vol. 86, pt. 1. Leipzig: Hirzel, 1934. Reprinted in his *Kleine Schriften zur Geschichte des Volkes Israel,* vol. 1, pp. 278–332. Munich: Beck, 1953. English: "The Origins of Israelite Law." In his *Essays on Old Testament History and Religion,* pp. 79–132. Translated by R. A. Wilson. Oxford: Blackwell, 1966.—Noth, Martin. *Die Gesetze im Pentateuch.* Schriften der Königsberger Gelehrten Gesellschaft, Geisteswissenschaftliche Klasse, vol. 17, pt. 2. Halle (Saale): Niemeyer, 1940. Reprinted in his *Gesammelte Studien zum Alten Testament,* pp. 9–141. Theologische Bücherei, vol. 6. Munich: Kaiser, 1957. English: "The Laws in the Pentateuch." In his *The Laws in the Pentateuch and Other Studies,* pp. 1–107. Translated by D. R. Ap-Thomas. Edinburgh: Oliver & Boyd, 1966.—Stamm, Johann Jakob. *Der Dekalog im Lichte der neueren Forschung.* Bern: Haupt, 1962. English: *The Ten Commandments in Recent Research.* Translated by M. E. Andrews. Studies in Biblical Theology, 2d series, vol. 2. Naperville, Ill.: Allenson, 1967.—Rost, Leonhard. "Die Schuld der Väter." In *Solange es "heute" heisst* (Festschrift Rudolf Hermann), pp. 229–233. Edited by Paul Althaus. Berlin: Evangelische Verlagsanstalt, 1957. Reprinted in his *Studien zum Alten Testament,* pp. 66–71. Beiträge zur Wissenschaft vom Alten und Neuen Testament, 6th series, vol. 1. Stuttgart: Kohlhammer, 1974.—Zimmerli, Walther. *Das Gesetz und die Propheten.* 2d ed. Göttingen: Vandenhoeck & Ruprecht, 1969. English: *The Law and the Prophets.* Translated by R. E. Clements. James Sprunt Lectures, 1963. Oxford: Blackwell, 1965.—Schulz, Hermann. *Das Todesrecht im Alten Testament.* Beihefte zur Zeitschrift für die Alttestamentliche Wissenschaft, vol. 114. Berlin: Töpelmann, 1969.—Hentschke, Richard. *Satzung und Setzender.* Beiträge zur Wissenschaft vom Alten und Neuen Testament, 5th series, vol. 3. Stuttgart: Kohlhammer, 1963.—Kilian, Rudolf. *Literarkritische und formgeschichtliche Untersuchung des Heiligkeitsgesetzes* (with bibliography). Bonner biblische Beiträge, vol. 19. Bonn: Hanstein, 1963.—Merendino, Rosario Pius. *Das Deuteronomische Gesetz* (with bibliography). Bonner biblische Beiträge, vol. 31. Bonn: Hanstein, 1969. —Rendtorff, Rolf. *Die Gesetze in der Priesterschrift.* Forschungen zur Religion and Literatur des Alten und Neuen Testaments, vol. 62. Göttingen: Vandenhoeck & Ruprecht, 1954.—Cf. also the bibliographies to §1 and §6.

§12 The First Commandment

At the head of the apodictic commandments of the Decalogue stands Yahweh's prohibition in Exodus 20:3 (= Deut. 5:7), which, literally translated, reads: "There shall not be for you other gods over against me" (Noth.

Knierim) or "in defiance of me" (Köhler). This commandment is continued in verses 5–6 by an expansion in which Yahweh describes himself for a second time (vss. 5*b*–6). The significance of this expansion has already been discussed in § 11. As Exodus 34:14 shows, this description refers back to the first commandment. The use of Yahweh's two arresting descriptions of himself in verses 2 and 5*b*–6, which bear the burden of justifying this first commandment, fully expresses the thematic significance of the first commandment. Obedience to Yahweh, the one God, who delivered Israel out of slavery and is jealous of his own uniqueness, defines the fundamental nature of the Old Testament faith.

There are two striking features about Exodus 20:2 in its extended formulation:
1. No other god is mentioned specifically by name. The phrase "other gods" is a general formula embracing the entire world of the gods apart from Yahweh. This recalls the way treaties were formulated in the ancient Near East: the prohibition against entering into any kind of agreement with "another sovereign" can thematically dominate the individual stipulations.
2. The use of the colorless and neutral verb היה *hyh* in the formulation of the predicate ("there shall not be for you") also distinguishes the first commandment from all the rest, which prohibit or demand a specific act, addressing the listener in the second person. This formulation is unusual, and distantly recalls the absolute imperatives of the creator in Genesis 1:3, "Let there be light," 1:6, "Let there be a firmament," and, in the lack of agreement with the plural subject, especially 1:14, "Let there be luminaries in the firmament." This formulation obviously represents an ultimate distillation of a fundamental principle. Linguistically, its closest parallels occur in the deuteronomic and deuteronomistic documents.
The formulation of Exodus 34:14, which is probably earlier, is more concrete, prohibiting prostration before any other god—a point expressly added by the expansion in Exodus 20:5. A striking feature is the use of the singular, "another god" (אחר אל *ēl aḥēr*), found only here in the Old Testament. What is probably the earliest recognizable form of this commandment, Exodus 22:19 in the Covenant Code, which forbids sacrifices to other gods, is unfortunately garbled. According to Alt, the present form "Whoever sacrifices to gods shall be put to death under the ban" is based on an original "Whoever sacrifices to other gods shall surely die." Schulz suggests instead: "Whoever sacrifices to other gods shall be put to death under the ban."
The two passages cited raise doubt about ascribing the prohibition against worship of other gods to the deuteronomic period. On the other hand, it is unlikely that this prohibition had already been formulated during the nomadic beginnings of the people, when the host just delivered from Egypt could hardly have felt tempted to worship other gods. More weight attaches to Knierim's suggestion that Israel's obligation to worship Yahweh exclusively dates from the establishment of the twelve tribe system of Israel at Shechem, of which a reminiscence may be preserved in Joshua 24. A welcome confirmation of this hypothesis appears to be found in the strange ritual, associated with Shechem, of renouncing and burying "foreign gods" (הנכר אלהי *ĕlōhê hannēkār*) beneath the sacred tree at Shechem (Gen. 35:2, 4), which, as already mentioned (p. 55), seems to have been incorporated as a tradition of some antiquity into the ritual for the pilgrimage from Shechem to Bethel when the royal sanctuary was transferred to Bethel (1 Kings 12:29; cf. Amos 7:13). This theory would mean that in this act of decision, in which Yahweh took on the role of ישראל אלהי אל *ēl ĕlōhê yiśrā'ēl*, the first commandment was explicitly formulated for the first time.

As the earlier formulations express even more clearly than Exodus 20:2, the first commandment is not meant to be a point of doctrine requiring Israel to believe that nowhere in the wide world were there other gods to be found among other peoples. It has already been stated (p. 42) that initially Israel quite unabashedly presupposed the existence of other deities in other realms, just as Paul admits the possibility in 1 Corinthians 8:5: "If there be so-called gods, whether in heaven or on earth, as indeed there are many gods and many lords. . . ." Like Paul, however, it knew the crucial continuation: ". . . yet for us there is one God." In the first commandment the pronoun is emphatic: "There shall not be for *you* other gods." Israel shall not offer prostration and sacrifice to any other god.

We can observe how here, too, the challenges of history force a rigorous polemic exposition of the commandment. The Israel of the early period quite ingenuously applied the name and titles of the Canaanite high god El to Yahweh and interpreted what earlier tradition had said of encounters with the "God of the fathers" as a history of promise referring to Yahweh. Bitter opposition first breaks out clearly in relation to the figure of the god Baal (at Ugarit, the son of Dagan and also, indirectly, of El; cf. Kapelrud), whose special realm was fertility and meteorological phenomena and their associated ritual. The period of Ahab and his prophetic antagonist Elijah, when an attempt was made to naturalize the religion of Baal, initially in its Tyrian offshoot, which could easily, however, take root in Canaanite soil, became the first period of conflict. In the confrontation on Mount Carmel, as reported in 1 Kings 18, confession of Yahweh takes the form of anti-Baal polemic: "Yahweh is God, Yahweh is God." (18:39) In the polemic of Hosea, which is carried on in the early preaching of Jeremiah, the Tyrian background has vanished. Under the dynasty of Jehu, too, who owed his throne to his break with the pro-Tyre policies of Ahab and Jezebel, Baalism continued to extend its influence under the guise of apparent Yahwism. In their opposition to this, the prophets just mentioned give full weight to the first commandment as interpreted for their own age. Hosea's polemic, stamped with the seal of history in the downfall of the Northern Kingdom, makes Northern Israel the "idolatrous" kingdom *par excellence.*

During the Assyrian period, the wave of devotion to foreign gods breaks over Judah in a different way. 2 Kings 23:4ff. reveals how many symbols of "other gods" had been naturalized under the pressure of foreign political power, even finding a place in the Jerusalem Temple. At this point the deuteronomic corpus, in which opposition to foreign gods found its most vehement expression, became the obstinate champion of Yahweh against all worship of foreign gods. The outline of deuteronomic legislation in the narrower sense is especially instructive for the concrete interpretation given the first commandment in the period, since it reflects the two fronts on which the battle is now being fought. Deuteronomy 13 provides three examples of how prophets or "dreamers of dreams" could lead their own families or the populace of an Israelite town astray into worship of foreign gods. It requires inexorable punishment for those who lead the people astray, even if they can claim signs and miracles as their credentials (13:3). Deuteronomy 17:2–7 cites an analogous case, in which the most important requirement is careful inquiry of witnesses. Deuteronomy 13, which would be expected to stand at the head of the legislative corpus as an explication of the "first command-ment," is in fact preceded in Deuteronomy 12 by several variants of the so-called centralization law, which undoubtedly likewise purports to be a topical application of the first commandment. The idea that "no other gods" means "no other sanctuaries"—or, to put it in positive terms, that "one Yahweh" (to use the words of Deut. 6:4, the Shema, which is still an impor-tant liturgical text for Judaism) means "one sanctuary"—leads to the require-ment that even all the local sanctuaries of Yahweh be destroyed, except for the one "which Yahweh will choose as a dwelling place for his name." (12:11) In centralizing the worship of Yahweh at Jerusalem, the deutero-nomic reform seeks to live by the first commandment as interpreted for its own age.

The Holiness Code does not exhibit the rigid structure of Deuteronomy. Even here, though, a parallel to Deuteronomy 12 can be discerned in Leviticus 17, where the requirement is laid down that all sac-rifices must be brought to the entrance of the sacred tent. Otherwise, how-ever, Leviticus 17 is more concerned with the cultically correct way of offering sacrifice (so as to avoid the consumption of blood). The highly composite partial collection in Leviticus 19 prohibits resort to idols (here called אֱלִילִים ʾĕlîlîm), if not at the beginning, then at least in verse 4, among the introductory precepts. Leviticus 26:1 places this prohibition, formulated in the same way, once more at the head of the list. In the collection found in Leviticus 20, on the contrary, we hear at the very beginning a strict prohibi-tion against sacrifice to Molech. Pace Eissfeldt and others, who claim to find in the word מֹלֶךְ mōlek a term for a particular kind of sacrifice, we are actually dealing with a derogatory revocalization of the title "king" (melek) with the vowels of the word בֹּשֶׁת bōšet, "shame." Sacrifice of the firstborn to a deity termed "king," probably interpreted as Yahweh and having an altar in the valley of Hinnom (Jer. 19:2ff.), is for the priestly circles of the exilic and early postexilic period the most abominable form of idolatry; cf. also Ezekiel 20:25–26 and the discussion below, p. 210. The tendency of priestly thought to find worship of foreign gods especially serious, primarily because it re-sulted in cultic uncleanness, is probably also behind some of Ezekiel's ter-minology. In Ezekiel (as well as in some deuteronomistic passages) the foreign gods are called גִּלּוּלִים gillûlîm. The vocalization of this word probably represents a derogatory assimilation to the term שִׁקּוּצִים šiqqûṣîm, "abomina-tion." Etymologically, however, the word is probably related to the "excre-ment" (גְּלָלֵי gelʿlê-) of Ezekiel 4:12, 15, and refers to the false gods and the objects representing them as "dung."

The recapitulation of history in Ezekiel 20 is also informative about the significance of the first commandment. It begins with the "election" of Israel in Egypt. Yahweh's revelation of his name ("I am Yahweh your God") is followed first by his oath that he will lead his people out of Egypt into a fair land. This is followed immediately by a commandment, which is thus given a place at the very beginning of the history of God's election, in Egypt. The subject matter is limited to the first commandment, which is formulated in the priestly terminology just outlined and is underlined by Yahweh's motivating statement of his own name: "Cast away the abominations on which you feast your eyes (שִׁקּוּצֵי עֵינָיו *šiqqûṣê 'ênāw*) and do not defile yourselves with the idols (גִּלּוּלִים *gillûlîm*) of Egypt. I am Yahweh, your God." (vs. 7) Here there is no longer any mention of the local baals in Canaan and the great gods of the Assyrian Empire. The requirement that the firstborn be sacrificed is interpreted in 20:25–26 as a sinister ordinance, decreed by Yahweh himself but serving only to multiply sin. Just as in the Decalogue, however, the truly central requirement imposed in Egypt, at the fountainhead of Israel's history, is found in the first commandment, given concrete expression in this initial situation by special reference to the "idols of Egypt."

When we come to the late exilic prophet Deutero-Isaiah, we have entered a different world. He does not cite any legally formulated commandments, but the wealth of gods he had directly before his eyes in Babylonia has become an object of superior scorn. Alluding to Yahweh's power exhibited in history and his "word" that guides and shapes the course of history in advance (see above, p. 104), he depicts the impotence of the "gods" worshiped in their images. It is remarkable to see how at the very time Israel is set adrift in the pagan world, apparently helpless to the powers of the "gods," the truth comprehended in the first commandment becomes self-evident to the prophet, beyond doubt or discussion. According to 45:23–24, in time to come even the Gentiles will bow the knee and confess: "In Yahweh alone . . . are victory and might." Here we see once more an illustration of what was said at the outset of our discussion of "Yahweh's commandment": the instruction that imparts the first, the most central commandment imposed on Israel is gracious instruction that leads to salvation.

Knierim, Rolf. "Das erste Gebot." *Zeitschrift für die Alttestamentliche Wissenschaft* 77 (1965): 20–39.—Schmidt, Werner H. *Das erste Gebot.* Theologische Existenz heute, new series, vol. 165. Munich: Kaiser, 1969.—Alt, Albrecht. "Die Wallfahrt von Sichem nach Bethel." In *In piam memoriam Alexander von Bulmerincq,* pp. 218–230. Abhandlungen der Herder-Gesellschaft und des Herder-Instituts zu Riga, vol. 6, no. 3. Riga: Ernst Plates, 1938. Reprinted in his *Kleine Schriften zur Geschichte des Volkes Israel,* vol. 1, pp. 79–88. Munich: Beck, 1953.—Kapelrud, Arvid. *Baal in the Ras Shamra Texts.* Copenhagen: Gad, 1952.—Lohfink, Norbert. *Das Hauptgebot.* Analecta Biblica, vol. 20. Rome: Pontifical Biblical Institute, 1963.—Horst, Friedrich. *Das Privilegrecht Jahves.* Forschungen zur Religion und Literatur des Alten und Neuen Testaments, vol. 45. Göttingen: Vandenhoeck & Ruprecht, 1930. Reprinted in his *Gottes Recht,* pp. 17–144. Theologische Bücherei, vol. 12. Munich: Kaiser, 1961.—Eissfeldt, Otto. *Molk als Opferbegriff im*

Punischen und Hebräischen und das Ende des Gottes Moloch. Beiträge zur Religionsgeschichte des Altertums, vol. 3. Halle (Saale): Niemeyer, 1935.—Preuss, Horst Dietrich. *Verspottung fremder Religionen im Alten Testament.* Beiträge zur Wissenschaft vom Alten und Neuen Testament, 5th series, vol. 12. Stuttgart: Kohlhammer, 1971.—Cf. also the bibliographies to §6 and §11.

§13 The Prohibition against Images
(and against Misusing the Name of God)

Alongside the first commandment in Exodus 20, preceded and followed by Yahweh's repeated statement of his own name, we find the prohibition: "You shall not make a carved image for yourself." The continuation, whose textual linkage to the prohibition is controversial, represents a later elucidation: ". . . nor the likeness of anything in the heavens above, or on the earth below, or in the waters under the earth." The close association between the prohibition of foreign gods and the prohibition of images, which also occurs elsewhere, has added fuel to the fire of the continued debate whether the prohibition of images refers to images of Yahweh or to images of foreign gods.

The word פֶּסֶל *pesel* used in Exodus 20:4 refers initially to a divine image carved or chiseled out of wood or stone, or the non-metallic core of such an image. Later it is used less precisely for metal images as well (Isa. 40:19; 44:10). The formulation in Exodus 34:17, "You shall not make yourselves gods [or: 'a god'] of cast metal," has today been displaced by the strongly deuteronomic version of the first commandment in 34:14. The word מַסֵּכָה *massēkâ*, derived from the root נסך *nsk*, "pour," always refers to the metal image. The law of the altar (Exod. 20:24–26), which at an early stage probably introduced the legal corpus of the Covenant Code, has had a plural commandment placed at its beginning in verse 23: "You shall not make gods of silver with [= besides?] me, and gods of gold you shall not make." Once again the position at the beginning reveals the importance of the prohibition of images. We find it once more closely associated with the prohibition of idolatry in Leviticus 19:4*b* (Holiness Code): "You shall not make gods of cast metal (אֱלֹהֵי מַסֵּכָה *ĕlōhê massēkâ*) for yourselves"; cf. also Leviticus 26:1. The decalogue of curses in Deuteronomy 27 has its own special emphasis, placing the prohibition of images (secondarily?) at the head of the whole series of curses without any explicit prohibition of foreign gods: "A curse upon the man who carves an idol (פֶּסֶל *pesel*) or casts an image (מַסֵּכָה *massēkâ*), an abomination to Yahweh, the work of the hands of a craftsman, and sets it up in secret." (27:15) The secrecy of the act means that we cannot think in terms of a divine image set up publicly in Israel, which is what the previously mentioned passages probably referred to. It is also striking that the legal corpus Deuteronomy 12—26 does not contain any prohibition of images. For a discussion of the מַצֵּבָה *maṣṣēbâ*, see below.

It is definitely wrong to interpret the prohibition of images as though it represented a "higher spirituality" that gradually developed in Israel, rejecting materialistic images. Such a material/spiritual dualism is foreign to the Old Testament. It must also be stressed that the other religions of the ancient Near East did not harbor the vulgar belief that the deity was simply identical with the image set up in the temple. They believed rather that the deity took possession of the image and could thereafter be approached in it. In its prohibition of images, Israel radically rejected this belief. Behind this prohibition stands the knowledge, probably present very early, that Yahweh, whom Israel encountered as the lord of history in the historical act of deliverance from Egypt, remains a lord who cannot be captured in any representation or image. This is not because Israel conceived its God in abstract spiritual terms far removed from concrete visual form. The naive talk of Yahweh's countenance, his hands, his eyes, etc. contradicts such a notion very clearly. But Israel could never believe in Yahweh as a god who would simply enter into something made by human hands. Confrontation with the ancient Near Eastern notion of creation led to a clear formulation of the doctrine of creation peculiar to the Old Testament (§4). This belief was present in Israel from its very beginnings, and left its deposit in the strict prohibition against making an image of God in any form. Israel knew that Yahweh was never so ready to hand as the deity in the ritual forms of the ancient Near East, in which the image of the god was waited on, clothed, decorated, and fed, but also manipulated for mantic purposes. The strict prohibition of all forms of magic points in the same direction.

Now of course this knowledge did gradually permeate Israel with increasing clarity in the historical process. The Old Testament itself provides the evidence.

In the eyes of later historians, the Northern Kingdom was not merely the sinful kingdom in general: it was specifically the idolatrous kingdom. In the Deuteronomistic History, which played a special role in shaping this general estimate, the primary focus is on the two golden bulls that stood at the royal sanctuaries of Bethel and Dan. According to 1 Kings 12:28–29, Jeroboam I set these up with the cultic acclamation: "This is your god, who brought you up from Egypt." How was such a thing possible in an Israel that had known since its earliest days that Yahweh was superior to everything in the created world? A glance at the Jerusalem sanctuary, against which Jeroboam's measures were undoubtedly directed as a kind of "separatist" polemic, can help us here. The ark brought by David stood at Jerusalem as a sign of God's presence. There was no suggestion the ark, a chest, could be confused with Yahweh himself. It remained a "stool for his feet," while the cherubim above it constituted the "throne" of Yahweh. There is thus every reason to believe that Jeroboam's actions were not meant to suggest that the two ox-images were images that Yahweh himself would take possession of in the sense of images elsewhere in the ancient Near East. They, too, were probably interpreted as pedestals, thrones for the deity who is above them and clearly distinct from them. Only this interpretation explains how an Elijah and even an Amos could prophesy at Bethel without any explicit polemic against these images (2 Kings 2:2–3; Amos 7:10ff.). Not until Hosea, in the accounts that have been preserved, does there break through with sudden violence the awful realization that in the faith of the populace the image had become more than a mere pedestal, a footstool for the throne of the Lord who was intrinsically superior to any work of human hands. "Men kiss calves!" cries Hosea in one of his expressions of disgust (13:2). This gesture of adoration reveals to the prophet the sinister confusion that has taken place. The bull image, which was closely associated in the ancient Near East with fertility deities after the manner of Baal, naturally presented a temptation vastly different from that of the chest in the holy of holies at Jerusalem.

Behind the story of the golden calf in Exodus 32, in which Aaron, the brother of Moses, plays such a striking role, we can probably still make out the Bethel sanctuary legend of the golden ox. It was considered a cultic symbol introduced by an early priestly figure of the exodus period (once again the reference to the beginnings of Israel's history is typical). The cultic acclamation shouted in the presence of this image does not celebrate a fertility god; in Exodus 32:4 as in 1 Kings 12:28, it refers to the God who brought Israel out of Egypt. In its present form, of course, the narrative in Exodus 32 has turned into a bitter polemic against this image, which is unequivocally contrary to the will of Yahweh. In it the faith of the Old Testament deserts once and for all this cultic image that was capable of creating such dangerous confusion. The account in Judges 8:24ff. of the actions of Gideon, who had gone into battle crying "The sword of Yahweh!" should probably be interpreted along similar lines. The official interpretation of the ephod set up at Ophra (see above, p. 96) probably differed from the present account of it by the deuteronomistic narrator. Is it possible to suggest something similar for the cultic image at Dan, whose unholy early history is recounted in Judges 17—18, but which was served by a priestly family that traced its origins (Judg. 18:30?) back to Moses?

Furthermore, Jerusalem initially had no cause for any polemic against Bethel, as is shown by the well attested report that as late as the time of Hezekiah there was a bronze serpent in the Jerusalem Temple before which sacrifice was offered. Like the hypothetical early form of Exodus 32, Numbers 21:4-9 still shows that this image, whatever its actual historical origin may have been, was thought at Jerusalem to be a cultic symbol from the exodus period. According to the Jerusalem sanctuary legend, it was reputed to have been made by Moses himself. Numbers 21 reports all this quite unabashedly without any polemic follow-up. However, toward the end of the eighth century, immediately before the time of Hosea, this image, too, begins to become suspect as a cultic symbol in the Jerusalem Temple and is silently removed by King Hezekiah in the context of a cultic reformation (motivated by anti-Assyrian sentiments?), even though no one disputes the Mosaic origin of the symbol (2 Kings 18:4).

The polemic of Hosea and its subsequent confirmation in the fall of

Northern Israel also led to the elimination of another cultic symbol that the earlier period had found totally inoffensive. Israel had very early come to have serious reservations about setting up divine symbols of wood, called asherahs after the Canaanite deity Asherah; but because of this association of wood with a female deity (1 Kings 15:13), the earlier period had not the slightest reservation about setting up stones in a sacred place. Exodus 24:4 tells how Moses, in the context of the covenant ceremony at the foot of the mountain of God, set up twelve stones, one for each of the tribes of Israel. The tradition that the sacred stone at Bethel had been set up and anointed with oil by the patriarch Jacob (Gen. 28:18) was preserved without any polemic. The same is true of the "Stone of Help" (אבן העזר *eben hā'ēzer*) set up by Samuel (1 Sam. 7:12) and the stone set up at Shechem by Joshua (Josh. 24:26–27). Jeremiah 2:27 shows, however, that even these stones could leave room for superstition. Thus polemic beginning as early as Hosea also cast suspicion on the massebahs (מצבה *maṣṣebâ*) as cultic symbols; the prohibition of images made them intolerable. Deuteronomy 16:22 classes them with the asherahs (vs. 21) and expressly forbids their setting up. In Leviticus 26:1 this prohibition stands alongside the prohibition against setting up divine images.

In the case of the prohibition of images, too, we see that Deutero-Isaiah approaches the whole subject with an impressive superiority that seems no longer subject to the temptations of idolatry. Here—particularly in the secondary expansion Isaiah 44:9–20—ridicule is heaped on the credulity that could believe the deity to be present in an image. Granted that this ridicule cannot really do justice to the way religious images were used and understood in Babylonia, it is still impressive how totally free the faith of the Old Testament has become of any internal temptation to fall into idolatry, which is here associated directly with worship of the images of foreign gods. Once more this takes place at the time of Israel's utmost humiliation, when the Israelites are dwelling among a people devout in their use of idols.

In an expansion of the deuteronomic introductory discourses in Deuteronomy 4 we find reflection on the inner basis of the prohibition of images. It is once more characteristic that this reflection does not involve meditation on the hidden and mysterious nature of Yahweh, but concentrates on the initial experience of revelation. Because the people standing in the presence of Yahweh at the mountain of God did not see a form of any kind, but only heard the voice of Yahweh speaking from the fire, they are not to make any carved image (פסל תמונת כל סמל *pesel t˘mûnat kōl semel*), or the figure (תבנית *tabnît*) of any male or female creature, or (paraphrasing Exod. 20:4 at greater length) of any creature from the three regions of the world (Deut. 4:16–18). In the formulation of the prohibition of images placed at the beginning of the Covenant Code a similar line of argument seems to be intended; the prohibition is preceded in Exodus 20:22 by the statement that Yahweh spoke from heaven.

The antithesis in Deuteronomy 4 (not a visible image, but a word to be heard) raises the question whether people might not likewise take into their own possession the spoken word, above all the revealed name of God, and use it arrogantly for their own purposes. The Decalogue, in whose preamble Yahweh openly makes himself known in his name, confronts this sort of highhanded independence in its third commandment (Exod. 20:7): "You shall not pronounce the name of Yahweh your God for worthless purposes (לַשָּׁוְא *laśśaw'*)." This prohibition, behind which stands the warrant to use the name of Yahweh in its proper place, to praise him and to call on him for help, is meant to prevent any abuse. Thus in the law of Yahweh (1) all forms of magic are absolutely rejected. The list of abuses rejected in Deuteronomy 18:10–12 should doubtless also include misuse of Yahweh's name. (2) Leviticus 24:10–23, a didactic story into which an extended passage of legal instruction has been incorporated in verses 15–20, shows clearly how an unrestrained blasphemer, who "pierces" (נקב *nqb*) the name of Yahweh, is to be stoned by the community. Misuse of God's name also includes (3) perjury in the name of Yahweh, forbidden by Leviticus 19:12 (Ps. 24:4). (4) Should we also include in this context the profanation of Yahweh's name spoken of in Ezekiel 36:20, which Israel brings about as the "people of Yahweh" by putting the name of Yahweh into the mouths of the Gentiles through its bad conduct and the subsequent catastrophe? This idea undoubtedly goes beyond the immediate intentions of the third commandment, but it does reveal a final dimension of the peril that the name of God is subject to in the mouths of people, a peril Yahweh willingly accepted in the gift of his name.

In the late Old Testament period, dread of this commandment led to a refusal even to speak the name of Yahweh (see above, pp. 17–18). It may be asked whether this course does not relinquish the gracious warrant to use God's name contained in the preamble to the Decalogue. The New Testament community, which gained a new knowledge of the Father's name in the name of the "Son," experiences anew the privilege of invoking the Father "in the name of Jesus Christ."

Zimmerli, Walther. "Das zweite Gebot." In *Festschrift Alfred Bertholet zum 80. Geburtstag*, pp. 550–563. Edited by Walter Baumgartner. Tübingen: Mohr, 1950. Reprinted in his *Gottes Offenbarung*, 2d ed., pp. 234–248. Theologische Bücherei, vol. 19. Munich: Kaiser, 1969.—Bernhardt, Karl-Heinz. *Gott und Bild*. Theologische Arbeiten, vol. 2. Berlin: Evangelische Verlagsanstalt, 1956.—Zimmerli, Walther. "Das Bilderverbot in der Geschichte des alten Israel." In *Schalom: Studien zu Glaube und Geschichte Israels* (Festschrift Alfred Jepsen), pp. 86–96. Edited by Karl-Heinz Bernhardt. Arbeiten zur Theologie, 1st series, vol. 46. Stuttgart: Calwer, 1971. Reprinted in his *Studien zur alttestamentlichen Theologie und Prophetie*, pp. 247–260. Theologische Bücherei, vol. 51. Munich: Kaiser, 1974.

§14 Liturgical and Ritual Commandments

The faith of the Old Testament lives in the presence of the God who will not tolerate the worship of another god together with himself, who will not let himself be captured and "manipulated," either in an image or even in his revealed name "Yahweh." This faith does not live in a state of free spirituality, but in a life that has specific liturgical forms. The regulations governing the life of worship are known to be part of God's law.

Two points, however, need to be made: (1) The forms in which the faith of the Old Testament worships its God did not simply drop directly from heaven. Alongside material brought along as their ancient heritage by the tribes entering Canaan, we find forms that derive unmistakably from the new environment in which they found themselves. (2) In its worship, too, Israel lives in a historical process in which older material loses its significance and new accents make themselves heard. It cannot be our task here to provide a complete history of Old Testament worship; for such an account, see the work by Kraus. But any Old Testament theology must pay attention to the way in which the faith of the Old Testament hears the commandment of its God in its liturgical ordinances.

1. The Sabbath, the day of rest after six days of work, has already made its appearance in §4, in the context of P's creation account. There it was the day on which God rested after concluding his mighty labor of creation. There was no mention in that context of any "Sabbath commandment" applying to humans. Such a commandment appears in fourth place in the Decalogue as a commandment given to Israel by Yahweh. It is mentioned as early as the Covenant Code (Exod. 23:12; likewise Exod. 34:21). In the Holiness Code, cf. Leviticus 19:3; 23:3; 26:2. In P, it is solemnly associated in Exodus 31:12–17 (35:1–3) with the institution of Israel's sacred worship; according to 31:13 Yahweh expressly terms it a "sign between me and you in every generation that you may know that I hallow you" (cf. also 31:17). In Ezekiel 20, alongside the similar formulation in verse 12, verse 20 provides a freer paraphrase: "so that you will know that I am Yahweh your God." This makes it clear that the Sabbath is understood as a special sign of the setting apart (hallowing) of Israel, which is recognized as the people of Yahweh in its observance of this day.

The origins of the Sabbath are still obscure. Analogous features have been pointed out in Babylonian hemerologies, in which the first, seventh, fifteenth, twenty-first, and twenty-eighth of the month were considered unlucky days, when no important projects should be undertaken (*AOT²*, p. 329). These days are characterized by their dependence on the lunar cycle and their nature as days of ill omen. The former characteristic also holds for the fifteenth day of the lunar month, a day of special observance called *šabattu*. Meinhold claimed to find in the Sabbath what was originally a day of the full moon, because it occasionally appears parallel to the new moon (Amos 8:5 and elsewhere). Jenni thinks in terms of a market day. Kraus derives the Sabbath

from the prototype of the festal weeks at Passover (or the Feast of Unleavened Bread) and the
Feast of Booths (see below). For the Sabbath as found in the Old Testament, there is no
dependence on the lunar cycle and no hint of its being an unlucky day. Since the Sabbath is
observed quite independent of any sanctuary by abstinence from work, it has increased in
importance during the course of history.

In leaving every seventh day free for Yahweh as a kind of "fallow day,"
the Old Testament Sabbath honors the Lord of time. The Old Testament
itself provides two explicit motivations for this fallow day. The Decalogue
form in Deuteronomy 5:12–15 defines the purpose of this rest from labor:
". . . so that your slaves and slave-girls may rest as you do. Remember that
you were slaves in Egypt, and Yahweh your God brought you out with a
strong hand and an outstretched arm, and for that reason Yahweh your God
commanded you to keep the Sabbath." The reference to slaves gives the
Sabbath here, as in Exodus 23:12, a social motivation. Concern for the slaves
is itself based on recollection of Israel's own period of slavery in Egypt. By
keeping every seventh day free from work, the Israelite comes face to face
once more with the God who freed Israel when it was enslaved. In this way
the descendants of those whom Yahweh freed will have their eyes opened
to see those who are burdened by toil alongside them. The Decalogue form
in Exodus 20, on the contrary, is connected with the Priestly creation narrative, which concludes with the Sabbath as a day of rest for the creator himself.
Through it Israel comes to share in the privilege of rest enjoyed by the
creator himself, thus becoming a people set apart within Yahweh's creation,
called by Yahweh to himself, or, as Exodus 31:13 and Ezekiel 20:12 put it,
"hallowed." The privilege of this regulation governing the seventh day, to
be received with joy again and again from the hand of Yahweh, as may be
seen most impressively in Exodus 16:29 (Yahweh "gives" the Sabbath),
unexpectedly takes on the the character of a strict commandment as well,
inculcated under pain of death (Exod. 31:14; cf. Num. 15:32–36).

2. Alongside the Sabbath, recurring regularly throughout the year without any ties to the cycle of nature, we find the observance of certain festivals.
Of course in its earlier period Israel was familiar with the possibility of
appointing an observance *ad hoc:* a victory celebration following a victory in
battle (1 Sam. 18:6–7) or a day of penance when the land was imperiled by
enemies (1 Sam. 7:5–6; Jer. 36:9) or drought (Jer. 14). In addition, however, there are the regular festivals, which center on the agricultural harvest
and are thus clearly shown to be feasts originally celebrated by the inhabitants
of Canaan. Three such festivals, during which the male population is to
appear at the sanctuary, are mentioned in the earlier festival calendars (Exod.
23:14–17; 34:18–23 [where the Sabbath, still separate in 23:12, is included];
Deut. 16:1–17):

a) the Feast of Unleavened Bread (חג המצות *ḥag hammaṣṣôt*);

b) the Feast of Harvest (of grain) (חג הקציר *ḥag haqqāṣîr*), given the name Feast of Weeks (חג שבועת *ḥag šābū'ōt*) in Exodus 34:22; and

    c) the Feast of Ingathering (חג האסיף *ḥag hā'āsîp*), which is later termed the Feast of Booths (חג הסכות *ḥag hassukkôt;* Deut. 16:13).

The agrarian origin of these festivals is clear. The eating of unleavened bread for seven days was probably ordained in order to make a clear distinction between the newly harvested barley and the old grain of the previous year (to be used as sourdough leaven). At the Feast of Harvest (of wheat), Exodus 23:16 explicitly ordains that "the first fruits of your work in sowing the land" are to be offered (34:22 speaks even more specifically of "the first fruits of the wheat harvest"). And the Feast of Ingathering at the turn of the year clearly has reference to the grape harvest. In the earlier period this was the great annual festival. In Judges 21:19, when the Benjaminites seize the daughters of Shiloh while they are dancing in the vineyards, it is referred to simply as "the Feast of Yahweh" (חג יהוה *ḥag yahweh*). 1 Kings 12:32 shows that it was subsequently celebrated somewhat later in the year in the Northern Kingdom than in the South. Initially, however, it certainly did not have a fixed date, being celebrated according to the status of the harvest in each particular year.

As is characteristic of the Old Testament faith, during the course of Israel's history not only were new elements added to the old Canaanite festival calendar, but the inner motivation experienced a displacement. A glance at the prayer of the farmer who brings his first fruits to the sanctuary (Deut. 26) shows the direction in which this displacement moved. Instead of focusing on the harvest and the fertility of the land, understood (as discussed in §8) to be the gifts of Yahweh, the God of Israel, the prayer focuses on the God who brought Israel out of Egypt.

This change is especially impressive in the case of the first of the three festivals, to which the later period ascribed primacy, and which appears in the New Testament as the great festival for pilgrimage to Jerusalem (Jesus and Paul). This very early became associated with Passover, a pastoral custom probably dating from the period before the occupation of Canaan. According to Rost, we are dealing with an apotropaic ceremony performed by the semi-nomadic shepherds when the flock is about to change pasturage: the sacrifice of an animal and the use of its blood on certain objects guards the health of the flock and wards off the evil powers that would bring a murrain upon it. It is historically obscure how this custom came to be associated with the departure of the groups escaping from Egypt. In any case, the smearing of blood on the doorposts (Exod. 12:7, 22) and wearing of traveling garb (vs. 11) are subsequently bound up closely with the memory of the exodus from Egypt, when Yahweh slew the Egyptian firstborn with his destroying angel while protecting the Israelites and making their escape possible. The association of Passover with the seven days of unleavened bread may have resulted initially from the proximity of the two observances in the calendar. It is characteristic of the Old Testament faith, however, that when the two were combined victory went unequivocally to the component that emphasized the historical deliverance from Egypt. Even the eating of unleavened bread is now explained within this context. The departure from Egypt had to take place so suddenly, we are told, that the Israelite women, who had just prepared the dough to make bread but had not yet leavened it, omitted the leavening (Exod. 12:34), so that Israel ate unleavened bread during the exodus. The noctural Passover ceremony, in which an animal is slaughtered and its blood used for the blood ritual, now constitutes the ceremony introducing the week during which unleavened bread is eaten. The telescoping of the two ceremonies is already complete in the present text of Deuteronomy 16. The story of Josiah's reformation in 2 Kings 23:21–23 shows that the Passover celebrated at the central sanctuary in Jerusalem (now even the name "Passover" carries the day) became the characteristic festival of Josiah's reformation. But the postexilic legislation of P (Exod. 12:1–20) shows how the ancient custom of family celebration could maintain itself even after the centralization. According to the account of the synoptic Gospels, Jesus himself celebrates Passover in Jerusalem, but not at the Temple, choosing instead the table fellowship of his disciples, just as families were accustomed to celebrate it.

The transformation that affected the great fall festival is more obscure. While many assumed that the custom of dwelling in booths belonged to this festival from the beginning, Kraus prefers to assume an originally independent tent festival that later came to be associated with the fall festival. The victory clearly went to the historical perspective of Leviticus 23:39–43, where Israel is commanded to dwell in booths for seven days, "so that your descendants may be reminded how I made the Israelites live in booths when I brought them out of Egypt." In place of the reference to the harvest fruit that Leviticus 23:40 indicates are part of the observance and are even today used to deck the booths in the Jewish festival, we find here, too, a recollection of Israel's early history, when the Israelites dwelt in booths in the desert—however impossible it may seem to reconcile green branches and fruit with the march through the barren desert.

The "Feast of Weeks" was celebrated seven weeks after Passover: that is, on the fiftieth day, counting the initial day (thus the "Pentecost" of Acts 2:1). If the dating given by Exodus 19:1 (P) is not taken as the first step toward a historical interpretation, this feast was not historicized until after the Old Testament period, when it was celebrated in memory of the revelation at Sinai.

In all this we see how emphatically the faith in Yahweh the God of the exodus from Egypt was able to find expression in Israel's festival calendar even in instances where this calendar was originally based on totally different forms of belief. A further negative illustration of this tendency is the clearly minor role played in Israel's festival calendar by the feasts related to the heavenly bodies, which elsewhere in the ancient Near East were not unimportant. This holds true for the new moon, mentioned in 1 Samuel 20:5–6 as a day of special observance during the time of Saul and David, and still recognizable in the sacrificial regulations in Ezekiel 46:1ff. and Numbers 28:11ff. It holds true also for the New Year festival, which at Babylon, for instance, developed into a gigantic festival in which the divine and earthly kingdoms joined hands and the destinies of the coming year were determined in the council of the gods, assembled in the capital. Whatever passing significance this observance may have had at the royal court in Jerusalem, it was never able, contrary to Mowinckel's hypothesis, to gain a really important place in the festival calendar of Israel. Numbers 29:1–6 decrees special sacrifices and the blowing of trumpets for the first day of the seventh month, the autumnal New Year of ancient Israel. Leviticus 23:24–25 also mentions festal assembly and sounding of trumpets. Leviticus 25:9 (Ezek. 40:1) seems to point to the tenth day of the seventh month as the first day of the New Year. In comparison to the great annual festivals, however, the significance of these dates in the annual cycle of nature remains minor. Nor should it go unmentioned that the people Yahweh brought up out of Egypt nowhere in the Old Testament included in their festival observances a celebration of the death and resurrection of their God, nor any celebration of a divine marriage. That there was no lack of temptation to do this is shown not only by Ezekiel 8:14 but also by the penitential hymn in Hosea 6:1–2.

After the exile, the great Day of Atonement (יום הכפרים *yôm hakkippūrîm*), whose ceremonies are described in detail in Leviticus 16, came to occupy an important place in the festival calendar of Israel (Lev. 23:27–32; 25:9; Num. 29:7–11). Ancient elements of ritual, probably associated originally with the purification of the sanctuary and the priesthood, have here been incorporated into a great communal observance in which the high priest obtains for the people, who have been mortifying themselves through fasting, forgiveness for the sins of the past year. The scapegoat, bearing the sin of the community, is chased into the desert to the desert demon Azazel (hence the idiom "go to the devil"). By this ceremony the sanctuary, the priesthood, and the people are freed from sin. The increased importance of this festival is connected with the increased sense of the need for atonement on the part of the people after the exile. In the ritual of the great Day of Atonement, Israel experiences most forcibly in the priestly and liturgical sphere the willingness of its God to forgive even when his people have fallen into sin. In §21 we shall discuss the crisis apart from which this development cannot be understood.

The feast of Purim, which makes its first Old Testament appearance in the book of Esther, is of unknown origin. It came into being in the eastern Diaspora, after the model of a pagan observance. Within the context of the concerns of an Old Testament theology, its only significant feature is the appearance once more·of a great historical act of deliverance as the basis for a festival, however legendary the account may appear, and however limited the reference to help from the God of Israel may be, consisting of a single cryptic reference to "relief from another quarter." (Est. 4:14) The name of the festival contains the Akkadian word *pur,* "lot," as Esther 3:7; 9:24 indicate. The purpose of the festival is to celebrate the day chosen by lot first for the destruction, then for the deliverance of the Diaspora Jews.

The great festivals bring the community together at the sanctuary. They require special sacrifices, set forth in the regulations of P. Through the offering of tithes and first fruits the individual member of the community takes part in the observances to varying degrees throughout the year. The fulfillment of a "vow" (נדר *nēder*) and free-will sacrifice (נדבה *n*'*dābâ*) guarantee scope for free contributions. In P, Leviticus 1—7 exhibit a more definite differentiation of the various types of sacrifice, the most important being the "burnt offering" (עולה '*ôlâ*), the "cereal offering" (מנחה *minḥâ*), the "sacrifice" (זבח *zebaḥ*) or "peace offering" (זבח שלמים *zebaḥ š*'*lāmîm*), and, of particular importance in the postexilic period, the "sin offering" (חטאת *ḥaṭṭā*'*t*) and "guilt offering" (אשם *āšām*). For a further discussion, see pp. 149-150.

3. But Yahweh's law also imposes its demands directly on the individual, in daily conduct before the Holy One. We have already discussed the teaching function of the priest in §10d. This instruction includes not only protection of the holy, of the unapproachable area set apart by the presence of Yahweh, and its distinction from what is "ordinary" or "profane," but also supervision of the boundary between what is unclean, to be eschewed, invested as it were with dangerous negative power, and what is clean, open to use. See above, p. 97. This is the world of ritual regulations.

Especially unclean are the spheres of death (Num. 19), sexual secretions (Lev. 15), contagious leprosy (Lev. 13), and human excrement (Deut. 23:12–14; Ezek. 4:12*b*, 14–15). But the distinction between "clean" and "unclean" extends also to animals, fish, and birds. Deuteronomy 14 and Leviticus 11 provide lists of these, categorized as clean (available for human enjoyment) or unclean (forbidden). Whereas the taboo areas just listed are easily categorized on the basis of religio-historical analogies, such a categorization is more difficult in the case of the lists of unclean animals. Historical distinction from the customs of the indigenous population may have played a part. We now know on the basis of evidence from Ugarit that pigs were an important element in the retinue of Baal. Their "demonization" may have its origin in a deliberate attempt to distinguish Israel from Canaan, just as later the Christian church "demonized" the flesh of the horse, sacred to the Germanic tribes, as unfit for human consumption. Examination of the lists themselves, however, reveals no trace of these possible considerations. Instead certain categories are spoken of quite objectively (and in some cases with dubious accuracy—the hare is described as chewing the cud in Lev. 11:6): animals that chew the cud and those that do not, those that have cloven hooves and those that do not; those that have scales and those that have fins. No explanation at all is given for these criteria. Thus the eschewal of the animals listed as unclean becomes a pure act of obedience, not based on any profound rational insight. By observing the limits laid down here and keeping the purity regulations, people observe the commandment discovered by the priest and prescribed in his instruction, thus betraying their awe in the presence of Yahweh's ordinance.

But it can also be seen in the Old Testament how elements of this customary ritual purity can be made transparent to a very different understanding of guilt. In the ritual of Deuteronomy 21:1ff., for example, a specific sacrificial ritual cleanses an area that has been made unclean by the blood of a person slain by an unknown hand. At the same time, however, a prayer is recited that asks forgiveness in personal terms, praying for cleansing through Yahweh's personal will. In Psalm 51:9 the custom of using the hyssop plant for purification becomes an image for the forgiveness of sin, requested of Yahweh in a personal prayer. The preaching of the great writing prophets is especially radical in drawing the ritual customs into the sphere of personal social responsibility, e. g. in Isaiah 1:15-17.

Two ritual ordinances must be particularly stressed because they acquired special significance for the faith of the Old Testament. In the context of the law given to Noah after the Deluge, Genesis 9:4 strictly prohibits the consumption of animal blood. It is reasonable to see behind this prohibition the practice of drinking blood to increase one's power, frequently attested in the history of religions. In the words of Leviticus 17:11—"The vital force of a creature is in its blood"—the Old Testament itself expresses the notion that blood conveys power. But the faith of Israel violently rejects the practice of drinking blood. This rejection found its ritual expression in kosher butchering, which lets the blood escape through an incision. Each time an animal is slaughtered, the people are to recall that they do not have sovereign power over life, but must always recognize the prior rights of God. But in Leviticus 17:11, Yahweh himself says: "I have given it [the blood] to you to make expiation on the altar for yourselves; it is the blood, that is the vital force, that makes expiation"; in such an ordinance the power reserved by Yahweh to himself is bestowed in a new way upon humanity through his grace.

It is characteristic, however, that in Genesis 9:5-6 this prohibition against drinking the blood of animals is associated directly with the strict prohibition against shedding human blood. We shall return to this motif of protecting human life in §15. In the present context, it suffices to point out that for the priestly legislator the ritual commandment introduced by the catchword "blood" is directly associated with the commandment embodying reverence for human life. The bitter polemic of the priestly prophet Ezekiel against the "bloody city" of Jerusalem (22:1ff.) shows how far the limits of this law respecting human blood can be extended.

The second ordinance to be singled out is the requirement of ritual circumcision.

Here, too, we find a widespread practice common to many religions; as a "rite of passage," it guarantees the fertility of the male and is therefore usually found as an initiation ritual at the age of puberty. Israel shares this practice with related peoples of the ancient Near East. Anyone uncircumcised (the Philistines, for example, among Israel's neighbors) is felt to be ritually unclean.

Two passages in the Old Testament provide the justification for circumcision, each with a different emphasis. In Exodus 4:24-26, the episode is recorded in which Moses, returning to Egypt from Midian, is attacked during the night by Yahweh, who seeks to kill him. All that saves his life is the presence of mind of his wife Zipporah, who circumcises their son with an (archaic) flint knife and touches Moses' genitals with the foreskin. There is no explicit commandment here requiring circumcision. It is probably not by accident, however, that this episode, out of place as it is in its context (Yahweh is at the point of delivering Israel from Egypt through Moses), has been set in the time of Moses. Here, in a strangely abbreviated account no longer clear in all its details, the ritual is interpreted as a tutelary ritual. Any notion of guaranteeing fertility is excluded. It is also noteworthy that in the present context the ritual is not performed on Moses, whom Zipporah calls her "blood-bridegroom," but on their child.

P's account of how circumcision was initiated is much more clearly thought out. As has already been mentioned, Genesis 17 associates circumcision with the covenant between God and Abraham; in this context it takes on the function of a sign securing the covenant with Abraham in the flesh of everyone who belongs to this covenant. If we look back from this perspective on the original religio-historical significance of circumcision, two major differences cannot be missed: (1) According to the specific ordinance of Yahweh, circumcision is to take place on the seventh day after the birth of the child. This timing clearly distinguishes it from an initiation ritual of puberty. (2) It has become instead an initiation rite of a very different kind: it is a sacramental sign and pledge of Yahweh's promise to Abraham and his descendants. No reason is given why this should take the particular form of circumcision. The notion of purity may still play a role, as may perhaps be observed in Joshua 5:1ff., which tells how the people were circumcised upon entering the land. But it is impossible to miss the retreat from the realm of nature and vitalism and the increased emphasis on the themes of history and election.

In comparison to Exodus 4:24–26, circumcision has taken on infinitely greater significance in P. It is not one ritual among many, but the sign *par excellence* of belonging to the people of Yahweh. The increased importance of circumcision, its elevation to the status of being the sign of the covenant, is similar to the increased importance of the Sabbath law, its elevation to the status of being the sign of the sanctification (i. e., appropriation) of Israel on the part of Yahweh; both should probably be understood as responses to the historical challenges of the exile period, when Temple, cult, and territory had been lost. Sabbath and circumcision could be confessional symbols for a people in an alien environment, without Temple or territory.

At the same time, the same can be said of the importance attached to circumcision in P as can be said of the significance of the Sabbath. It is at once both a gift and a commandment. It is a sign of grace in that it grants access to the great promises given to Abraham; through this sign the people whose

God Yahweh would be are addressed. At the same time, however, Genesis 17:14 pronounces the anathema heard also in Exodus 31:14: whoever does not receive circumcision as commanded by Yahweh is to be cut off from the circle of his family.

In the case of the sign of circumcision, too, the ceremony performed on the flesh gradually became a symbol for the renewal of the heart to be effected by Yahweh; cf. Jeremiah 4:4; 9:24; Deuteronomy 10:16; 30:6; Leviticus 26:41; Exodus 6:12. See the discussion by Hermisson.

Kraus, Hans-Joachim. *Gottesdienst in Israel.* 2d ed. Munich: Kaiser, 1962. English: *Worship in Israel.* Translated by Geoffrey Buswell. Richmond: John Knox, 1966.—Landsberger, Benno. *Der kultische Kalender der Babylonier und Assyrer.* Leipziger semitistische Studien, vol. 6, pts. 1–2. Leipzig: Hinrichs, 1915.—Meinhold, Johannes. "Zur Sabbathfrage." *Zeitschrift für die Alttestamentliche Wissenschaft* 48 (1930):121–138.—Jenni, Ernst. *Die theologische Begründung des Sabbatgebotes im Alten Testament.* Theologische Studien, vol. 46. Zollikon: Evangelischer Verlag, 1956. —Rost, Leonhard. "Weidewechsel und altisraelitischer Festkalender." *Zeitschrift des Deutschen Palästinavereins* 66 (1943):205–216. Reprinted in his *Das kleine Credo und andere Studien zum Alten Testament,* pp. 101–112. Heidelberg: Quelle & Meyer, 1965.—Alt, Albrecht. "Zelte und Hütten." In *Alttestamentliche Studien Friedrich Nötscher zum sechzigsten Geburtstag,* pp. 16–25. Edited by Hubert Junker and Johannes Botterweck. Bonner biblische Beiträge, vol. 1. Bonn: Hanstein, 1950. Reprinted in his *Kleine Schriften zur Geschichte des Volkes Israel,* vol. 3, pp. 233–242. Munich: Beck, 1959.—Mowinckel, Sigmund. *Psalmenstudien. II: Das Thronbesteigungsfest Jahwäs und der Ursprung der Eschatologie.* 1922. Reprint. Amsterdam: Schippers, 1961.— Hermisson, Hans-Jürgen. *Sprache und Ritus im altisraelitischen Kult.* Wissenschaftliche Monographien zum Alten und Neuen Testament, vol. 19. Neukirchen: Neukirchener Verlag, 1965.

§15 Yahweh's Commandments Governing Social Relationships and Property

In Israel, Yahweh called his people to be his own. Not only did he set them apart from the nations round about them by means of liturgical and ritual symbols, but, as the early legal corpus of the Covenant Code shows, he made them subject to his will in all aspects of life, in their treatment of other people and of material goods. The great pre-exilic writing prophets are bitter accusers of a people who think they can satisfy Yahweh by observing the ritual and liturgical symbols and get around the commandments of Yahweh in their treatment of others and their attitude toward property.

1. In the Decalogue, a series of commandments deliberately covering a wide range of topics, the commandments dealing with conduct towards other people and their property, follow upon the four commandments that are "religious" in the narrower sense without any discontinuity. There is no hint of any distinction assigning the commandments to "two tables." The Sabbath commandment is followed by the commandment to honor one's father and mother; the same juxtaposition occurs in Leviticus 19:3. This commandment has the historical continuity of the generations in its purview. Since the mother is also included (and even mentioned first in Lev. 19:3),

it will not suffice simply to speak of a patriarchal society here. This commandment, cited time and time again in the Old Testament with particular emphasis, expresses not a patriarchal principle but the historical character of the Old
Testament attitude. Every individual comes from somewhere. No one creates his or her life: they receive it from others. Therefore they must never
forget reverence for those from whom their life derives.

Anyone who strikes his father or mother or reviles them (belittles them?) commits a capital
offense (Exod. 21:15, 17). This offense appears in the dodecalogue of Deuteronomy 27 in verse
16. It is characteristic of Jerusalem, the bloody city (Ezek. 22:7). Deuteronomy 21:18–21
decrees that a disobedient son who will not obey his father and mother should have public
complaint lodged against him before the elders of his town and be stoned. On the other hand,
it must not be overlooked that this is the only commandment of the Decalogue that includes
a promise (Eph. 6:2–3). Those who respect this ordinance of Yahweh are promised possession
of the land.

Now anyone who would conclude that the ultimate purpose of this
commandment is glorification of the family must consider Deuteronomy
13:7–12, which speaks of brother, son, daughter, and wife, albeit not father
or mother. When any of these family members entices anyone into worshiping foreign gods, all familial solidarity is cast to the winds: the harshest
judgment must be carried out. There is nothing wrong with making the
commandment to honor one's parents subordinate to the first commandment;
as Jesus puts it in a different context in the New Testament, "No one is
worthy of me who cares more for father or mother than for me." (Matt.
10:37) Above the sequence of generations made up of earthly parents stands
the lord and giver of all life, who refuses to let any purely human authority
be absolute.

2. A similar point can be made with respect to the commandment "You
shall not commit murder," in which Yahweh protects the life that he has
given from any arbitrary attack.

The verb used in Exodus 20:13, רצח *rṣḥ,* is not the usual word for "kill," but means a
wanton, uncontrolled attack on the life of someone else (Stamm). The Old Testament keeps
watchful guard on human life, which is a blessing from God. In the context of the Noachian
laws, the shedding of human blood is forbidden on the grounds that humans are made in the
image of God. In Genesis 9:6, an artistically framed legal maxim, consisting of two triple verses
arranged chiastically, emphasizes God's command: "He that sheds the blood of a man, for that
man his blood shall be shed." Exodus 21:12 includes the slaying of another human being in the
list of capital crimes; cf. also Leviticus 24:17, 21*b*. According to Deuteronomy 21:1–9, when
there is a murder for which expiation cannot be made, a special expiation ritual must be
performed for the town in question. Even a person who commits unintentional manslaughter
cannot simply be absolved by human agency. In such a case Yahweh himself places his hand upon
the person by granting asylum at his altar. In the detailed regulations governing the right of
asylum (Num. 35:9ff.; Deut. 19:1–13; Josh. 20), which are also concerned to make it impossible
to abuse this right, we find a striking regulation in Numbers 35:25, 28 (P): unintentional
homicides must remain where they have taken sanctuary until the death of the anointed high
priest. This ordinance conceals the principle that the death of the high priest expiates the blood
shed by the homicide.

It would likewise be wrong to interpret this commandment as embodying the notion of the absolute sanctity of human life. What is protected is not life itself, but the life accorded a person by Yahweh. The Yahweh war, in which Israel goes forth to battle against its foes, presents no problems for the Old Testament; neither does the judicial execution of a criminal. This means that the faith of the Old Testament sees human life under the hand of God, whose will stands superior to any human life in preserving the people of Yahweh from their foes and in maintaining the justice enshrined in his decrees. Of the self-sacrifice of someone who is perfectly righteous on behalf of a sinner, which will one day begin to cast doubts on war and capital punishment, the Old Testament contains only a faint hint in Isaiah 53.

3. Another commandment of the Decalogue prohibits interference in someone else's marriage. Precisely in the realm of sexual ethics Israel very early recognized how it differed from Canaan. Talk of a "folly in Israel," of something that is "not done in Israel," occurs at an early date in the context of responsible sexuality; see above, p. 46.

Priestly thought considers adultery primarily within the category of (cultic) impurity (Ezek. 18:6; 22:11). Leviticus 18 and 20 discuss prohibited sexual relationship in detail (Elliger). Capital punishment for adultery is already presupposed in Genesis 38. Marriage is established by betrothal (Deut. 22:23–24). The Old Testament knows nothing of any law requiring monogamy. One of a series of images in Ezekiel 23 even speaks of Yahweh's marriage with two women. Nor is it forbidden to dismiss a woman from a marriage. Deuteronomy 24:1–4 stipulates that an innocent woman who is dismissed must be given a note of divorce, which gives her legal protection. But a couple thus divorced may not remarry. Old Testament law vigorously impugns all intercourse between homosexuals as well as bestiality (Lev. 18:22–23; 20:13, 15–16). Especially after the time of Hosea and Deuteronomy, it is equally hostile to all religously tinged cultic prostitution, which in Canaan was associated with the "sacred marriage of the deity." None of these prohibitions imply any hostility to the body; they are stated against the background of an artless affirmation of the human body and sexuality. Here, too, the Old Testament is ingenuously "worldly," but in the sexual realm, too, it knows the world only as Yahweh's creation, and human conduct as being responsible to Yahweh; see above, §4.

4. Conduct with respect to the property of others is the subject of the eighth and tenth commandments of the Decalogue (Exod. 20:15, 17; Deut. 5:19, 21).

For the "coveting" of the last commandment of the Decalogue, Herrmann has shown that חמד *ḥmd* does not refer primarily to inward craving, but to the unjust machinations by means of which someone else's property can be deviously appropriated, as illustrated by the actions of Jezebel in 1 Kings 21. In the deuteronomic version, the notion of an inward state of mind was added by the introduction of the verb אוה *'wh*.

Here, too, it is important not to find something like the notion of the "sanctity of private property" in the commandment. God's protection of the property of others is based on the idea that God gave the property in the first place, and that his gift is inviolable. That property rights also have their limits is made abundantly clear in the prophets; in Isaiah 5:8 and Micah 2:1ff., we find a violent attack on land speculators "who add house to house and join field to field, until not an acre remains, and you alone are left in possession of the land." Such conduct contravenes God's own apportionment of the land, which has as its goal a house and portion of land for everyone in Israel. Therefore the intervention of God is announced: he will demolish these godless claims to private ownership.

The law of the jubilee year in Leviticus 25 belongs in this context, regardless of when it came into being or how it was enforced. Here we have legislation setting forth in great detail how every fifty years the land that has been alienated in the interim to alleviate financial distress shall revert to its former owners, and how servitude arising out of debt shall be canceled, so that everyone receives once more the portion alloted by Yahweh.

5. The ninth commandment of the Decalogue addresses the realm of jurisprudence. In the prohibition of "false evidence," an element is singled out that is absolutely necessary for the proper administration of justice. Only when the witness, clearly constrained by Yahweh's righteous will, does full justice to the truth in giving testimony can the judicial process really uphold the law that protects everyone.

The judicial process is already dealt with in the Covenant Code, which contains a special code for judges (Exod. 23:1-3, 6-9), where the topics discussed include spreading false rumors, fear of the powerful, and the temptation to accept a bribe. The short code for judges in Leviticus 19:15-16, which once more is emphatically based on Yahweh's personal appearance ("I am Yahweh"), is striking in its stress on fairness toward both parties, on equal treatment for the poor and for the mighty. Deuteronomy contains ordinances regulating the judicial process in 16:18-20; 17:8-13. In the Holiness Code (Lev. 19:35-36), the demand for true weight and true measure is appended to the demand for justice in the judicial process. The motivating clause, with remarkable abruptness, makes personal reference to Yahweh, who delivered Israel out of Egypt.

In the context of regulating the judicial process, both the Covenant Code and the Holiness Code reveal an awareness that Yahweh wishes to see not just ruthless pursuit of justice for oneself, but also a readiness to help the "enemy." In Exodus 23:4-5, for example, conspicuously interrupting the ordinance of the code for judges, we hear the command to take an "enemy's" stray animal back to him, and to help to its feet an enemy's ass that has collapsed under its burden. Deuteronomy 22:1-4 suppresses any mention of an "enemy," speaking instead of the "brother" for whom this is to be done. In Leviticus 19:17-18, on the other hand, immediately following the regulations governing the judicial process, we find two laws that begin with negative prohibitions and turn into positive admonitions: "You shall not nurse hatred in your heart [i. e., in secret] against your brother. You shall reprove your neighbor frankly and so you will have no share in his guilt. You shall not seek revenge, or cherish anger towards your kinsfolk; you shall love your neighbor as yourself. I am Yahweh." The concern here obviously goes beyond the possessions that Yahweh grants to his people: it has in mind the graciousness he intends for all of them. Therefore people who are angry with their neighbor and plan revenge must be willing to act out of love instead when they stand face to face with Yahweh ("I am Yahweh").

6. Such admonitions to be concerned for the "enemy" are not common in the Old Testament; but beginning with the rules for judges in the Covenant Code we frequently enounter admonitions to protect the poor and the weak.

In this context certain classes are singled out: the poor; the "stranger" (גר *gēr;* better translated "resident alien"), who owned no land and therefore had no legal rights, being dependent instead on the patronage of a free Israelite; and the widow and orphan, who likewise are at a disadvantage in judicial proceedings involving free men. They must not be oppressed (Exod. 22:20–23; 23:6, 9; Lev. 19:33). It is Yahweh who will heed their cries. When a debtor's cloak is heartlessly taken in pledge and kept overnight, Yahweh will hear the cries of the debtor when he freezes at night (Exod. 22:25–26; for further restrictions on property taken as security, cf. Deut. 24:6, 10–13). In this context, too, we find the prohibition against taking interest, reiterated intransigently throughout the entire Old Testament. This commandment is not concerned with commercial loans in the modern sense, in which money is borrowed to set up production, but with consumer loans in which the poor are forced to borrow grain or fruit or even money just to keep body and soul together. Another's need shall never be the occasion for the wealthy to enrich themselves. Deuteronomy 23:21 allows a single exception: a foreigner (נכרי *nokrî,* not גר *gēr*) may be charged interest. Here we are probably concerned with foreign traders and merchants, who never became needy "neighbors" for Israel like the "strangers" (resident aliens) who lived as "neighbors" in Israelite society. In Deuteronomy the landless Levite is added to the list of the needy; it is stressed that he shall be brought along with the rest of the poor to the sacrificial meals at the central sanctuary (Deut. 12:12 and *passim*). It is likewise Deuteronomy that prescribes that every third year the tithes shall be brought not to the sanctuary but directly to the Levite, the resident alien, the orphan, and the widow (Deut. 14:28–29).

Yahweh is the God who brought Israel out of slavery in Egypt and gave the Israelites freedom. Even in the (perhaps later) additions to the Covenant Code, but especially in Deuteronomy we hear how this fundamental experience is recalled, the experience through which Israel came to know its God.

Exodus 22:20 recalls this experience when it forbids oppression of the resident alien: "You were yourselves aliens in Egypt." Exodus 23:9 puts it more fully: "You know how it feels to be an alien; you were aliens yourselves in Egypt." In Deuteronomy, this reminiscence occurs in the context of the regulations governing slavery. Deuteronomy 15:15 (cf. also 24:17–18) goes beyond Exodus 21:1ff., decreeing that when a Hebrew slave is freed he must be given means to support himself: "Remember that you were slaves in Egypt and that Yahweh your God redeemed you; that is why I am giving you this command today."

In positive terms, active responsibility for the resident alien is expressed most fully in Leviticus 19:34: "The resident alien shall be treated as a native born among you, and you shall love him as a man like yourself, because you were aliens in Egypt. I am Yahweh your God." Here the two elements are totally associated once more: reference to historical experience and reference to Yahweh in his personal appearance, declaring himself to be the God of Israel.

7. In summary we shall single out a few features that characterize the ethos demanded in the law of Yahweh, before going on in Part IV to the response of obedience as described in the Old Testament.

The elements cited in §§ 11–15 show that, whatever the faith of the Old Testament, in its understanding of Yahweh's law, may have in common with its environment and other religions, it has a very special sense of being called to obedience by the God who made himself known to Israel at the outset by his act of deliverance.

a) First and foremost the law of Yahweh is concerned with Israel. In Deuteronomy, a document of particular significance for the shaping of the Old Testament pronouncements, the sense that Israel is the holy people chosen by God undergoes a particularly extensive development, as von Rad has shown. Polemic against the Old Testament has repeatedly used this restriction to Israel to reinforce its attacks. Deuteronomy 23:20–21 is frequently quoted in this context; enough has been said above to enable it to be understood. Deuteronomy 14:21 stipulates that the Israelites are forbidden to eat meat that has not been properly slaughtered; resident aliens may eat it, however, and it may be sold to foreigners. Here it is impossible to miss the distinction of Israel as a special entity, described as the people of Yahweh, obligated to observe their special ritual ordinance. But when we come to the non-cultic question of responsibility for the "stranger" (= resident alien) who has become a "neighbor," even Deuteronomy speaks unequivocally: "You must love the stranger [= resident alien], for you once lived as strangers in Egypt." (Deut. 10:19) The Old Testament knows nothing of the love for those who are far distant that forgets one's neighbor, but it does reckon with the possibility that someone who is distant can become a neighbor. In the New Testament, cf. also Galatians 6:10.

b) The law of Yahweh is addressed first and foremost to Israel as a nation. It does not take the individual as its point of departure, but the community affected by Yahweh's call. This community is to be holy, because Yahweh is holy (Lev. 19:2). We therefore search the Old Testament in vain for an ethics of individual self-realization or a morality that takes as its point of departure the individual Israelite as the primary element in the history of Yahweh and his people. The law of Yahweh applies to the community, and of course also therefore to the individual member of this community. It is inappropriate to speak of Old Testament "collectivism." When Ezekiel 18 gives voice to explicit polemic against a resignation based on the argument of collective fate, in which the sons must atone for their fathers' sins, form-critical analysis shows that this polemic is not to be understood as something totally new. In Ezekiel 18:5ff., Ezekiel is arguing on the basis of series of legal dicta already shaped by use in the Jerusalem Temple, however the prophet may go on to modify them in the specific situation. Cf. below, p. 213. The constantly recurring debate over whether the Decalogue is addressed to the individual or to the people as a whole can only make it clear how self-evidently the appeal to the individual is here set in an appeal to all Israel. The analogous observation can be made in the discussion of the "I" in the Psalms, where it is fundamentally impossible to maintain the distinction between the individual "I" and the community of the people of God. Similarly, there is no individual morality to be distinguished from responsibility in and for the community.

c) Because the individual Israelite has concrete personal life in the context of Israel, the people of Yahweh, the law cannot be reduced to a morality of subjectivity, according to which the good will of the individual would suffice and intention alone would be crucial, however the actual deed might appear. Despite all that will be said in the following section about the total attitude on which every action is based, the demands of Yahweh call for conduct that will stand the test in the concrete communal life of Israel. This point has already been touched upon in our discussion of the tenth commandment. Here it will be illustrated once more in the context of the ninth commandment.

There is nothing in the Decalogue requiring truth in general or forbidding lying in general. The ninth commandment deals with the concrete situation of the judicial process, in which a witness who belongs to the people of Yahweh is obligated not to say anything that would stand in the way of the justice required by Yahweh between his people. The requirement of truthfulness is based here on the need for truthful evidence if a neighbor is to be delivered.

By way of contrast, it is striking how even a Jeremiah, so sensitive to the "lies" of the people, readily accedes to Zedekiah's request not to reveal to the leaders of the people the true content of his conversation with the king (Jer. 38:24ff.). Jeremiah's half-truth does not harm anyone close to him, but it does protect the king, whom he had refused to spare from having to learn the truth. He does this freely because he is not constrained by any abstract notion of truth, but only by concern for his neighbor.

In noting the Old Testament attitude toward "truth," we must even go a step further and link what has just been said with our discussion under (a) above. In its attitude toward the truth, Israel senses that it operates within the context of God's attitude. When it is Yahweh's will to judge his enemies in his wrath, it is not for Israel to insist on the "truth." This approach is especially glaring when Yahweh is about to punish Egypt for refusing to let his people go. Israel is commanded to borrow vessels from the Egyptians without any mention of the intent to rob them (Exod. 3:22; 11:2; 12:35). Cf. also the actions of Elisha in 2 Kings 8:8ff. It is clear that when the event on the cross demolishes once for all the friend/enemy distinction maintained in the Old Testament, new light is cast on "speaking the truth." But there is probably still significance that transcends the Old Testament in the Old Testament approach, in which all truth-speaking demands not only an inward truthfulness, but also concern for the neighbor who will be affected by the truth spoken. This concern remains valid in both Testaments. To speak the truth is to stand in a relationship of fidelity that is aware of its obligation to its neighbor and cannot disregard specific actions and their effects upon others. A cold, fanatical devotion to the truth, blind to its effect on others, concerned only with objective facts, not with human beings, can hardly claim to be what the Bible demands. In this emphasis on responsibility toward one's neighbors, the Old Testament champions the standard of אמת ĕmet, "trustworthiness, fidelity, truth."

These remarks about what Yahweh requires now lead quite directly to a discussion of the response that people are expected to make to God, and, more broadly, the kind of life lived "in the presence of Yahweh" in all its variety.

Stamm, Johann Jakob. "Sprachliche Erwägungen zum Gebot 'Du sollst nicht töten.' " *Theologische Zeitschrift* 1 (1945):81–90.—Elliger, Karl. "Das Gesetz Lev. 18." *Zeitschrift für die Alttestamentliche Wissenschaft* 67 (1955):1–25. Reprinted in his *Kleine Schriften zum Alten Testament*, pp. 232–259. Theologische Bücherei, vol. 32. Munich: Kaiser, 1966.—Zimmerli, Walther. *Die Weltlichkeit des Alten Testaments*. Kleine Vandenhoeck-Reihe, vol. 327 S. Göttingen: Vandenhoeck & Ruprecht, 1971.—Herrmann, Johannes. "Das zehnte Gebot." In *Sellin-Festschrift; Beiträge zur Religionsgeschichte und Archäologie Palästinas*, pp. 69–82. Edited by Anton Jirku. Leipzig: Deichert, 1927.—Hejcl, Johann. *Das alttestamentliche Zinsverbot*. Biblische Studien, vol. 12, pt. 4. Freiburg: Herder, 1907.—Bertholet, Alfred. *Die Stellung der Israeliten und der Juden zu den Fremden*. Freiberg: Mohr, 1896.—Hempel, Johannes. *Das Ethos des Alten Testaments*. Beihefte zur Zeitschrift für die Alttestamentliche Wissenschaft, vol. 67. 2d ed. Berlin: Töpelmann, 1964.—Jacob, Edmond. "Les bases théologiques de l'éthique de l'Ancien Testament." In International Organization for the Study of the Old Testament. *Congress Volume, 1960*, pp. 39–51. Supplements to Vetus Testamentum, vol. 7. Leiden: Brill, 1960.—Van Oyen, Hendrik. *Ethik des Alten Testaments*. Geschichte der Ethik, vol. 2. Gütersloh: Mohn, 1967.

IV. Life before God

It is reasonable to ask whether a section on "life before God" belongs in an Old Testament theology. Especially in a theology that takes as its point of departure the principle that the Old Testament faith derives from Yahweh's "statement" about himself in history. But our discussion has shown how the faith of the Old Testament knows its God not in an absolute transcendence but rather in his approach to Israel and the world, and how the Old Testament, in what it has to say about God, thinks of itself as a book of God's words addressed to people. And it is also true that in the "response" God expects from those he addresses God himself can be recognized as in a mirror.

This "response" is found in people's obedience to the commandments of God as formulated in his law. But it is also found when Israel submits to the gracious governance of its God, even when no specific commandments are formulated (§16). Yahweh's nature is also recognizable in those situations when people turn to him in thanksgiving or petition (§17). Even in situations in which individuals, sensible of their relationship to the creator, order their daily course according to reasonable decisions, making thankful and obedient use of the gifts given them by Yahweh, their creator, it is possible to recognize the God who guides their lives (§18).

§16 The Response of Obedience

As Parts II and III have made clear, Yahweh's love for his people has two aspects, which are inseparable from each other. It expresses itself in Yahweh's gracious guidance, beginning with his deliverance of Israel out of the house of bondage in Egypt, and subsequently in all his gifts bestowed on Israel and the world. But the gift always implies a requirement. This imperative aspect takes concrete form in the words of Yahweh's commandments, which expect very specific actions in obedience to them.

The response of obedience itself has two aspects. In the first place, it consists of obedience to the concrete requirements of the law as elaborated in Part III.

In this context, an important role is played by "hearing" (שׁמע *šmʿ*, which can also mean "obey"), "observing" (שׁמור *šmr* in the sense of "keep, follow"), and "doing" (עשׂה *ʿśh;* cf. the stereotyped formulas of the Sinai episode [Exod. 19:8; 24:3; and 24:7 in conjunction with שׁמע *šmʿ*]). They refer to a clearly delineated act of obedience.

Likewise, the response of faith consists of the acceptance and proper stewardship of the gifts given by Yahweh, which Israel receives within the framework of having its history guided and governed by its God. It is not always clear in any particular case at what point precisely the gift to be received with pure hands turns into the commandment that requires active obedience. The discussion to follow will illustrate this point clearly with reference to certain specific passages.

1. Yahweh, who comes to his people, wishes to have his nature reflected in theirs. This point is made especially clear in the statement that introduces the core of the legal material in the Holiness Code: "You shall be holy, because I, Yahweh your God, am holy (קדושׁ *qādôš*)." (Lev. 19:2) Here the closeness between Yahweh's gift and his commandment is unmistakable.

The designation of Yahweh as "holy" probably represents the borrowing of a Canaanite notion. At Ugarit, El, for example, receives the predicate *qdš* (Schmidt). Israel associated with this term its sense of Yahweh's lordship and exclusivity. In Exodus 19:6 (Deut. 14:21*aβ*; 26:19), Israel is referred to as a "holy people." Deuteronomy 14:2 underlines this indicative statement by explicit reference to Yahweh's election. In Exodus 31:13 and Ezekiel 20:12, the Sabbath is referred to as the special sign of the election that makes Israel holy. At this point there is projected upon Israel something of the nature of Yahweh, who is called the Holy One, most powerfully in the Trisagion of the seraphim in Isaiah 6:3 (Ps. 99). At the same time, however, the people are called upon in Leviticus 11:44–45; 20:26 to demonstrate this very holiness through specific actions in their life before God. As the thematic statement of a legal corpus, Leviticus 19:2 introduces a plethora of individual precepts: by following them, Israel is to demonstrate its holiness. Deuteronomy 28:9 even makes Yahweh's setting up of his holy people conditional upon their keeping his commandments. The tension created by this use of the holiness predicate clearly voices the admonition: Become what you are through what Yahweh has done.

2. The projection of Yahweh's divine nature upon the community living before God, and at the same time the unmistakable tension between gift and commandment, indicative and imperative, can be seen even more clearly in the term צדקה (צדק) *ṣdāqâ (ṣedeq)*, translated very imperfectly as "righteousness." This circumstance conceals the fundamental theological problem of "divine and human righteousness."

Recent studies have shown clearly that the "righteousness" predicated of Yahweh must not be confused with the blindfolded "justice" that strictly apportions to every person the reward or punishment he or she deserves according to an objective norm that stands above all parties. When the Old Testament speaks of "Yahweh's righteousness," it means rather the social bond existing between him and his people and Yahweh's actions based on this bond. The plural form צדקות יהוה *ṣidqôt yahweh,* found as early as the Song of Deborah (Judg. 5:11; also 1 Sam. 12:7 and Mic. 6:5), is best rendered "saving acts." The singular forms צדקה *ṣdāqâ* and צדק *ṣedeq* are often used in the Psalms and in Deutero- and Trito-Isaiah, which come from the milieu of the Psalms, to refer to Yahweh's beneficent order, which can be recognized even in the realm of nature. According to Jepsen, the masculine form צֶדֶק *sedeq* means "rightness," "order," while the feminine form צְדָקָה *ṣ̌dāqâ* means the "conduct that aims at right order." Schmid prefers to understand the term in its various ramifications on the basis of its Canaanite background, where it expresses the harmony of the world in all its different realms.

Now it turns out that the term "righteousness," which characterizes the sphere of divine justice, understood in Israel with specific reference to Yahweh, becomes likewise the central term for human justice. The extent to which Israel sees this human justice as a reflection of Yahweh's justice is illustrated especially well in the twin acrostic Psalms 111/112. The former extols the glorious acts of Yahweh; the latter, the actions of the person who fears God. In verse 3 *b*, each of them uses precisely the same words to refer to both God and the person before God: "His 'righteousness' is forever."

If we go on to ask for a more detailed description of human righteousness, the fact cannot be overlooked that it is associated with keeping the commandments. Ezekiel 18:5ff., for example, describes righteous persons in terms of their conduct with respect to a series of commandments: "Consider the man who is righteous and does what is just and right. He never feasts at mountain-shrines, never lifts his eyes to the idols of Israel, never dishonors another man's wife. . . ." According to this passage, it is individuals' right actions, according to the norm of the law, that constitute their "righteousness."

But the list culminates surprisingly in the repeated formula: "Such a man is righteous; he shall live." The first half of this statement is composed formally in the style of a priestly "declaration," like those found above all in the legislation governing leprosy in Leviticus 13 (Rendtorff). Here it pronounces a general verdict upon the man. Von Rad has pointed out that more is involved here than an analytic statement. The declaration must be seen in the context of the priestly entrance liturgies, which pronounce the general divine verdict of "righteousness" upon the pilgrim, who has been examined on some of the marks of the righteous person. Thus we see in Psalm 24:4–5 how the one "who has clean hands and a pure heart, who has not set his mind on falsehood, and has not committed perjury" is granted entrance to the Temple; it is further said of him: "He shall receive a blessing from Yahweh, and righteousness from God his savior." Here "righteousness" is clearly something received at the sanctuary, not simply achieved by the individual. Genesis 15:6 states that Abraham believed in God and "it was counted as righteousness"; von Rad has shown elsewhere that this statement is connected with "righteousness" accorded by declaration. We see especially clearly in Job 33:26 how God restores "righteousness" to the sinner who has been warned by his illnesses and then prays to God.

In sum, all talk of human "righteousness," like that heard at the sanctuary, is like the talk of Israel's "holiness": there is obvious tension between what the law given by Yahweh seriously requires on the one hand, and on the other the concomitant superabundance that is an unearned gift. Neither aspect can simply be eliminated in favor of the other. The law that in the great legal corpora of Deuteronomy and the Holiness Code culminates in the alternatives of salvation and perdition, that confronts people with a promise and a threat, is not to be abrogated. But Israel is also familiar with the will of Yahweh to exercise a beneficent "righteousness" over Israel, only rarely (as in Ps. 7:12) associated with his wrath: "God is a 'righteous' judge, and a God who is daily angered." Israel, living before God, knows that it is called to the "righteousness" that is indispensable for real "life." Therefore the theme of "righteousness" also dominates the prayers of the Psalms. At the beginning of the psalter there is placed, like a call to decision, the twofold image of the "righteous" person and the "wicked," who is blown away like chaff at the judgment (Ps. 1), so that the worshiper will always keep in mind that the prayer of the devout can never evade the question of being in the right before Yahweh.

3. Deuteronomy grounds Yahweh's election of the patriarchs on a simple reference to Yahweh's love; see above, p. 45. The images of marriage and childhood, which involve the notion of divine love, are also used to describe the relationship of Yahweh to Israel. "When Israel was a boy, I loved him; I called my son out of Egypt." (Hos. 11:1) Besides the verb אהב 'hb, "love," used in this passage, the relevant terminology includes the noun חסד ḥesed, which refers to the "grace" appropriate in the context of a specific social bond, and רחמים raḥămîm, which means natural love like that of a mother for her child. One of Yahweh's solemn adjectival predicates is רחום וחנון raḥûm weḥannûn (Exod. 34:6 and elsewhere).

Once again it is appropriate to cite the conclusion of the twin Psalms 111/112, where verse 4b applies the same adjectival predicate to Yahweh and to the righteous person. Here the notion is probably of compassion toward one's neighbor; elsewhere, most clearly once again in the parenetic sections of Deuteronomy, the emphasis is on human love for God. The full exposition of this theme in Deuteronomy 6:5 admonishes listeners to love Yahweh with all their "heart and soul and strength." But when this loving is immediately associated with keeping the commandments, with serving Yahweh and going by his ways (Deut. 10:12; 11:22; cf. also the Decalogues: Exod. 20:6; Deut. 5:10), we can see how human love for God cannot simply be equated with God's love for Israel. Israel's reply is a response to Yahweh's initiative. The love for Yahweh referred to here is never simply free intrusion into the presence of God, but an approach to God along the road he has cleared. We will speak later about the "fear of God" that is associated with love for him.

Besides Deuteronomy, it is primarily several of the Psalms that speak of people's love for God (18:2 רחם rḥm; 116:1 אהב 'hb [?]; 31:24 אהב 'hb). That it is also possible to speak of loving the commandments of Yahweh (119:47) shows once more how love follows the summons of Yahweh along the paths which he maps out. Deuteronomy 30:6 transcends everything else that is said, speaking of this love in terms reminiscent of the New Testament talk of the charisma of love in 1 Corinthians 13 and calling it a consequence of a circumcision of the heart performed by God himself. Thus the Old Testament already suggests, if not especially often, at least in crucial passages, that people must respond to Yahweh's love with their own love.

4. Amos 3:2 used the verb "know" to describe Yahweh's election of Israel. Jeremiah, too, according to 1:5 realizes that Yahweh "knew" him and thus made him his prophetic instrument. Now if knowledge of Yahweh also plays a significant role in the life of people before God, it must be stressed even more than in the case of "love" for God that the human response of

knowledge does not share in the creative power of the Lord who chooses his people, but can only return to Yahweh along the road that he himself has pioneered.

In his study of the priestly torah (see the bibliography of §10d), Begrich has argued convincingly that the term "knowledge" (דַּעַת *da'at*) was applied particularly to priestly expertise in knowing the proper torah. Above and beyond this observation, however, we see that the "knowledge" that has Yahweh as its object cannot possibly be limited to purely intellectual understanding, but includes a decidedly personal component. What the Old Testament means by "knowledge" is not the theoretical objective knowledge that abstracts as much as possible from the thing or person before it, but the knowledge that takes full account, up to and including its corporeality. For example, sexual intercourse can be described in the Old Testament, as elsewhere in the ancient Near East, as "knowledge" of a woman. Knowledge of Yahweh is therefore not limited to technical priestcraft and general theology, but includes at the same time the intensely personal aspect of acknowledgment. This helps explain Hosea's polemic against the priests: "My people are ruined for lack of knowledge—you have rejected knowledge, and I will reject you from serving me as priest. You have forgotten the torah of God, and I, your God, will forget your sons." (4:6) On the other hand, it will not do to filter the cognitive component entirely out of priestly knowledge, since knowledge also comprises the religious message of Israel's early traditions; cf. the controversy between Wolff and Baumann. Hosea, for instance, can lament that "there is no fidelity, no love (חֶסֶד *ḥesed*), no knowledge of God in the land" (4:1), and maintain that Yahweh takes more pleasure in love (חֶסֶד *ḥesed*) than in sacrifice, and more pleasure in knowledge of God than in burnt offerings (6:6). The charisma of the king who will save Israel includes the "spirit of knowledge." (Isa. 11:2)

As we have shown (p. 20 above), alongside this direct talk of knowledge of God we find in Ezekiel and also in certain passages outside that book a "knowledge formula" with a very different structure, which plays its major role in the "proof-saying." Here the announcement of some act of judgment or deliverance that God is about to do is followed by the statement: "They shall know that I am Yahweh." Here the name of Yahweh does not follow the verb יָדַע *yd'* as direct object, but is embedded in a nominal clause used as object, which has its primary locus in the self-introduction, like the formula that begins the Decalogue. In this context it becomes especially clear that the knowledge occurring in the "life before God" is not the creative knowledge that establishes a new truth; it follows after Yahweh's actions in history. When humans perceive the emergence of God in these events, they are led to acknowledge the "truth" of Yahweh. Such an instance of knowledge/acknowledgment is depicted vividly in the contest upon Mount Carmel, where Elijah calls upon Yahweh, the "God of Abraham, Isaac, and Jacob," and asks: "Let it be known today that you are God in Israel and that I am your servant." (1 Kings 18:36) Such acknowledgment of Yahweh characterizes people's true life before God.

5. In Deuteronomy the requirement to love Yahweh was linked with the requirement to fear him. Far beyond the limits of Deuteronomy, this fear of Yahweh plays an important role in E (Wolff), in circles antedating the writing prophets, in a series of Psalms, and above all in wisdom literature, where it practically becomes the supreme requirement. It is strikingly absent in P and Ezekiel. The juxtaposition of these two concepts may at first seem surprising. If love appears to bring people into the presence of Yahweh, "fear" appears to remove them from this presence.

Now it is doubtless true that the "fear of Yahweh" repeatedly recalls the distance that separates creatures from their creator and Lord. In all periods of its history, Israel has had a sense of awe before the Lord, who transcends all Israel's power to love and understand, and whose encounter from time to time produces uncontrollable terror (Volz). Israel encountered the mysterious side of God in its worship, which never eliminated the element of "holiness." Even when licensed into the very presence of Yahweh, people have felt something of terror (Gen. 28:17; Isa. 6:5; Amos 3:8). In its wisdom musings (Ecclesiastes) and its attempts to understand the mysteries of human destiny (Job), Israel never evaded the terror evoked by Yahweh's impenetrability.

But it is a striking fact that, in all its talk of the fear of Yahweh, the faith of the Old Testament never was diverted into mere trepidation before God. This is probably in part because in Yahweh Israel knew that it confronted a Lord in whom it encountered not only mystery and arbitrary caprice, but a Lord who had promised to be Israel's God and who, in his law, had shown Israel the way that made life before him possible. Therefore in the Old Testament "fear of God" often becomes synonymous with obedience to the commandments of Yahweh.

It is no accident that the Holiness Code often cites the "fear of God" as a positive summary of commandments inculcating reverence for the weak or the aged: "You shall not treat the deaf with contempt, nor put an obstruction in the way of the blind. You shall fear your God—I am Yahweh." (Lev. 19:14) "You shall rise in the presence of gray hairs, give honor to the aged, and fear your God. I am Yahweh." (Lev. 19:32) In the story of the sacrifice of Isaac (E) it is a very concrete and specific command from God that Abraham obeys, whereupon God concludes: "Now I know that you fear God; you have not withheld from me your son, your only son." (Gen. 22:12 [E]) This fear of God can also be found among citizens of other nations who display a genuine reverence toward certain basic rules governing proper human conduct. In the case of the midwives of the Israelites in Exodus 1:17, who refuse to kill the male children, it is not totally clear whether the reference is to Israelite or Egyptian women; but according to Genesis 42:18, Joseph appears to his brothers (who stand in fear of the Egyptian vizier) in the guise of a foreigner when he says to them, "I, too, fear God."

Yahweh's law summons people into his presence. Obedience to his will promises life. This explains how the talk of fear of God as the proper attitude for people before Yahweh can, quite surprisingly, take on a decided note of confidence. "Fear of God" becomes quite generally a term for the piety that brings people within the orbit of Yahweh's protection: "In the fear of Yahweh there is confidence and trust, even for children he [Yahweh] is a refuge. The fear of Yahweh is a fountain of life, so that one may escape the snares of death." (Prov. 14:26–27) Thus one might almost say: whoever fears Yahweh need have no fear, but whoever does not fear Yahweh must have fear. "The wicked are wracked with anxiety all their days, the ruthless man for all the years in store for him," says Eliphaz the Temanite (Job 15:20). How wisdom speaks of the fear of Yahweh will have to await detailed discussion in §18.

6. The term "belief" or "faith" is sometimes used to describe the proper response of people to what Yahweh does. It does not occur frequently, but it is found in a few momentous passages. As in the case of the "fear" of

Yahweh, we are no longer dealing with an attitude that reflects Yahweh's own attitude. The term refers instead to the way a person who is weak derives stability from someone else, who is strong.

The notion of mere "holding an opinion," which is one of the senses of the English word "believe," is totally absent from the Hebrew הֶאֱמִין *heʾĕmîn*. This word derives from the root אמן *ʾmn*, "be firm, stable, secure," familiar to everyone from another derivate, "amen," which can be used as a response to emphasize a curse (Deut. 27:15–26; Num. 5:22), a royal command (1 Kings 1:36), a wish (Jer. 28:6), or even a prayer (Ps. 41:14 and elsewhere, concluding a subsidiary collection of Psalms). One theory holds that הֶאֱמִין *heʾĕmîn* should be understood as a declarative hiphil, so that belief represents a responsive "amen" to a promise made by Yahweh. Against this theory, it must be pointed out that the word is usually constructed not with the expected accusative but with the preposition בּ *bʾ*, "in," and sometimes with לְ *lʾ*, "to." According to Wildberger, it is to be understood intransitively; when used with בּ *bʾ* in theological contexts, it means "find security in," "place trust in." Thus the statement in Genesis 15:6 (quoted in Rom. 4 and Gal. 3) about Abraham, to whom, though childless, God promised descendants like the stars of heaven in number, is to be understood as meaning: "Abraham found security in Yahweh, and Yahweh accounted this as righteousness." This "finding security" in Yahweh makes people "righteous" in the eyes of God. The absolute use of the term, in which Smend claims to find the origin of talk about "faith" in the Old Testament, occurs in Isaiah. In an hour of great danger, Isaiah promises King Ahaz that the plans of the enemy will miscarry, using an elegant pun that employs the root אמן *ʾmn* twice: "If you do not believe, you will not endure"; or, literally, "If you do not find security [i. e., in Yahweh's promise], you will not be secured [= preserved]." (7:9) And Isaiah 28:16 refers to Yahweh's establishment of Zion (see above, pp. 76–77): "He who believes will not waver." Belief or faith means security, repose within God's promise. But because this promise is spoken through men sent by Yahweh, Exodus 14:31 can say that the people believed Yahweh *and* his servant Moses. Exodus 4:1, 5; 19:9 speak of Moses alone as the messenger to be believed. 2 Chronicles 20:20 calls upon the people to believe Yahweh and his prophets. Psalm 119:66 speaks of God's commandments as the object of "belief."

In none of these passages is "belief" or "faith" to be understood as passive quietism. Jonah 3:5 says that the people of Nineveh, when they heard Jonah's message, "believed God and ordered a public fast and put on sackcloth, high and low alike." Belief effects repentance and conversion. In Exodus 4:1, 5 it is signs that evoke belief among the people. Isaiah, too, offers the hesitant Ahaz such a sign (7:10ff.). In Exodus 14:31 the great event of deliverance from the Egyptians is patent to the eyes of all. According to the Old Testament, then, Yahweh now and then gives belief the aid of a sign or even direct vision. But Genesis 15:6 shows very clearly how people must venture to believe even contrary to what they can see with their own eyes— what kind of evidence is the view of the starry heavens that is given to Abraham? And yet it is possible to say that faith bears knowledge within it. Isaiah 43:10 states that Israel must be Yahweh's witness, "that they may gain insight and believe and know that I am He." But Psalm 106:12 clearly states the purpose of belief: "Then they believed his [Yahweh's] promises and sang his praises." Belief sings God's praises.

Barth, Christoph. "Die Antwort Israels." In *Probleme biblischer Theologie* (Festschrift Gerhard von Rad), pp. 44–56. Edited by Hans Walter Wolff. Munich: Kaiser, 1971.—Schmidt, Werner H. "Wo hat die Aussage: Jahwe 'der Heilige' ihren Ursprung?" *Zeitschrift für die Alttestamentliche Wissenschaft* 74 (1962): 62–66.—Jepsen, Alfred. "צדק und צדקה im Alten Testament." In *Gottes Wort und Gottes Land* (Festschrift Hans-Wilhelm Hertzberg), pp. 78–89. Edited by Henning Graf Reventlow. Göttingen: Vandenhoeck & Ruprecht, 1965.— Schmid, Hans Heinrich. *Gerechtigkeit als Weltordnung*. Beiträge zur historischen Theologie, vol. 40. Tübingen: Mohr, 1968. —Zimmerli, Walther. "Zwillingspsalmen." In *Wort, Lied und Gottesspruch* (Festschrift Joseph Ziegler), vol. 2, pp. 105–113. Edited by Josef Schreiner. Forschung zur Bibel, vol. 2. Würzburg: Echter Verlag, 1972. Reprinted in his *Studien zur alttestamentlichen Theologie und Prophetie*, pp. 261–271. Theologische Bücherei, vol. 51. Munich: Kaiser, 1974.—Rendtorff, Rolf. *Die Gesetze in der Priesterschrift.* Forschungen zur Religion und Literatur des Alten und Neuen Testaments, vol. 62. Göttingen: Vandenhoeck & Ruprecht, 1954.—Von Rad, Gerhard. " 'Gerechtigkeit' und 'Leben' in der Kultsprache der Psalmen." In *Festschrift Alfred Bertholet zum 80. Geburtstag,* pp. 418–437. Edited by Walter Baumgartner. Tübingen: Mohr, 1950. Reprinted in his *Gesammelte Studien zum Alten Testament,* pp. 225–247. Theologische Bücherei, vol. 8. Munich: Kaiser, 1958.—Idem. "Die Anrechnung des Glaubens zur Gerechtigkeit." *Theologische Literaturzeitung* 76 (1951):129–132. Reprinted *ibid.,* pp. 130–135.—Zimmerli, Walther. "χάρις" In *Theologisches Wörterbuch zum Neuen Testament,* vol. 9, cols. 366–377 (with bibliography). Edited by Gerhard Kittel and Gerhard Friedrich. Stuttgart: Kohlhammer, 1973. English: "χάρις" In *Theological Dictionary of the New Testament,* vol. 9, pp. 372–387. Translated by G. W. Bromiley. Grand Rapids, Mich.: Eerdmans, 1973.—Wolff, Hans Walter. " 'Wissen um Gott' bei Hosea als Urform von Theologie." *Evangelische Theologie* 12 (1952/53):533–554. Reprinted in his *Gesammelte Studien zum Alten Testament,* pp. 182–205. Theologische Bücherei, vol. 22. Munich: Kaiser, 1964.—Baumann, E. " 'Wissen um Gott' bei Hosea als Urform der Theologie?" *Evangelische Theologie* 15 (1955):416–425.—Wolff, Hans Walter. "Erkenntnis Gottes im Alten Testament." *Evangelische Theologie* 15 (1955):426–431.—Idem. "Zur Thematik der elohistischen Fragmente im Pentateuch." *Evangelische Theologie* 29 (1969):59–72. English: "The Elohistic Fragments in the Pentateuch." *Interpretation* 26 (1972):158–173. Reprinted in *The Vitality of Old Testament Traditions,* pp. 67–82. Edited by Walter Brueggemann. Atlanta: John Knox, 1975. —Volz, Paul. *Das Dämonische in Jahwe.* Sammlung gemeinverständlicher Vorträge und Schriften, no. 110. Tübingen: Mohr, 1924.—Becker, Joachim. *Gottesfurcht im Alten Testament.* Analecta Biblica, vol. 25. Rome: Pontifical Biblical Institute, 1965.—Wildberger, Hans. " 'Glauben': Erwägungen zu האמין." In *Hebräische Wortforschung* (Festschrift Walter Baumgartner), pp. 372–386. Supplements to Vetus Testamentum, vol. 16. Leiden: Brill, 1967.—Smend, Rudolf. "Zur Geschichte von האמין." *Ibid.,* pp. 284–290.

§17 Israel's Sacrificial Worship: Praise of Yahweh and Cry for Help

The praise of God makes plain upon earth who this God is. In its present form, Psalm 22:4 appears to make a daring change in the description of Yahweh as being enthroned on the cherubim: "You are the Holy One, enthroned on the praises of Israel." This is how the faith of the Old Testament knows its God: he is the Holy One of Israel (Isa. 1:4; 5:19, and elsewhere)—but despite his unapproachable holiness, he is not unapproachably distant; he is the God whose majestic throne is the praise of his people. Thus the Old Testament corpus includes a book that has been given the title תהלים *thillîm,* "praises" (Buber's translation).

Anyone who examines the individual Psalms in the book that bears this title will soon realize that although the genre of "praises" constitutes a significant portion of the book, there is an even greater number of hymns of supplication (תפלות *tʿpillôt*), or, to use the commonly accepted term introduced by Gunkel, "laments." The title of the book obviously includes in the praises on which Yahweh is enthroned the "cry" heard in the supplications.

Modern study of the Psalms has made it clear that they cannot be looked upon as the free poetic outpourings of the religious heart. They have many points of contact with the liturgical life of the congregation of Yahweh; the polemic of the prophets, for example, shows that "songs" or "hymns" (Amos 5:23) and "prayers" (Isa. 1:15) formed part of the worship in the sanctuary. It is true that the detailed superscriptions found today over many of the Psalms speak of individual crises (in the life of David), which point to an origin for the Psalm in question outside the sanctuary. Only once is a liturgical occasion mentioned (Ps. 92: "For the Sabbath"). But other headings to many of the Psalms, for the most part not totally clear, as well as the ascriptions to the guilds of Temple singers, the Asaphites and Korahites, point at least to a later use of the Psalms in Temple worship. The information in Chronicles about the Temple music and the explicit citation of the Psalms, as in the account of a liturgical occasion in 1 Chronicles 16, but above all the conventional phraseology of many idioms, with parallels in other literatures of the ancient Near East (cf. *AOT²*, pp. 12–18, 241–281; *ANET,* pp. 365–400; Falkenstein-von Soden), make it absolutely certain that the Psalms were associated with the cult.

If, then, we are to speak of praise and supplication as Old Testament forms that give additional insight into Yahwism, we cannot omit a brief survey of the background against which we hear these concrete verbal manifestations. What has been said in earlier contexts about the gift of Yahweh's presence (§9) and the function of the priests (§10d) also belongs to this background.

Unfortunately, the instructions for the sacrificial worship of the community, which probably constituted the focus of the celebrations in the sanctuary (Num. 28—29), say very little about the intentions of the worshipers expressed in the sacrifices. The sacrificial legislation of P is primarily content with describing the ceremonial of the sacrificial rites, i. e. the concrete outward form of ceremonial, so that one might conclude on the basis of it alone that no words, spoken or sung, were involved. A survey of everything that is reported about the sacrificial system does, however, permit us to say something about three fundamental points given expression in the sacrifices. Alongside the intention of celebrating communion with Yahweh in the sacrificial meal stands the purpose of honoring God with gifts and, with clearly increased emphasis in the postexilic period, of expiating transgressions.

Communion with Yahweh is found primarily in the form of sacrifice, attested from the earliest period, referred to as זבח *zebaḥ* (literally "slaughtering"; usually rendered simply as "sacrifice" or "offering"). According to 1 Samuel 1, for example, Elkanah goes up to the sanctuary at Shiloh every year with his two wives and his children in order to prostrate himself (השתחוה *hištaḥăwâ*) before "Yahweh of hosts" and offer sacrifice (זבח *zbḥ*). The sacrificial ritual of Leviticus 3 defines precisely which portions of the sacrifice, here referred to as זבח שלמים *zebaḥ šəlāmîm,* are to be burned upon the altar for Yahweh. 1 Samuel 1 goes on to depict graphically how the family of the man offering the sacrifice gathers for the meal in which each is given a portion and eats in the presence of Yahweh. It may be surmised that the atmosphere of joy that permeates the accounts of sacrifice in Deuteronomy 12:5–7 and else-where, where all kinds of sacrificial rituals are vaguely included, derives primarily from this זבח *zebaḥ* sacrifice, celebrated in the context of a communal meal. Deuteronomy is very con-cerned that on these occasions the poor and the local Levites not be forgotten. P's use of the fuller expression שלמים זבח *zebaḥ šlāmîm* probably derives from the later association of the sacrificial meal with a "concluding sacrifice," referred to initially merely as שלמים *šlāmîm* (Rendtorff).

The עולה *'ôlâ*, "burnt offering" or "whole offering," on the other hand, is the form of sacrifice in which the entire animal is offered to Yahweh by being burnt upon the altar. The ritual for this sacrifice is found in Leviticus 1. The feminine participle עולה *'ôlâ*, literally "rising up," was probably connected originally with the noun מנחה *minḥâ*, "gift" or "offering." This word is used in Judges 3:17, for example, in the totally secular sense of tribute offered to a political superior. The "burnt offering" is therefore called the "tribute that rises [to heaven in the fire]." This clearly expresses the purpose of the "tribute." This recalls the situation in Deuteronomy 26:1ff., where the farmer brings gifts of his produce to the sanctuary, and the priest receives the basket containing the gifts and places it before the altar of Yahweh. In this tribute the subject attests his reverence for the sovereign, to whom he is indebted for his property. Later, in the sacrificial system of P (Lev. 2), the מנחה *minḥâ* came to be distinguished as a "food offering" or "grain offering" from the "burnt offering," which involved animal flesh. As their position in the first two chapters of Leviticus shows, the burnt offering and food offering came later to take precedence over the זבח *zebaḥ* meal. Vows, first fruits, tithes, etc. also fall into the category of tribute.

During the later period, which had experienced the crisis of the exile and come to have a new sense of the fundamental need for expiation on the part of the people of Yahweh, two further forms of sacrifice attained great importance: the sin offering (חטאת *ḥaṭṭā't*) and the guilt offering (אשם *ašām*). On the more important sacrificial occasions they usually appear as additions to the tribute offerings. In respect to their mode, they are related to the עולה *'ôlâ*. The rituals for these two forms are recorded in Leviticus 4 and 5; it is rather difficult to differentiate the significance of these two offerings. As propitiatory offerings, they both lend a note of expiation to the intention of simple tribute. It is characteristic that we do not encounter these two forms in the detailed sacrificial lists of joyous celebrations in Deuteronomy. But they dominate the great Day of Atonement, which took on such importance in the postexilic period and in its very designation (see above, p. 129) contains an element of expiation (כפר *kpr*).

These three elements can be isolated only indirectly: communion, in-volving a joyous celebration; tribute, offered as homage; and propitation, springing from a sense of repentance. In the Psalms, however, the people of Yahweh open wide their mouth and clearly state what brings them before their God.

It has already been shown that when Israel opens its mouth the cry of the faithful to their God occupies an important place. The various prayer forms include: speaking, "stroking the countenance of Yahweh," asking, calling, crying, groaning, moaning, lamenting, weeping, and wailing. This terminology reveals the unrestrained vitality of this prayer over its whole range, which may also be called an "outpouring of the heart."

If we are to define the particular nature of this Biblical supplication, which, as we have said, exhibits in its language many points of contact with the psalmody of the rest of the ancient Near East, there are at least three features that can be singled out as being distinctively Old Testament; in the context of Israel's prayer, they reveal Yahweh, the God of Israel, as the unique addressee.

1. All prayer growing out of the Old Testament faith is definitely limited by the first commandment. When the faith of Israel cries out, there is only one who is addressed. Israel never has the chance and never makes the attempt to flee to other helpers or mediators. There is no prayer to the angels of Yahweh, who are mentioned in the Psalms (Ps. 91:11–12), or to the king, such as we find in the so-called monotheism of the period of Akh-en-Aton in Egypt. Here we find no trace of the variety of supplication encountered elsewhere in the ancient Near East, where one god may be asked to intercede with another and where the supplicant, besides addressing the deities known by name, for safety's sake includes "the god" or "goddess whom I do not know" (Falkenstein-von Soden, p. 225). The consistency of the Psalms is unprecedented: it is Yahweh and Yahweh alone to whom all prayers and supplications are addressed.

2. The second point is in fact implied by the first. Despite all the mystery that shrouds God's governance, which is quite familiar to the supplicants of the Psalms, and despite all sense of God's unfathomable majesty, he is not the "unknown God." He is the Yahweh of the introduction to the Decalogue, who has made himself known to his people in his delivering love. Even when the supplicant sits in darkness and laments "that the governance [literally: 'the right hand'] of the Most High is so altered" (Ps. 77:11, after the *Zürcher Bibel*), he remonstrates with God on the basis of what he did for the fathers in days gone by. Cf. also Psalms 22 and 89.

This knowledge includes a sense of Yahweh's "righteousness" (cf. the discussion on pp. 142–144 above), which is seen from various angles. In the so-called "penitential Psalms" (as ecclesiastical tradition calls Pss. 6, 32, 38, 51, 102, 130, and 143), we see the terror evoked by the Holy One who brings the sinner before the bar of his judgment; but in the midst of this terror, the hope is expressed that Yahweh will not abandon the lost sinner and the Israel that cries out to him from the depths. On the other hand, we also find the assurance that Yahweh will not forsake the one who confesses him and is unjustly oppressed by enemies. Schmidt has discussed a group of Psalms based on the prayers of the innocent accused person awaiting the divine decision (e. g., Pss. 7, 17, and 26). When the supplicant in these Psalms speaks of his innocence and "righteousness," the reader should always recall what was said above in our discussion of the righteousness of Yahweh and the "excess" in his gifts. In these passages we do not hear the voice of the rigidly self-righteous Pharisee of Luke 18:9–14, but that of the Old Testament believer, who takes refuge in the God who expresses his righteousness in what he gives. The priestly "declaration" at the sanctuary gate, spoken with the authority that comes from Yahweh, has told him that it is Yahweh's will to accept him, to vouchsafe him blessing and "righteousness" (Ps. 24:5). And so he dares appeal to Yahweh's "constancy" (חֶסֶד

ḥesed) (Pss. 17:7; 26:3, and elsewhere). When he cries out, he knows, despite all the perils that encompass him, that he is protected by the presence of Yahweh (Ps. 27:1ff.) as by a shield (Ps. 5:13). And so he can venture to take the epithet "Shepherd of Israel" by which Yahweh is known and apply it quite personally to himself, speaking of the care of this shepherd, who leads him to fresh pasturage and through the perils of the dark valleys (Ps. 23). The faith of the Old Testament knows its God by name, the God who promised to be Israel's own God, and knows that, "for the sake of his name" (Ps. 23:3; 25:11, and elsewhere), he will not allow Israel to fall.

3. At the same time, it is clear that the prayer of the Old Testament supplicant is also subject to the third commandment. The "name of Yahweh" has been revealed to the faith of the Old Testament believer. He may— indeed must—call upon him without hesitation. How totally different is the mystery surrounding the secret name of the sun god Re in the Egyptian myth of Isis and Re (*ANET*, pp. 12–14)! But there is also another difference: the name never becomes a technical device by which the supplicant tries to coerce the God of Israel. In the case of many personal and moving psalms from Babylonia, it can be observed that they were used subsequently as formulas in the context of magical rites. Now while it is true that we still find in the Psalms faded remnants of magical formulas (Nicolsky), none of the Psalms appears to have been used in a magical context. According to Hempel, a magical incantation includes not only the mention of the deity's name, which is used as a word of power, but also frequent repetition of the text and its whispered recitation. Exodus 3:14, the only passage in which an attempt is made to cast some light on the meaning of the name "Yahweh," contains an imperious refusal to countenance any abuse of the name. Even when the faith of the Old Testament approaches its God in impassioned prayer, it knows him to be the free God who will not countenance any abuse of his name. "I am who I am." This knowledge dominates all the prayers of the Psalms. We even look in vain for any hints that the Psalms could be prayed like litanies. The repetition of a refrain in the strophic poems Psalms 42—43; 80 can hardly be considered evidence of such use, and the responses in the hymn Psalm 136 fall in a different category. When 1 Samuel 1:13 speaks of Hannah praying silently, only moving her lips, the entire context shows that we are dealing with anything but an attempt to constrain God by means of magical prayer. Furthermore, as Hempel again has shown, this elimination of any element of magic is particularly well illustrated by the formal transformation exhibited by the elements of blessing and curse, which would be the most likely to retain some sense of constraint. Within the Old Testament, the magical curse or blessing formula turns more and more clearly into a prayer of blessing or cursing. For an example of a curse, see the particularly harsh Psalm 109, a plea for vengeance; for an example of a

blessing, see the form for the blessing to be pronounced by the high priest in Numbers 6:24–26.

The faith of the Old Testament believer is dominated by the knowledge that Yahweh has freely made himself known to his people in his name: "I am Yahweh, your God, who brought you out of Egypt, out of the house of bondage." Therefore supplication in the Old Testament never turns into a mere independent transaction with God, which would reduce him to an "object" and make use of him as a "power" to be wielded in devout godlessness. Every cry for help is stated personally: "You, Yahweh." In this form of address the Old Testament faith pays homage to its God even when it cries out from the abyss of despair and is dominated by "why?" and "how long?"

It is in that agonized cry of "why?" in Psalm 22, that was to be the cry of Christ on the cross (Matt. 27:46; Mark 15:34), that we see how the supplication leads up to the thanksgiving that will be offered when the supplicant is delivered and the assembly is called on to give thanks: "I will make known your name to my brethren, and will praise you in the midst of the assembly." (vs. 23) Here we find the opposite pole of Old Testament prayer, which gave its name to the entire psalter. The praise and thanksgiving of the community and of the individual within the community, which declares the honor of Yahweh before everyone, is heard against the background of the cries of the oppressed, who know God as a deliverer and as a righteous judge. The bridge from the one to the other is the form called the "thanksgiving of the individual" by Gunkel and "narrative praise" by Westermann. In this form it is still possible to recognize very clearly an association with a particular form of sacrifice. The term תּוֹדָה *tôdâ* refers both to a hymn of thanksgiving, whether spoken or sung (Ps. 50:14), and to a thank-offering (Amos 4:5). Psalm 30 shows how an individual, looking back on a crisis that is past, expresses his thanksgiving in the company of those he has invited to share in the thank-offering with him. In Psalm 107 it is the various groups within the community that have experienced deliverance (from a dangerous journey, from prison, from sickness, for a storm at sea) who are called upon to give thanks. This form of thanksgiving hymn makes it very clear that even in the case of the individual Yahweh's aid does not achieve its purpose until it leads to praise of Yahweh in the assembly.

In this context we must mention the particular form of doxology in which someone who has sinned "gives glory to Yahweh" in confessing the sin, thus confessing it by praising Yahweh (Achan in Josh. 7:19). The strange hymnic interpolations in Amos 4:13; 5:8; 9:5–6 have been interpreted by Horst and by Wolff in his commentary as such doxologies deriving from the community that transmitted and preserved the prophetic text, in which they confess the righteousness of God's judgment (according to Wolff, God's judgment upon the altar at Bethel in particular).

But this brings us already to the great "hymn" form (to use Gunkel's term), which constitutes a recognizably independent genre. The hymn, which has its *Sitz im Leben* in the liturgical praises of the assembled community, includes, as Crüsemann has shown, various groups of forms differing in origin and genesis. The imperative hymn achieved dominance within the Old Testament and subsequently came to incorporate elements from other genres. In its narrative it extols the gracious deeds Yahweh has done for his people and calls on them to praise him. Such narrative is the authentic response of Israel to the actions of Yahweh it experiences. By way of the contrast, the hymn that glorifies Yahweh with participial predications is strikingly similar to the hymnody of the rest of the ancient Near East. Crüsemann (pp. 136–150) has collected a wealth of parallels, including the creation of heaven and earth, the stars, dominion over the sea, earthquakes and meteorological phenomena, a throne in heaven, creation and maintenance of humans and animals; but also righteousness and mercy, help for the weak, punishment of the godless, and dominion over the nations. He has also argued convincingly that the application of all these demonstrations of power to Yahweh took place initially through the addition of the polemic formula "Yahweh (of hosts) is his name"; cf., for example, the passages from Amos just mentioned. This opens the way at once for the praise of Yahweh as expressed by Old Testament faith to invade all the realms in which Israel's neighbors praised their gods. Here in the context of praise we find the original locus, in all its vitality, of what was said in §4 about the wide horizon claimed for Yahweh's act of creation and kingship, and in §8 about the conviction that Yahweh is also the one who gives the land with its blessings. The people of Yahweh did not formulate these insights in intellectual speculation; in praising their God they confessed his name and introduced his name into all the praise of the gods that they encountered among their neighbors. But this proclaiming of his name in order to confess him reveals a faith that in all those domains it is Yahweh himself who reveals himself to the world. Just as the faith of the New Testament, encountering the Christ of God, confesses that there is no other name under heaven given to people by which they may be saved (Acts 4:12), so the faith of the Old Testament, experiencing the sovereign power of its God in the name Yahweh, confesses that there is no other god with power in any of these realms. "He who forges the mountains and creates the wind . . . Yahweh is his name." (Amos 4:13) This human doxology is a response to what the faith of the Old Testament, to which the dominion of Yahweh has been made known, perceives in all things: "I make the light, I create darkness, author alike of prosperity and trouble—I am Yahweh." (Isa. 45:7)

This discussion shows that, however gloriously people might frame Yahweh's praises, these do not draw their life from human eloquence and art, but merely reflect what humans have seen and heard of Yahweh through all his actions in nature and in history.

When I discussed the supplications in the laments of the psalter, I said at the outset that there was no source to address from which help might come other than the one source: "My help comes from Yahweh, who made heaven and earth" (Ps. 121:2), and that this very singleness of focus implicitly contains the praise of Yahweh. This applies also to the explicit praise of Yahweh. It, too, can be addressed only to the One, whether we are dealing with the praise of the entire community or with the individual calling on his own soul to praise Yahweh, as in Psalm 103. Whenever a hymn speaks of those other divine powers, whose existence is by no means denied on theoretical grounds, it can only be with reference to the One who will call their actions to judgment (Ps. 82), or in a spirit of superiority that mocks their impotence (Pss. 115:4–8; 135:15–18).

Gunkel, Hermann, and Begrich, Joachim. *Einleitung in die Psalmen.* Göttinger Handkommentar zum Alten Testament, supplement to section 2. Göttingen: Vandenhoeck & Ruprecht, 1933. —Falkenstein, Adam, and von Soden, Wolfram. *Sumerische und akkadische Hymnen und Gebete.* Bibliothek der alten Welt: der alte Orient. Zurich: Artemis, 1953.—Rendtorff, Rolf. *Studien zur Geschichte des Opfers im Alten Israel.* Wissenschaftliche Monographien zum Alten und Neuen Testament, vol. 24. Neukirchen: Neukirchener Verlag, 1967.—Schmidt, Hans. *Das Gebet der Angeklagten im Alten Testament.* Beihefte zur Zeitschrift für die Alttestamentliche Wissenschaft, vol. 49. Giessen: Töpelmann, 1928. Nikolskii, Nikolai (Nicolsky, Nicolaj). *Spuren magischer Formeln in den Psalmen.* Beihefte zur Zeitschrift für die Alttestamentliche Wissenschaft, vol. 46. Giessen: Töpelmann, 1927.—Hempel, Johannes. "Die israelitischen Anschauungen von Segen und Fluch im Lichte altorientalischer Parallelen." *Zeitschrift der deutschen Morgenländischen Gesellschaft* 79 (1925):20–110. Reprinted in his *Apoxysmata,* pp. 30–113. Beihefte zur Zeitschrift für die Alttestamentliche Wissenschaft, vol. 81. Berlin: Töpelmann, 1961.—Westermann, Claus. *Das Loben Gottes in den Psalmen.* 3d ed. Göttingen: Vandenhoeck & Ruprecht, 1963. English: *The Praise of God in the Psalms.* Translated by K. R. Crim. Richmond: John Knox, 1965.—Horst, Friedrich. "Die Doxologien im Amosbuch." *Zeitschrift für die Alttestamentliche Wissenschaft* 47 (1929):45–54. Reprinted in his *Gottes Recht,* pp. 155–166. Theologische Bücherei, vol. 12. Munich: Kaiser, 1961.—Crüsemann, Frank. *Studien zur Formgeschichte von Hymnus und Danklied in Israel.* Wissenschaftliche Monographien zum Alten und Neuen Testament, vol. 32. Neukirchen: Neukirener Verlag, 1969.

§18 Mastery of Everyday Life and Its Concrete Secrets (Wisdom)

Life before God is not limited to the explicitly "religious" sphere. There is also the realm of everyday life with its jobs to be done, its decisions to be made without a divine commandment to regulate each step, interpersonal relations with spouse and child and friend, conduct toward superiors and inferiors. Here, too, people face everywhere the question of how to evaluate the situation correctly and what their appropriate conduct should be.

The Old Testament is an unabashedly human book in that it provides

a place in its canon for what is briefly termed "wisdom literature," which
deals for the most part with this everyday realm. In § 10f the figure of the
"wise man" was discussed, and we saw that the Old Testament claims not
only that the wisdom of the highly placed political counselor, but also that
the skill of the craftsman and the science of the farmer, are charismata given
by God. We must now examine in more detail the theological understanding
of wisdom whose literary deposit is found primarily in Proverbs and Ecclesiastes, but in the broader sense includes also the book of Job and a series
of Psalms (for example Pss. 37 and 73).

It was already mentioned in § 10f that wisdom has more international affinities than any
other part of the Old Testament, and that a wealth of related material has come to light in the
ancient Near East.

In Sumeria, Babylonia, and Assyria, for example, we find lists that initially define the stock
vocabulary of the language, but at the same time, with the purpose of understanding the world,
set up a kind of inventory of the things existing in the world, listing the various classes of things
as exhaustively as possible. We also find collections of proverbs, disputations in which various
concepts from the realm of nature or civilization defend their usefulness, didactic discourses, and
poems reminiscent of Job and Ecclesiastes in which human suffering is examined. In Egyptian
literature, alongside the onomastica claiming to list exhaustively all things in the world, we find
primarily the so-called "instructions." As a rule, these have an older figure (king, vizier, official)
instructing a younger figure (son, disciple) in proper conduct in various situations. Nor are the
elements of meditation on life and lamentation lacking in Egypt. There was a particular affinity
between Israel and Egyptian wisdom, as can be determined indirectly from Solomon's marriage
with a member of the Egyptian royal house and directly from Proverbs 22:17—23:12, where
an excerpt from the Egyptian Instruction of Amenemope has been incorporated with minor
revisions into the collection of proverbs under the title "Sayings of the Wise." (22:17[?]) The
material added by the editor is naturally revealing for the particular self-understanding of Old
Testament wisdom.

In recent studies of Egyptian "wisdom" (the term is borrowed from Old Testament wisdom), the concept of *maat*, already mentioned on p. 39 above, has taken on particular importance. It can be rendered as "truth," "justice," or, best of all, "world order" (Gese). It includes
both the order of the cosmos and the order of human life. But *maat* is thought of not only as
a concept but also as a divine being. In the system of Heliopolis, Maat is the daughter of the
sun god Re. "In the 'primordial age' she came down to humans as the right order of all things"
(Brunner, *HO*, I.2, p. 93). She can be pictured as the child standing before the creator god
Atum, a graphic depiction of the tender relationship between the creator and his daughter.
Through Maat all things have their existence. When a man properly subordinates all he does
to Maat, he will set his life in proper order and thus achieve success. Thus the apparently quite
secular admonitions found in the Egyptian instructions take on a religious overtone. By engaging
in conduct that strives for success by conscious attention to the proper ordering of life, a man
also becomes a part of the order determined by Maat, grounded ultimately in the deity.

Attempts have been made to treat the Sumerian term *me* in Mesopotamia as equivalent to
the Egyptian *maat*, but it does not take on the importance of its Egyptian counterpart.

A glance at the statements made in the wisdom literature of the Old Testament shows that
there is a strong will at work here seeking to understand the objects in the world around it.
Unfortunately we know fewer details about the *Sitz im Leben* of wisdom tradition in the Old
Testament than elsewhere in the ancient Near East, where court and temple schools were the
preferred sites for "education." It has been suggested (Hermisson, von Rad) that in Israel, too,
there were "schools" where the art of framing wisdom aphorisms was practiced. But the
consonantal script of Hebrew, immeasurably easier to learn than the cuneiform and the hiero-
glyphs of the great civilizations of the ancient Near East, may have made it possible from the
outset for Israel to enjoy more open "schooling," less class centered. There is also the potentially
more "democratic" intellectual tradition of Israel, which does not see any divine kingship at the

earthly royal court, and, on the basis of its understanding of Israel as the "people of God," tends more to make the individual Israelite a full-fledged member of society.

The Old Testament does not contain any examples of wisdom lists as a pure genre. But Solomon's songs and proverbs "about the tree, from the cedar of Lebanon to the hyssop that grows on the wall" (1 Kings 5:13) may well have been based on list lore (Alt). Von Rad has also suggested a similar background for the list of the works of creation in Job 38ff. On the other hand, the numerical proverbs in Proverbs 30 clearly exhibit groupings organized in broad categories: things that are particularly greedy (30:15–16); phenomena that are especially strange and hard to understand (30:18–19); unbearable people (30:21–23), etc. Here individual observations like those found in the maxims of 10:1—22:16 are collected in coherent groups under particular numbers, usually increasing in value. May we conjecture behind this organization a question, posed in school or even asked as a riddle, asking for such lists of similar things?

In their various forms of parallelism, the proverbs exhibit the purpose of recognizing certain regularities in the realms of nature and humanity, behind their artful pleasure in originality, which is unmistakable, especially in the use of imagery and metaphor. One thing is always being set in relationship to another; see, for example, the collocation of natural phenomena in Proverbs 30:24–28, which share the characteristics of industry and order. But the recognition of these regularities is not purposeless, an intellectual game: the purpose behind recognizing hidden regularities is to illuminate the rules governing one's own conduct and thus achieve "life" through correct conduct.

The hidden purpose behind instructing oneself and others and acquiring values becomes clear when a comparative proverb weighs one statement with another and finds one superior: "It is better . . ." (12:9; 15:16–17, and elsewhere). This form implies the admonition to seize what is better and eschew what is worse. Such an "admonition" can then be linked in a two-line form with a motivation clause, containing an observation expressed in the form of a statement. "Do not keep company with drunkards or those who are greedy for the fleshpots; for drink and greed will end in poverty, and drunken stupor goes in rags." (23:20–21)

The Egyptian religious mind believed that the mysterious order of Maat lay behind all the rational observations of the everyday world, and therefore sensed the presence of a divine order even in the rational mastery of the daily problems of life. It is clear from the outset that on this point the faith of the Old Testament senses the presence of a different power from that sensed by the Egyptian faith. In the rationally recognized order and regularity of its daily life it can know only the One, who was also the only one to whom its supplications and praises were addressed: Yahweh.

Here, however, we come to the real theological problem of how to incorporate "wisdom" properly into an Old Testament theology. The faith of the Old Testament stands under the confession of Yahweh, the God of Israel, who led Israel out of the house of bondage in Egypt. Wisdom literature does indeed speak of Yahweh as the Lord who stands over the order and regularity of daily life. But it never mentions his particular involvement in the history of Israel, his guidance of his people. Nor is the greatness of the people of Yahweh ever mentioned. Not until the Wisdom of Sirach (Ecclesiasticus), which is later than the Old Testament, does the perspective include Yahweh's involvement with Israel (Ecclus. 44ff.). Thus the question arises whether in its wisdom lore and approach to the world Israel comes upon a second source of revelation, independent of the first.

At this point we must recall what was said in §4, which was just cited in our discussion of the hymn-form in the Psalms. When it entered the promised land, Israel entered a world in which high gods were praised as creators of the world and the glory of their creation was displayed. As our examination of the hymn showed, Israel entered this world with the polemic confession: "Yahweh is his name." Using this confession, Israel in turn sang the praises of creation in the words borrowed from this world. Now, however, they were understood with reference to the One God Yahweh; there was no second realm with any second god to be praised. This process was more than formal and intellectual. What happened was that Israel opened the entire world of creation and entered it with its faith in Yahweh, by subordinating the realms it discovered there to Yahweh. This is the locus of wisdom lore, whose international character, as we have seen, was well known to Israel.

The observations of the industrious ant (Prov. 30:25) and the miraculous flight of birds through the air (30:18–19) could have been made anywhere. The Hymn of Akh-en-Aton (*AOT*², pp. 15–18) provides a good illustration of this process as it applied to hymns. It contains many observations of the natural realm, some of which came to be repeated in Psalm 104 by ways that are not entirely clear. Here praise is addressed not to the almighty Sun, but to Yahweh, the Lord, who placed the sun in the heavens.

But the same thing holds true for observations in the human realm: laziness brings poverty (Prov. 10:4); sudden wrath engenders strife (15:18); a foolish son is a disgrace to his parents (10:1). These observations, too, could be borrowed in the context of a created world now ascribed to the creative act of Yahweh. Thus an excerpt from the Egyptian Instruction of Amenemope could be incorporated into the collection of proverbs that came as a whole to be ascribed to Solomon, king in Israel. Here, too, it is impossible to miss the introduction of the cry "Yahweh is his name" into this material. Even in the superscription the Old Testament redactor includes a comment on the meaning of wisdom instruction that is not found in the Egyptian original: "I would have you trust in Yahweh, and so I tell you these things this day." (22:19) To the admonition not to rob the poor, heard in Amenemope 2, Proverbs 22:23 adds the motivation: "For Yahweh will take up their cause and rob him of life who robs them." The same process is repeated with the admonition not to alter boundaries. What Amenemope 6 forbids by reference to the moon god, Proverbs 23:11 bases on the statement: "For their guardian [or 'redeemer'] is powerful, who will take up their cause against you"; the term אֵל gōʾēl clearly refers to Yahweh. Thus "Yahweh is his name" is spoken in the wisdom of

Proverbs, without changing any of the individual admonitions that can be pronounced quite as well by Old Testament wisdom as by Egyptian wisdom.

Comparison with the foreign original permits us here to observe the actual process of accommodation. The same process took place throughout the entire book of Proverbs: when the observations or instructions approach the boundary line where human considerations reach their limit and the hidden background of the "order" that affects all things becomes visible, in every instance it is Yahweh who is mentioned. His blessing brings riches (10:22); his governance gives refuge to the blameless (10:29); in his sight false scales are an abomination, but correct weights are pleasing (11:1); his eyes see all (15:3); before him the depths of the underworld lie open—how much more the hearts of people (15:11)! When a person makes plans, it is really Yahweh who governs the course of events (16:9); from him comes the decision when people cast lots (16:33); when people think they have done right he tests their hearts (21:2). In clarity it is recognized that face to face with him no human wisdom, understanding, or counsel (עֵצָה *ēṣâ*) can avail (21:30). Everywhere he is clearly the One in whose presence all human intellectual activity takes place. In him it finds its absolute limit; but in him it also finds reward when it has followed his will. Thus even in the many observations that wisdom makes in the natural world, which have no direct bearing on the service of God in the narrow sense or on his commandments, wisdom is aware of operating within the realm of Yahweh's creation. Even though "Israel" and its unique history never makes an appearance, so that knowledge, counsel, and understanding operate in the realm of what is common to all people, the "man" (אָדָם *ādām*) under consideration here is still the creature of Yahweh; Israel's awareness of this fact was discussed in §4. The creator (עֹשֵׂה *ʿśh*) is specifically mentioned in Proverbs 14:31; 17:5 (Eccles. 12:1 uses בָּרָא *brʾ*).

Related to this observation is the fact that the term "fear of Yahweh" (discussed on pp. 145–146 above) plays a fundamental role in proverbial wisdom. In the organization of the book of Proverbs as a whole it is placed thematically at the beginning of the whole body of wisdom instruction: "The fear of Yahweh is the beginning of knowledge"; cf. also 9:10; 15:33 (Ps. 111:10; Job 28:28). It must be recalled that there is associated with this talk of the fear of Yahweh, as we observed in Deuteronomy, an element of trust and confidence. This element also comes very much to the fore in the wisdom use of the expression "fear of Yahweh" in the book of Proverbs. "A strong man who trusts in the fear of Yahweh will be a refuge for his sons; the fear of Yahweh is the fountain of life for the man who would escape the snares of death." (14:26–27)

Koch has attempted to find in the Old Testament some trace of a sphere within which an act brings about its own consequences: by a kind of internal law, evil brings evil upon the evildoer, just as good befalls the one who does good. Gerhard von Rad has modified this perspective to read: "A good result means a good act." He maintains that this, too, is an element of wisdom lore. He emphasizes that such a sense means a world that is Yahweh's creation. It must be firmly maintained that such an awareness constitutes the actual basis for the knowledge of the world exhibited by the book of Proverbs and is not merely a peripheral element added as a kind of religious ornament.

The subordination of all wisdom to the name of Yahweh probably also accounts for the immeasurably greater emphasis on the contrast between the righteous and the godless in the book of Proverbs than in other wisdom literature of the ancient Near East. In many aphorisms it has replaced the "wise/foolish" antithesis, which is proper to wisdom literature. Even in its rational observations of everyday life, wisdom moves within a world known to be determined by Yahweh's demand for righteousness.

All this means that the world which the wise man of Proverbs seeks to comprehend in his aphorisms and master in his maxims governing human conduct is a world of hidden order. Despite the reserve with which God acts in his world, it remains, as the world of Yahweh's righteousness, obedient to principles of order that are decreed by God; they do not function automatically, but are maintained by Yahweh. The success of many human undertakings is uncertain: "A horse may be made ready for the day of battle, but victory comes from Yahweh." (21:31) This uncertainty, however, does not impugn the validity of the principle that good conduct produces good results, even though people may err in their intentions and judgments (21:2).

It is an inescapable fact that such a sense of fixed order in the world leads to delight in the significance of such wisdom. In the eyes of those who concern themselves with it, wisdom appears as an independent entity, which can even be personified and described in action. In Proverbs 1:20ff., wisdom appears on the streets preaching repentance. In 9:1ff., she is a hostess inviting people to her table. She finally becomes an entity already present alongside Yahweh at creation—not, certainly, as a second creator, but probably as the first among creatures. In Proverbs 8:30, following the exposition of 8:22ff., wisdom says of herself: "Then I was alongside him [the creator] as a child and was a [his?] delight each day, playing in his presence continually." It has been suggested that in this passage we hear an echo of the previously mentioned notion of Maat as the child of the creator god Atum.

At this point, however, we begin to sense problems. Is wisdom not in danger of being exalted to the status of mediator between Yahweh and the faith of Israel? Is it not possible for her to lead astray those who have sat at her table? Of course it is emphasized over and over again that the fullness of wisdom is inaccessible to humans. Job 28:1–27 paints a particularly impressive picture of wisdom dwelling in a place inaccessible to humans, more inaccessible even than the metals they know how to mine from the depths of the earth. Only God knows the way to her (vs. 23). But when she can be depicted calling out in the streets (Prov. 1:20ff.), when her invitation to her laden table can be described so graphically, is there not a danger that the wise man who has intercourse with her (von Rad has impressively described the erotic overtones of this relationship) will think that through this intercourse he gains possession of the secret order of the world? It is no accident that Jeremiah 9:22 warns: "Let not the wise man boast of his wisdom, nor the valiant of his valor. . . ." Just as it is the specific temptation of political and military might to imagine a godless security (Isa. 28:15), so it is the ever-present temptation of the wise to feel secure about the world and everyday life because they "know" about both. Like Isaiah 5:21, Proverbs 3:7; 26:12

recognize that the wise man is especially subject to the danger of being "wise in his own eyes."

At this point, we find within the corpus of Old Testament wisdom literature itself a fundamental protest in Ecclesiastes and Job, two otherwise very different works.

"Ecclesiastes" or "the Preacher," an anonymous wisdom teacher of the late Old Testament period (12:9), constructs his argument on the basis of actual experience. The tone of his meditation is usually one of cool, distant, and rational observation (but cf. 2:18, 20). The proper function of the wise man is to take his experiences and observations seriously. "The wise man has eyes in his head, but the fool walks in the dark." (2:14) It is inappropriate to dismiss the Preacher as a "skeptic." He, too, makes his observations within a world that he considers incontestably God's world. Although he avoids mentioning Yahweh by name, it is manifest that in all his penetrating questions he honors in his own fashion the majesty of the one alongside whom there is no other with comparable power. Thus in his own fashion he moves within the framework of the first commandment of the Decalogue—and probably, in his own special way, the second and third as well.

The position against which he directs his critical and polemic wisdom is clearly defined in 8:16–17: "I applied my mind to acquire wisdom and to observe the business which goes on upon earth . . . and always I perceived that God has so ordered it that man should not be able to discover what is happening here under the sun. However hard a man may try, he will not find out. The wise man may think that he knows, but he will be unable to find the truth of it." There are wise men who think they comprehend the order of God's world. The argument of Ecclesiastes makes it quite clear that he is not polemicizing against a wisdom that has become "godless." He finds himself confronted with wise men who are concerned with God's world and seek to glorify God in all their discoveries and statements about the hidden order of the world.

At the very center of Ecclesiastes' discussion stands a sense of the "proper moment." The expansive treatment of "everything in its season" in 3:1–9, containing two series of seven pairs, followed by the meditation in verses 10–15, exhibits even outwardly the significance of this knowledge. The right moment for an undertaking had been a subject for discussion not only in Egyptian wisdom, but also in the Old Testament wisdom of Proverbs. "There is joy for a man in the answer of his mouth, and a word at the right time [literally 'in its time'], how lovely that is!" (Prov. 15:23)

Other wisdom literature (cf. especially Ecclesiasticus and von Rad's discussion) found no particular difficulty for the wise man in recognizing the right moment. It is no accident that Ecclesiastes begins the series in 3:2 with the statement: "There is a time to be born and a time to die." He comes to far more radical conclusions. No one can control the moment of his birth or of his death; in like fashion, recognition and therefore also mastery of the particular moment are totally outside the realm of human possibility. This autonomy of the moment extends even to such very personal things as love and hate, where people think they are most their own masters (9:1). It is true that God has placed "eternity" (עוֹלָם *ōlām*) in the hearts of people, probably meaning the desire to transcend the particular moment and master intellectually the order of the ages. But the true knowledge of this order—which Ecclesiastes knows to be good (it has been suggested that 3:11 borrows from what is said in Gen. 1)—continues to be beyond human grasp. "I have seen the business God has given men to keep them busy. He has made everything good in its time. Moreover he has put eternity into men's hearts—but no comprehension of God's work from beginning to end."

All the details of Ecclesiastes' observations are to be understood in the light of this basic recognition. If people think they can discern an order of justice in the world, so that the good person prospers and the wicked meets disaster, this view is contrary to the observation that the good person may suffer disaster while the wicked prospers (7:15). When a wise man maintains that wisdom brings worldly success, Ecclesiastes maintains the possibility that "speed does not win the race nor strength the battle; bread does not belong to the wise, nor wealth to the intelligent, nor success to the skillful; time and chance govern all." (9:11) A besieged city in which a wise man dwells who could save it is lost because no one thought to consult the poor wise man (9:13ff.). If wisdom extols the great value of industrious labor, it is contradicted by the dubious restlessness of the compulsion to achieve (4:4–6) and the fact that a man without relations may lose all the reward of his labor (4:7–12). Above all, however, human mastery of time is repeatedly called into question by death, which brings all labor to naught and brings smiles to a man's heirs (2:18–23 and elsewhere). Thus, weighing values against each other, encounter with death when it comes is better—because more genuine—than encounter with life (7:1ff.).

In this context Ecclesiastes raises the question of what might be the deeper meaning of our inability to gain mastery of time and all the things behind which the wise man apparently finds such good order. In 3:14 he replies: "God has done it all in such a way that men must fear him." Here and elsewhere he returns quite surprisingly to the old demand of Old Testament wisdom: the fear of God is the beginning of wisdom. This fear of God —and here Ecclesiastes makes a statement unprecedented in wisdom literature—knows that humanity cannot gain mastery over life by being "over-righteous" or by being "over-wicked," in other words by devout or godless excellence. Therefore people should eschew both and thus show that they truly "fear God" (7:16–18).

From this perspective we can understand why Ecclesiastes does not reach a dreary resignation as his conclusion, but can surprisingly admonish us to accept what good is given us at any moment and enjoy it: "And yet I saw that this comes from the hand of God. . . . God gives wisdom and knowledge and joy to the man who pleases him, while to him who displeases him is given the trouble of gathering and amassing wealth only to hand it over to someone else who pleases God." (2:24, 26) This also explains why Ecclesiastes can exhort the young man who does not yet have to bear the burdens of age to enjoy his youth and thus in his youth remember his creator (11:9—12:7). This knowledge that all things are in the hands of God, which confronts a man when he is burdened by evil (7:29; 8:11), makes it possible for the man who has renounced his own "over-righteousness" to exercise merciful restraint when he hears his slave cursing him (7:21–22).

Ecclesiastes presents a broad spectrum surveying life in all its variety. The book of Job, by contrast, deals with an acute crisis in the life of a single righteous man—a crisis like that reflected in the laments of the Psalms. The framework narrative presents a righteous man who firmly maintains his faith in God, overcoming all temptations arising from a wager in heaven between God and the accusing angel (Satan).

Within this framework narrative has been inserted, undoubtedly by another hand, an exciting dialogue between Job and three of his friends who come to comfort him. And in this dialogue there appears once more the problem of the wise mastery of life, now reduced to the problem of why God ordains suffering. There is no mention here of any personified wisdom mediating God's order of the world. The three friends, however, probably represent increasingly adamant proponents of belief in the evident "righteousness" of God in his dealings with people. The dialogue begins with comforting recollections of how Job once comforted the oppressed (4:3–5) and a reference to the God who stands as the righteous one over all creation. It develops into an increasingly harsh direct attack upon Job, insisting that his suffering must be due to a transgression he has not admitted (22:1ff.). This is demanded by belief in the "order" maintained by a righteous God.

In the face of this argument Job appears as an unbridled rebel. He goes over to the offensive, first attacking his friends, then more and more turning from his friends and crying out against God himself for his suffering and against the assigning of his suffering to a rational place in the order of the universe. The words he casts in God's face are harsh, bordering on blasphemy; he calls God a cruel God, who plays games in his omnipotence with the impotence of his creation, and laughs when his creatures perish in suffering and despair (9:22–23). Job refuses throughout to recognize this God as the defender of an order based on just recompense as depicted by his friends. He challenges God at the bar of justice and finally confronts God in a mighty oath of purgation (chapter 31) in which he asserts his innocence. He does not mean innocence in the absolute sense. Job, too, knows that the human race is sinful, and he is no exception. But he refuses to recognize the rationalistic calculation that would make him, suffering beyond measure, into a sinner beyond measure.

Despite all this rebellion, it is apparent from other statements that Job's wisdom, too, moves within the framework of the Old Testament notion of God the creator. Job reveals that behind the God his friends display to him he knows another God—the God who cannot forget his creation. In a prayer that sounds utopian he wishes that God would hide him in the realm of the dead until his anger subsides, and then summon him when his wrath has abated: "Then you would summon me, and I would answer you; you would long to see the work of your hands." (14:15) Later his speech becomes more assured: he prays that his blood will not be covered, i. e., that his case be continued, and gives his reason: "For look! My witness is in heaven; there is one on high ready to answer for me. My friends mock me, my eye looks to God in tears, that he vindicate man against God, a man against his friend." (16:19-21) Against the God of his friends he appeals to the God he knows as his "witness" in heaven, who will vindicate him. This faith is voiced most powerfully in 19:25, where, despite all the textual uncertainty that characterizes the following verses, we hear the unambiguous statement: "I know that my redeemer (גֹּאֵל gō'ēl) lives and that my advocate (אַחֲרוֹן aḥărôn) will arise upon the dust." In Proverbs 23:11 a reference to the גֹּאֵל gō'ēl, meaning Yahweh, was inserted into the Egyptian original in order to express the idea that the poor person has a friend. Elsewhere the term refers to the man who carries out blood vengeance (Num. 35:12, 19ff.). In Job the term is unmistakably used in its full legal sense. After a murder, the avenger, as the victim's next of kin, takes up the cause of the life that has been snuffed out and sees to it that accounts are settled by the death of the murderer. Thus Job stands here as a dead man, but he knows there is one who will take up his cause even after death and demand his rights. How this process is pictured concretely, whether the continuation, as some translations have it, really speaks of seeing God after death, remains uncertain. What is stated clearly is that Job, the apparent rebel who refuses to understand his suffering as being part of the necessary order of things, here transcends everything that is not understood and confesses the God who will stand up for his rights as his next of kin, seeing that blood vengeance is carried out—in fact, as his "redeemer," to use an interpretative translation. Can we not see here the God known to Israel since the deliverance in the exodus? If so, however, Job is more than a rebel. He is the "poor man" who does not forsake his faith even when he cannot understand his fate.

After the discourses of Elihu in chapters 32—37, which are a later addition that attempts to understand Job's suffering as God's means of education, chapters 38—41 describe how God appears to Job in a violent storm. Job's appeal to God has not gone unheeded. But the content of God's speeches is not what we would expect from the challenge in 29—31. God does not vindicate Job by saying "He is righteous," but confronts him with the majesty and mystery of his creation, asking him whether he was present at the creation of the world and whether he can fathom its mysteries. This is clearly a rebuke to contentiousness that has passed acceptable limits. Job accepts the rebuke and explicitly submits to God. But then in 42:7 comes a surprise: God compares what Job has said with what his friends have said, and concludes that the friends spoke incorrectly, unlike "his servant" Job. The apparent rebel, who refused to accept the calculated order of his friends and the God who maintains the order, is vindicated rather than his friends. In all his contentiousness, Job did more honor to the living God than did his friends. It is totally inappropriate to push this concluding verdict of God upon the dialogue between Job and his friends into an epilogue by a different hand and try to understand the dialogue without this final verdict. Even if, as is not impossible, this verdict belonged to an earlier stratum of the Job narrative containing a different form of the dialogue between Job and his friends, the final recension of the book sets this verdict upon the entire dialogue. What Job has said and what God has said—reminding Job of his limits—have both been vindicated. In the faith of the Old Testament, no rational order, however sublime, can mediate the direct confrontation between the God who acts mysteriously and yet "righteously" and his creation, comprehending it in an orderly system. "I am who I am."

In conclusion, we must take a look at Psalm 73. Here it is not Job, suddenly afflicted with suffering, but a troubled faith, more like that of Ecclesiastes, that does not understand the order of Yahweh's world in which the godless can prosper. The answer that the Old Testament believer finds here does not come, as in Job, through contentious dialogue. Instead, the psalmist says that he came into the "sanctuaries of God" (מִקְדְּשֵׁי אֵל *miqdᵉšê ēl*), where he came to realize that Yahweh sets the godless on slippery ground (vss. 17–18). Did the worshiper receive assurances in the Temple that gave him final certainty? Or is the term "sanctuaries of God" to be understood metaphorically as God's "holy governance," as the *Zürcher Bibel* does? In any case, it is once again clear here that faith, assailed by its inability to comprehend God's "order" in the experiences of everyday life, finds its way to the bold confidence which confesses that it will cleave to God as its "portion" even when heart and body fail. Once again we find a limiting statement, not further elaborated: verse 24 not only confesses the assurance that God will guide the speaker with his counsel (עֵצָה *ēṣâ*), but also looks forward to being carried away in glory. Here, as in Job, leave is taken of any rationalistic wisdom. Totally defenseless, the Old Testament believer commits his life entirely into the hands of God and finds in the fear of God (the term is not used here) the true wisdom that leads to life. In these same terms the faith of the New Testament will speak of human and divine wisdom in the encounter with Jesus Christ (1 Cor. 1:18ff.).

Schmid, Hans Heinrich. *Wesen und Geschichte der Weisheit.* Beihefte zur Zeitschrift für die Alttestamentliche Wissenschaft, vol. 101. Berlin: Töpelmann, 1966.—Gressmann, Hugo. "Die neugefundene Lehre des Amen-em-ope und die vorexilische Spruchdichtung Israels." *Zeitschrift für die Alttestamentliche Wissenschaft* 42 (1924):272–296.—Gese, Hartmut. *Lehre und Wirklichkeit in der alten Weisheit.* Tübingen: Mohr, 1958.—Hermisson, Hans-Jürgen. *Studien zur israelitischen Spruchweisheit* (with bibliography). Wissenschaftliche Monographien zum Alten und Neuen Testament, vol. 28. Neukirchen: Neukirchener Verlag: 1968.—Von Rad, Gerhard. *Weisheit in Israel.* Neukirchen: Neukirchener Verlag, 1970. English: *Wisdom in Israel.* Nashville: Abingdon, 1972. Cf. *Evangelische Theologie* 31 (1971):680–695.—Alt, Albrecht. "Die Weisheit Salomos." *Theologische Literaturzeitung* 76 (1951):139–144. Reprinted in his *Kleine Schriften zur Geschichte des Volkes Israel,* vol. 2, pp. 90–99. Munich: Beck, 1953.—Von Rad, Gerhard. "Hiob 38 und die altägyptische Weisheit." In Society for Old Testament Study. *Wisdom in Israel and in the ancient Near East* (Festschrift H. H. Rowley), pp. 293–301. Edited by Martin Noth and D. Winton Thomas. Supplements to Vetus Testamentum, vol. 3. Leiden: Brill, 1955. Reprinted in his *Gesammelte Studien zum Alten Testament,* pp. 262–271. Theologische Bücherei, vol. 8. Munich: Kaiser, 1958. English: "Job XXXVIII and Ancient Egyptian Wisdom." In his *The Problem of the Hexateuch and Other Essays,* pp. 281–290. Translated by E. W. Trueman Dicken. New York: McGraw-Hill, 1966.—Zimmerli, Walther. "Ort und Grenze der Weisheit in Rahmen der alttestamentlichen Theologie." In *Les Sagesses du Proche-Orient ancien.* Paris: Presses Universitaires de France, 1963. Reprinted in his *Gottes Offenbarung,* 2d ed., pp. 300–315. Theologische Bücherei, vol. 19. Munich: Kaiser, 1969.—Koch, Klaus. "Gibt es ein Vergeltungsdogma im Alten Testament?" *Zeitschrift für Theologie und Kirche* 52 (1955):1–42.—Hempel, Johannes. "Das theologische Problem des Hiob." *Zeitschrift für systematische Theologie* 6 (1929):621–689. Reprinted in his *Apoxysmata,* pp. 114–173. Beihefte zur Zeitschrift für die Alttestamentliche Wissenschaft, vol. 81. Berlin: Töpelmann, 1961.

Genesis 3 has been repeatedly interpreted as reflecting the "doctrine of the fall of man." Thanks to Augustine's misinterpretation of what Romans 5:12 says about Adam *("in quo omnes peccaverunt"),* this chapter has been thought to speak of "original sin," as though the human race springing from Adam share almost physically "in Adam," in his sin as a hereditary property conceived almost biologically.

In view of this interpretation, it must appear surprising that the Old Testament (apart from distant echoes in Ecclesiastes) never speaks of such a "doctrine." Genesis 3 is therefore making a different point. It is not proclaiming a timeless universal truth, but speaking in concrete metaphor. The metaphor, however, does express a universal truth that transcends the immediate narrative complex.

Furthermore, Genesis 3 must not be read in isolation. The primal history of J is characterized by a whole sequence of stories about sin: Genesis 4 recounts Cain's murder of his brother and Lamech's unbridled vengeance; Genesis 6:1–4 tells about the marriages with angels, leading immediately to the Deluge (6:5–9, 17). It is also reasonable to include in this deliberate concatenation of disaster stories the cursing of Canaan (9:18–27), even though Yahweh, the God of Shem, is "blessed" in 9:26, as well as the story of the Tower of Babel. Each of these stories casts light in its own way on one particular aspect of what this enigmatic break between God and humanity means and on God's response to it. The following points are being made:

a) Genesis 3 does not tell the story of just one individual in the course of human history but of the first man, whose designation "Adam" ("man") is subsequently taken as a proper name. The point is undoubtedly to provide an exemplar of human conduct before God. Paul is not off the mark in Romans 5 when he compares Christ, the new man, with the "man" of Genesis 3.

The same can be said of Genesis 4:1ff., where the first "brother" (the catchword is emphasized) appears, and of 11:1ff., where the first large group of people working together appears.

b) The sudden appearance of sin does not derive causally from God's good creation according to Genesis 3.

Part of man's sinful flight from the presence of God is his desire to blame God: "The woman you gave me for a companion, she gave me fruit from the tree and I ate it." (3:12) The so-called Babylonian Ecclesiastes, for example, speaks in very different terms: "The king of the gods, Narru, the creator of men, the renowned Zulummar, who pinched off their clay, the queen who formed them, Princess Mama, bestowed crafty speech upon mankind, lies and untruthfulness they gave to mankind for all time" (quoted from O. Loretz, *Qohelet und der Alte Orient* [1964], pp. 104–105). The Old Testament Ecclesiastes speaks quite differently in 7:29. It would also be a misinterpretation of the radical statement in Isaiah 45:7 to see it as transferring blame or "guilt" to Yahweh. Cf. the further discussion under (g).

V. Crisis and Hope

In the life of humanity before God as described in the Old T
there is reflected the reality of the God of Israel. In what has bee
to this point, however, we have not yet caught sight of the ultim
that reveals fully the nature of Yahweh, the God of Israel and crea
creation. We have not yet examined the terrible crisis in which
narrator records that "Yahweh was sorry he had made man" (Gen.
a prophet calls his child "Not-my-people" to shatter the ears of ever
the statement of how Yahweh feels about his people Israel (Hos.
must now discuss explicitly this crisis and the way the faith of
Testament sees the judgment and salvation of God as they apply to
in the life of humanity (§19) and of the people of God (§§20–21
it thinks about the future of the world (§22).

§19 Humanity between Judgment and Salvation (Primal Hi

The fundamental reflections of the Old Testament faith on
apart from and before the unique history of Israel with its God ar
the primal history. Gese has shown how not just individual eleme
primal history, but the whole sequence of creation, primal age, d
new beginning after the great crisis can be found in Sumerian histo
The question now is what is being said about the transaction bet
and humanity when this historical narrative speaks of Yahweh as
its history.

1. We have already discussed in §4 how J attempts in his ou
of the beginnings of history (Gen. 2:4b–25) to illustrate Yahwel
care for man, whose good he wishes. There follows immediately
3 the account of the fall in the garden of God.

The traditional elements of this narrative are also found, in far more myth
in the oracle against the King of Tyre in Ezekiel 28:11–19. Greek mythology a
divine garden whose fruits are jealously protected by its owner (Hera), which
by a powerful man (Hercules); this story of the garden of the Hesperides ("th
in the evening," i. e. at the western edge of the world) probably contains echoes o
material.

c) According to Genesis 3, the nucleus of sin does not consist merely in the transgression of an objective norm, but in man's disregard for his divine Lord, who has showered him with blessings.

Initially, of course, Genesis 3 speaks of the "taboo" tree and its fruit in the midst of the garden. But the real interpreter of what is going on is the serpent, who explains: "God knows that as soon as you eat it, your eyes will be opened and you will be like God, knowing both good and evil." Under this interpretation the sinful act that follows means rejection of the giver and man's change from the role of recipient to that of giver. The strangely blurred episode of the marriages with angels (6:1–4; see the discussion on p. 61 above) was probably also understood as demolishing the God-given relationship between heaven and earth. And we can see clearly in 11:1ff. how human strength, brought together for a single purpose, seeks in hybris to pave the way to heaven itself.

d) The primal history of J illustrates uncannily the rapid growth of evil, which spreads like a drop of oil on water.

The break with God is followed (not "self-evidently," but once more frighteningly and incomprehensibly) by the break between brothers, by the wild self-assertion of the vengeful Lamech, by the blurring of the boundary between heaven and earth, by disrespect for father and abuse of collective national might. It has been suggested that the story of David exhibits a similar internal progression: the murder and adultery committed by David (2 Sam. 11—12) are followed in the next breath by sexual promiscuity and murder among David's children (2 Sam. 13). Nowhere, however, is a causal relationship posited between the new sin and what preceded, which would lift the burden of guilt.

e) The tendency of sin to conceal and disguise itself appears in bold relief, especially in Genesis 3—4.

The man hides among the trees when God approaches (3:8). With an air of hypocritical respect he tries to make excuses when God asks where he was: "I was afraid because I was naked, and I hid myself." (3:10) In the case of Cain, a lie is coupled with a frivolous play on words when Yahweh asks him where his brother the shepherd is: "I do not know; am I my brother's keeper [=shepherd]?" (4:9) In 3:12, the retreat has been cynically transformed into an accusation against God: "The woman you gave me. . . ."

f) At the same time, sin shows in horrible distortion how man was created for life with others, and how even here it is not good for him to be alone (2:18).

"She gave me fruit from the tree and I ate it," says the man (3:12) when God asks him whether he has eaten from the tree, pointing to the companion God gave him out of careful consideration. "The serpent tricked me, and I ate," says the woman (3:13), pointing to the beast which, according to 2:18–19, God had likewise created for the benefit of man. Thus man misuses the creation God has given him, employing it as a shield behind which to seek protection.

g) To the basic question of how evil comes into the world the primal history gives no answer. In common with all the rest of the Old Testament, it does not make the slightest attempt to take refuge in a dualistic or pluralistic universe. Guilt is left to stand unexplained as guilt, in all its harshness.

We very early find attempts to see Satan, God's hostile counterpart, behind the serpent of Genesis 3 (cf. Rev. 12:9; 20:2). Whatever the preliminary history of the mythological material in Genesis 3 may be, this interpretation clearly does not accord with the intentions of J, who at the very outset explicitly includes the serpent among "the beasts of the field that Yahweh Elohim had made." The serpent is thought of here simply as a snake, not as a hostile divine power in disguise. The subsequent curse condemning the serpent to eat dust and go upon his belly makes this clear. The eschatological description of the coming paradisal peace (Isa. 11:6–8) also provides evidence from the opposite perspective; one feature is the elimination of the hostility between people and the serpent. Examination of the story in Genesis 4, which is closely associated with Genesis 3, is also significant. No serpent appears in Genesis 4. But Cain's transgression is preceded by a warning from the mouth of Yahweh himself, the interpretation of which is linguistically uncertain. Strikingly echoing Genesis 3:16, 4:6–7 says: "Why are you so angry and cast down? Is it not true, if you do right, then you may raise it up [?], but if you do not do right, sin crouches at the door. It is eager for you, but you must master it."

It is reasonable to ask why the serpent is introduced at all in Genesis 3. Couldn't the story have been told like the story of Cain? One reason, of course, is the availability of specific narrative material. But closer examination also shows that in both instances, first by the introduction of the serpent, second by the interpolation of Yahweh's warning, the man is given scope to make a free decision. Sin does not simply overwhelm the man like a fate to which he has fallen victim; it confronts him initially as a temptation: in Genesis 3, it is embodied in the serpent; in Genesis 4, it is brought to light by the words of Yahweh. Given this scope for free choice, each man seizes the opportunity to disobey. Only this free choice makes it possible to take each man's guilt seriously. It was not necessary for them to sin. Humans are not simply guilty by nature; sin and guilt are alien to them, they come to them as temptation. But neither is sin part of a dualism, a fundamental principle hostile to God from the beginning of time.

We can see how the Old Testament wrestles with this problem, which is probably not amenable to logical solution. 2 Samuel 24:1 ventures to draw the mystery of temptation directly into the realm of Yahweh's will, making reference to the wrath of Yahweh, when it states: "Once again the Israelites felt Yahweh's wrath, when he incited David against them and gave him orders that Israel and Judah should be counted." The rest of the narrative shows how David fully confesses his guilt and how his conscience afflicts him on account of it. The later account in Chronicles is concerned like Genesis 3 to preserve scope for human freedom and make it clear that the temptation comes to David from without. The figure of Satan is introduced, possibly as an "interpretation" based on Zechariah 3:1ff. (cf. Willi in the bibliography to §20): "Now Satan, setting himself against Israel, incited David to count the people." (1 Chron. 21:1)

When the term "Satan" appears in the Old Testament, it should not be associated with a dualistic world view or a doctrine of two eons. At first it refers to a human accuser; later it comes to mean an accuser from the divine realm, who brings guilt to light, in some cases by instigating it.

"Satan" is basically not a proper name but a functional term. The verb שׂטן *śṭn* means "show enmity." Thus שׂטן *śāṭān* can mean a political opponent. In 1 Samuel 29:4, the Philistines send David back before attacking Saul so that he will not become an "adversary" in the battle. 1 Kings 11:14, 23, 25 lists the "adversaries" who rise up against Solomon during his reign. At the same time, the word can take on the overtones of "tempter." In 2 Samuel 19:23, David berates the sons of Zeruiah, who sought to induce him to take vengeance, calling them his "adversaries," "satans."

Zechariah 3:1ff. and Job 1—2 show how Yahweh also has a "Satan" or "Adversary" in the realm of the angelic powers that wait upon him; this figure acts as a kind of "public prosecutor," taking note of everything that does not appear to be in order and investigating it with critical questions. In Zechariah 3:1ff. it is the uncleanness of the high priest, brought about by the exile, that the Satan brings to the attention of God. In Job 1—2, it is the critical inquiry whether the only reason Job is so devout is that he is prosperous. In 1 Chronicles 21:1, the only passage where the term "Satan" appears without an article as a proper name, the provocation of Satan actually incites David to sin when he is tempted (unlike Job 1—2).

In all of these passages, nothing is done to dissociate evil from disobedience. Again and again the Old Testament shows that, although severe temptation makes sin appear almost inescapable, its commission is always a matter of human responsibility. The mystery of sin remains unclarified; in the last analysis, it can be spoken of only in the form of a religious confession. In the judgment doxology (see above, p. 153), we have heard how people glorify God even when confessing sin. Psalm 51:7, where the worshiper confesses that his mother conceived him in sin, must not be understood as an attempt to transfer guilt to one's ancestors. Just as Isaiah's horrified exclamation, in which he confesses not only that he is a man of unclean lips, but also that he dwells in the midst of a people with unclean lips (6:5), is not meant to transfer his guilt to a collective "people," so, here, too, all that is being said is that everyone is inextricably bound up in sin. The same point is made in the story of the first man's disobedience to God.

Yahweh cannot overlook this action on the part of the man. The most sinister formulation of Yahweh's reaction is found in Genesis 6:6, where J states: "Yahweh was sorry that he had made man on earth." Does this not mean the end of the human race? The primal history speaks of a chain of blows Yahweh delivers in judgment, responding to the rebellion of his creation. His judgment takes the form of a direct sentencing; it must not be reduced to the neutral process of an action involving its own consequences. According to Genesis 3, God imposes in his judgment specific plights that are still inextricably bound up in the life of creation as we know it. Here, too, however, the Old Testament merely gives illustrations, not a comprehensive account.

In the animal world, Genesis 3:14–15 speaks of the enigmatic crawling of the serpent on its belly, its eating dust, and the profound hostility that will exist between it and humanity. Anyone who sees a serpent will try at once to stamp on its head, and whenever a serpent sees a person, it will attempt to strike and set its poisonous fangs in the person's heel. The church later claimed to find a "protevangelium" here, according to which one born of woman would one day put to death the serpent, taken as Satan in the New Testament sense; such an interpretation imports notions into Genesis 3 that are not found in the text.

In the case of the woman, the punishment includes the pain of childbirth and bondage to her husband (a given of patriarchal society), to whom she nevertheless feels drawn.

In the case of the man, we see at once that he must labor as a farmer, producing the fruits of the soil by the sweat of his brow, all the while realizing that in the end he will return to dust. At the conclusion of the paradise story this latter punishment, banishment from the place of life, takes concrete form in the man's banishment from the garden of God and thus from access to the tree of life. The guard at the entrance to the garden denies for all time humanity's return there. Genesis 6:1–4 describes the restriction placed on human life in the context of a totally different tradition, citing an explicit decree of Yahweh that human life may not exceed 120 years.

The details of the Cain tradition suggest an original locus in the semi-nomadic life of the Kenites. In its present context, the emphasis is on the homeless wanderings of the fratricide, who can never settle down in peace. The narrative manifestly has a profound psychological transparency.

J tells his story most expansively in the account of the Deluge, where God's regret that he created people takes the form of a universal catastrophic flood.

The Canaan episode points more specifically to the particular circumstances of the Canaanite world, where during the time of David Israel became the rulers, the Canaanites their subject servants.

The story of the Tower of Babel once again has a universal problem in view, which even today still afflicts the nations: the different languages spoken by different nations are a source of divisiveness preventing people from working together in peace.

These are the severe consequences of the curse as touched on by J. Alongside them, however, J's portion of the narrative in Genesis 3—11 reveals an enigmatic divine restraint. The man and woman are threatened with death on the day they eat from the forbidden tree (2:17), but their lives are not taken on the day they sin. In fact, the description of the woman's punishment speaks of childbirth and the future, so that in 3:20 the man ventures to give her the name חַוָּה ḥawwâ, Vulgate Heva, English "Eve," "because she became the mother of all who live." When the fratricide Cain pleads with Yahweh in desperation, Yahweh protects him by means of a (tatooed?) sign, "in order that anyone meeting him should not kill him." (4:15) At the beginning of the great Deluge we hear the sinister statement that God regretted ever having made people; but Yahweh himself (not, as the Babylonian epic has it, the cunning of another god working against the god who caused the flood) carefully preserves not only an entire human family but enough living creatures from all animal families to insure the whole world a future. And Yahweh's final decision, in the context of which he explicitly acknowledges that "the inclinations of man's heart have been evil from his youth up," leads up in 8:21-22 to a total preservation of life on earth.

In all of this we have a foretaste of what is explicitly stated in Genesis 12:1-3 in the call of Abraham. Yahweh plans a new future of blessings for the world, which is in many ways under a curse and has no righteousness of its own that could move God to make such a decision. In Abraham the bearer of this new blessing is made visible. How the nation of Israel is anticipated in his figure and Yahweh's promise has been discussed in §3.

Thus J understands and attests the meaning of Israel's existence according to God's will: to bring a blessing into a world marked by the afflictions of God's judgment because of its alienation from him. J does not go into detail about how this blessing is to take effect in a world afflicted with death, pain, enmity between various groups of creatures, and lack of understanding among nations. That the problem remained acute is demonstrated by Isaiah 11:1-8; 25:8a and other passages that must be discussed later.

2. J was composed in the early period of the monarchy; the outline of P brings us into the period following the great catastrophe of Israel. It has

been pointed out in another context that P's introduction in Genesis 1:1—2:4*a* with its detailed account of the creation of the world betrays a noticeably different interest and purpose from that of J. The question of humanity and the riddle of human existence recede in favor of the problem of God's great design for the world and the people of Yahweh. P does not include the stories of the fall and the first fratricide, which cast such a sharp spotlight on the nature of people; neither does it mention the episode of the angelic marriages, the Canaan incident, or the Tower of Babel. Only the detailed account of the Deluge, linked by means of the genealogical lists in Genesis 5 and 11:10ff. with the story of the world's beginning and the incipient history of Israel, intervenes between the account of creation and the story of Abraham.

The six days of God's creation conclude in 1:31 with the summary statement: "And God saw all that he had made, and it was very good." When God alone acts, everything is "very good." In 6:11, however, at the beginning of the Deluge account, after ten generations of human history have elapsed, we encounter a terrible new observation: "Now God saw that the whole world was corrupt and full of violence (חָמָס *ḥāmās*)." In addition, we find the statement, clearly phrased in contrast to 1:31: "And God saw the earth, and behold, it was corrupt, for all flesh had lived corrupt lives upon earth." (6:12) This reference to "violence" on earth intrudes quite unexpectedly alongside the opening observation in 1:31. Only the statement that Enoch "walked with God" and was therefore taken away by God, in a list that is otherwise dominated by nothing more than names and numbers (Gen. 5), gives the slightest hint that other things on earth might not be taking place "with God."

It has been stated (Köhler) that P says nothing about the fall of man. This statement is correct to the extent that P does not contain any lengthy story of the fall after the manner of Genesis 3. But the fact of a universal fall into sin in all its unmotivated irrationality is if anything stated even more trenchantly by P than by J. The fall also appears more inclusive in P than in J, because "all flesh" is involved. This phrase is probably meant to include the animal world as well, in which the "violence" of the strong against the weak is as widespread as in the human world.

This universality of the fall is also expressed in the account of the Deluge that is God's response to the alienation of the world. J had pictured the great Deluge as a downpour lasting forty days, something like a catastrophic flood. In P, it affects the very foundations of the world created and ordered in Genesis 1. "All the springs of the great abyss were broken through and the windows of the sky were opened." According to Genesis 1:6–7, the ordering of chaos to form the created world began with God's placing a "firmament" or vault between the earth and the "water above it," and his assigning a fixed place to the "water below it"—fixing for the deep a boundary that it might not pass, Psalm 104:9 adds. Now these waters, and with them chaos, threaten once more to invade the ordered world. P puts the theological question in much more fundamental terms than J: does the corruption of the world, primarily represented by the corruption of humanity, which was given lordship over the lower orders of creation, have the power to annul God's initial decision to create the world, so that the world described in Genesis 1 will be swallowed up once more by chaos?

Now P recounts not only how God delivers a single devout man from the flood, and with him representatives of all types of animals, but also how he seals his affirmation of the post-Deluge world by means of a covenant (see above, p. 56). God wishes to continue to have dealings with his creation—even though now (and here Gen. 9:2-3, even without any mention of the serpent, recalls 3:15 [J]) the peace of paradise no longer exists between man and beast. The animal world is now afflicted with fear of humanity. Now homicide also exists in this world (recalling Gen. 4), so that an authority with power to punish must be established to requite such bloodshed (9:4-6). But once again the blessing of fertility is pronounced over this world (9:1, 7). And the appended table of nations in P (10:1-7, 20, 22-23, 31-32) is meant to illustrate how the descendants of Noah branch out into a multiplicity of nations "by families and languages, with their countries and nations." (10:31; cf. 10:5, 20) In this account the variety of nations and languages attests a world blessed by God.

But according to P (Gen. 17) God sets Abraham apart from the rest of humanity on this earth that he has graciously preserved, and through Abraham Israel, to be a nation especially close to him, among whom he is to be worshiped rightly.

Gese, Hartmut. "Geschichtliches Denken im Alten Orient und im Alten Testament." *Zeitschrift für Theologie und Kirche* 55 (1958):127-145. Reprinted in his *Vom Sinai zum Zion*, pp. 81-98. Beiträge zur evangelischen Theologie, vol. 64. Munich: Kaiser, 1974.—Steck, Odil Hannes. *Die Paradieserzählung.* Biblische Studien, vol. 60. Neukirchen: Neukirchener Verlag, 1970.—Kluger, Rivkah Schärf. "Die Gestalt des Satans im Alten Testament." Ph.D. dissertation, Zurich, 1948. Reprinted in Jung, Carl Gustav. *Symbolik des Geistes.* Psychologische Abhandlungen, vol. 6. Zurich: Rascher, 1948. English: *Satan in the Old Testament.* Translated by Hildegard Nagel. Studies in Jungian Thought. Evanston, Ill.: Northwestern University Press, 1967.—Von Rad, Gerhard. *Die Priesterschrift im Hexateuch.* Beiträge zur Wissenschaft vom Alten und Neuen Testament, 4th series, vol. 13. Stuttgart: Kohlhammer, 1934.

§20 The Crisis of Israel in the Historical Narratives

The primal history of the world is followed in Genesis 12—50 by the early history of the patriarchs of Israel. The rest of the Pentateuch recounts the history of the people of Yahweh before their entrance into Canaan, and the portion of the canon known as the "Former Prophets" (Joshua—2 Kings) covers the period to the end of the monarchy. Are "blessing" (J) and "God's presence" (P) the dominant motifs of this continuation of the story?

1. The extent to which the patriarchal narratives in Genesis 12—50 are dominated by the broad promise that a single individual will multiply to become a nation and occupy the land of Canaan has been discussed thematically in §3. The narrative, especially J, depicts the patriarchs in realistic terms

as human beings whose lives show human anxiety (Abraham: Gen. 12:10–20 [J]; 20 [E]; Isaac: Gen. 26:6ff.), impatience over the delayed fulfillment of the promise (Abraham: Gen. 16 [J]), cunning and trickery in the case of Jacob himself (Gen. 25:27–34; 27; 30:25ff.), and domestic violence in the case of Joseph's brothers (Gen. 37); cf. also Genesis 34 and 38. But all this is sustained by God's will to achieve his purpose, even if he has to take long detours in the Jacob story. It is probably not by accident that Jacob, having tricked Esau, is tricked in turn by Laban (Gen. 29). In the Joseph story, which exhibits wisdom influence, the superiority of God's design over human intentions is stated almost thematically in Genesis 50:20, where Joseph says to his brothers: "You meant to do me harm; but God meant to bring good out of it."

2. The story of Israel's early history before the entrance into Canaan is likewise recounted with a strong sense of purpose in Exodus—Numbers (Deuteronomy). This period stands under the guidance of Yahweh, which has as its goal Israel's occupation of the promised land. Here, too, however, the nation brought out of Egypt by Yahweh is depicted very realistically as a problematic nation, inclined to disobedience. Only rarely do we find transgressions of the fundamental commandments of Yahweh laid down in the Decalogue: the apostasy in worshiping Baal Peor, which transgresses the first commandment (Num. 25:1ff.); violation of the prohibition against images (Exod. 32); or the exemplary narratives in Leviticus 24:10ff. and Numbers 15:32–36 dealing with violations of the third and fourth commandments. Far more typical are the repeated incidents of faithless pusillanimity or obstinate rebellion against God's guidance, the purpose of which is to lead Israel into the land of promise.

This tendency begins in Egypt, when Moses' initial intervention with Pharaoh merely leads to the imposition of harsher terms of forced labor on the Israelites (Exod. 5:20–21). At the Sea of Reeds, immediately before the act of deliverance celebrated in the earliest hymn of Yahweh's people (15:21), it takes on concrete form once more in direct repudiation of God's deliverance of Israel from Egypt (14:11–12). And this murmuring against Moses (לון *lûn;* Exod. 15:24; 17:3, and elsewhere) is repeated whenever the people experience a shortage of bread, meat, or water in the wilderness. Exodus 16:3 (P) speaks of homesickness for the "fleshpots of Egypt"; in Exodus 17:3 and Numbers 20:4, Moses is accused of having brought the people out of Egypt into the wilderness to see them die there. Numbers 11:1 says more generally that the people "complained" (אנן *nn* hithpael). Numbers 11:4–6 (20:5) lists in detail the delicious foods of Egypt, to which the scanty ration of manna given by Yahweh in the wilderness is compared unfavorably, leading up to the explicit demand: "Give us meat to eat" (Num. 11:13, 18) and the question: "Why did we ever come out of Egypt?" (vs. 20) When the spies sent to explore the land return and report the resistance to be expected, the people's rebelliousness expresses itself in an open decision to pick a new leader and return to Egypt (Num. 14:2–4 [P]). In Numbers 16:12–14, Dathan and Abiram stand on the verge of blasphemy when they apply the predicates of the promised land to Egypt, from which Yahweh had brought them out: "Is it a small thing that you have brought us away from a land flowing with milk and honey to let us die in the wilderness?" The resistance to Moses' leadership on the part of Miriam and Aaron in Numbers 12, and against the position of Moses and Aaron on the part of the Korahites in

Numbers 16:3, is of rather different nature. In Deuteronomy, cf. 1:27; 9:7ff. For a discussion of the entire question, see the work by Coats.

The books of Exodus—Numbers (Deuteronomy) reveal the response of Yahweh to the people who faithlessly mistrust his guidance, suspect it, and even rebel against it openly. When we survey the entire narrative, we see that Yahweh's response is to remain faithful to his cause and to his promise. At the conclusion of Deuteronomy, the people brought out of Egypt stand on the threshold of the promised land; in the narrative of the book of Joshua they will cross this threshold and take possession of the land. We also see how Yahweh delivers the faint-hearted people from the Egyptians, feeds them when they are hungry, and gives them water when they thirst, even when they complain and murmur to him about their hunger and thirst. Despite their stubborn resistance, their attempts to go back, and even their blasphemous praise of Egypt, the very place they had been delivered from, Yahweh guides them into the land flowing with milk and honey.

At the same time, we see that Yahweh does not do this in patient equanimity; he blazes with wrath when his honor is impugned.

According to Numbers 25:3–4, when the first commandment is violated, Yahweh's wrath blazes and a virulent plague decimates the Israelites (vs. 9). Judges arise against those who violate the second, third, and fourth commandments. But this is not all. Yahweh's judgment strikes the complainers of Numbers 11:1, the people demanding meat in Numbers 11:4ff., and the clan of Dathan and Abiram (Num. 16); the people who despise the manna as "miserable fare" are punished with a plague of snakes (Num. 21:6). For those who hesitate in the face of the spies' report, entrance into the land is delayed for an entire generation.

Yahweh's wrath blazes with particular violence in Exodus 32:10 and Numbers 14:11–12, where he threatens initially to destroy the entire nation and offers Moses the chance to become a great nation, thus striking an entirely new path for fulfillment of his promise. In both cases it is only the importunate intercession of Moses on behalf of his people that reminds Yahweh how his honor would be impugned in the eyes of the nations if he were to cause his people, whom he had brought out of Egypt, to perish in the wilderness (Exod. 32:11–12; Num. 14:13–16). It is the appeal to the old promise made to the patriarchs (Exod. 32:13) and recollection of Yahweh's earlier revelation of himself (Num. 14:17–19; cf. Exod. 34:6–7) that keep him from destroying his people in judgment. In Exodus 32:34, furthermore, we hear the sinister threat of judgment to come in the future. In all of this we face the dangerous reality in the second preamble to the Decalogue, in which Yahweh revealed himself not to the outside world, but to his very own people, who are destined to be a blessing for the world and enjoy special closeness to God.

One further point: According to Numbers 20:12, God's wrath strikes Moses himself, who has not acted according to Yahweh's will, so that he is prevented from entering the promised land. The reflection of the author who retells this story in Deuteronomy 1:37 turns this wrath into wrath that strikes Moses on account of the people, so that he shares the fate of the generation that perishes in the wilderness. Here we can perceive a striking solidarity uniting the messenger sent by Yahweh to his people with those who fall victim to the judgment of Yahweh's wrath. We shall encounter this solidarity elsewhere in a different form (see below, pp. 223–224).

3. With Deuteronomy begins the great complex of the Deuteronomistic History, which extends to the end of 2 Kings (Noth). This historical narrative, which in certain passages incorporates much earlier material and has itself been subject to later revision, was written in the period when Israel, in the political form of two separate states, suffered total collapse. It is intended as a historical accounting of Israel before Yahweh.

The deuteronomistic narrative begins at the point where Yahweh gives the law to his people; in Deuteronomy this event is embedded in the great promise of the land. The fulfillment shows how Yahweh remains faithful to his promise. But then a mysterious decline sets in among the people to whom the land has been given. The period of the judges with its cycles of deserved oppression and gracious deliverance is followed by the monarchy, the beginnings of which are very problematical in the eyes of Yahweh. In the election of David as well as Jerusalem and its Temple, Yahweh gives Israel new assurances of salvation. But with Solomon, after glorious beginnings, apostasy from Yahweh continues. In the Northern Kingdom with its high places and image worship, this apostasy leads to catastrophe in the Assyrian period. The south, with the Davidic dynasty and Jerusalem, whose kings Asa, Hezekiah, and Josiah are distinguished for their obedience to the commandments of Yahweh, while Manasseh is distinguished by the extent of his godlessness, receives a longer probation. Finally, however, Yahweh's destroying judgment strikes the Southern Kingdom. The monarchy and the Temple are destroyed by Nebuchadnezzar, and the upper classes deported. The account ends with the brief statement, offered without explicit theological interpretation, that Jehoiachin, who had been deported in 597, was released from prison and restored to honor through the amnesty of Nebuchadnezzar's successor.

a) This account, within which Smend claims to be able to distinguish a nomistic editorial stratum and Dietrich a prophetical stratum, is dominated initially by avowal of Yahweh's faithfulness toward his people. At the beginning of the book of Joshua, Yahweh promises to Joshua in a thematic discourse that as long as he lives no one will be able to stand against him, and that he will give the people the land promised by Yahweh to their fathers as their heritage (1:5–6). An exuberant retrospective summary in 21:43–45 states that Yahweh gave Israel the land and security on every side, just as he had sworn to the people's forefathers. "Not a word of Yahweh's promises to the house of Israel went unfulfilled; they all came true." Cf. also 23:14. Just as in former times Yahweh heard the cries of his people when they were oppressed in Egypt, so in the period of the judges he repeatedly hears the cries of the people in distress and sends them deliverers (Judg. 3:9, 15; 10:12). And the prayer spoken by David in 2 Samuel 7:18–29 in thanksgiving for the promise given him through Nathan exhibits in the deuteronomistic expansion of verses 22–24 particular amazement at the great deeds Yahweh has done for his people. The same theme is heard in Solomon's prayer at the dedication of the Temple in 1 Kings 8:15ff., now with special emphasis on the place from which Yahweh has spoken: "My name shall be there." (vs. 29) The blessing associated with this place will extend even to "the foreigner, the man who does not belong to thy people Israel," when he comes and prays toward this place where the divine name is present (vss. 41–43).

b) According to Deuteronomy, however, the God who exhibits this faithfulness is known by Israel to be the God who has made his will known to his people. A reminiscence of the moment when Israel left Horeb, the mountain of God (Deut. 1:6), begins the great discourse of Moses that constitutes the beginning of the whole Deuteronomistic History; the core of this discourse is the proclamation of "statutes and ordinances" in Deuteronomy 12—26, probably to be understood as a more detailed exposition of the Decalogue already proclaimed to the people at the mountain of God (Deut. 5:6–21). According to the Deuteronomistic History, however, this proclamation of the law at the beginning is not all. During the great assembly at Shechem told of in Joshua 24, Joshua requires the people to decide whether they will obey Yahweh or not and gives them "a statute and an ordinance." At the great turning point of the incipient monarchy, Samuel exhorts the king and the populace to remain obedient to Yahweh. Within the testament of David, the Deuteronomistic History has inserted in 1 Kings 2:2–4 an exhortation to Solomon to keep the commandments. And in the period of the monarchy it is the prophets who from time to time remind Israel to keep the commandments enjoined on their forefathers (2 Kings 17:13). For a discussion of the entire topic, see Dietrich.

c) The actual verdict of this deuteronomistic "accounting" of the history of Israel is that the people have been disobedient. This disobedience is not a timeless universal truth; it expresses itself in concrete historical events. In the period of the judges, the Israelites begin to do what is evil in the eyes of Yahweh by violating the first commandment, whose fundamental significance is well known to the Deuteronomistic Historian. They worship baals, forsake Yahweh, the God of their fathers, who brought them out of Egypt, and follow after other gods, the gods of the Gentiles. They worship Baal and the Ashtaroth (Judg. 2:11–13). In demanding a king they have rejected not Samuel but Yahweh himself, whom they refuse to have as king over them (1 Sam. 8:7). And when Yahweh does give Israel kings, it is not only the ambiguous figure of Saul, the first king, who comes to grief for refusing to exterminate the enemy as reported by the source at hand, but Solomon, the son of David, the king of special promise and builder of the house in which Yahweh causes his name to dwell, who sins against the first commandment according to the account formulated by the Deuteronomistic Historian himself. According to 1 Kings 11:4–8, in his old age his foreign wives lead him astray by persuading him to set up altars and offer worship to Astarte of the Sidonians (Phoenicians), Milkom of the Ammonites, Chemosh of Moab, and other foreign gods, thus opening the gates for the transgressions of the kings who follow him. The kings of the Northern Kingdom are routinely charged with the "sin of Jeroboam," i. e. worship of the bull images at Bethel and Dan (1 Kings 12:26ff.), when there is nothing more specific such as the mention of the Baal of Tyre as an object of worship in the source account of Ahab and Jezebel (1 Kings 16:31–32). The kings of the Southern Kingdom are judged instead primarily by the criterion of the basic commandment of Deuteronomy and are accused of worshiping at high places. Additional offenses, likewise from the perspective of the law of Deuteronomy, can include the setting up of masseboth and asherim, as well as promotion of cultic prostitution (1 Kings 14:23; 15:12–13). Ahaz and Manasseh are singled out as having sinned by "causing their sons to pass through [be sacrificed in?] the fire." (2 Kings 16:3; 21:6) Manasseh is further charged with having introduced, under Assyrian pressure, the cultic symbols of the "host of heaven." (2 Kings 21:5; cf. 23:4–5)

If we ask why these transgressions were committed, the Deuteronomistic History cites the phenomenon of "temptation," in this case involving a very specific historical nexus. Intermarriage with the Canaanites turns into a snare for Israel. Just as Solomon was tempted by his foreign wives to worship alien gods, so Israel is brought to ruin by mixed marriages with the indigenous Canaanite population. Such passages as Joshua 23 and Judges 2:10ff. show how this consideration even made it necessary to revise the original account of the occupation of Canaan in the Deuteronomistic History (Smend). The account spoke originally of the extermination of the entire indigenous population, exhibiting the total fulfillment of Yahweh's promise; Joshua 13:1*bβ*-6 and Joshua 23 now speak of an indigenous remnant, in the face of which Israel must remain obedient to Yahweh by eschewing any marriage relationship. Alongside the argument that this "remnant" was left in the land to "test" Israel (Judg. 2:21–22; 3:1*a*, 4), we find in Judges 3:2 the totally secular explanation that Yahweh left them in the land to teach the Israelites to make war. The notion of temptation then leads to the strict legal separation enjoined through-out the deuteronomic corpus. Despite Schmitt's arguments, this legislation can hardly date from the early period of Israel. Apart from this reference to temptation through the Canaanites, the Deuteronomistic History, like the primal history, offers no explanation for the disobedience of Israel. Here, too, inability and unwillingness to hearken obediently to Yahweh are let stand as the great riddle of human life.

d) Such disobedience, however, is subject to Yahweh's judgment. During the period of the judges, the sending of "oppressors" (Judg. 2:14), which leads the oppressed in turn to repent and cry out for help, still has something of an "educational" nature about it. Yahweh's mercy carries the day repeatedly. Later the blows strike harder. According to 1 Kings 11:14ff., the borderlands of Solomon's kingdom are first taken from him in consequence of his idolatry. Then the prophet Ahijah of Shiloh predicts that ten tribes of the Israelite kingdom will be taken from Solomon's son. He is the first in the series of prophets, named and nameless, who now appear throughout the history of the monarchy and give to the deuteronomistic narrative its peculiar structure of "promise and fulfillment." 1 Kings 12:1ff. then tells how the kingdom is divided. After two centuries during which the Arameans are occasionally sent by Yahweh to scourge the Northern Kingdom, it goes to destruction. 2 Kings 17:7–23 contains the deuteronomistic reflection on this event, which is interpreted as the judgment of Yahweh upon Northern Israel's obdurate refusal to repent. In verses 19–20, however, a reflection on Judah, which will not keep the commandments of its God, has been interpolated into the discussion of Israel. In the events of Judah even after Solomon (1 Kings 11:12, 32, 34, 36), it was occasionally possible to say that Yahweh would continue to show mercy on account of David his servant (1 Kings 15:4; 2 Kings 8:19; 19:34; 20:6); but according to 2 Kings 21:1–18 the actions of Manasseh impose on Judah such a burden of guilt that even the reformation of the devout king Josiah can no longer avert judgment. Nebuchadnezzar becomes the instrument of Yahweh's wrath, as Yahweh now banishes even Judah from his presence "because of all the sin that Manasseh had committed and because of the innocent blood that he had shed." (2 Kings 24:3)

This is the historical verdict of the Deuteronomistic History upon Israel. According to Noth, it is to be understood as the account of an event in the past—a general confession on the part of Israel, no longer looking forward to any future. Von Rad, however, in that short concluding episode of Jehoiachin's pardon, claims to hear yet another echo of the promise to David that "moves like a refrain through the history of Judah and restrains its much deserved judgment 'for the sake of David' " (*Deuteronomium-Studien,* 63). Should this protective mercy not make itself heard once more at the end, in the gracious pardon of Jehoiachin, as a demonstration of Yahweh's power over the catastrophe? Wolff, on the other hand, prefers to understand the whole Deuteronomistic History as a call to repentance. Not a single passage ventures to suggest a concrete future, not even in the promise to David. But the situation remains open in the eyes of Yahweh; every Israelite is expected to be ready for genuine repentance and return to Yahweh, whatever Yahweh brings to pass.

At the conclusion of this historical verdict on Israel, composed by the Deuteronomistic Historian from the depths of catastrophe, we must recall that the faith of the Old Testament knows Yahweh as the living Lord—living in his grace and mercy as well as in his wrath. History experienced in the light of his presence therefore never takes on the features of a neutral fate. It always remains a history that is in the hands of the living God. It is therefore appropriate for the Deuteronomistic Historian to recount a history, still open before the living God of Israel, illustrating Israel's profound sinfulness. It is not impossible that the concluding story of the mercy shown the descendant of David does indeed hint at the question (although there is no explicit mention of it) of whether Yahweh might indeed be prepared to pave the way for a new future even beyond this present death of Israel, in order to be faithful to his word. In any case, such a future would be his own free decision.

4. In addition to the Deuteronomistic History, the Old Testament contains the Chronicler's account of Israel's history; in the Hebrew canon, it is found at the end of the third section. It begins with an extensive genealogical introduction, starting with Adam (1 Chron. 1—9), followed next by the story of Saul's death (1 Chron. 10, following 1 Sam. 31) and then the history of David (1 Chron. 11—29), in which the preparations for building the Temple, the regulations governing its worship, and the transfer of office to Solomon occupy considerable space (1 Chron. 22—29). The history of the monarchy that begins with Solomon, after the division of the kingdom under Rehoboam, is restricted to events in Judah and Jerusalem, the small kingdom of the Davidic dynasty (2 Chron. 1—36). The concluding mention of Cyrus's edict (2 Chron. 36:22ff.) is repeated verbatim at the beginning of the book of Ezra, raising the question whether Ezra and Nehemiah, which precede Chronicles in the Hebrew canon, do not constitute an organic part of the Chronicler's history.

When the Chronicler's history is compared with the Deuteronomistic History, besides passages that are borrowed verbatim, we find noteworthy additions in the story of David; there is no parallel to 1 Chronicles 22—29. The Chronicler omits the negative features of the story of Solomon (1 Kings 11) and elaborates on the accounts of kings who were faithful to Yahweh always or occasionally: Asa (2 Chron. 14—16), Jehoshaphat (2 Chron. 17—20), Hezekiah (2 Chron. 29—32), Josiah (2 Chron. 34—35), etc. Above all, he emphasizes a much stricter law of retribution. In the case of Manasseh, for example, the most infamous of all the kings of Judah, who according to 2 Kings 21:11-15 had richly deserved the catastrophe that eventually befell Judah, we read that he was punished by the Assyrians, whereupon he repented and returned to his throne. Thus the unusual length of his reign appears justified in the eyes of God.

Recent opinions on the overall interpretation of the Chronicler's history have diverged sharply. Willi finds two different works of one and the same author in 1 and 2 Chronicles on the one hand and Ezra—Nehemiah on the other. By means of a painstaking analysis of 1 and

2 Chronicles, he attempts to show that these two books are to be understood as "interpretations" of the corresponding portions of Samuel and Kings. According to Willi, the author of the books of Chronicles was already familiar with the two first parts of the Hebrew canon (Torah and "Prophets") as canonical scripture. He attempts to "expound" them in the peculiar situation of his own period by interpreting "scripture" on the basis of "scripture." In explicit opposition to Willi, Mosis follows the majority of recent interpreters, maintaining that 1 and 2 Chronicles together with Ezra—Nehemiah constitute a single work that expresses its own unique historical perspective. "The structure of the work organizes the stories of Saul, David, and Solomon within the framework of three great historical periods: an age of wrath and judgment, an age that looks forward to salvation and enjoys its preliminary realization, and a future age of final and complete salvation; this structure serves to give insight into the nature of history as the history of Israel and therefore also of the 'Gentiles' before Yahweh, but above all into the nature of the Chronicler's own age as an age of incipient salvation" (p. 203). Ackroyd proposes a much more complex structure. He finds in the repeated alternations of contrasted sovereigns (Ahaz— Hezekiah—Manasseh—Josiah—Jehoiakim) a "skilful patterning," alongside which a "more subtle pattern of apostasy and repentance, obedience and faith, disobedience and unbelief" (p. 105) is frequently employed within the accounts of the individual rulers. This pattern shows that the Chronicler, like the Deuteronomistic Historian, does not wish to be read simply as a historian, but as a theologian.

Despite the overlap of 2 Chronicles 36:22–23 with Ezra 1:1–3*a*, a distinction between Chronicles on the one hand and Ezra—Nehemiah on the other is supported both by their striking sequence within the Hebrew canon and by their different treatments of prophecy. It is noteworthy that in Ezra only the two figures of Haggai and Zechariah are mentioned in connection with the building of the Temple (5:1; 6:14), both of whom are found in the canon of the Prophets. Nehemiah limits itself to two derogatory remarks about contemporary prophets (6:7, 14). In contrast, 1 and 2 Chronicles, like the Deuteronomistic History, are full of crucial references to prophets, named and unnamed. Chronicles in fact mentions such prophetic figures (often referred to by the term חֹזֶה *ḥōzēh*) even more frequently than the Deuteronomistic History. The point may well be an even greater emphasis on the fulfillment of the divine promise in Deuteronomy 18:15, 18, according to which no period of Israel's history will ever be without prophets. There seems even to be a distant echo of the notion, found explicitly in the rabbinic period, of a succession of prophets from a single family, with the son succeeding to his father's prophetic office (Willi, 217, n. 9). Even more clearly than in the Deuteronomistic History, the prophets are depicted functionally as proclaimers of God's law after the manner of Moses, whose authority they bear. In 2 Chronicles 20:20, for example, the demand for (obedient) faith of Isaiah 7:9 is extended so as to apply to the prophets: "Hold firmly to your faith in Yahweh, your God, and you will be upheld; have faith in his prophets and you will prosper." For Moses, cf. Exodus 14:31.

The Chronicler's exaltation of the Davidic line has already been discussed (p. 92). In an age of exhaustion, the purpose of the Chronicler's account is clearly to revive hopes in the promise given to David.

It has likewise been pointed out (pp. 114–115) that Chronicles also traces the institution of the Temple musicians back to David. The marked emphasis on the Temple cult in Chronicles led earlier scholars to maintain a one-sided dependence of Chronicles on P; von Rad has demonstrated convincingly that "more Deuteronomic than Priestly elements" are found in Chronicles (134). More emphasis is placed on the tradition of the ark and the Levites than on the tradition of Moses, the tabernacle, and the Aaronic priesthood, which so dominate P. This observation confirms Ackroyd's statement that the Chronicler is concerned to unite previously separate theological schools.

2 Chronicles likewise depicts the overall history of the monarchy in Judah as a history moving relentlessly toward catastrophe on account of the sins of the kings of Judah. The measures taken by the faithful kings, depicted in much greater detail, can do nothing to halt the process. For an overall theological estimate of the narrative, however, it is not accidental that at the conclusion of 2 Chronicles the pardon of Jehoiachin (2 Kings 25:27–29) has been replaced by the edict of Cyrus directing that the Jerusalem Temple be rebuilt and allowing the exiles to return for that purpose. The promise to David here takes second place to the renewed possibility of worshiping Yahweh once more in the sanctuary at Jerusalem. In this possibility, which incorporates the concerns of Deuteronomy as well as those of P, Yahweh makes known once more his "yes" to his people that transcends the catastrophe of his judgment.

Coats, George W. *Rebellion in the Wilderness.* Nashville: Abingdon, 1968.—Noth, Martin. *Überlieferungsgeschichtliche Studien. I: Die sammelnden und bearbeitenden Geschichtswerke im Alten Testament.* 2d ed. Tübingen: Mohr, 1957.—Smend, Rudolf. "Das Gesetz und die Völker." In *Probleme biblischer Theologie* (Festschrift Gerhard von Rad), pp. 494–509. Edited by Hans Walter Wolff. Munich: Kaiser, 1971.—Dietrich, Walter. *Prophetie und Geschichte.* Forschungen zur Religion und Literatur des Alten und Neuen Testaments, vol. 108. Göttingen: Vandenhoeck & Ruprecht, 1972.—Schmitt, Götz. *Du sollst keinen Frieden schliessen mit den Bewohnern des Landes.* Beiträge zur Wissenschaft vom Alten und Neuen Testament, 5th series, vol. 11. Stuttgart: Kohlhammer, 1970.—Von Rad, Gerhard. *Deuteronomium-Studien.* Forschungen zur Religion und Literatur des Alten und Neuen Testaments, vol. 40. Göttingen: Vandenhoeck & Ruprecht, 1947. English: *Studies in Deuteronomy.* Translated by David Stalker. Studies in Biblical Theology, no. 9. Naperville, Ill.: Allenson, 1950.—Wolff, Hans Walter. "Das Kerygma des deuteronomischen Geschichtswerks." *Zeitschrift für die Alttestamentliche Wissenschaft* 73 (1961):171–186. Reprinted in his *Gesammelte Studien zum Alten Testament,* pp. 308–324. Theologische Bücherei, vol. 22. Munich: Kaiser, 1964. English: "The Kerygma of the Deuteronomic Historical Work." In *The Vitality of Old Testament Traditions,* pp. 83–100. Edited by Walter Brueggemann. Atlanta: John Knox, 1975.—Willi, Thomas. *Die Chronik als Auslegung.* Forschungen zur Religion und Literatur des Alten und Neuen Testaments, vol. 106. Göttingen: Vandenhoeck & Ruprecht, 1972.—Mosis, Rudolf. *Untersuchungen zur Theologie des chronistischen Geschichtswerkes.* Freiburger theologische Studien, vol. 92. Freiburg: Herder, 1973.—Ackroyd, Peter R. "The Theology of the Chronicler." *Lexington Theological Quarterly* 8 (1973):101–116.—Von Rad, Gerhard. *Das Geschichtsbild des chronistischen Werkes.* Beiträge zur Wissenschaft vom Alten und Neuen Testament, 4th series, vol. 3. Stuttgart: Kohlhammer, 1930.

§21 Judgment and Salvation in the Preaching of the Great Literary Prophets

We have seen in §10e how the freedom of the God of Israel, whose name is "I am who I am," is reflected especially clearly in the person and office of the prophets. In addition, in the "word of Yahweh," which it is the particular function of the prophets to convey, Israel is confronted most directly with the God who also encounters Israel in his gifts and his commandments. It is therefore no accident that the essential features of the Old Testament faith in God are most sharply etched in the words of the prophets.

The prophetic movement of the great literary prophets grew upon the soil of the mantic and visionary charisma that initially can give advice in the minor concerns of private everyday life. Characteristically, however, this charisma developed in the Old Testament by becoming increasingly concerned with matters affecting "Israel" and those responsible for the populace. Even pre-literary prophecy demonstrates a special concern for the monarchy in Israel and Judah. As the accounts in 1 Samuel 9—11; 16 and 2 Samuel 7; 1 Kings 11:29ff. show, Israel's historical memory cannot even conceive of the establishment of the monarchy without the active participation and crucial legitimation of the prophetic word. But it is also the greatest of the pre-literary prophets, Elijah, after some earlier precursors, who radically impugns a royal house that has transgressed the principle of exclusive Yahwism by engaging in Tyrian and Canaanite religious politics (1 Kings 17ff.).

The great literary prophets then take the final and decisive step, challenging not merely a royal house but Israel, the people of God, as a whole, questioning its legitimacy before Yahweh, its God, who has shown his love for Israel in gifts and commandments. The tension implicit in the initially peaceful juxtaposition of gift and commandment is here actualized in the sharpest terms. Or would it be better to say that the second preamble to the Decalogue now rises in menace against the first?

a) Literary Prophecy of the Eighth Century

1. Amos, a shepherd from Tekoa in Judah, makes his appearance in Northern Israel without any apparent links with the past. It is true that from him we still hear an attack on the reigning king, Jeroboam II, under whom the country was experiencing a period of prosperity following a long period of oppression by the Syrians (2 Kings 14:25–27): "Jeroboam shall die by the sword." (Amos 7:11) In 7:9, the attack is expanded to include the entire "house of Jeroboam." But this threat, which was probably the primary reason the high priest of Bethel denounced Amos to the royal court, is embedded

in both passages in a threat against Israel: "Israel shall be deported far from their native land." In the concluding attack on Amaziah, the high priest at the royal sanctuary in Bethel (vs. 17), there is no longer any mention of Jeroboam, but the message of judgment against Israel is repeated verbatim.

When Amaziah orders Amos to leave Bethel, Amos concludes that Amaziah suspects him of complicity with prophetic groups from Judah; instead, he vigorously asserts his claim to have been called by Yahweh himself: "Yahweh took me as I followed the flock and said to me, 'Go and prophesy to my people Israel.' " (7:15) This is all Amos says about his call. In 3:8, however, we can hear clearly the menacing force of the divine word of judgment that the prophet hears: "The lion roars; who is not terrified? Yahweh speaks; who will not prophesy?" The immediacy of the prophet's encounter with Yahweh can also be recognized in the series of four visions, arranged in pairs (7:1–8; 8:1–2), followed in 9:1–4 (1, 4*b*?) by a climactic oracle depicting Yahweh himself in his sanctuary carrying out judgment upon Israel. In his visions the prophet also hears menacing words. Particularly impressive is the pun that transforms the "fruit" (קַיִץ *qayiṣ*) shown to the prophet in his vision into a threat of the "end" (קֵץ *qeṣ*) in 8:1–2. Amos proclaims the end of Israel as the message entrusted to him by Yahweh to deliver.

Scholars have made various attempts to go beyond the prophet's own words in seeking the deepest reasons for his appearance as a prophet, arriving at diverse conclusions: (1) He has been understood as the representative of a sudden new moral outrage over the injustices suffered by the people (Duhm, 1875). His prophecy of judgment is therefore a postulate of his ethos. (2) An attempt has been made to understand his God in terms of the category "absolutely other" (Weiser, 1929). (3) Würthwein has cited violation of the covenant law as the cause that forced Amos to speak out. Bach has attempted to pursue this approach further and show that the violation involved primarily the ancient apodictic law of Israel (as defined by Alt). In this interpretation of Amos as a cult prophet (espoused also by Reventlow), Bentzen has gone even further, claiming to find in Amos 1—2 (oracles against the transgressions of the neighboring nations) a ritual corresponding to the attacks on foreign nations in the Egyptian "execration texts." (4) Wolff is undoubtedly correct in maintaining that knowledge of imminent judgment is initially an elementary fact. He does not, however, accept the explanation of cult prophecy, preferring to understand Amos's wrath as deriving from the ethos of tribal wisdom. (5) Schmid finds in Amos's polemic the verbal expression of a universal human sense of divine order.

The words addressed to Israel are formulated harshly: "You alone have I known among all the nations of the world; therefore will I punish you for all your iniquities." (3:2) This statement shows that for Amos Yahweh's judgment springs directly from his relationship with Israel. The polemic exaggeration of 9:7 cannot be cited to the contrary; here, in order to guard against any confidence of being God's chosen people nourished by the exodus credo, Israel is set on a par with the surrounding nations that Yahweh had likewise led forth from foreign places of origin. Cf. the related attack of John the Baptist against comfortable reliance on descent from Abraham in

Matthew 3:9. Amos 3:2, by contrast, illustrates the terrible "election logic" of the prophet. The special nearness of Israel to its God leads Yahweh to conclude that Israel has special responsibilities. The prophet has a kind of "fundamental certainty" (Schmidt) that Yahweh judges the world; his judgment concerns Israel precisely because he has a special relationship with them.

In the prophet's description of the approaching judgment, it is striking how blurred and diverse the expected phenomena are in detail. Locusts (7:1) and drought (7:4) are threatened, although Yahweh does not carry out the threat. Earthquake (2:13; cf. 1:1) and plague (6:9–10) stand alongside the threat of deportation at the hands of enemies (4:3; 5:27; 6:7; 7:11, 17). Central to all the predictions, however, is the prediction of the "Day of Yahweh" (5:18–20). No matter how the judgment will appear when it is realized in history, it will involve encounter with Yahweh himself, who will pass through the midst of his people (5:17). There are no other descriptive elements describing the Day of Yahweh. It is the day on which all that matters is Yahweh's presence. The people obviously expect that Yahweh's presence will mean he has come to their aid (an idea possibly deriving from the notion of the Yahweh war [von Rad]). The prophet counters this belief with the presence of the judge, before whose judgment neither the palaces of the aristocrats (3:11, 15), nor the altars (3:14) and holy places (5:5) will remain oases of safety.

But even if judgment is a "fundamental certainty" for the prophet, it is not visited on Israel as an incomprehensible fate. Amos describes at great length the various loci of disease in the body politic of Israel. His allusion to the heartless acceptance of a poor person's cloak as security (2:8) derives directly from the requirements of the Covenant Code (Exod. 22:25). But his charges go far beyond the explicit demands of earlier legislation. In the very luxury enjoyed by the rich the prophet sees the heedless agglomeration of human selfishness. He mounts his ruthless attack not by citing the letter of the law as laid down in earlier formularies, but by freely actualizing the ancient meaning of the law of Yahweh in new circumstances, thereby announcing the coming of the God long known to Israel. Thus the polemic against the luxurious sacrificial cult of Amos's day takes issue explicitly with the ancient statutes of the people wandering in the wilderness (5:25).

The question of whether Amos sees a coming salvation of his people on the part of Yahweh once the imminent judgment is past has been discussed repeatedly. In 9:11–12 a Judahite voices the expectation that the Davidic kingdom will be restored and that the remnant of Edom will be subject to it. Amos 9:13–15 depicts the coming fertility of the land and reconstruction after exile. In neither passage do we hear the voice of Amos. Contrary to Wolff (commentary *ad loc.*), however, the torah in 5:14–15 should probably be ascribed to the prophet. Verse 15 states: "Hate evil and love good; enthrone justice in the gate; perhaps (then) Yahweh the God of hosts will have mercy on the remnant of Joseph." The "no" of Amos (Smend) is uncompromisingly harsh. The prophet must announce the end of Israel. But this end is not simply a fate that unfolds as predicted. When it is announced in the most fundamental terms as the "Day of Yahweh," we hear in the midst of it: "I, Yahweh." What the prophet announces is a confrontation with the living God. But because it is the living God, there is still room for a "perhaps" in the message of the prophet. Yahweh is still the personal lord of the announced judgment. In the first two visions of the prophet we could hear that Yahweh has the power to heed intercession, just as in the following visions he has the power to put an end to intercession. The prophet's call to do good cannot go beyond the "perhaps," peripheral to his admonitions, of divine restraint towards a "remnant" in the midst of God's judgment. But this "perhaps" guarantees the freedom of the God who comes to judge.

2. Not long after Amos, Hosea comes forward to prophesy against Northern Israel, of which he was probably a citizen. In the thematic richness of his message he far surpasses Amos and appears to anticipate Isaiah. In many passages, however, the sometimes extremely bad state of preservation does not permit a precise understanding of his oracles. Traditio-historically, he stands in the line of the pure Northern Israelite tradition. The credo of the exodus and wilderness constitutes the foundation for everything he says about Israel. The Zion tradition is foreign to him; the mention of David (3:5) is an interpolation from the hand of a later Judahite redactor, whose work can also be found in other references to Judah.

There is no account of Hosea's call. Instead, his book begins in chapters 1—3 with a subsidiary collection comprising a group of oracles (chapter 2) set in the framework of two accounts of symbolic actions (chapters 1 and 3). The accounts of symbolic actions address the theme of Israel's conduct toward Yahweh, which resembles that of a promiscuous (1:2) and adulterous (3:1) woman, whom the prophet takes as his wife at Yahweh's behest "at the beginning, when Yahweh spoke to him." (1:2) The oracles of judgment and salvation in chapter 2 deal with the same theme.

It is impossible to resolve with certainty the question whether the third-person account in chapter 1 and the first-person account in chapter 3 deal with marriage to one and the same woman or with two distinct marriages. The hypothesis that both passages deal with a marriage to the same woman is supported by the fact that both chapters refer to Israel and by the notion of Yahweh's inner faithfulness. This hypothesis, however, requires us to interpret 2:4 as referring to the prophet's divorce from his wife and 3:1ff. as an account of his return to the same wife. Since 3:1ff. contains no hint of such a "return" to the same wife, and in fact the MT of 3:1 ("Go again and love a woman . . .") points to a totally new event, many have concluded that there was a second marriage with a different woman, similar in character. A third possibility, finally, has been suggested: chapters 1 and 3 may be considered variant (third-person *vs.* first-person) accounts of one and the same event, a single marriage. In this case, the two accounts would be viewing the same marriage and its history from different perspectives.

The moral offensiveness of what is recounted raised the question even in ancient times whether we are dealing here with a symbolic action that was actually carried out or in fact with an allegory. Consideration of the purpose of symbolic actions (see above, pp. 103–104), as well as comparison with Isaiah, whose giving symbolic names to his children corresponds to the sequel to the marriage in Hosea 1 and was undoubtedly actually carried out (Isa. 7:3; 8:1–4), contradicts this hypothesis. More recent scholarship has attempted to evade the difficulty by suggesting that Hosea did not discover his wife's unfaithfulness until after their marriage, whereupon he came to understand the marriage *ex post facto* as a symbolic action commanded by Yahweh. But such reconstruction of the personal story of a Hosea who is initially unsuspecting and then horrified to discover the truth carries little conviction. A more likely solution is that the account refers to Hosea's marriage to a woman who had participated in certain baalistic customs popular among the people (sexual promiscuity at the sanctuary to insure fertility) and then interprets the marriage symbolically as referring to the relationship between Yahweh and Israel. This is the approach taken by Rost and Wolff; Rudolph takes a different approach. The statements in Hosea 4:4ff. favor such an interpretation.

The difficulty of reconstructing the biographical background to Hosea 1 and 3, which recurs with full force in the symbolic actions of Ezekiel, stands in contrast to the observation that the theological message of all the statements can be clearly recognized. This contrast leads to the realization that the author of the account of the symbolic actions is not interested in biographical details or the precise reconstruction of what actually took place in the symbolic actions. The biographical record has been swallowed up totally by the author's purpose of presenting the prophet's message and is sometimes almost unrecognizable.

In the case of Hosea, too, it seems that we can find traces of pre-literary prophecy, which in Elijah, its most powerful exponent, directed radical criticism against the royal house, in the background of his message. Hosea's first son is given the name "Jezreel," "for in a little while I will punish the line of Jehu for the blood shed in Jezreel and put an end to the kingdom of Israel." (1:4) This refers to the murders connected with the revolution of Jehu, which is reported with approval in a section of the Deuteronomistic History (2 Kings 9). But then there takes place immediately, as in the case of Amos, the extension to Israel, the entire people of God, that is typical of the literary prophets: Hosea's second child is named לֹא רֻחָמָה *lōʾ ruḥāmâ*, "Not Pitied" ("for I will never again show pity to the house of Israel"); and the third, climactically, is named לֹא עַמִּי *lōʾ ʿammî*, "Not My People" ("for you are not my people, and I am not for you"). This means, although the actual word used in Amos 8:2 does not appear, the "end" of Israel, which owes its existence to its being the "people of Yahweh."

It has been suggested that 1:9 originally read not "for you" but "(not) your God." If so, we would have here an explicit renunciation of the covenant formula in its precise wording from the mouth of Yahweh. Thus through the names of the prophet's children Yahweh speaks to Israel, of which he says in 11:1, recalling the credo of the exodus: "When Israel was a boy, I loved him; out of Egypt I called my son." And in both 12:10 and 13:4 we hear the solemn words of the first preamble to the Decalogue: "I have been Yahweh your God since your days in Egypt." In 13:4 (possibly paraphrasing the first commandment of the Decalogue in the form of a promise), there is added: "You know no god but me, and there is no other savior than I."

Israel is "not my people" because it has scorned the fundamental precepts of Yahweh and acted contrary to his commandments. We hear another echo of the Decalogue in 4:2: "Cursing and cheating and murder and theft and adultery. They commit adultery and pile one deed of blood upon another." There are specific references, no longer totally comprehensible, to violation of the covenant at Admah, a site on the Jordan (6:7), and to murder on the road to Shechem (6:9). But we also hear a more profound voice that goes beyond the individual commandments and speaks of a fundamental attitude: "There is no faithfulness (אמת *ĕmmet*) or love (חסד *ḥesed*), no knowledge of God (דעת אלהים *da' at ĕlōhîm*) in the land." (4:1) Hosea speaks of the last of these with particular urgency. We have already pointed out (pp. 144–145) that "knowledge of God" applies not only to intellectual "knowledge" but also to "acknowledgment" in the total conduct of the person concerned. The priests should be the particular guardians of such knowledge; the fact that they have failed their commission lays them open to a brutal attack in 4:4ff. At the same time, however, the profound disregard for Yahweh that betrays the absence of "knowledge" of him is revealed in the charge that the priests have not acted to restrain the "promiscuity" (זנה *znh*) of the women (probably baalized Yahweh worship) that takes place on the "high places," but have actually encouraged it. In this cult it is man in all his sensuality who is lord. Yahweh, who would like to be present with his people in genuine faithfulness, remains unknown, even when his name is spoken.

Hosea links this charge with a highly developed view of history. Israel's lapse into baalistic excesses stands out against the background of a favorable beginning: "I came upon Israel like grapes in the wilderness, I looked on their forefathers with joy like the first ripe figs; but they resorted to Baal-peor and consecrated themselves to a thing of shame [= Baal]." (9:10) Numbers 25 recounts an offense at this site, near the crossing of the Jordan. For Hosea it becomes the exemplary transgression that involves Israel in baalism. In 13:5–6, this apostasy is illuminated from another angle: "I knew [= chose] you in the wilderness; when they had pasture, they were filled, but when they were filled, they grew proud; and so they forgot me." The passage from the barren wilderness to the bounteous countryside that was the land of Baal, the passage from poverty to riches, is here recognized—in a way that has broader revelance to human life—as the place where God is forgotten. For Hosea, this forgetting of Yahweh includes other arbitrary actions on the part of contemporary Israel: devotion to the bull image at Bethel and other cultic symbols, in which a lack of "knowledge of God" is betrayed (10:5; 13:2); wilfullness in making political decisions, exemplified by the making of kings without inquiring into Yahweh's will (8:4); appeal to foreign powers for help (12:2). According to Alt, 5:8–6:6 comprises a short collection of oracles relating to the Syro-Ephraimite war (see the discussion of Isaiah below), revealing in its attack upon both Israel and Judah the inner bankruptcy of both states.

In this context, the questionable character of the patriarch Jacob, already noted in the patriarchal narrative of Genesis, where, however, it is incorporated into the optimistic account of Yahweh's promise, can be taken out of context as the terrible prototype of Israel's depravity. To cheat his brother and contend with God was Jacob's nature (12:4). No attempt is made to construct a theology of history that would reconcile the golden age of the wilderness with this primordial inclination of Israel toward evil in the figure of the patriarch. In 12:13–14, the prophet Moses who brought Israel out of Egypt is contrasted in a play on words as one who tended Israel with Jacob, who did service and tended sheep to win a wife. If these verses really do come from Hosea, they attest at most his high esteem for prophetic leadership.

All of this explains the announcement of God's judgment, which reveals that Israel is no longer the people of Yahweh and no longer deserves his mercy and pity. In Hosea's prediction of judgment, the natural catastrophes still found in Amos diminish in importance. But in Hosea, too, the haziness of the oracles predicting judgment (already noted in the preaching of Amos) shows itself, although in a different way. As the contemporary historical situation would lead one to expect, he speaks of conquest by the Assyrians (10:6). But we also find the threat of a return to Egypt (8:13). Both are juxtaposed in 11:5, where the contradiction is apparent. In addition, 2:16 predicts a return to the wilderness, and 12:10 a period of dwelling in tents as in the old days. But in Hosea just as in Amos this haziness in the description of the judgment stands in contrast to the absolutely unequivocal statement that the judgment will mean encounter with Yahweh. "I will be like a panther to Ephraim, like a lion to the house of Judah; I will maul the prey and go, carry it off beyond hope of rescue," says Yahweh to both opponents in the Syro-Ephraimite war (5:14). Again we hear the emphatic first-person pronoun, the "I" of Yahweh. Judgment is not catastrophic fate, but confrontation with the living God.

As the living God, however, he calls Israel to true obedience. Hosea 6:1ff. describes the worship of the people as they come before Yahweh with a moving hymn of repentance. But Yahweh recognizes how transitory the love (חסד *ḥesed*) of the people is, which vanishes "like the morning mist, like the dew that vanishes early." Elaborate worship is not what Yahweh commands. "Love is my desire, not sacrifice, not whole-offerings but the knowledge of God." Hosea, too, can use imperatives to express God's call: "Sow for yourselves in righteousness (צדקה *ṣdaqâ*), and you will reap what love deserves; break up your fallow—'knowledge' [?]—to seek Yahweh." (10:12) Here, too, we may ask whether such a summons makes any sense in the face of the announced end of the covenant and of Yahweh's mercy.

Hosea knows nothing of the whispered "perhaps" of Amos. Instead there erupts from his lips the same realization betrayed in the expansion of the second preamble to the Decalogue: wrath and love cannot be held in abstract balance. "How can I give you up, Ephraim, how surrender you, Israel? How can I make you like Admah or treat you as Zeboyim? [Gen. 19 speaks here of Sodom and Gomorrah.] My heart is changed within me, my remorse kindles already. I will not let loose my fury, I will not again destroy Ephraim; for I am God (אֵל *ēl*) and not a man, the Holy One (קָדוֹשׁ *qādôš*) in your midst and not a destroyer [?]." (11:8–9) Here the love of God, with all its passion, breaks through in all its illogicality (or, more accurately, its own peculiar logic). In a way that is quite unique this love is incorporated into Yahweh's designation of himself as the "Holy One." If chapter 14 derives for the most part from Hosea, we find the prophet in verses 5–8 giving a more detailed description of the future Yahweh intends for his people once the judgment is past.

This is the context in which the symbolic actions of chapter 3 and the corresponding oracles of 2:16ff. belong. This second account of the prophet's marriage to an adulterous woman, commanded by Yahweh as a symbolic action and here described as it actually takes place, represents this marriage, whatever its relationship to the marriage described in chapter 1, in terms of education leading to purification. The imposition of a waiting period on the prophet's wife means that Israel must live "many a long day without king or prince, without sacrifice or massebah, without ephod or teraphim," until it repents and returns trembling to its God. Hosea 2:16–17 takes up the notion of return to the wilderness, to the place where Israel's golden age had its beginning in the presence of God after the exodus from Egypt. Here, in extreme poverty once more, the people will be completely dependent on their God. He will speak to their heart and restore their vineyards. The valley of Achor, which had become a place of disaster when Israel first entered into Canaan (through circumstances recorded in Josh. 7), will become the "Gate of Hope." What will take place then is described in 2:21–22 as a new betrothal, in which Yahweh himself will provide the bride-price that Israel does not have in the days of Hosea: righteousness, justice, love, faithfulness, knowledge of Yahweh. And 2:25, even if not formulated by the prophet himself, says quite in the spirit of what has gone before that Yahweh himself will say to "Not My People": "You are my people," and "Not My People" will respond: "My God."

This is Hosea's message, when the Northern Kingdom of Israel is facing collapse, concerning the people of Yahweh, who founder on the commandment of their God and are faced with the judgment of rejection from his presence. Their only hope lies in the possibility that, once the judgment is past, Yahweh may turn the judgment into a new beginning through his own free grace.

3. Isaiah, the Judahite contemporary of Hosea, represents a very different tradition. He is a Jerusalemite. In his preaching the traditions elaborated
in §9 and §10c play a vital part. His prophecies parallel the entire history
of the last four decades of the eighth century, politically so momentous,
during which Northern Israel perished as an independent entity and Judah
came close to the brink of catastrophe. In the thematic breadth of his preaching he is related to Hosea. Unlike Hosea's oracles, however, Isaiah's prophecies can for the most part be assigned to specific phases of his ministry. If
Hosea surpasses Isaiah in the often disconnected passion of his preaching,
Isaiah surpasses Hosea in his rhetorical creativity, which exhibits an unusual
brilliance of linguistic invention.

All phases of Isaiah's prophecy exhibit a particular stress on the proclamation of Yahweh's actions in the history of his people and the Gentile
world, which is more often the subject of Isaiah's prophecy than of Hosea's.
This emphasis is especially clear in the account of Isaiah's call (Isa. 6).

The influence of this call can be noted in three ways in Isaiah's subsequent preaching:

1. In the Temple Isaiah experiences the presence of Yahweh. Therefore for Isaiah and his
circle of disciples Zion (the name is not mentioned in Isa. 6, but appears in the later oracles of
Isaiah) is the special dwelling place of God (8:18), where the precious cornerstone is laid for
what is to come, which faith looks forward to (28:16).

2. Isaiah's experience in the Jerusalem Temple continues to influence his message. In the
praise of the seraphim, he hears Yahweh called "Yahweh of hosts" (6:3; cf. 1:24; 2:13; 3:1,
etc.), the ancient name associated with the ark, in praise of the God whose glory fills the whole
earth. He uses the ritual category of impurity to articulate his own sinfulness: "Woe is me! I
am lost, for I am a man of unclean lips and I dwell among a people of unclean lips; yet with
these eyes I have seen the King, Yahweh of hosts." In a ceremony of cultic reconciliation he
experiences purification. Subsequently it is above all the category of holiness, expressed in the
Trisagion of the seraphim, that informs Isaiah's entire preaching concerning Yahweh, whom he
has seen as "King."

3. At the same time, however, the prophet's exclamation of terror shows clearly how strong
is his sense of unity with his people when confronted with the Holy One. It is characteristic of
Isaiah's preaching to call God the "Holy One of Israel" (1:4; 5:19, 24; 30:11–12; 31:1), a
designation reflecting all the inner tension of the relationship. The "Holy One," before whom
everyone unclean is lost, is at the same time the God who has bound himself to Israel. With
all Isaiah's marked dependence on the theologoumena of Jerusalem traditions, it must not be
overlooked that, at a time when "the two houses of Israel" (8:14) are still in existence, he
acknowledges in this designation the "God of Israel," whom he can also call the "Mighty One
of Israel" (אביר ישראל *ăbîr yiśrā'ēl*) in 1:24, recasting the ancient designation of the patriarchal
God. In 9:3 he also refers to Gideon's victory in a Yahweh war over the Midianites, a victory
that was won in the Northern Kingdom of Israel. With all his attachment to Zion, Isaiah
nevertheless has "all Israel" in mind in his theology.

In his call experience, the prophet receives a terrible commission: by his
preaching he is to harden the hearts of his people. The only protest Isaiah
can venture is a subdued "How long?" Yahweh replies implacably with a
reference to the imminent total devastation of the land. In similar fashion,
1 Kings 22:19ff. had spoken of the lying spirit in the mouth of Ahab's
prophets, which hardened his heart as he went forward to his doom. Even
if it is reasonable to suggest that Isaiah's commission was formulated in

consequence of events during the Syro-Ephraimite war (Schmidt), it nevertheless reveals in any case how Isaiah, like Amos, can proclaim the inevitable
catastrophe of his nation.

Here, too, however, it must be insisted that the prophet's message to his
people is not Cassandra's announcement of a fate that is sealed, but encounter
with the living God. That encounter is never fate.

Thus we see Isaiah go forth to proclaim his message in very specific
words of accusation and challenge. Isaiah's oracles are influenced perceptibly
by the oracles of Amos (Fey), in both themes and forms, especially in Isaiah's
early preaching; but in them Isaiah's own unique tones are also heard with
increasing clarity, and these are to be understood on the basis of his experience at the time of his call, when he encountered the majesty of the Holy
One, before whom all human hybris must vanish. Indeed, Isaiah's characteristic attack is just here—against every situation in which people assert their
autocratic independence.

In an oracle much more elaborately developed than Amos 5:21ff., he attacks the autocratic
temple cult of the "princes of Sodom" and "people of Gomorrah": "Who asked you to trample
my courts?" The oracle concludes with a concrete admonition to do what is right and champion
the weak (1:10–17). The indictment against the elders and princes in 3:14 sounds quite like the
words of Amos, but bears the specifically Isaian accent of lese majesty: "What do you mean by
crushing my people!" In 22:15–18, Isaiah attacks a high official who has proudly constructed
a magnificent tomb in the rocks. Isaiah's attack on the women of Jerusalem in 3:16–17, 24—
4:1, which recalls Amos 4:1–3, clearly illustrates his typical change of emphasis: judgment is
proclaimed against the women of Jerusalem not for their acts of social injustice but for their
arrogance in their fashionable pretentiousness, in massive "exchange" phrases that lead up to
ingenious wordplays ("instead of perfume the stench of decay, instead of a girdle a rope"). In
the "Song of the Vineyard" (5:1–7) we find an oracle that, in its gradual revelation of deeper
and deeper dimensions, can hardly be surpassed in the formal art of rhetoric. Starting in the style
of a flirtatious love song, it moves on to legal argument and finally to brutally frank and
inexorable proclamation of judgment, on grounds (quite in the manner of Amos) of disregard
for justice and righteousness (משפט צדקה *mišpāṭ, ṣᵉdāqâ*) and expressed in brilliant wordplays
(which might be faintly echoed by such pairs as "good/blood," "right/blight"). It has also been
suggested that we hear the peculiarly Isaian accent in the recasting of the refrain found in the
great strophic poem 9:7—10:4; 5:25–29 (?), which unfortunately cannot be completely recon-
structed in its original form. In place of the chiding "Yet you did not come back to me" of Amos
4:6ff., Isaiah uses the same verb to refer to the Lord who comes in judgment: "For all this his
anger has not turned back, and his hand is stretched out still." Subsequently Isaiah, like Hosea,
turns his attack increasingly upon the autocratic tendencies of the people to engage in politics
and make alliances without consulting Yahweh (30:1–2; 31:1). What ignorance of Yahweh's
true sovereignty is revealed when in the Syro-Ephraimite war Ahaz "rejects the waters of Shiloah
[the aqueduct at the foot of Mount Zion, probably referring to the God who dwells in Zion]
which run so softly and gently" and turns to the Assyrians, or later when the Israelites call on
Egypt for help, although "the Egyptians are men, not gods, their horses are flesh, not spirit"
(31:3)!

The judgment for such disregard of the Holy One is inexorable. Like
Hosea, Isaiah knows nothing of such catastrophes—so obvious to the rural
mind—as drought, famine, or locusts. The prophet of the royal city of Judah,
the keen observer of political events, appropriately depicts judgment as the

collapse of all forms of political authority (3:1ff.). In addition, once more like Amos, he takes up the central threat of the imminent Day of Yahweh. Again, however, in comparison to Amos 5:18–20 he makes a typical modification. The encounter with Yahweh, which constitutes the focal point of everything that will take place on that day, is depicted in 2:12–17 as total collapse of everything that was high, in the realms of both humans and nature. "Then man's pride shall be brought low, and the loftiness of man shall be humbled, and Yahweh alone shall be exalted on that day"—the "Day of Yahweh of hosts."

The early oracles of the prophet, down to the oracle of the "Day of Yahweh," speak of the coming judgment in somewhat vague terms. With the increasingly menacing entrance of the Assyrians into the political world of Syria and Palestine, Isaiah's oracles refer to them more and more clearly as the agents of Yahweh's judgment. In 7:18–19 (which is not to be emended as some critics have suggested) Yahweh is nevertheless depicted as whistling for both the fly from the streams of Egypt and the bee from the land of Assyria; in this juxtaposition we see once more the prophet's lack of concern with the specific details of what is to come. The message to be heard is that it is Yahweh who whistles for the enemies that will cover the land.

The freedom of the "Holy One of Israel" is also illustrated quite astonishingly, and in a way not found elsewhere among the prophets, in the announcement of Assyria as the instrument of judgment. In the brutal conduct of the Assyrians in their conquered territories, their inhuman method of deporting large portions of the population, their flaying and impaling and hanging of the conquered populace, which the Assyrian victory documents in their palaces have conveniently depicted for posterity, but above all in their blasphemous arrogance toward the God of Israel, the prophet sees the hybris against God of those who were called to be his instrument. And so Yahweh's judgment will also strike the Assyrian, who boasts of his totalitarian methods (10:5ff.). In Yahweh's land, upon Yahweh's mountains, he will be broken (14:24–27). No matter what happens in the course of history, Yahweh's plan will have the last word. Isaiah's preaching is dominated by talk of the "plan" or "purpose" (עֵצָה *eṣâ*) of the Holy One of Israel (5:19; cf. 14:26–27; 28:29), which remains secure despite the ambitious plans of the nations (8:10) and is carried out even though human eyes cannot penetrate the strangeness of what is done (28:21) and the wisdom of the wise fails before the wonderful mystery.

But there is still another side to this royal proclamation of Yahweh's perpetual freedom that has not yet been stated with sufficient clarity. This can be observed in a short survey of the prophet's preaching in its various historical phases.

The prophet's early preaching, probably recorded primarily in chapters

2—5, echoes in many ways the preaching of Amos against Northern Israel. It announces to Judah and Jerusalem imminent judgment and the Day of Yahweh. In his early years, Isaiah named one of his sons Shear-jashub, "A Remnant Shall Return" (7:3). Like 6:12–13a, which resembles Amos 5:3 and was originally probably an independent oracle, this name is to be interpreted as a sinister threat, like the names of Hosea's children. Decimation of the populace is imminent.

The events of the year 733 seem to prove that the prediction of divine judgment upon Judah and Jerusalem was true. In this year Judah is fallen upon by her two neighbors to the north, Aram and Israel. In their army they have a "son of Tabeel" who promises to go along with their plans for an alliance against Assyria. He is to be made king in Jerusalem in place of Ahaz, who is to be deposed. Isaiah 7—8, however, which dates from this period, reveals a surprising change in God's message. According to 7:3ff., Isaiah and his son Shear-jashub are to go to King Ahaz, who has been intimidated, and encourage him: "Be on your guard and keep calm, do not be afraid. . . ." In Deuteronomy 20:3–4, this is the function performed by the priest before a Yahweh war (see above, p. 62). And an oracle in the indicative is added concerning the plans of the enemy kings: "This shall not happen now, and never shall." Whence comes this unexpected shift to a promise of deliverance? The enemy kings think that, as one of their war aims, they can simply replace the descendant of David in Jerusalem with a foreigner bearing an Aramaic name. Isaiah counters this human arrogance that simply dismisses the promise to David (2 Sam. 7). Thanks to Yahweh's decision, the situation has been altered; now Ahaz and Jerusalem are faced quite unexpectedly with the chance to take refuge in Yahweh's promise of salvation. At this point we hear the momentous word "faith" (= confident reliance on Yahweh): "Have firm faith, or you will not stand firm" (see above, p. 147). In typically Isaian fashion, the name of the prophet's son takes on a new meaning in this context: it now contains the summons to be the "remnant" that returns to Yahweh.

The theologoumenon of the "remnant," which Müller thinks can be traced to the experience of wars of annihilation, probably antedates Isaiah (1 Kings 19:18 [Elijah]; Amos 5:15, etc.). Subsequently, in Zephaniah and elsewhere, it took on particular significance, especially in the self-understanding of those who had survived the catastrophe of Jerusalem and the exile.

We see in 7:10ff. how Ahaz rejects the offer; and according to 7:17, even though Yahweh will avert the immediate threat, Ahaz will once more be struck by God's judgment.

In this context, Isaiah announces to the king, in place of the sign that Ahaz himself has rejected, the imminent birth of a child, who shall be named Immanuel. The Hebrew text refers to the young mother as an עלמה *'almâ*, "young woman"; this was erroneously rendered by the LXX as *parthénos,* with the implications of a "virgin birth" that is totally alien to the MT. Interpretation of the child Immanuel is debated. Various theories suggest that he was another son of the prophet himself (8:3–4 undoubtedly speaks of such a son, born during the crisis of the Syro-Ephraimite war, named "Speed-Spoil-Hasten-Plunder"), a son of Ahaz, a future messianic figure, etc. (Stamm, Hammershaimb, Wolff). In any case, it is clear that the name "Immanuel" has beneficent significance. According to 7:16, the kings whose advance now seems so menacing will be totally gone by the time the boy begins to be able to distinguish good from evil. The name is certainly not to be interpreted as the mother's cry of terrible distress, or even as "God be with us," a cry of desolation. What does remain a matter of debate is whether "Immanuel" has beneficent significance beyond the immediate situation and is to be associated with the messianic oracle in 9:5–6.

We hear nothing from the prophet in the period following the events of 733. He and his children, however, remain "signs and portents in Israel." But his "teaching" is "sealed up" among his circle of disciples (8:16–18). The threat of Assyria hangs over Judah and Jerusalem once more.

If Alt is correct in suggesting that 8:23*b* belongs with 9:1–6, we hear in 8:23*b*—9:6 an oracle of salvation from the period between 733 and 722, addressed to the provinces of Northern Israel separated from the heartland of Ephraim in 733 and trampled by the boots of the Assyrian army. There are two significant points: the change to an anti-Assyrian attitude, and above all the full development of the promise of a descendant of David who will bring salvation. The faith in the validity of the divine promise to the house of David implicit behind 7:1–9 here expands into a full description of a coming savior king. The first of his four new throne names ("Wonderful Counselor") in particular contains echoes of Isaian language about how Yahweh acts. On the "wonder," cf. 29:14; on "counsel" (or "purpose"), see above, p. 193. He is further described as the savior king through whom will be fully realized the "justice and righteousness" no longer found in Judah and Jerusalem according to the Song of the Vineyard (5:7).

Isaiah's authorship of 11:1–8 is even more contested; there are also no clues to help date the passage more precisely. Here we find the striking image of a future king who will spring forth from the stump of Jesse. This image clearly presupposes God's judgment on the house of David. Once this judgment is past, Yahweh will send from the same house a ruler endowed with the true spirit of kingship. In the list of his endowments, the old dynamistic features of the "spirit" take a back seat to the charismata of wisdom, counsel, fear of God, and just judgment. The picture of paradisal peace extending even to the animal world, in which even the primordial feud between humanity and the serpent will be resolved, hints at the expectation of an end to the primordial suffering of creation depicted in Genesis 3:15 and 9:2–3 as the primal curse.

These passages display the fully developed expectations for the promise to the house of David current with Isaiah (and his school). In his later preaching, the expectation of Zion's deliverance comes increasingly to the fore. But this expectation is not to be taken in the sense of the massive unshaken faith in the Temple that Jeremiah must later attack in his Temple Sermon (Jer. 7:4, 10). The threat of Assyria remains, especially after the collapse of the rest of the Northern Kingdom in 722. According to chapter 20, for three years during the Ashdod rebellion (713–711) Isaiah goes naked and barefoot to illustrate how the Egyptians and Ethiopians, on whom Judah set its hopes as allies, will be taken into captivity naked and barefoot by the Assyrians. In the probably somewhat earlier oracle dating from the year of Ahaz's death (14:28–32) yet another totally different idea is heard. Faced with the threat of a new enemy incursion (by the Assyrians) from the north, Isaiah replies to the Philistine emissaries: "Yahweh has fixed Zion in her place, and the poor among his people shall take refuge there." Refuge in Zion is promised only to the poor, i. e., those who have renounced all forms of hybris. During the final phase of Isaiah's ministry, after Judah had taken the occasion of the transition from Sargon to Sennacherib (705) to revolt against Assyria, this message is directed against Judah and Jerusalem themselves. The presumptuous self-confidence of the politicians in Jerusalem is depicted in 28:14ff.: they think they have made a treaty with death and with hell, so that nothing can befall them. The prediction of the catastrophic results of these policies is preceded in 28:16–17a by these mysterious words from the mouth of Yahweh: "Look, I am laying a stone in Zion, a block of granite, a precious cornerstone for a firm foundation; he who has faith shall not waver. I will use justice as a plumb-line and righteousness as a plummet." To be poor, to have renounced hybris—so 28:16 interprets the words of 14:32—is what it means to "have faith." But faith would imply renunciation of the hectic mobilization and riding about described in 30:15–17, which can only lead to being pursued. "Come back, keep peace, and you will be safe; in stillness and in staying quiet, there lies your strength. But you would have none of it."

Isaian authorship of the great image of the pilgrimage of the nations to Zion, where God will instruct them in the ways of peace, is uncertain. It is found in Micah 4:1–3(4) as well as in Isaiah 2:2–4(5). There can be no doubt, however, that the belief that the law keeping peace among the nations will one day go forth from Zion is more appropriate to the circle around Isaiah than to that around Micah.

We finally come to the question of how all these elements come together in the preaching of Isaiah: prediction of Yahweh's harsh judgment upon his people who will not repent, together with a sense of the promise Yahweh has given to the place of his presence, which is a reality for the poor, for those who have faith and confidence. The oracle against Ariel (i. e., the city of the fire upon Yahweh's altar) in 29:1–7(8), which should not be fragmented, probably points the way. We hear a lament that the city of Yahweh's fiery altar, the city where David encamped, is under siege. It is Yahweh himself who has besieged her, who will set her ablaze indeed, so that all will be brought low in the dust (the old theme of the Day of Yahweh is once again present in full force). Then, however, Yahweh will fall upon the hosts of the hostile siege army so that they vanish like the dust, and the horde of nations encamped around Ariel will be swept away like a dream. There is no longer any mention of a royal messianic figure.

The last datable oracles of the prophet in 1:4–9 and 22:1–14 bring us to the time of Sennacherib's catastrophic attack in the year 701. According to Sennacherib's own reports, which are confirmed by 2 Kings 18:13–16 as well as by Isaiah's words, he laid waste to the entire countryside and, although he did not enter Jerusalem itself, forced the capitulation of Hezekiah, imposed a crushing tribute, and reduced the territory of Judah to the immediate environs of Jerusalem. The legend of Isaiah (chapters 36—37), a product of the Isaian school, saw in these events the miraculous deliverance of the city expected by Isaiah. In 22:1ff., Isaiah himself speaks sadly of the opportunity, lost once again, to be called out of this "day of tumult and of trampling upon the Lord, Yahweh of hosts" and into "weeping and beating the breast, shaving the head and putting on sackcloth," that is, what would finally have been an act of abasement before the Most High.

Thus at the end Isaiah stands once more before the mystery of his people's hardness of heart and the mystery of Yahweh's plan, which nothing can obstruct. The strange parable of the plowman in 28:23–29 recounts in its first strophe the various operations of the plowman as he plants his field; in its second, it depicts the various ways the crops are harvested, and confesses devoutly, in the face of this mysterious variety: "This, too, comes from Yahweh of hosts, whose purpose (plan) is wonderful, whose wisdom is great." It looks as if we can recognize here the meditation of the prophet on the mysteries of God's governance.

Thus Isaiah speaks of the freedom of the Holy One of Israel, who, though hidden to human eyes, unhesitatingly pursues his goal in the impenetrable mystery of his history with his people. But the prophet speaks thus not with stoic equanimity, but rather—as his statements in 8:16–18; 22:4, as well as 5:18–19 and 30:8–11 show—as one who is himself assailed, who suffers the anguish of the "Holy One of Israel" for his people.

4. Not Jerusalem itself but the countryside of Judah was the home of Micah of Moresheth, a town in the "lowlands" near the territory of the Philistines. He was a contemporary of Isaiah; according to 1:5–7 (if indeed these verses derive from Micah; cf. Fritz), he must have begun his preaching before the fall of Samaria (722). Jeremiah 26:18 confirms that he was still preaching when Hezekiah was on the throne. His closeness to Isaiah is indicated by the fact that like the latter he inveighs against the system of

landed estates and its injustices (2:1–2). The countryman living at a distance
from the city can be recognized in his statement that in both north and south
the cities (Samaria and Jerusalem; 1:5) constitute the focuses of sin. In massive invectives he speaks of the cruelty of the upper classes (3:2–4), the
venality of the prophets "who promise prosperity in return for a morsel of
food, who proclaim holy war against those who put nothing into their
mouths" (3:5), the unjust and venal rulers, priests, and prophets in Jerusalem, who lull themselves into a blasphemous sense of security, saying "Is not
Yahweh among us? Then no disaster can befall us." (3:11) These are the
same charges of violations against righteousness and justice that we heard
from Amos and the early oracles of Isaiah; they are spoken by a man who
can say of himself: "I am full of strength [a later hand has added 'of the spirit
of Yahweh,' in the sense of the earlier prophetical 'spirit' theology], of justice
and power, to denounce his crime to Jacob and his sin to Israel." (3:8) Of
his own call to be a prophet Micah says nothing.

But Micah, too, is a messenger of what Yahweh is about to do, not a
social critic. In an oracle that is unfortunately textually quite corrupt, dated
by Donner in the period between 724 and 722, by Elliger in the year 701,
he uses a series of wordplays on place-names in the "lowlands," his own
homeland, to depict the devastating invasion of the enemy. If we may follow
Alt's interpretation of 2:1–5, the prophet foresees a new distribution of the
land, which will dispossess the "property-butchers of the capital" who have
disobeyed Yahweh, taking from them the rewards of their dealings. The
most merciless judgment, however, as Jeremiah 26:18–19 shows, is reserved
for Mount Zion itself; there is no way to reconcile Micah's predictions with
Isaiah's expectations for the place of God's presence: "Therefore, on your
account, Zion shall become a ploughed field, Jerusalem a heap of ruins, and
the Temple hill a rough heath." (3:12) A good hundred years later, in the
time of Jeremiah, the elders of the countryside in Judah still recall that when
Hezekiah, the king of Judah, and all Judah heard this word from Micah "they
feared Yahweh and besought Yahweh that he might repent of the evil that
he had spoken against them."

Of Micah's oracles, which seem to have impressed his Judahite contemporaries more than the oracles of Isaiah, little has been preserved; most of
what remains is found in Micah 1—3. If 6:1–8 also derives from Micah, the
prophet would appear in verses 1–5 as the prosecutor in a legal case against
his people. Verses 6–8, in the form of a priestly entrance liturgy, bring to
our attention Yahweh's instructions to his people who are ready to offer
untold sacrifices, and refer to the commandment made known to Israel long
before: "Do justice (משפט *mišpaṭ*), love loyalty (חסד *ḥesed*), and walk humbly
[or carefully?] (הצנע לכת *haṣnēaʿ leket*) with your God." It has been suggested that we have here a summary of what Amos, Hosea, and Isaiah have
to say about the will of Yahweh.

Whether the messianic prophecy in 5:1ff. derives from Micah himself is a matter of debate. In its present form it has undoubtedly been subject to revision. If the future "ruler of Israel" is expected to come out of Bethlehem, "the least among the territories of Judah," this notion fits in well with Micah's renunciation of Jerusalem. At the same time, however, there is an inescapable note of trust in the faithfulness of Yahweh, who does not simply turn his back on his previous actions. David came from Bethlehem. With a clear allusion to the choice "in days gone by" of one who is to come, a shepherd is expected who will keep watch over Israel "in the strength of Yahweh." Here, too, in a fashion quite different from what was seen in Isaiah, the announcement of something new, in which Yahweh will bring his work to completion, is connected with a sense of present judgment, which leads initially into the depths.

Duhm, Bernhard. *Die Theologie der Propheten.* Bonn: Marcus, 1875.—Weiser, Artur. *Die Profetie des Amos.* Beihefte zur Zeitschrift für die Alttestamentliche Wissenschaft, vol. 53. Giessen: Töpelmann, 1929.—Würthwein, Ernst. "Amos-Studien." *Zeitschrift für die Alttestamentliche Wissenschaft* 62 (1949/50): 10–52. Reprinted in his *Wort und Existenz,* pp. 68–110. Göttingen: Vandenhoeck & Ruprecht, 1970.—Bach, Robert. "Gottesrecht und weltliches Recht in der Verkündigung des Propheten Amos." In *Festschrift für Günther Dehn,* pp. 23–34. Edited by Wilhelm Schneemelcher. Neukirchen: Verlag der Buchhandlung des Erziehungsvereins, 1957. —Bentzen, Aage. "The Ritual Background of Amos 1,2—2,16." *Oudtestamentische Studiën* 8 (1950):85–99.—Reventlow, Henning Graf. *Das Amt des Propheten bei Amos.* Forschungen zur Religion und Literatur des Alten und Neuen Testaments, vol. 80. Göttingen: Vandenhoeck & Ruprecht, 1962.—Wolff, Hans Walter. *Amos' geistige Heimat.* Wissenschaftliche Monographien zum Alten und Neuen Testament, vol. 18. Neukirchen: Neukirchener Verlag, 1964. English: *Amos, the Prophet.* Translated by F. R. McCurley. Philadelphia: Fortress, 1973.—Schmid, Hans Heinrich. "Amos: Zur Frage nach der 'geistigen Heimat' des Propheten." *Wort und Dienst* 10 (1969): 85–103. Reprinted in his *Altorientalische Welt in der alttestamentlichen Theologie,* pp. 121–144. Zurich: Theologischer Verlag, 1974.—Schmidt, Werner H. "Die prophetische 'Grundgewissheit.'" *Evangelische Theologie* 31 (1971):630–650.—Smend, Rudolf. "Das Nein des Amos." *Evangelische Theologie* 23 (1963):404–423.

Wolff, Hans Walter. "Hoseas geistige Heimat." *Theologische Literaturzeitung* 81 (1956):83–94. Reprinted in his *Gesammelte Studien zum Alten Testament,* pp. 232–250. Theologische Bücherei, vol. 22. Munich: Kaiser, 1964.—Rost, Leonhard. "Erwägungen zu Hos. 4,14f." In *Festschrift Alfred Bertholet zum 80. Geburtstag,* pp. 451–460. Edited by Walter Baumgartner. Tübingen: Mohr, 1950. Reprinted in his *Das kleine Credo und andere Studien zum Alten Testament.* Heidelberg: Quelle & Meyer, 1965.—Rudolph, Wilhelm. "Präparierte Jungfrauen? (Zu Hos. 1)." *Zeitschrift für die Alttestamentliche Wissenschaft* 75 (1963): 65–73.—Alt, Albrecht. "Hosea 5,8—6,6: Ein Krieg und seine Folgen in prophetischer Beleuchtung." *Neue kirchliche Zeitschrift* 30 (1919):537–568. Reprinted in his *Kleine Schriften zur Geschichte des Volkes Israel,* vol. 2, pp. 163–187. Munich: Beck, 1953.

Zimmerli, Walther. "Verkündigung und Sprache der Botschaft Jesajas." In *Fides et communicatio* (Festschrift Martin Doerne), pp. 444–454. Göttingen: Vandenhoeck & Ruprecht, 1970. Reprinted in his *Studien zur alttestamentlichen Theologie und Prophetie,* pp. 73–87. Theologische Bücherei, vol. 51. Munich: Kaiser, 1974.—Schmidt, Johann Michael. "Gedanken zum Verstockungsauftrag Jesajas (Is. VI)." *Vetus Testamentum* 21 (1971):68–90. —Fey, Reinhard. *Amos und Jesaja.* Wissenschaftliche Monographien zum Alten und Neuen Testament, vol. 12. Neukirchen: Neukirchener Verlag, 1963.—Müller, Werner Ernst. *Die Vorstellung vom Rest im Alten Testament.* 1939. Reprint, with additional material by Horst Dietrich Preuss. Neukirchen: Neukirchener Verlag, 1973.—Stamm, Johann Jakob. "La prophétie d'Emmanuel." *Revue de*

Théologie et Philosophie 32 (1944):97–123.—Idem. "Neuere Arbeiten zum Immanuel-Problem." *Zeitschrift für die Alttestamentliche Wissenschaft* 68 (1956):46–53.—Wolff, Hans Walter. *Frieden ohne Ende: Eine Auslegung von Jes. 7,1–7 und 9,1–6.* Biblische Studien, vol. 35. Neukirchen: Neukirchener Verlag, 1962.—Alt, Albrecht. "Jes. 8,23—9,6: Befreiungsnacht und Krönungstag." In *Festschrift Alfred Bertholet zum 80. Geburtstag,* pp. 29–49. Edited by Walter Baumgartner. Tübingen: Mohr, 1950. Reprinted in his *Kleine Schriften zur Geschichte des Volkes Israel,* vol. 2, pp. 206–225. Munich: Beck, 1953.

Donner, Herbert. *Israel unter den Völkern.* Supplements to Vetus Testamentum, vol. 11. Leiden: Brill, 1964.—Fritz, Volkmar. "Das Wort gegen Samaria." *Zeitschrift für die Alttestamentliche Wissenschaft* 86 (1974):316–331.—Elliger, Karl. "Die Heimat des Propheten Micha." *Zeitschrift des Deutschen Palästinavereins* 57 (1934):81–152. Reprinted in his *Kleine Schriften zum Alten Testament,* pp. 9–71. Theologische Bücherei, vol. 32. Munich: Kaiser, 1966.—Alt, Albrecht. "Micha 2,1–5: ΓΗΣ ΑΝΑΔΑΣΜΟΣ in Juda." In *Interpretationes ad Vetus Testamentum pertinentes* (Festschrift Sigmund Mowinckel), pp. 13–23. Edited by Arvid Kapelrud. Oslo: Land og Kirke, 1955. Reprinted in his *Kleine Schriften zur Geschichte des Volkes Israel,* vol. 3, pp. 373–381. Munich: Beck, 1959.

Cf. also the bibliography to §10d.

b) Prophecy at the Beginning of the Exile

With the catastrophe of 701 begins a period of more than half a century in which nothing is heard from the great literary prophets. History seems to have come to a stop for the remnant of Israel, ruled by Assyria, which, during the unusually long reign of Manasseh, suffered all the bitter religious consequences of being totally in thrall to Assyrian power. The word of God was silent. Things begin to change in the period of Assyria's incipient collapse and the new historical changes it signaled, which were subsequently to bring Judah to destruction. Once again, as in the case of Amos, it is during the reign of a particularly able king, recognized as righteous even by literary prophecy (Jer. 22:15b), that a new prophetic voice is heard, whose message is recorded in the corpus of the literary prophets.

Of the prophets involved, the voices of Zephaniah, Nahum, and Habakkuk are scarcely audible. The collection of prophetic writings contains only fragments of their work, distorted by much later editing. We will devote most of our attention to the preaching of Jeremiah and Ezekiel, who was himself part of the first group to be deported to Babylon.

1. Zephaniah's ministry should probably be dated in the early period of Josiah's reign. He actualizes the familiar picture of the imminent Day of Yahweh found in Amos and Isaiah. On a broad canvas he depicts both its universal dimensions and its specific effects on Jerusalem and its inhabitants. When the prophet calls for deeds of righteousness and singles out the humble (2:3), it has been suggested that we are hearing an echo of Isaiah's preaching. As in the case of Isaiah, the proclamation of judgment upon the nations

extends from Israel's immediate neighbors in Palestine to the great powers in Cush (Ethiopia and Egypt) and to Nineveh (Assyria). In its present form, Nahum's preaching is directed primarily against Nineveh. According to Jeremias, however, Nahum's original oracle, besides the threat against Assyria, contained an announcement of judgment against an Israel that worships foreign gods, violates the rights of the weak, trusts in its own skillful diplomacy, and lives in arrogant disregard of Yahweh. Habakkuk, the latest of these three minor prophets, announces the imminent invasion of the Chaldeans (Neo-Babylonians), probably speaking shortly before 605. According to Jeremias, here, too, a later exilic editor has eliminated what was originally an attack on the godless in Israel. Habakkuk 2:1ff. is significant on two accounts. In the first place, it gives us a glimpse of the almost ritualized "lookout" kept by a cult prophet "watching" for the word of God to come forth. In the second place, with its exhortation to wait patiently when God's oracle is delayed, it provides yet another reference to the freedom of Yahweh's word, which comes forth when and as Yahweh wills.

2. The determination of Jeremiah's own message encounters no small difficulty in the observation that substantial sections of the oracles in the book that bears his name have an unmistakable deuteronomic stamp, in both language and ideology (Mowinckel's source "C"; studied by Thiel from the perspective of redaction history). Even Jeremiah 1, the account of the prophet's call, which contains unmistakably Jeremian material, is not free of this influence. With a directness that leaves no room for a personal decision and against which the prophet's struggle is unavailing, it is revealed to Jeremiah in the thirteenth year of Josiah that even before his birth he was "known" (i. e., chosen) and "consecrated" (i. e., set apart) and appointed to be a "prophet to the nations." The worldwide scope of prophecy, which surfaced so violently in Isaiah's preaching, is here presupposed at the very beginning of the prophet's commission. In the initial commission "to tear down and to uproot, to destroy and to demolish, to build and to plant," if indeed these words do come from Jeremiah himself, a totally different tone is struck from that heard in Isaiah 6: at the very outset a commission to rebuild is visible beyond the prophetic announcement of disaster, even though only faint traces of it are recognizable in the prophet's subsequent preaching. In contrast, the two tersely reported visions, which are formally very reminiscent of the visions in Amos 7—8, clearly record the prophet's own message. After the fashion of Amos 8:1-2, an object seen by the eye is transformed through a kind of pun into a word heard by the ear: the שָׁקֵד *šāqēd* ("almond branch") brings to the prophet's ears the statement that Yahweh "keeps watch" (שֹׁקֵד *šōqēd*) over his word. For this prophet, too, the "word of Yahweh" is the great reality that determines his commission. That Yahweh "keeps watch" over his word means that his earlier message of

judgment upon the remnant of Israel in Judah is not forgotten. In a second vision, whose actual content is hard to reconstruct, the prophet sees a pot boiling over from the north; this vision leads directly into the midst of Jeremiah's early preaching.

a) This early phase, to be dated in the period before Josiah's reformation, appears with particular clarity in chapters 2—6. In it the prophet announces judgment upon Judah and Jerusalem in the form of an invasion by a mysterious "foe from the north."

There are echoes of Isaiah's preaching here (Isa. 14:31). But Jeremiah, a Benjaminite living at Anathoth, north of Jerusalem, is influenced particularly by the preaching of Hosea. Jeremiah's internal emotional conflict makes him personally reminiscent of Hosea. Like Hosea, Jeremiah speaks of a golden age of Israel during the wilderness period, which ended when Israel entered the fertile land and became devoted to Baal, or, as Jeremiah is fond of saying in his polemic, to "vanity, emptiness" (הבל *hebel*). Like Hosea, he refers less to social injustices than to the inward faithlessness of the heart (שקר *šeqer*, "lie," is one of his favorite rebukes). Like Hosea, he finds this faithlessness particularly in the baalized cult of the high places, where there is revealed the licentiousness of the unruly people, who run around like a camel in heat (2:23–24). Like Hosea, he maintains that not even the most moving hymns of repentance can disguise this faithlessness (3:21ff.). In a wealth of rapidly changing images his accusation against the sinful people pours forth. In a dramatic sequence of scenes in which one horrified voice follows hard on another the catastrophe of approaching judgment through the foe from the north is depicted.

In the oracles belonging to this first phase there is no lack of imperatives calling on the people to repent and change their ways. Borrowing verbatim one of Hosea's images (see above, p. 189), 4:3–4 begins: "Break up your fallow ground, do not sow among thorns, circumcise yourselves to the service of Yahweh, circumcise your hearts, men of Judah and dwellers in Jerusalem." The note of concern for the heart of his people and true obedience cannot be missed. Despite the harshness of the envisioned disaster, despite the lament over the people's "uncircumcised" ears (6:10), despite God's command to pour out his wrath upon the children in the street and the young men in their gangs (6:11), it is clear that Yahweh has not slammed the door. In all that comes, the Living One knocks at the door of the hearts of his people, waiting to be heard and obeyed.

b) The next striking observation is that none of the genuine oracles of Jeremiah can be interpreted with certainty as referring to the deuteronomic reform instituted by Josiah in 622. This means that Jeremiah became neither a partisan nor an opponent of the reform. Yahweh's word concerning Judah through his prophet is silent on this subject, which undoubtedly caused a radical upset in the life of the people.

Indirect evidence suggests strongly that Jeremiah was on friendly terms with the circles that instigated the reform. According to 26:24, it was Ahikam, the son of the reform chancellor, who protected Jeremiah after his "Temple Sermon," which almost cost him his life. According to 36:10, Baruch read from the scroll containing the words of Yahweh in the room of Gemariah, another son of the reform chancellor, who also appears to be wholly on Jeremiah's side in verse 25. And Jeremiah is also closely related to Gedaliah, the son of Ahikam and grandson of the reform chancellor, who was appointed governor by the Babylonians after the fall of Jerusalem and was later slain by a nationalistic prince belonging to the royal house (chapters 40—41). The positive reference to King Josiah in the oracle against Jehoiakim (22:15–16) points in the same direction. But nothing is mentioned beyond Josiah's righteousness and his advocacy on behalf of the poor. Nothing is said about the reform of the cult. It is not the prophet's office to address this subject.

This period probably does include the summons to "apostate" Israel to return (3:6–13) and the so-called Book of Comfort for Ephraim in those portions of chapters 30—31 that can be ascribed to Jeremiah. In the summons to return we have before our eyes the whole wretched story of "faithless" Judah, which echoes the early preaching of Jeremiah. None of this is retracted in the period of the reformation. But now there is no proclamation of judgment against Judah, but only a call to repentance addressed to what had been Northern Israel and is now an Assyrian province. The basic stratum of the Book of Comfort is addressed to Ephraim; it was later expanded by the addition of statements addressed to Judah. In the Ephraim section, coming salvation is announced to the defeated northern territories. Here, too, there is an unmistakable revival of Hosea's message (cf. 31:20 with Hos. 11:8–9). Josiah's expedition into the north has been seen as something akin to an attempted political realization of Yahweh's promise formulated by the prophet.

Jeremiah's silence during the actual period of the reformation raises the question whether we may not be dealing here with the same idea expressed by the "perhaps" of Amos 5:15, but appearing now in different form. It can be asked whether Yahweh holds back from sending the prophet to announce the doom of his sinful people (3:6ff. shows that this verdict upon Judah has not been reversed) as an expression of expectancy. Might the repentance and return of his people finally persuade him to "have mercy on the remnant of Israel"? God's desire to deal mercifully with Israel achieves full expression in 3:16ff. and chapters 30—31. Wolff has shown how the prophet's call to repentance goes forth against the background of God's gracious will; cf. 3:12, 14, 22.

c) Later, however, at least by the time of Jehoiakim's accession, the prophet's proclamation of judgment is once again in evidence.

The words concerning Jehoahaz, who was deported to Egypt (22:10 [11–12]), still express pure sorrow without any trace of polemic. But the beginning of Jehoiakim's reign brings us to the Temple Sermon (Jer. 7:1–15 [chapter 26]), which attacks the godless sense of security based on faith in the Temple and announces that the Jerusalem Temple will meet the same fate as the temple at Shiloh. In the fourth year of Jehoiakim (605), the Neo-Babylonian Nebuchadnezzar invaded the Syro-Palestinian world at Carchemish; with him reappeared the menacing power of Mesopotamia, which, under different leadership, had been Yahweh's instrument of judgment in the time of Isaiah. In this year Jeremiah received the command to write down on a scroll all the words he had previously proclaimed and bring them to the ears of the people: "Perhaps the house of Judah will be warned of the calamity that I am planning to bring on them, and every man will abandon his evil course; then I will forgive their wrongdoing and their sin." Jeremiah 36 recounts the passion narrative of the word of Yahweh, given concrete form in the scroll, at the hands of Jehoiakim, who burns the scroll. To justify this action, he says: "Why have you written here that the king of Babylon will come and destroy this land and exterminate both men and beasts?" (36:29) The oracles of Jeremiah contained in the scroll probably spoke of the "foe from the north" without further specification. In the meantime, history had given the prediction concrete shape: Jehoiakim can understand the threat of the foe from the north only as the threat of Nebuchadnezzar's approach. According to 2 Kings 24:1, he had unwillingly become Nebuchadnezzar's vassal; after three years of obedience, he broke away once more at the first opportunity.

From now on, Jeremiah's message is absolutely unequivocal. Jeremiah 36:30–31 shows that in this specific context the word of Yahweh could be directed once more against the king himself. Cf. also the collection of oracles "to the royal house of Judah" in 21:11—23:8. These, however, like Amos 7:10ff. and Hosea 1 immediately expand their horizon to include a threat against the entire remnant of God's people in Judah and Jerusalem. In 22:24–30 the prophet attacks Jehoiachin, who had been deported to Babylon. In the years that follow, Jeremiah devotes all his efforts to making the people willing to humble themselves under the judgment that has befallen them in the person of Nebuchadnezzar.

He calls for such submission in the fourth year of Zedekiah, when certain voices, supported by prophets in Jerusalem, seductively announce an imminent turning point in history and a conspiracy against Babylon is undertaken in Jerusalem with emissaries from neighboring countries. Jeremiah goes around with a yoke over his shoulders. With renewed authority he predicts the death of the prophet who opposes his message (see above, p. 106). He calls for such submission in his letter to the exiles deported in 597, whom he calls upon to settle down indefinitely in exile and pray for the good of the land in which they find themselves. Most forcefully, he calls for such submission in 589–587, when Nebuchadnezzar's army stands before Jerusalem. Only by capitulating can the king and populace at least save their own lives. But the same message is behind the admonition not to flee to Egypt after the murder of Gedaliah (42:1ff.). That the Babylonian is the executor of Yahweh's judgment is finally still the message when the prophet, carried off to Egypt against his will, announces Nebuchadnezzar's coming to Egypt to the refugees there who think they have escaped the Babylonians (43:8—44:30). Throughout all these events we hear the same unequivocal message: Yahweh is judging his people. Submit to the power that Yahweh has placed as lord of the nations and executor of judgment over his disobedient people for a period of three generations (27:7) or seventy years (25:12; 29:10).

This raises the question whether Jeremiah has any notion of a future and a restoration in store for Israel. The passages pointing in this direction in Jeremiah's own words are few. The symbolic action involving the two baskets of figs (Jer. 24) shows that the prophet's expectations along these lines centered on those who had been exiled to Babylonia. Only with those who had suffered the full force of Yahweh's judgment would any possible future be found. In the midst of the siege of Jerusalem, immediately before its catastrophe, Yahweh instructs him to buy a field at Anathoth from a relative who offers it to him as next of kin. In this act he hears God's promise: "The time will come [once more] when houses, fields, and vineyards will be bought and sold in this land." (32:15) If 29:11 is actually from Jeremiah, his letter to the exiles contains the promise that Yahweh's purpose for his people is "prosperity and not misfortune, a future [lit. 'end'] and hope." If 23:1ff. contains Jeremian material, the invective against the evil shepherds is followed by hope for good shepherds, indeed for a branch of David's line who will maintain justice and righteousness in the land and bear the royal name "Yahweh is our Righteousness [= our Salvation]." Here it is hardly possible to miss the muted polemic against the king named Zedekiah ("Yahweh is my Righteousness [= my Salvation]"). But in Jeremiah's own preaching this expectation of a righteous king hardly stands out as a major theme. The promises in Jeremiah 33 are undoubtedly of later origin.

Jeremiah 31:31–34, written in deuteronomic language, should probably be included among the later additions to the words of Jeremiah. It contrasts the old covenant made with the fathers at the time of the exodus from Egypt with a new covenant. The primary feature of the latter is that no one will have to teach anyone else to know Yahweh; the law will be written on people's hearts. This image depicts the new form that will be taken by the free obedience to Yahweh's commandment that springs from people's own internal impulses. To this same context of hopeful expectations, which contrast something new to what has gone before, belong the statements in 16:14–15 (= 23:7–8) to the effect that in days to come people will not swear by Yahweh who brought Israel out of Egypt, but by Yahweh who brought the descendants of the house of Israel "out of the land of the north and out of all the lands to which he had dispersed them."

Jeremiah's proclamation of judgment does not exhibit the same wide-ranging multidimensionality as the proclamation of Isaiah. His announcement of judgment is more unvarying. In his reflections on the prophets, which with his struggle against the false prophets occupy incomparably more space in his writings than in the writings of his predecessors, he sees the true prophet of Yahweh as being characterized "from earliest times" by a message of "war, famine, and pestilence." (28:8)

The unique contribution of Jeremiah's prophecy lies elsewhere. In it we see in an unprecedented way how the messenger of Yahweh's word, who enables Yahweh to be present in his word in the midst of his people, becomes a figure of shared suffering.

We already see in Jeremiah 1 how the prophet, suspecting the suffering in store for him, at first tries to refuse Yahweh's commission. The explanations of the coming judgment then illustrate his intense personal suffering under the incomprehensible obduracy of the people, who can no more change their ways than the leopard can change its spots or the Nubian his skin (13:23). Above all, however, in the accounts of Jeremiah's early ministry we can see how the prophet, envisioning the invasion of the foe from the north, feels their attack in his own trembling body: "Oh, the writhing of my bowels and the throbbing of my heart! I cannot keep silence. I hear the sound of the trumpet, the sound of the battle-cry. Crash upon crash, the land goes down in ruin, my tents are thrown down, their coverings torn to shreds. How long must I see the standard raised and hear the trumpet call?" (4:19–21) What he sees in his prophetic vision strikes him to the quick, and he cannot hold back his tears: "If I go out into the country, I see men slain by the sword; if I enter the city, I see the ravages of famine." (14:18) In his oracles the question form occupies an extensive place. Only in his writings do we find the emphatic form of the triple question (no less than eight times): "Is Israel a slave? Was he born in slavery? If not, why has he been despoiled?" (2:14)

But shared suffering also appears in other contexts than the announcement of judgment. It is not by accident that the book of Jeremiah (composed by his friend Baruch?) contains several passion narratives involving the prophet: the episode telling how he was put in the stocks (20), his peril after the Temple Sermon (26), the attacks of other prophets upon him (28—29), the passion narrative of the word of Yahweh recorded on a scroll (36), and finally the detailed account of events during the siege of Jerusalem (37—38) and after the murder of Gedaliah (42—44). These accounts cannot simply be ascribed to an awakening biographical interest. As chapter 36 illustrates especially well, they depict the suffering of the word of Yahweh and the suffering of the prophet on account of the word of Yahweh entrusted to him.

Even more striking is the fact that the oracles of the prophet include descriptions of his most private internal sufferings, recounted before Yahweh and lamented to him, the so-called "confessions" of Jeremiah.

The similarity of these passages to the laments in the Psalms has always been a matter of note, and has occasionally led scholars to deny their genuineness. Since Baumgartner's study, however, this view has been untenable. As in the Psalms, in Jeremiah's laments we find "enemies" against whom he inveighs passionately. We can see the persecution he suffered from his own relatives and also at Anathoth. But in these laments we can also see how Jeremiah drew life from his message, how it enabled him to pray for God's forbearance toward those threatened with judgment and was then repaid with their persecution, evoking passionate outbursts of anger.

The human persecutor is not the only enemy. There are sinister passages in the laments where Yahweh himself is subject to the accusations of the prophet who can no longer understand his purposes. In 15:15–18, expressions of utter rapture at having received the word of God are interspersed in a way not subject to the constraints of logic with bitter accusations that Yahweh has profoundly isolated his prophet by sending his word to him and laying his hand upon him, and set him apart from the normal life of joy and sorrow (16:1ff.). We are suddenly listening to a bitter indictment of Yahweh. In remarkable fashion, we twice hear Yahweh's reply to such an indictment: a reply that does not give quiet comfort but gives sharp correction and demands repentance (15:19–21) or even says that what the prophet has undergone so far is nothing compared to what is in store for him (12:5–6). The confessions end in 20:7–18 with the prophet's admission that he wanted to escape from his office and cease speaking in the name of Yahweh, but was then compelled once more to speak by a force that shook his body like a fever. Finally he curses the day of his own birth.

Never is a word spoken to alleviate his suffering, which strikes him as the riddle of prophetic life. Only twice, it seems to me, do we see how the prophet's suffering becomes transparent to him. In 12:7–8, Yahweh says in sadness: "I have forsaken the house of Israel, I have cast off my own people. I have given my beloved into the power of her foes. My own people have turned on me like a lion from the scrub, roaring against me; therefore I hate them." This statement suggests that Yahweh himself suffers when he brings judgment upon Israel. The same idea is expressed more openly in chapter 45, in an oracle with which Jeremiah comforts his faithful companion Baruch when the latter laments all the suffering he has been undergoing with Jeremiah: "What I have built, I demolish; what I have planted, I uproot. You seek great things for yourself. Leave off seeking them." (45:4–5) Here we can see, behind all the incomprehensible suffering of the world, the ultimate depth that constitutes the background of this suffering: Yahweh himself suffers in the judgment that he must execute upon his people. In the suffering of the prophet is reflected the suffering of God for his people. Thus the prophet's suffering becomes a part of his message.

3. Despite the many features that Ezekiel has in common with Jeremiah, this prophet, one of the group that had already gone into exile with King Jehoiachin in 597, is a fundamentally different figure. He exhibits none of Jeremiah's agitated suffering. According to 3:9, Yahweh makes his brow "like adamant, harder than flint." This is also the nature of Ezekiel's message. He has none of Isaiah's powerful eloquence, none of the human emotion that seems to make Jeremiah so much more directly accessible. Instead, this prophet with his priestly background has a special sense that Yahweh, despite the blows he is inflicting on his people, which at first glance appear so harsh, is in the process of revealing himself not just to this people, but to the entire world of the nations. The proof-saying, which characterizes Yahweh's actions as a mode of his free emergence ("They shall know that I am Yahweh"; see above, p. 20), is a characteristic form of divine utterance in the book of Ezekiel. This prophet's message has inclined some, *ceteris imparibus,* to call him the Calvin of the prophets: he is concerned above all else to defend the honor of Yahweh's name. This message, however, comes from the lips of a man who, in the forms taken by his prophetic experience, recalls in many ways the prophetic experiences common among the pre-literary prophets. An outstanding role is played by symbolic actions and visions that spontaneously run their course. In addition, the unaffected account of how the "spirit" or "hand" of Yahweh comes upon Ezekiel and enraptures him distinguishes him from the earlier literary prophets.

In his entire ministry, this prophet is a figure who takes the message of judgment proclaimed by the pre-exilic literary prophets and crowns their work by expressing it in the most uncompromising terms; by forcing Israel to face this confrontation with its God, he also helps Israel to survive the catastrophe of death and go forward toward new life.

The prophet's call (1:1—3:15) is reminiscent of Isaiah's call: both have a vision of Yahweh in all his glory upon his throne. The surprising element in the case of Ezekiel is that this now takes place not in Jerusalem but in distant exile by the river Kebar, probably the "large canal" beside which the exiles in the settlement of *tel abîb* gathered to worship (Ps. 137:1). Later editorial work on the part of Ezekiel's school has expanded the account of this appearance of Yahweh's "glory" (1:28) and rendered some passages obscure. The form in which the prophet then receives his commission to proclaim the word shows that we are already in the period when prophecy was expressed in fixed written form. (Did the prophet personally witness the scene described in Jer. 36 in the Jerusalem Temple?) The prophet is given a scroll "written all over on both sides with dirges and laments and words of woe" to eat—the translation of a metaphor (Jer. 15:16) into a vivid experience, a transformation not unique to this occasion. In the description of the contents of the scroll we can recognize the harsh message of the prophet, which he is to proclaim to the "rebellious house" (בית מרי *bêt mᵉrî;* 2:5, 7 and elsewhere). The message will evoke "dirges and laments and words of woe." Especially noteworthy is the repeated statement that Ezekiel is to proclaim "These are the words of the Lord Yahweh" (2:4; 3:11) "whether they listen or whether they refuse to listen." (2:5, 7; 3:11) The prophet's success in delivering his message is not to be judged by whether the people listen to him. His real responsibility, clearly reflected here, is to deliver the message in any case.

From Ezekiel, too, we hear the coming Day of Yahweh announced (Ezek. 7). The mountains of Israel, which had witnessed the worship of the high places in the predeuteronomic period, are threatened with destruction (Ezek. 6). Above all, however, the prophet's message, communicated in sometimes obscure symbolic actions and oracles, concentrates on the imminent fall of Jerusalem, the focal point of the "house of Israel." The name "Zion" does not appear. All those to whom the prophetic message is addressed, including Jerusalem, are called "Israel," the term for the nation as a whole.

Ezekiel 7, with its detailed description of "the day" (i. e., the Day of Yahweh), appears to be an elaboration of the catchword in Amos 8:2, "The end has come." Such persistent and detailed elaboration of a specific theme or image distinguishes Ezekiel strikingly from Hosea and Jeremiah, whose own oracles exhibit an extravagant wealth of kaleidoscopic imagery. The oracle about "death upon the mountains of Israel" in Ezekiel 6 depicts death reaping its grim harvest on the very high places where worship was offered.

The coming siege of Jerusalem and its fall constitute the theme of Ezekiel 4—5, a composition comprising three signs, in which 4:1–2 (3) illustrates the beginning of the siege, 4:9*a*, 10–11 its height, and 5:1–2 (3–4*a*) its end. The symbolic action of "packing up for exile" in 12:1–6 represents the deportation of the populace of Jerusalem; it has been expanded secondarily by interpretative material referring to the fate of King Zedekiah. The image of the "forest in the south" that is consumed by fire also signifies (according to the interpretation given in 21:6ff.) the conflagration of Jerusalem. By contrast, the symbolic action involving the two roads in 21:23ff. represents the advance of Nebuchadnezzar against Palestine and the decision of the king, arrived at by lot, to attack Jerusalem first rather than the capital of the Ammonites. The sinister image (suggested by Jer. 1:13–14?) of the cauldron containing pieces of meat, which is set over the fire until all its liquid has boiled away and the cauldron itself begins to glow from the heat (24:3ff.) depicts the fate of those who are trapped in the "cauldron" of Jerusalem. Ezekiel's use of the image of smelting (22:17–22) also belongs in this context. According to

24:15ff., the sudden death of the prophet's wife at the command of Yahweh becomes a symbolic representation of the fall of Jerusalem. Just as Ezekiel sits motionless and numb, unable to carry out the usual ceremonies of mourning, so the people will sit motionless and numb after the fall of Jerusalem, when the sons and daughters left behind by the exiles fall by the sword and overwhelming grief and anguish make them incapable of mourning.

When Ezekiel's message of judgment is compared with that of Isaiah or Jeremiah, we note a striking absence of any further hope for a real change in the course of history. For this prophet, already in Babylonia with the "vanguard" of those struck by God's judgment, all that is left is to depict the final plunge into the abyss by even the remnant left in Jerusalem. The various phases of this fall can be seen in chapter 19 in the retrospective lament for the deported kings.

More agitated are the accusations the prophet levels against Israel and Jerusalem, which make the harsh judgment of Yahweh comprehensible. But they, too, exhibit a harsh finality that no longer finds room for forgiveness for the land of Israel, for the city of Jerusalem and its sacred focal point, the Temple, or for Israel's king and his prophets.

We have already mentioned how the land of Israel was described in chapter 6 in terms of its high places where the people went after idols. Ezekiel's characteristic term for idols (גלולים *gillûlîm*) expresses, as already mentioned above (p. 118), all the revulsion of a priest for everything unclean. An all-out attack is made on Jerusalem, the "bloody city," in 22:1–16, where the prophet goes down a list (probably stereotyped) of transgressions referred to as "capital crimes" (see above, p. 134) and charges Jerusalem with having committed all of them. Ezekiel's attack on the sanctuary in Jerusalem is pressed in chapter 8, where the prophet is transported to Jerusalem and conducted by a road that leads up to the Temple itself and is shown four abominations: an altar far from the sacred precincts; worship of figures carved on the wall; women lamenting the Babylonian vegetation god Tammuz on the very threshold of the Temple; and men shamelessly turning away from the site of the divine presence to the east (toward the rising sun) in front of the entrance to the Temple building. The four transgressions are meant to express a totality to which there corresponds a totality of judgment. According to chapter 9, this judgment is carried out by six figures of destruction, who, "beginning at the sanctuary," slay everyone in the city who has not been marked by a seventh, priestly figure. This saved "remnant" of those "who groan and lament over the abominations practised there" (in Jerusalem) is not found anywhere else in the genuine oracles of the prophet (44:6ff. is undoubtedly from a different hand). In the context of chapters 10—11, which have been subjected to major editorial revision, the judgment culminates in the departure of Yahweh's glory from the Temple.

In 22:23–31, a "class sermon" has been appended to the charges against the bloody city and the image of the smelter: the various classes are charged with neglect of their duties, the princes (?), the priests, the officers, the prophets, the rural aristocracy. The prophets, both men and women (the latter engaged in the practice of magic), are attacked in Ezekiel 13. The harshest and most concrete charges, however, are leveled against King Zedekiah, who did not keep his vassal oath, sworn by Yahweh, to the Babylonian king and who therefore faces judgment. Cf. also 21:30–32.

These forms of attack take specific individual transgressions as their point of departure. In addition we find a unique feature of Ezekiel's preaching: large-scale historical schemata in which Israel is charged with sin in the temporal dimension of its history. Preliminary stages can be found in Hosea,

Isaiah (1:21–26), and Jeremiah. But Ezekiel, living in exile with the entire history of Israel complete before his eyes to meditate upon, far surpasses his predecessors in the breadth with which he depicts this history and above all in the absolute rigor of his charges. Unlike his three predecessors, he cannot find any period in which Israel exhibited genuine love for its God. The imagery for these schemata, which are often extended metaphors, was taken by the prophet from traditional material.

Chapter 15 cannot be considered a fully developed historical schema. The prophet uses the venerable image of a vine for Jerusalem, but now treats it merely as a piece of wood to show how totally useless the city is, especially after having been "charred" during the events of 597. Thus he destroys all Jerusalem's pride in being God's chosen city, a pride expressed through this same image (Ps. 80) when the vine is thought of in terms of the noble fruit it bears. In Ezekiel 16 and 23, it is the marriage image borrowed from Hosea and Jeremiah that the prophet develops. In 16, Jerusalem is depicted as a foundling, exposed at birth and taken in by Yahweh: the city's Canaanite parentage leads us to expect nothing better than the wicked lasciviousness Jerusalem has exhibited in its participation in godless cults. "Like mother, like daughter," maintains the proverb in 16:44. In Ezekiel 23, the image is elaborated along the lines of Jeremiah 3:6ff. so as to refer to the two kingdoms of Israel, here depicted as two bedouin girls named Oholah and Oholibah. Their sexual debauchery even in Egypt is described in terminology that draws on the ancient credo. As in Jeremiah, the conduct of the younger sister is depicted in darker terms than that of the Northern Kingdom, whose fall should have served as a warning to her sister. Unlike Jeremiah 3, however, the whole section leads up to an accusation that the Southern Kingdom is reviving its ancient fornication with Egypt in its Egyptian conspiracies, which according to chapter 17 also determine the conduct of Zedekiah. This historical transgression turns "Egypt," which, within the context of the credo, recalls Yahweh's initial miracle on behalf of his people, into a catchword for the present sinfulness of Israel itself. The narrative contained in 20:1–31, recounted without benefit of imagery, cannot be surpassed for its radical approach to Israel's history. It limits itself to describing the period of the exodus and Israel's wanderings in the desert (27–29 constitutes a later addition), and reveals how even in Egypt and again in the first and second generations of the desert Israel rebelled against Yahweh and disobeyed his commandments. Therefore Yahweh had to threaten increasingly severe punishment. According to 20:23–24, Yahweh decides as early as the end of the desert period to scatter Israel among the nations. He even—an unprecedented statement unique in the Old Testament—gives Israel commandments that are not good, by which they could not win life. Here he has in mind the commandment that all human firstborn are to be sacrificed, the literal fulfillment of which (as by Ahaz and Manasseh; see above, p. 178 can only be viewed as a terrible sin. Here the prophet acknowledges the enigmatic fact that a commandment given by God can be an occasion of human sin, an enigma that Paul, too, reflects on after his own fashion in the light of the revelation of Christ (Rom. 7).

In these historical schemata all the self-righteousness of Israel and Jerusalem is radically shattered. The sinfulness of the present is not just an episode but a revelation of what has been at work in Israel since the beginnings of its history. What Hosea has to say about the patriarch Jacob (12:4) is here applied to the entire history of Israel.

Therefore the total execution of God's judgment is inescapable. Ezekiel 33:21–22 recounts tersely how an eyewitness brings the prophet news of the fall of Jerusalem. Ezekiel's mouth, until that moment incapable of speech, is opened once more. The prophet's renewed ability to speak has a deeper significance. According to 12:21–25 and 12:26–28, the unbelieving people had denied the immediacy of the demonstration of Yahweh's judgment. Now the truth of Yahweh's word has been demonstrated and the prophet who had proclaimed this word can once more "open his mouth" in confidence (cf. 29:21).

The oracles against the foreign nations in Ezekiel 25—32, including the oracles against Egypt in 29—32, which the unusually abundant chronological references date quite close to the fall of Jerusalem, exhibit few points of contact with any specific message for Israel. The haughtiness of Egypt as a great power and of Tyre as a center of commerce, the seductive policies of Egypt toward the house of Israel, and the gloating of Israel's neighbors over the fall of Jerusalem are here threatened with judgment by Yahweh, who is also lord of the Gentile nations. Taken as a whole, however, Ezekiel's preaching concerning the nations remains somewhat schematic and cannot be compared to Yahweh's personal intercourse with his own people.

Even after 587, it can be seen that the prophet continues in all severity to threaten Yahweh's judgment whenever people do not truly accept his judgment or, out in the countryside, engage in a dangerous "Biblicism," comforting themselves by recalling Abraham and evading God's judgment (33:24).

At the same time, however, an entirely different note is suddenly struck. When the people around the prophet, shattered by the catastrophe, have ceased to believe in any future (33:10; 37:11), Yahweh begins to speak with a new voice. The most powerful example is 37:1–14; the imagery of this passage once more grows out of the despairing statement in 37:11, which is overheard by the prophet, for whom it becomes a visionary reality. The prophet is commanded to proclaim the word of Yahweh over a field full of desiccated skeletons. As he speaks, the dead bones begin to turn into living bodies; this vision is interpreted to him as a promise that Yahweh means to bring the house of Israel forth from their graves once more. The category of new creation (although the word "create" is not used), in which Yahweh after the manner of Genesis 2:7 turns dead bones once more into bodies and breathes the breath of life into them, is used as a way of understanding the newly promised life of Israel.

Other oracles of the prophet, which have manifestly been expanded in the tradition of his school, depict this coming life in its totality. In a symbolic action that recalls the earlier symbolic actions of the prophet, two pieces of wood are joined together, one inscribed "Judah and his associates of Israel," the other "Joseph and all his associates of Israel," thus announcing the reunification of the two separated portions of Israel. They will once more be a single nation. And they will have one king, Yahweh's servant David, to be their shepherd. Here and in chapter 34, where the good shepherding of Yahweh is contrasted at length to the evil shepherds of Israel, and the coming of the one shepherd David is announced, there is no further speculation over the possibility and nature of this David redivivus. Like the blessing of fertility once more to be bestowed on the land, which will even include peace among the wild beasts (34:28), this lies in the power of the Lord of Israel, who makes all things new.

Of particular importance for the later (late exilic) prophet Deutero-Isaiah is Ezekiel 20:32–44, God's counter to the wicked history of Israel's beginnings. Once more this oracle takes as its point of departure an Israel

that presumes itself lost and that wants to be left alone: "Let us become like
the nations and tribes of other lands and worship wood and stone." But here,
too, Yahweh commands his prophet to announce his new act of creation,
which begins once more from the beginning. "I will reign over you with a
strong hand, with arm outstretched and wrath outpoured." This is the only
passage in which Ezekiel speaks of Yahweh ruling as king. His kingship will
be demonstrated in a new exodus, in which the scattered people of Israel will
be gathered out of all the nations. The echo of earlier exodus terminology
is unmistakable, as is the unique emphasis of Ezekiel. Yahweh will bring them
out into the "wilderness of the peoples," just as he once brought their
ancestors into the "wilderness of Egypt." There he will confront them. Like
a shepherd he will pass them "under the rod"—in Matthew 25:32-33, Jesus
speaks in similar terms of dividing the sheep from the goats when the Son
of Man comes to judgment. But the destination to which they will be led is
Yahweh's "holy hill, the lofty hill of Israel," where Israel will offer pleasing
sacrifices to its God and recall the time of its sinfulness with profound shame.

The expectation of a new sanctuary received its full development in the great concluding
vision of the book of Ezekiel, which has been enriched secondarily by much later material. The
prophet beholds the new sanctuary of Israel high upon the mountain, laid out with regular
dimensions and with a clear distinction between what is sacred and what is profane. Here the
expectation of something new is interwoven with the planning of the exiles, which probably
went as far as concrete sketches. The crucial point, however, is made in 43:1ff. The prophet sees
how the glory of Yahweh returns to this place and hears how Yahweh promises to dwell in the
midst of the Israelites forever. Proceeding from this place of God's presence the prophet then
sees a river (the mythological element of the river of paradise found in Gen. 2:10-14 and Ps.
46:5 is here given a specific eschatological interpretation), which swells from a tiny stream to
a mighty torrent. With its healing power it even restores the Dead Sea, that geographical enigma
of the land of Yahweh, so that fish abound in it. A later hand has added a new division of the
land to this vision of the territory surrounding the sanctuary, making corrections in the ancient
apportionment to the tribes of Israel (see above, p. 66). Besides the portions of the twelve tribes,
a thirteenth is set apart as a "sacred reserve," with room for the Temple, the priests, and the
Levites, and also, at a proper distance from the sacred center, for "the city" and the territory
of the prince. The final supplementer (48:30-35) has abolished the separation between "city"
and sanctuary, as do Deutero- and Trito-Isaiah, and given the city with its twelve gates the name
"Yahweh is there."

But the rebuilding involves more than externals. There is a corresponding promise that Yahweh will remake the innermost nature of humanity,
taking his people's hearts of stone out of their bodies and giving them hearts
of flesh, so that they may be enabled to keep his commandments (11:19-20;
36:25ff.). This is the same promise made in Jeremiah 31:31ff., stated in
somewhat different terms. A new, eternal covenant of salvation is also mentioned in Ezekiel 16:60; 34:25; 37:26, in contexts that can be ascribed to
editorial expansions made by the circle of the prophet's disciples.

How does Yahweh come to offer his people a new beginning after their
boasting has been so totally confounded? Ezekiel answers this question quite

directly. The history of Yahweh with his people is recapitulated once more in 36:16ff. Because of Israel's uncleanness, this history had to end with their being scattered among the Gentiles. The malicious comment of the Gentiles is recorded: "These are the people of Yahweh, and they had to leave his land." (36:20) But then Yahweh has regrets on account of his holy name, which is profaned among the Gentile nations by Israel. Therefore Yahweh begins once more with a new beginning: "It is not for your sake, you Israelites, that I am acting, but for the sake of my holy name, which you have profaned among the peoples where you have gone. I will hallow my great name, which has been profaned among those nations. When they see that I reveal my holiness through you, the nations will know that I am Yahweh." This is not the tone of irresistible love found in Hosea and Jeremiah. Neither is it the majesty of divine purpose spoken of by Isaiah. But when we read here that Yahweh has regrets on account of his name, we must accept without discussion that his name is "Yahweh, the God of Israel." To this name he remains faithful. Because he remains faithful to his name and thus to himself, he does not reject his people so as to begin something different somewhere else; even in his new beginning he remains "Yahweh, the God of Israel." This is the message of the prophet of the early exile.

One aspect of this message has not yet been touched on. Ezekiel is living among the exiles. Their resignation he counters by announcing that Yahweh is about to do something new in the new exodus, the new Temple, and the new hearts he will give his people. Their question must be: Then what must we do today? Ezekiel 18 and 33:10–20 show how the prophet deals with this question. Both units take as their point of departure words spoken by the demoralized people, so that it is not appropriate to deny Ezekiel's authorship of them on form-critical grounds and postulate a "Deutero-Ezekiel" (Schulz). Ezekiel 18:2 cites a cynical and sarcastic proverb: "The fathers have eaten sour grapes, and the children's teeth are set on edge." Could not this sense of resignation very well derive from the prophet's preaching that Israel had been radically rebellious from the beginning? The discussion in 18:1–20 attempts to destroy this fatalism by using three generations (father, son, and grandson) to illustrate how Yahweh accords life or death to each individual depending on his own personal obedience or disobedience. A series of commandments is used to clarify the meaning of obedience and disobedience. The initial points in 18:5–9 show that this series derives from the practice of the Temple, where the individual was questioned about his conduct and was then accorded the priestly declaration, "He is righteous, he may enter into the realm of life" (see above, p. 143). By means of such a series of commandments the prophet seeks to make clear to the inquirers in exile what the will of Yahweh is and how it includes the promise of life for each individual, regardless how his father may have lived.

But it was also possible for the individual not to set himself cynically apart from his "fathers," but rather to be very personally aware of his own guilt and to confess it. Thus we hear in 33:10: "We are burdened by our sins and offenses; we are pining away because of them; we despair of life." In this situation the prophet proclaims Yahweh's will even more audaciously. In Yahweh's eyes, even a person's past does not bind the person as an inexorable fate. "As I live, says Lord Yahweh, I have no desire for the death of the wicked. I would rather that a wicked man should mend his ways and live. Give up your evil ways, give them up; O Israelites, why should you die?" Then, after the casuistic fashion of school instruction, both 18:21ff. and 33:12ff. discuss in detail how one's past does not fatalistically determine one's present. The righteous man who supposes that his righteousness of yesterday lets him take the path of the godless today will not live; neither is it necessary that the godless man who repents today and seriously returns to Yahweh (in this context 33:14–15 cites the same two specific commandments already found in 18:7) should perish on account of his wickedness of yesterday.

Yahweh's merciful love for the individual opens the door to life in the present moment. This statement expresses the fact that even behind the inflexible preaching of Ezekiel, totally dominated by the honor of Yahweh's name, Yahweh remains the God of Israel, who does not demand the death of the wicked but calls them to repentance and return.

This sense of Yahweh's merciful love stands out, finally, in a striking second definition of the prophet's calling. The full account is found in 33:1–9, but the redactor of the book has appended a shorter recension in 3:16–21 to the first account of Ezekiel's call. The prophet is told that he is to understand his office as a watchman or warner. This image was already used in Jeremiah 6:17 for the prophets in general. Like the watchman on the wall who warns a city of approaching danger, Ezekiel is personally obligated to warn the individual whose unrighteousness is endangering his life and thus bring him to repentance. How strange a God this is, who appoints men to give warning of his own approach so that his judgment can be stayed! The second call of the prophet is clearly linked to the call at the beginning of his ministry (recounted in 1:1—3:15) by the appearance once more of reflection on his sphere of responsibility. He is to give warning. Whether his warning is heeded is not his responsibility. But woe to him if he fails to give warning!

This is the mandate of the prophet Ezekiel in the period of reorganization and of expectant waiting for the salvation announced to the people by Yahweh. To Ezekiel's message to Israel is added his ministry to the individual Israelites who look forward with him expectantly to the future.

Jeremias, Jörg. *Kultprophetie und Gerichtsverkündigung in der späten Königszeit.* Wissenschaftliche Monographien zum Alten und Neuen Testament, vol. 35. Neukirchen: Neukirchener Verlag, 1970.

Mowinckel, Sigmund Olaf. *Zur Komposition des Buches Jeremia.* Videnskapsselskapets skrifter; II. Hist.-filos. klasse, 1913, no. 5. Kristiania: Dybwad, 1914.—Thiel, Winfried. *Die deuteronomistische Redaktion von Jeremia 1—25.* Wissenschaftliche Monographien zum Alten und Neuen Testament, vol. 41. Neukirchen: Neukirchener Verlag, 1973.—Bach, Robert. "Bauen und Pflanzen." In *Studien zur Theologie der alttestamentlichen Überlieferungen* (Festschrift Gerhard von Rad), pp. 7–32. Edited by Rolf Rendtorff and Klaus Koch. Neukirchen: Neukirchener Verlag, 1961.—Gross, K. "Hoseas Einfluss auf Jeremias Anschauung." *Neue kirchliche Zeitschrift* 42 (1931):241–255, 327-343.—Wolff, Hans Walter. "Das Thema 'Umkehr' in der alttestamentlichen Prophetie." *Zeitschrift für Theologie und Kirche* 48 (1951):129–148. Reprinted in his *Gesammelte Studien zum Alten Testament,* pp. 130–150. Theologische Bücherei, vol. 22. Munich: Kaiser, 1964.—Herrmann, Siegfried. *Die prophetischen Heilserwartungen im Alten Testament.* Beiträge zur Wissenschaft vom Alten und Neuen Testament, 5th series, vol. 5. Stuttgart: Kohlhammer, 1965. —Kremers, Heinz. "Leidensgemeinschaft mit Gott im Alten Testament." *Evangelische Theologie* 13 (1953):122–140.—Baumgartner, Walter. *Die Klagegedichte des Jeremia.* Beihefte zur Zeitschrift für die Alttestamentliche Wissenschaft, 32. Giessen: Töpelmann, 1917.—Von Rad, Gerhard. "Die Konfessionen Jeremias." *Evangelische Theologie* 3 (1936):265–276. Reprinted in his *Gesammelte Studien zum Alten Testament,* vol. 2, pp. 224–235. Theologische Bücherei, vol. 48. Munich: Kaiser, 1973.—Stoebe, Hans Joachim. "Seelsorge und Mitleiden bei Jeremia." *Wort und Dienst* 4 (1955):116–134.

Zimmerli, Walther. *Ezechiel: Gestalt und Botschaft.* Biblische Studien, vol. 62. Neukirchen: Neukirchener Verlag, 1972.—Idem. Bibliography in Biblischer Kommentar, vol. 13, pp. 120*-130*.—Schulz, Hermann. *Das Todesrecht im Alten Testament.* Beihefte zur Zeitschrift für die Alttestamentliche Wissenschaft, vol. 114. Berlin: Töpelmann, 1969.

Cf. also the bibliographies to §10d and §21c.

c) Late Exilic and Postexilic Prophecy

1. In Deutero-Isaiah, during the late exilic period when Israel was living through the darkest night of its history, we encounter the "evangelist" (i. e., bearer of good news) of the Old Testament. In his tumultuously exultant message he seems worlds apart from Ezekiel. And yet it is unmistakably true that elements of Ezekiel's message, albeit in a totally different guise, achieve their full flowering in him (Baltzer; for discussion of the form of the oracles, see especially Begrich).

There is no narrative account, not even a separate superscription, to introduce the unknown author of Isaiah 40—55. It seems that only in 40:6–8 do we find a hint of his encounter with Yahweh at his call. In this passage, as in all the rest of the collection of oracles, there is no trace of any visionary element. Everything has become auditory. He hears the divine summons, "Preach (cry)!" He responds with a confession of human helplessness: "What shall I preach (cry)?" However the following passage is assigned— whether it begins with further statements of human helplessness (as the *Zürcher Bibel* translates) or whether everything that follows, including what appear to be later additions, is God's reply (as most exegetes maintain)—it is clear in any case that the divine reply contrasts human perishableness, which resembles the flowers that fade, to God's word, which endures forever. Yahweh spoke in similar terms to Jeremiah in his initial vision (Jer. 1:11–12), saying that he was keeping watch over his word. And in Ezekiel we repeatedly hear the formalized statement that what Yahweh says, he does (12:25, 28; 17:24, and elsewhere).

The enduring validity of God's word constitutes a fundamental element in the message of Deutero-Isaiah, as is shown in the first place by the forensic polemic against the gods, which demonstrate the superiority of Yahweh by referring to his word, which governs the course of history (see below). It is also indicated by 55:8–13, a discussion of the word of Yahweh that concludes the entire collection. The word of Yahweh, we hear in this passage, proceeding from the exalted thoughts of Yahweh that surpass all human understanding, resembles the snow and rain that fall upon the earth and do not return without engendering fertility there. The word of Yahweh is the real power that shapes history, remaining constant in the midst of change. The contrast between perishable humanity and the enduring reality of Yahweh is a confession deriving from Israel's hymnology (Ps. 103:14–18); the special emphasis on Yahweh's word as that aspect of his reality that encounters people derives unmistakably from earlier prophetic experience. In its own history Israel learned by experience that it was not the policies of its kings and their armies that made history, but the word of Yahweh proclaimed by the pre-exilic prophets. The word of Yahweh plays the same role in the Deuteronomistic History.

Isaiah 55:12–13 describes the joyous exodus of Israel (from exile), amid the rejoicing of nature, as a consequence of the divine word. The same event is represented in the initial words of 40:3–5 as something overheard by the prophet from the heavenly realm: "There is a voice that cries: Prepare a road for Yahweh through the wilderness, clear a highway across the desert for our God." There follows a description of how the glory of Yahweh will be revealed on this road, created by the leveling of mountains and valleys, so that all creation shall see it. Other oracles fill out the details of the event that is only outlined here. Isaiah 40:9–11 depicts Yahweh as a careful shepherd, arriving with his spoil (an image with overtones of the victorious general): he carries the lambs in his bosom and cautiously leads the ewes. In other passages depicting this event we can recognize the notion of the great processions of the gods, with which the exiles were vividly familiar from their environment, especially in the context of the great Babylonian New Year's festival. It is associated with the idea of the march through the desert separating Babylonia from the Israelite homeland. The event of a new exodus is depicted throughout, far surpassing the exodus from Egypt.

Here Deutero-Isaiah incorporates the message of Ezekiel 20:32ff., which in turn had its prototype in Hosea's expectation of a new period in the desert followed by a new entrance into Canaan (Hos. 2:16–17). But what Ezekiel had described in prosaic narrative style is celebrated by Deutero-Isaiah in joyous poetic vignettes like individual snapshots. That these events are antitypes of the events that took place during the first period in the desert, as already suggested in Ezekiel 20:36, is fully emphasized. Isaiah 43:16ff. underlines the superiority of the "new" (antitype) to the "old" (type). This superiority is not meant to be interpreted in a polemical or didactic sense, as though Israel were being cut off from its ancient history with Yahweh and being confronted with something totally new (von Rad). The equation with the exodus is meant rather to maintain the link between the new history and the old, however superior the glory of the new may be, thus expressing the faithfulness of Yahweh, who remains true to his cause.

Other features, too, reappear enhanced. Israel shall not go forth "in urgent haste" (חִפָּזוֹן *ḥippāzôn*) as before (cf. Exod. 12:11; Deut. 16:3). Just as the pillar of fire of God's presence protected the people then, so now Yahweh will go before Israel and be their rearguard (52:12). In the desert, Israel will not only find water running from the rock to slake their thirst (48:21; cf. Exod. 17:5–6; Num. 20:7ff.), but will see the barren desert itself transformed. There will be pools of water, and trees will grow there to give shade. All of this, however, takes place because of Zion, the great goal of the new exodus. There the watchmen and messengers of joy are already proclaiming the kingship of Yahweh with rejoicing, so that the very ruins of Jerusalem break forth in exultation and all the ends of the earth see the salvation of the God of Israel. But the ruins are not the last word. Zion will be rebuilt in all its glory (54:11–12). Jerusalem, barren and desolate, will behold in amazement how the ingathering of the Diaspora (43:5–6) gives her so many children that there is no longer room for them in her tent (54:1–3). The reproach of widowhood is taken away from her, "for your husband is your maker, whose name is Yahweh of hosts." (54:4–6) This is the comfort of Israel, which Deutero-Isaiah is fond of formulating after the manner of a priestly oracle of favor (for example, 41:8–13; Begrich). "Comfort, comfort my people" is also the cry heard by the prophet in the heavenly assembly, with which the collection of his oracles begins (40:1–2).

The prophet uses the term "redeem" (גָּאַל *g'l*) to describe this action on the part of Yahweh. The expression derives from clan law, where it refers to the repurchase of someone who has been sold into slavery for debt. For a discussion of its use in the law of blood vengeance, see the treatment of Job 19:25 on p. 164 above. The term expresses both the initial tie between Yahweh and his people and the subsequent enthrallment of Israel by alien powers, from which Yahweh now "redeems" his people. In the context of this imagery it is possible to speak of the huge ransom that Yahweh is prepared to pay for his people (43:3–4). Objectively, what is meant is the breaking of the power of Babylon, which is holding Israel captive. In chapter 47 this event is announced in a vivid oracle against Babylon. But the image of redemption also implies a reference to the "debt" that brought Israel into servitude and has now been paid. It might be possible to misread 40:2 as suggesting that Israel had freed itself of this "debt" by its own power, but 43:22–28 makes it unmistakably clear that Deutero-Isaiah, like Ezekiel and the earlier writing prophets, knows that Israel cannot point to any righteousness of its own to justify its release: it is a free act of Yahweh's sovereign grace that redeems Israel and bestows a new future. Deutero-Isaiah adopts the cultic polemic of the pre-exilic writing prophets for his own purposes, stating that Israel did not really weary itself by calling on Yahweh and offering sacrifice, but did indeed burden Yahweh by its actions: "You burdened me with your sins and wearied me with your iniquities." Like Hosea before him,

Deutero-Isaiah refers to the patriarch Jacob as the prototype of sinners: "Your first father transgressed, your spokesmen rebelled against me . . . so I sent Jacob to his doom and left Israel to execration." Now, however, Yahweh's countervailing action is announced; once more we hear the sovereign insistence on the first person singular: "I alone, I am He, who for his own sake wipes out your transgressions, who will remember your sins no more." Cf. also the repeated "for my own honor" in 48:11 (למעני למעני *ḥma'ănî ḥma'ănî*), which corresponds to the "not for your sake" of Ezekiel 36:22 (למענכם לא *lō' ḥma'ankem*). The exultant announcement of imminent deliverance also permits no doubt that it derives solely from the gracious decision of the God of Israel, quite apart from any merit on the part of Israel. Calling Jacob "chosen" and Abraham the "friend" of Yahweh (41:8) cannot obscure the fact that, although Israel has eyes and ears, it is a blind and deaf people with respect to Yahweh. The echo of Isaiah 6:9–10 in 43:8 (cf. 42:18) cannot be missed.

The message of Deutero-Isaiah initially appears to focus on the eschatological miracle of the new exodus, which transforms the desert. Then, however, it becomes strangely historicized. *Pace* Begrich, it is probably incorrect to speak of a "disappointment" that led the prophet to despair of his great expectations. Instead, what we have here is a repetition of what we have already seen in Isaiah's concentrating of his proclamation of the Day of Yahweh into a warning about the Assyrians and Jeremiah's changing of his vague early reference to the foe from the north into specific talk of Babylonia. Deutero-Isaiah's proclamation of the new exodus, derived from Ezekiel, takes on concrete form in his reference to Cyrus, the king of Persia, whom Yahweh employs as an instrument of deliverance.

The coming of Cyrus is spoken of in various contexts. The most audacious is an oracle in which Yahweh addresses Cyrus directly; in its introductory formula, Cyrus is referred to as the "anointed" of Yahweh, for whom Yahweh will open every gate (45:1–7). In this oracle, Cyrus is promised Yahweh's aid in his battles. Yahweh will do this for the sake of Israel his chosen, "that men from the rising and the setting sun may know that there is none but I: I am Yahweh, there is no other." In 44:24–28 we find a great hymnic self-predication in which Yahweh, using the participles typical of hymnic style, depicts himself as creator of the universe and the Lord of history, who frustrates the signs of the (Babylonian) false prophets but fulfills his own servants' prophecies, who makes Cyrus the instrument of his purpose and causes Jerusalem to be rebuilt. Without mentioning Cyrus by name, 48:12–15 refers in the context of divine self-glorification to the "friend of Yahweh" who will wreak Yahweh's will on Babylon. The image of Cyrus as a bird of prey in 46:11 probably derives, like 41:2–3, from his rapid victories over the Medes and over Croesus of Lydia, which amazed the contemporary world. He can also be alluded to without being mentioned by name in disputations and forensic oracles that are more polemic in tone. The prophet may have composed 46:9–13 in answer to protests from the ranks of his own people, who found the unorthodox message of Cyrus as the "anointed" unseemly. The forensic discourses in 41:1–5 and 41:21–29, on the contrary, are clearly aimed at the gods of the Gentile world, especially in the Babylonian environment of the exiles. Faced with the insistent question as to which of them is able to determine history by predicting its course, they are shown to be powerless. Here, as in Ezekiel, Yahweh's action in history, illuminated and predicted by his word, is cited as the actual proof that Yahweh alone is God.

Yahweh's mighty demonstrations of his power and his glory in all that takes place are the concerns of this prophet, who draws so extensively on the language and ideas of hymns in framing his message. As already mentioned in §4, the praise of the creator is all-embracing. "I make (יצר *yṣr*) the light, I create(ברא *br'*) darkness; I effect (עשה *'śh*) prosperity, I create (ברא *br'*) trouble. I, Yahweh, do (עשה *'śh*) all these things." (45:7) Deutero-Isaiah goes beyond Genesis 1, including darkness and trouble totally within the power of the creator. But creation is universal in time as well, embracing all of history. The creation (ברא *br'*) of the ends of the earth (40:28), the constellations (40:26), and human beings (45:12), the fashioning of Israel (43:1) in the past are as much the work of the creator as the deliverance of the imminent future (45:8), which pours forth like the rain of the heavens and blossoms like flowers. The collection of oracles extolling the majesty of the creator (40:12ff.), whose position near the beginning of the collection as a whole is undoubtedly deliberate, also contains mocking polemic against the image worship of the author's Babylonian surroundings. Although here, too, considerable material has been added by later hands (e. g. in 44:9–20), the polemic against the Gentile gods and their images is part of the genuine message of Deutero-Isaiah, which triumphantly glorifies the first and second commandments of the Decalogue. Knowledge of the truth expressed in these two commandments becomes in Deutero-Isaiah an element of comfort for deported Israel, groaning under the oppression of the splendid array of Babylonian gods and saying, "My way is hidden from Yahweh, and my cause has passed out of God's notice." (40:27) "Yahweh has forsaken me, the Lord has forgotten me." (49:14)

Yahweh counters this despair with his gracious "I, I": "I am Yahweh, I myself, and none but I can deliver." (43:11) According to 54:10, Yahweh's actions include the assurance that even though the mountains and hills may shake, Yahweh's favor and covenant will not depart from Israel. What is happening to Israel is likened to what happened after the great Deluge, the "waters of Noah." Then Yahweh swore (P speaks of a "covenant"; see above, p. 174) that "the waters of Noah" would never again cover the earth; now, after the period of wrath, we hear Yahweh's oath that his favor is absolute and enduring (54:9). Unlike Jeremiah 31:31ff. and the corresponding passages in Ezekiel, there is no mention here of a new covenant; the prophet speaks instead of the constancy of the old covenant, which seemed to have been abrogated when "for a moment" Yahweh deserted Israel and hid his face from them (54:7–8). Now, however, the old covenant is confirmed by the "new thing" that Yahweh promises to do now that the old is past.

We have already noted passages in some of Deutero-Isaiah's oracles where he addressed the Gentile world around him as the realm in which the people will come to know Yahweh through his redemption of Israel. A few similar passages were already met with in Ezekiel. In Deutero-Isaiah, however, such statements constitute a whole new theme, of incomparably greater importance. It is true that we still hear some statements to the effect that the Gentile nations will come to Israel as servants—for example, when the Diaspora returns (49:22–23). But a new note is sounded in 45:14. When the nations come to Israel as tributaries, they confess: "Surely God is among you and there is no other, no other god." In 45:18–25 the prophet uses a broad canvas to depict how, impressed by the God who speaks and acts in history, the "survivors of the nations" and the "ends of the earth" are summoned to share with Israel in God's salvation. In this context we hear Yahweh's oath, which is borrowed by the christological hymn in Philippians 2:10–11: "By myself I have sworn, from my mouth righteousness [=salvation] has issued, a promise that will not be broken: to me every knee shall bend and by me every tongue shall swear." It is a strange phenomenon: during the period of the exile, at the very time when Yahweh is hidden far from the eyes of Israel (Perlitt), when 45:15 states, "Truly, you are a hidden God, O God of Israel, the deliverer," proselytes from the "nations" approach Israel, defeated but still bearing witness to so mighty a Lord, that they may confess in a new way, "I belong to Yahweh" and have the name of Yahweh tattooed on their hands as a sign that they belong to him. That this actually took place is attested by Zechariah 8:20–23; Isaiah 56:1–8. In 44:1–5, it is promised to Israel as a blessing. It seems that we have here a final extension of the patriarchal blessing in Genesis 12:2–3 to the Gentile world. In this process Israel plays a special role: its duty is to be a witness. According to the forensic discourse in 43:8–12, this "blind and deaf people" is to be a "witness" for Yahweh. None of Israel's own actions, not even its acts of devotion, make it a witness, but only the fact that it has experienced in its own history the hand of Yahweh acting by virtue of his own free grace and "bears witness" to this experience. Through this witness ("you are my witnesses whether there is any god beside me"; 44:8) Israel will completely fulfill its destiny as the chosen servant of Yahweh (43:10) in the Gentile world. This idea is expressed most audaciously in 55:1–5, where the promise to David is also extended to the entire nation—possible after Cyrus has been given the title of "Yahweh's anointed." There is no promise of any royal messiah in Deutero-Isaiah. David, who ruled over an empire that included alien nations, is reinterpreted in 55:4 as a "witness for the nations" in his reign (the ancient title נגיד nāgîd reappears here). Through him the power of Yahweh is made known to the nations. According to Deutero-Isaiah, the "promises to David" (cf. Ps. 89:50) mean that all Israel is now to become Yahweh's witness, so that nations hitherto unknown will come running to Israel because of the Holy One of Israel, a designation of Yahweh that links Deutero-Isaiah with Isaiah in a way that is traditio-historically obscure.

We may note with surprise that, in contrast to earlier prophecy, the oracles of Deutero-Isaiah contain no exhortations to social justice. Only in 44:21–22 and 55:6–7 do we find an exhortation to Israel and to the wicked, calling on them to return to Yahweh. Both admonitions stand totally within the light of Yahweh's great act of deliverance, proclamation of which is the real office and function of this "evangelist." "I will sweep away your sins like a dissolving mist, and disperse your transgressions like clouds; turn back to me, for I have ransomed you."

We have not yet discussed one component of Isaiah 40—55, which is probably the most controverted portion of the Old Testament: the so-called Servant Songs, first defined by Duhm as comprising Isaiah 42:1–4; 49:1–6; 50:4–9; 52:13—53:12. They speak of a "servant of Yahweh" (עֶבֶד יהוה *ebed yahweh*) who receives a commission far transcending Israel and is brought to suffering and death by his obedience, but is acknowledged anew by Yahweh as his servant.

The interpretation of these passages is beset by a host of problems. Duhm proposed that the four passages just mentioned should be eliminated from Deutero-Isaiah as an independent element. Mowinckel sought to support this argument by pointing out that these passages interrupt the series of catchwords that can be observed elsewhere in Deutero-Isaiah. This theory, however, has not gone uncontested. The question has also been raised whether 42:5–9; 49:7, 8–13; 50:10–11 must not likewise be viewed in the context of the Servant Songs—sections that in part closely resemble the oracles of Deutero-Isaiah in language and thought.

Even more important are the problems associated with the content of these passages. In the "servant of Yahweh" are we to see Israel, as in 41:8ff., for example? This identification is stated explicitly in 49:3. In 42:1, the LXX inserts "Israel," thus attesting an ancient tradition pointing toward this interpretation. In this case, the songs that speak of an individual servant should be interpreted in the sense of a "corporate personality" (Robinson), just as Ezekiel 16 and 23, for instance, refer to the national community under the figure of an individual. But this interpretation runs up against a major difficulty: in 49:5–6, the servant is quite unmistakably entrusted with a mission to Israel at the outset, which is later expanded. Thus the servant cannot be identical with Israel. An interpretation that would find a contrast here between an ideal Israel and the real Israel finds no textual support.

The interpretation that finds an individual in the figure of the servant is compelled to treat the "Israel" of 49:3 as an early gloss after the fashion of the LXX addition to 42:1. This interpretation itself has two variants, depending on whether the "servant" is seen as a royal or as a prophetic figure. The decision in favor of a royal figure has suggested the introduction of ideas associated with the divine king and the ritual of the suffering king. In the actual texts, it might seem that the royal office is spoken of most clearly in 42:1–4, which describes the establishment of justice throughout the world. But the hypothesis of a royal ideology common to the entire ancient Near East, in which the king also represents a royal penitent, has been increasingly challenged in recent years. Furthermore, the preparation of the servant's mouth (49:2) as well as the training of his tongue and ear (50:4–5) are more suggestive of a prophetic function. The existence of an ancient tradition supporting this interpretation is attested by 61:1–3, the introduction to which refers back unmistakably to 42:1, and whose "sending" terminology suggests a prophetic figure. The unmistakable connection with the confessions of Jeremiah also points in this direction. This observation has led some scholars to ask whether the description of the "servant" does not actually describe the very office and function of the evangelist Deutero-Isaiah himself (Mowinckel, 1921; Begrich). It must be acknowledged, however, that at least the final great section 52:13—53:12 far transcends any specific individual fate, and speaks in ultimate terms of a figure larger than life.

The earliest phase in the story of the servant is found in 49:1–6, where the servant himself, in the form of a proclamation addressed to the entire world, tells how Yahweh called him from the moment of his birth and trained his mouth. The echo of Jeremiah 1:5, 9 cannot be missed. The following lament of the servant over the failure of his ministry and the fruitlessness of his efforts recalls the confessions of Jeremiah. In particular, the servant's report of Yahweh's response to his lament recalls the response in Jeremiah 12:5–6, where the prophet's burden, far from being lightened, is to be increased. In 49:5–6 we hear the response of Yahweh, who had formed his servant in the womb for his service "to bring Jacob back to him": "It is too slight a task for you, as my servant, to restore the tribes of Jacob, to bring back the descendants of Israel: I will make you a light to the nations, to be my salvation to earth's farthest bounds." It has been suggested that we find here in the original commission given to the servant a description of precisely what Deutero-Isaiah did in his preaching. If 49:8–13 is to be included in this unit, we have an even clearer reference to the proclamation of the new exodus. This commission to proclaim salvation is now extended to a commission that is to encompass the entire world of the Gentile nations.

This extended commission is presupposed in 42:1–4, where Yahweh himself introduces his servant, upon whom he has bestowed his spirit. It has been suggested (Begrich) that the images of crying aloud in the open streets, of the bruised reed and the smoldering wick, derive from specific legal symbols. However this may be, it is clear that in any case the servant is entrusted with a striking message of mercy and of restraint before the bar of judgment (a flame that is almost extinguished, a staff already broken). It is probably against this background that we should understand the מִשְׁפָּט mišpāṭ, "justice" (used here in a rare absolute construction), that the servant is called on to establish throughout the world. It is tempting to follow Begrich in seeing here the mercy that has just been shown quite concretely to Israel and is now to be established throughout the world as the way in which Yahweh acts. If we can include here the following unit (42:5–7 [8–9]), this ministry of the servant makes him the "mediator of the covenant for the nation" (also in 49:8; Stamm), echoing the ancient function of Moses. His extended commission then goes further, making him a "light to all peoples" (also in 49:6).

The symbols of salvation found in 42:3 are strikingly transferred to the servant himself in verse 4: "He will not be extinguished or broken." Here we have a remote suggestion of what is fully developed in the two final

Servant Songs. In 50:4–9, the servant himself tells how God trained his tongue and his ear for God's service. Does he have in mind Jeremiah 1:6–7 and Ezekiel 2:8 when he emphasizes explicitly that he was not rebellious (מרה *mrh*), but offered his back to the lash and did not turn away his face from spitting and insult? In words that Paul repeats in Romans 8:33, he confesses his trust in Yahweh, who will stand beside him to plead his cause against his enemies.

These statements culminate in the great passage 52:13—53:12. Yahweh's first-person words about his servant in 52:13–15 and 53:11*b*–12 constitute a frame surrounding 53:1–11*a*, a confessional description of the servant's fate from the mouth of a community that stands in awe before Yahweh's mystery. There is no room here for any biographical interpretation that would refer to Deutero-Isaiah himself or any other prophetic or royal figure from Israel's history; the passage speaks in terms of ultimates. There is no mention of Israel here. Those who benefit from the saving act depicted here are termed, with a generality that is both startling and vague, the "many" (רבים *rabbîm;* 53:11, 12*b* [also 52:14–15; 53:12*a* in a different sense]). In the framework passages Yahweh fully recognizes his servant, who, in an unprecedented event, is exalted from a terrifying and horrible debasement, thus receiving his reward for his submission to the very point of death. In 49:7 similar words from Yahweh were already heard concerning "one who thinks little of himself, whom every nation abhors, the slave of tyrants." The community confesses its initial total failure to understand the significance of the servant, whom they thought punished by God in his suffering, which caused everyone to despise him. Then, however, they realized that in all his suffering he bore the burden of their own sins: "The chastisement he bore is health for us and by his scourging we are healed." The image of the lamb led to slaughter from the confessions of Jeremiah (11:19) reappears in a new sense: it no longer represents hatred for the prophet's enemies but rather the willing submission of the servant. Confronted with this way that leads to death and disgraceful burial with the wicked, however, the community here acknowledges the certainty that Yahweh will recognize his suffering servant, will grant him life, a future, and promote his own cause through him.

Two sacrificial terms help us understand the function of the servant. In 53:10, we read that he gave his life as a "sacrifice for guilt" (אשם *ăšām*); cf. p. 150 above. And the entire process is illuminated by the phrase "bear guilt" (נשא עון *nāśā' 'āwōn*). According to Leviticus 10:17, the animal sacrificed as a sin-offering "bears" or "takes away" the guilt of the community. Above all, according to Leviticus 16:22, on the great Day of Atonement the scapegoat chased out into the desert to Azazel, upon which the guilt (and punishment) of the community is placed, bears away this guilt. Here, too, there is a striking point of contact with the prophet of the early exilic period, who lay sick for days bearing the guilt of Israel (Ezek. 4:4–8).

In the confessions of Jeremiah, which seem to "anticipate" remarkably the songs of the servant of Yahweh in Deutero-Isaiah, both in the way they have been interspersed by a redactor among the other oracles of the prophet and in their actual content, the suffering of God's messenger remains an unsolved enigma. Only the suggestion of participation in Yahweh's own suffering could make any sense of the prophet's agony. In the songs of the servant of Yahweh in Deutero-Isaiah, the riddle of the man who suffers even while fully acknowledged by Yahweh is explicated in terms of these two priestly categories. Yahweh himself affirms the suffering of his servant as "bearing the sin" of the "many."

In these Servant Songs the prophet's message once more reveals in maximum concentration the nature of the profound crisis involving Israel and the "many." Guilt bars the way to Yahweh for his own people and the "many." But the Servant Songs go on to show what the "justice" of Yahweh is in the light of this situation of Israel and the "many" before God. The surprising restraint before the bar of judgment spoken of in 42:1–4, the task of "restoring" and "bringing back" the tribes of Jacob and the preserved of Israel, the commission to be a "covenant mediator for the people"—these are the narrower tasks of the servant. To be a "light for the nations" and to bring the salvation of Yahweh to the ends of the earth is his broader task. The final song clearly associates this function with the servant's "bearing the sins of the many" in fulfillment of Yahweh's will.

In the merciful love that Yahweh, the God of Israel, shows to his shattered people he also seeks to have his salvation shine upon the Gentile nations and to have the sins of the "many" taken away through the agency of his servant. This purpose here receives its ultimate expression. It would not be wrong to state that in the preaching of the two exilic prophets, however their messages differ in detail, there is revealed most fully in the depths of Israel's crisis who Yahweh, the God of Israel, is. All the rest of what the Old Testament goes on to say afterwards represents an intensification of the crisis dimension (apocalypticism) or subsequent interpretation (as in Trito-Isaiah), but never surpasses the actual statement of what is said here.

2. In his edict of restitution, Cyrus decreed that the Temple be rebuilt. During the reign of Cambyses at the latest, sizable groups of exiles returned to Jerusalem from Mesopotamia. Immediately after this return, we find in Haggai and Zechariah another highly topical prophetic message. These two prophets address the community of repatriated exiles, entangled in the initial problems of reconstruction, calling on them to rebuild the Temple. This was the primary task commanded by Cyrus. In addition, in Ezekiel's description of the salvation to come the new Temple dominated the picture of the new

beginning. If this commandment is obeyed, Haggai promises an age of prosperity that will include the natural world and an influx of riches from the Gentiles, brought about by a cosmic catastrophe. In Zerubbabel, the commissar belonging to the house of David appointed by the Persian king, Haggai sees and proclaims the messianic ruler chosen anew by Yahweh's grace, who is to rule over the age to follow the imminent collapse of the world empires and their armies. In a series of what were originally seven night visions (1:7—6:8) Zechariah likewise sees the destruction of the world powers and the repopulation of Jerusalem, which Yahweh himself will protect as a wall of fire. Using the image of a lampstand flanked by two olive trees he introduces two figures anointed by Yahweh, the descendant of David and the high priest, who serve before Yahweh. He sees the wicked purged from the land, "godlessness," symbolized by the figure of a woman, carried off to Shinar, i. e. Babylonia. A concluding vision shows him how the horsemen who rode forth throughout the world in the initial vision, only to report that all was well, ride forth once more. He hears the cry that those going forth to the land of the north will "give rest" to the "spirit" of Yahweh there. It remains a point of controversy whether this refers to an outpouring of the spirit upon the exiles who are still in Babylon or upon the entire world, in particular the untamed land of the north, an ourpouring that brings rest (or, following Horst, a new universal Sabbath) to the world, or whether the word רוח *rûaḥ* should here be translated as "wrath," following the LXX, in which case it is God's judgment of wrath upon the godless land that is being proclaimed. An impressive eighth vision (3:1-7) has been interpolated as the fourth in the series. It depicts how the high priest Joshua, wearing filthy clothes, is accused by Satan, but is reinvested and clothed in new raiment by Yahweh. The office of high priest, which is the sole subject of this passage, is legitimated by the explicit promise of jurisdiction within the sanctuary and access to the divine presence. In certain passages of the individual sayings interpolated before, after, and in the midst of the visions, it may be that we hear echoes of Deutero-Isaiah's message, restated in terms of a later chance to return. As in Haggai, exalted promises are made to Zerubbabel, the descendant of David, who is given the messianic designation "branch" (צמח *ṣemaḥ;* 3:8; 6:12), which derives from Jeremiah 23:5-6 (33:14-16). The symbolic action depicted in 6:9ff., the present text of which has been subject to editorial revision, describes how Zechariah sets out to make a crown for Zerubbabel out of contributions of silver and gold; after the hypothetical recall of Zerubbabel, the name of Joshua, the high priest, is substituted. The oracle of Zechariah in its original form resembled the vision of the lampstand in 4:1ff., describing the peaceful coexistence of the reigning descendant of David and the high priest. Here is foreshadowed the expectation of two messiahs that later achieved full development at Qumran.

3. Alongside this concrete messianic expectation in Haggai and Zechariah, the nucleus of so-called Trito-Isaiah (Isaiah 56—66), a collection that can hardly derive as a whole from a single hand, contains a non-messianic message that is clearly dependent on Deutero-Isaiah. The prophet, now obviously preaching back in the land, keeps alive the great expectation of salvation that will come to Jerusalem (especially chapter 60). The building of the Temple plays only a minor role—66:1-2 actually appears to polemicize against it. Alongside the passionate message of imminent salvation proclaimed to the humble and brokenhearted (in Luke 4:16ff., Jesus takes 61:1ff. as the text of his first messianic sermon at Nazareth), we find passages of equally passionate crying to Yahweh, imploring him to rend the heavens and cause his salvation to appear upon earth (63:15—64:11). In 57:14ff., Deutero-Isaiah's call to prepare the way for Yahweh is recast in the form of an admonition; chapter 58, for example, contains an entire torah dealing with the question of what kind of fasting is pleasing to God. When the loosing of unjust fetters, the setting free of those who have been crushed, the sharing of food with the hungry, and clothing the naked are commanded as the kind of fasting that is pleasing to God, the richest heritage of earlier prophecy is linked with the jubilant gospel of Deutero-Isaiah.

4. The element of rejoicing is largely absent in the anonymous book of Malachi. We find instead a remarkably dialectical argument containing, among other things, a violent attack on a priesthood that has grown disobedient and a renewal of the ancient prophetic message that Yahweh's day of judgment is imminent. In a concluding oracle, the returning prophet Elijah plays the role of harbinger of this judgment. This notion, too, becomes part of the New Testament message (Matt. 11:14; 16:14; 17:10-12, and elsewhere).

It is an unmistakable fact that the high prophecy that had plumbed the depths of the relationship between Yahweh and his people in its full profundity falls silent after the exile. In the period of Ezra and Nehemiah, the deuteronomic requirement of separation from everything pagan takes on particular significance in concrete obedience to the law, which Ezekiel had demanded in the context of proclaiming a great salvation for Israel. The specific instance is the dissolution of mixed marriages. At the same time, the priestly cultic legislation keeps alive the knowledge that Yahweh's community is always totally dependent on his atoning mercy. In the Chronicler's retelling of Israel's history from Saul to the exile and the edict of Cyrus, there emerges clearly Israel's faith in the kingship of Yahweh realized in the house of David.

In the apocalyptic movement, a late fruit of the prophetic sense of Israel's crisis, there arises yet another formulation of the message against the background of the entire world.

Baltzer, Dieter. *Ezechiel und Deuterojesaja.* Beihefte zur Zeitschrift für die Alttestamentliche Wissenschaft, vol. 121. Berlin: De Gruyter, 1971.—Begrich, Joachim. *Studien zu Deuterojesaja.* 1938. Reprint. 2d ed. Theologische Bücherei, vol. 20. Munich: Kaiser, 1969.—Zimmerli, Walther. "Der 'neue Exodus' in der Verkündigung der beiden grossen Exilspropheten." In *Maqqél shâqédh* (Festschrift Wilhelm Vischer), pp. 216–227. Montpellier: Causse Graille, Castelnau, 1960. Reprinted in his *Gottes Offenbarung*, 2d ed., pp. 192–204. Theologische Bücherei, vol. 19. Munich: Kaiser, 1969.—Idem. "Der Wahrheitserweis Jahwes nach der Botschaft der beiden Exilspropheten." In *Tradition und Situation* (Festschrift Artur Weiser), pp. 133–151. Edited by Ernst Würthwein and Otto Kaiser. Göttingen: Vandenhoeck & Ruprecht, 1963. Reprinted in his *Studien zur alttestamentlichen Theologie und Prophetie*, pp. 192–212. Theologische Bücherei, vol. 51. Munich: Kaiser, 1974.—Perlitt, Lothar. "Die Verborgenheit Gottes." In *Probleme biblischer Theologie* (Festschrift Gerhard von Rad), pp. 367–382. Edited by Hans Walter Wolff. Munich: Kaiser, 1971.—North, Christopher Richard. *The Suffering Servant in Deutero-Isaiah.* 2d ed. London: Oxford, 1963.—Zimmerli, Walther. "παῖς θεοῦ." In *Theologisches Wörterbuch zum Neuen Testament*, vol. 5, cols. 653–676. Edited by Gerhard Kittel and Gerhard Friedrich. Stuttgart: Kohlhammer, 1954. English: "παῖς θεοῦ." In *Theological Dictionary of the New Testament*, vol. 5, pp. 654–677. Translated by G. W. Bromiley. Grand Rapids, Mich.: Eerdmans, 1967.—Mowinckel, Sigmund Olaf. "Die Komposition des deuterojesajanischen Buches." *Zeitschrift für die Alttestamentliche Wissenschaft* 49 (1931):87–112, 242–260.—Robinson, Henry Wheeler. "The Hebrew Conception of Corporate Personality." In Internationale Tagung alttestamentlicher Forscher, Göttingen, 1935. *Werden und Wesen des Alten Testaments*, pp. 49–62. Edited by Paul Volz, Friedrich Stummer, and Johannes Hempel. Beihefte zur Zeitschrift für die Alttestamentliche Wissenschaft, vol. 66. Berlin: Töpelmann, 1936.—Kaiser, Otto. *Der Königliche Knecht.* 2d ed. Forschungen zur Religion und Literatur des Alten und Neuen Testaments, vol. 70. Göttingen: Vandenhoeck & Ruprecht, 1962.—Mowinckel, Sigmund Olaf. *Der Knecht Jahwäs.* Giessen: Töpelmann, 1921.—Stamm, Johann Jakob. "berît 'am bei Deuterojesaja." In *Probleme biblischer Theologie*, pp. 210–224. Edited by Hans Walter Wolff.—Zimmerli, Walther. "Zur Vorgeschichte von Jes. 53." In International Organization for the Study of the Old Testament. *Congress Volume, 1969*, pp. 236–244. Supplements to Vetus Testamentum, vol. 17. Leiden: Brill, 1969. Reprinted in his *Studien zur alttestamentlichen Theologie und Prophetie*, pp. 213–221. Theologische Bücherei, vol. 51. Munich: Kaiser, 1974.—Idem. "Zur Sprache Tritojesajas." In *Festschrift für Ludwig Köhler*, pp. 62–74. Bern: Büchler, 1950. Reprinted in his *Gottes Offenbarung*, 2d ed., pp. 217–233. Theologische Bücherei, vol. 19. Munich: Kaiser, 1969.—Michel, Diethelm. "Zur Eigenart Tritojesajas." *Theologia viatorum* 10 (1955/56):213–230. Cf. also the bibliographies to §§ 4, 10d, and 21b.

§22 Old Testament Apocalypticism

1. The message of the two exilic prophets shows Israel in its most profound crisis, revealing unmistakably the true nature of the people of Israel and their God. We find expressed with special intensity the fact that Israel lives through Yahweh's demonstration that he is a God of judgment and of mercy and through his faithfulness to the relationship revealed in historical encounter and described in his name: "Yahweh, the God of Israel." At the same time, however, we find hints in Ezekiel and direct statement in Deutero-Isaiah that the redeemer of Israel, as creator of the universe and all the nations upon earth, also claims sovereignty over the entire Gentile world and wishes to have his salvation known from the "ends of the earth." (Isa. 52:10)

In the phenomenon of apocalypticism, represented in fully developed form within the Old Testament by the book of Daniel, there is openly expressed the expectation of a final crisis engulfing the world, when God's sovereignty will be established through giving of kingly power to the "saints of the Most High" (7:27) and an eternal kingdom will be established by the "God of heaven." (2:44) The statements of the book of Daniel are in accord with the rest of the Old Testament in their central concern for the course of history in the Gentile world and within the people of God; the mysteries of nature and the heavenly regions have not yet taken on the significance they will acquire in postcanonical apocalyptic literature. The present discussion is concerned exclusively with Old Testament apocalypticism, without considering later changes.

Vielhauer has listed the following as the general characteristics of apocalyptic literature: apocalypses (there is no specific term for the genre in the Old Testament) usually circulate pseudonymously. The speaker is no longer a prophet appearing publicly and speaking in his own name with authority. This phenomenon is illustrated by the fact that the apocalyptic writer can receive his revelations while bent in study of the text of traditional "scripture," which has thus become a kind of "canon." Dreams and visionary experiences play an important role. Alongside the dreamer or visionary, we find the figure of the skilled interpreter, who may belong to either the human or heavenly realm. In the visionary's vision there is revealed the future course of history. A *vaticinium ex eventu* "predicting" events already past may constitute the more or less lengthy introduction to the intended message of the apocalyptist, which deals with his own contemporary world. In such protracted divine prophecy history appears as being long predetermined in God's plan. Now it unrolls as planned, so that calculation of its future course becomes an important element. As is clear in the book of Daniel, however, we are not dealing with general inquiry interested in calculating the course of history, but rather with a calculation looking forward to the end of the phase of history in which the apocalyptist is speaking. What matters is the "end," when the realized sovereignty of God will appear. Because this "end" marks the beginning of something qualitatively new, an element of dualism with respect to the world and its history can occur. Two qualitatively different ages, called "eons" following Greek terminology, are contrasted: the new eon replaces the old. It has already been mentioned that the perspective is worldwide. The apocalyptist thinks in universalistic terms. Since the old eon, in which the apocalyptist speaks, stands in sharp contrast to the new eon, which brings salvation, Vielhauer goes on to emphasize pessimism over the present world as an essential feature of apocalypticism.

2. It must not be overlooked that many of these elements find their prototypes in the prophecy of the preceding period and in the apocalyptic overtones present in the later redactional history of some of the prophetic books.

a) Ezekiel 38—39 announces the invasion of Gog, the chief prince of Meshech and Tubal (northern Asia Minor). He will come from the north with his armies to invade the land of Israel, which has just been resettled by Jews returning from the exile, but will perish mysteriously "upon the mountains of Israel." The birds of the air are summoned to a great sacrificial feast. In this prediction Jeremiah's message concerning the foe from the north, coupled with Isaiah's assurance that Assyria will meet defeat upon the mountains in the land of Yahweh, attains its final form. In a fashion that is unusual for the rest of Ezekiel's prophecy as well as for that of his predecessors, an event in the more distant future is predicted, to follow the return to the land, itself a future event for Ezekiel's contemporaries.

This takes place because an earlier prophetic oracle, which the author (Ezekiel?) considers not completely fulfilled, must be realized. This expectation that an unfulfilled divine promise must come to pass signals an important element in apocalypticism.

b) The visionary features already present in the earlier prophets take on much greater importance in Ezekiel and especially in Zechariah. The figure who leads the prophet through the temple that he sees in his vision (Ezek. 40ff.) and gives brief explanations (40:4 [45–46]; 41:4) is replaced in the night visions of Zechariah by an angelic interpreter who explains what is incomprehensible. In the night visions of Zechariah, Yahweh is no longer seen directly; at best, he is perceived indirectly in his words (1:13). The prophet's commission has become much more indirect in the night visions. Nothing of this appears in the logia that accompany the visions. It will also be noted that individual night visions can terminate in an open commission to preach (1:14) or with a divine oracle in the first person (2:9; 5:4; 6:8 [?]). Furthermore, with his night vision recorded in 4:1–6aα, 10aβ–14 as well as with the symbolic action described in 6:9–15 and individual logia the prophet intervenes quite concretely in his own contemporary history with a messianic proclamation addressed to his own age (analogous to Hag. 2:20–23). All these considerations suggest that it is inappropriate to follow Gese in calling the cycle of night visions the first Old Testament apocalypse (Chr. Jeremias).

c) The element of a crisis that engulfs the world is prefigured in the earlier descriptions of the Day of Yahweh. Daniel's phrase "time of the end," which he uses frequently to suggest the eschatological nature of the coming crisis, has its precursor in Amos's message that the "end" has come, as well as in Ezekiel 7 and other prophetic passages. The book of Joel, whose great theme is the Day of Yahweh, deserves particular mention in this context. The first half of the book (1:4—2:17) is devoted to a prophecy of disaster. Taking a plague of locusts as its point of departure, it proclaims the invasion of an army as a judgment upon Israel and calls for true repentance. But then in its second half (2:18—4:17) it turns to assurance of deliverance for Israel in a great act of judgment upon the nations in the "valley of Jehoshaphat." Cosmic convulsions characterize this day of judgment. In the outpouring of the spirit of Yahweh upon all flesh, the sons and daughters of Israel, the irruption of something totally new can be discerned. Joel derives much of his message from the earlier prophets. Ezekiel's prophecy is recalled in particular by the use of proof-saying terminology to describe what God is about to do as a proclamation of Yahweh in his special relationship with Israel: "You shall know that I am present in Israel, that I and no other am Yahweh your God." (2:27) "You shall know that I am Yahweh your God, dwelling in Zion my holy mountain." (4:17) Here we also meet the phrase "I, Yahweh" once more. With his call to repentance and his concrete assurance of salvation to Israel, Joel still belongs to the company of the prophets. But his announcement of the great judgment upon the nations and the eschatological outpouring of the spirit link him with apocalyptic thought.

d) The so-called Apocalypse of Isaiah (Isa. 24—27), which still presents unsolved problems of literary structure and origin, leads in a different manner into apocalyptic thought patterns. The description of the terrible Day of Yahweh, when the earth will be laid waste, follows a different course from that taken by Joel in depicting an event with two aspects. It has been suggested that the account of God's judgment, which concludes with the execution of his sentence (chapter 24), in a sense prefigures the juxtaposition of Daniel 10 and 11 in including in this judgment both the "host of heaven" and the "kings of the earth." The distinction of two stages can also be observed: the powers brought to judgment are first imprisoned in the depths, where "after many days" they receive their final punishment. In contrast to this judgment there stands on the other side great salvation. Echoing and transcending the initiating experience of

Israel as described in Exodus 24:9–11, "all nations" (does this refer to those that have been protected from the judgment or to a "remnant" delivered from the judgment?) are now invited to the "great universal feast of God's epiphany" (Plöger, p. 94) upon the mountain of God, where, according to 24:23, Yahweh has manifested his kingship "in glory" before his elders. I have the feeling that this extension of universal salvation to the nations echoes the message of Deutero-Isaiah. To the statement that when this happens Yahweh "will wipe away the tears from every face and remove the reproach of his people from the whole earth" another hand, probably later, has added: "he will swallow up death forever." (25:8*a*α) Even the primal curse of Genesis 3:19 (see above, p. 171) will be abolished in the future when the great final crisis has passed. In these statements the Apocalypse of Isaiah goes far beyond anything heard in Daniel.

e) Zechariah 12—14 appears to travel a similar course from a great judgment upon Jerusalem to the subsequent judgment of Yahweh upon the nations and their gathering to worship Yahweh (Lutz). More precisely, the events depicted in 12—14 repeat themselves. The attack of the nations on Jerusalem/Judah and its frustration are depicted in 12:1—13:6. The subsequent outpouring of the spirit focuses attention on the mysterious figure of a man "whom they have pierced (slain)" and ritual lamentation for him. Has Isaiah 53 influenced this description, whose specific reference still remains unknown? This internal change in the people is followed by an age of salvation characterized not only by the renunciation of idols but also by the firm rejection of all forms of ecstatic prophecy. A sword song (13:7-9) based entirely on quotations from Ezekiel, Isaiah, Jeremiah, and Hosea provides the transition to the second chain of events, which begins with the profound humiliation and affliction of Jerusalem. Then Yahweh appears upon the Mount of Olives, which is cleft asunder beneath his feet as he comes to the aid of Jerusalem. From this time on, the remnant of the nations that has been delivered from annihilation in battle will go up to Jerusalem every year for the Feast of Booths to worship the king, Yahweh of hosts. Here is fulfilled not only the kingship of Yahweh but also the uniqueness of Yahweh expressed in Deuteronomy 6:4 (Zech. 14:9).

Here, as in Joel and Isaiah 24—27, we can observe at every point how earlier Biblical passages are drawn upon. In the last analysis, this borrowing is not just a literary mannerism; it represents a profound motif—the burning desire that all the ancient promises be fulfilled.

3. After all these preliminary stages, we come in the book of Daniel to the full flowering of an apocalyptic message that exhibits the various elements characteristic of apocalypticism. It is surely more than mere accident that the book of Daniel received its final form in an age when the community was once more in the midst of a mortal crisis. The great prophets had already shown that times of crisis led to the outspoken disclosure of humanity's true situation before God.

During the Maccabean crisis, the apocalyptist took over the role played by the prophet during the crisis of the eighth through the sixth centuries. He cloaks his own person behind the pseudonym of Daniel, an exile of the Neo-Babylonian period not to be identified with the Daniel of Ezekiel 14:14, 20 and 28:3. Daniel 9 shows the apocalyptist bent in study over the text of the book of Jeremiah, whose prediction of seventy years of distress he does not understand. The angelic interpreter Gabriel then shows him that this refers to seventy weeks of years. Several visions seen in dreams trouble King Nebuchadnezzar (chapter 2) or Daniel himself (chapters 7—8); the wise interpreter Daniel unravels their meaning for the king, or an angelic interpreter explains their meaning to Daniel himself. Finally, in chapters 10—12, Daniel is given his instructions without any obscuring imagery in an encounter in broad daylight with a divine messenger whose description recalls the description of the beings in Ezekiel 1. In similar fashion, alongside the metaphorical discourses of Ezekiel 16 and 23, Ezekiel 20 presents an undisguised account of the history of Israel. In the case of the prophet, however, we see that he clearly reports past history as events that are past, whereas the restrospect of the apocalyptist appears in the guise of a vision of the future. This phenomenon can be observed most clearly in chapter 11, where he records the history of the Ptolemaic and Seleucid Empires with exceptional precision down to the year 167 (or possibly even 164), but then speaks of a third Egyptian campaign on the part of Antiochus Epiphanes and of the latter's death in a prediction that did not come to pass. The account of what is yet to come follows smoothly upon the narrative of past events, which is itself recounted in the future tense.

To structure the historical presentation, elements from elsewhere in the ancient world are drawn upon. Daniel 2 and 7, for example, use the schema of four ages attested with minor changes in Hesiod. It occurs in the Hindu doctrine of *kalpa* in the context of a cyclic theory of history and has been proposed as the basis for P's outline of history in the Old Testament (see above, p. 55). In Daniel it has been transformed into the notion of four kingdoms (Rowley) and associated, especially in Daniel 2, with the idea of the decreasing worth of the kingdoms. As in Hesiod, this latter idea is expressed by the decreasing value of the metals of which the statue seen in the dream is made. The accounts of ancient historians suggest that in the sequence Babylonians—Medes—Persians—Greeks the Assyrians were originally mentioned instead of the Babylonians. The first three elements of the schema probably take shape in the Medo-Persian sphere (Baumgartner). The use of animals to symbolize political entities (Dan. 7 and 8) finds a prototype in Ezekiel 19. In Daniel 8, this notion is linked with traditions of astral geography, according to which each land was assigned to one of the signs of the zodiac (Persia=Aries; Syria =Capricorn). The four monstrous animals rising out of the primal sea and wind have been associated with the mythological cosmogony familiar from Sanchuniaton by way of Eusebius and Philo Byblios (Eissfeldt). The description of at least the four beasts in Daniel 7 is probably influenced by familiarity with representations of hybrid creatures in Mesopotamia. The use of horns to symbolize political powers has a clear prototype in Zechariah 2:1–4, in Zechariah's night visions.

The term "ancient of days" found in Daniel 7:9, 13 has been associated with predicates of the Canaanite god El found at Ugarit. Undoubtedly the description of his appearance, as well as that of the awesome angel in Daniel, has been more than a little influenced by elements from the visions of Ezekiel. When we come to the figure resembling a "son of man" appearing with the clouds of heaven (Dan. 7:13–14), it is uncertain whether and to what extent we should consider analogies from elsewhere in the ancient Near East or merely the comparison to Ezekiel (1:26 alongside 2:1) (Colpe). The extensive development of angelology beyond what is found in Zechariah likewise raises the question of the extent to which foreign (Iranian?) influences are involved. Besides the angelic interpreter familiar from Zechariah, we find in Daniel 10 angels, likewise termed "princes" (שׂרים *śārîm*), assigned to the various nations: "the prince of the kingdom [or 'kings'] of Persia" (10:13 LXX), "the prince of Persia" (10:20) alongside the "prince of Greece (יון *yāwān*)." The notion of tutelary angels assigned to the various nations has an Old Testament prototype in Deuteronomy 32:8 (?; LXX). The juxtaposition of the "host of heaven" and the "kings of the earth" in Isaiah 24:21 is reflected in the juxtaposition of Daniel 10 and 11. The heavenly battle, hid from human eyes, among the angels of the nations, with Michael, "one of the chief princes," fighting especially on behalf of Israel (10:13, 21) finds its counterpart in the battle of the earthly kings, recounted in strictly historical terms in Daniel 11. These angelic figures embody the reality of "powers" transcending the realm of human actions.

The New Testament, too, can speak of angels and powers (Rom. 8:38). In the "Gabriel" of Daniel 8:16, one of the angelic interpreters is mentioned by name.

Within the framework of a "theology of the Old Testament," however, we must go beyond the individual outward features and historical background of apocalyptic ideology and inquire into the fundamental purpose of this strange form of discourse, and ask what it really has to say about the God of Israel and his dealings with his world and his people.

The book of Daniel is not homogeneous; it was put together out of existing material, probably with revisions and interpolations. Its author, who probably gave the book its present form during the period of persecution under Antiochus IV, took already extant material going back to the time of Alexander and possibly even to the Persian period and incorporated it into the legendary section of the first half of the book and probably also into chapter 7, revising it in chapters 2 and 7 from the perspective of his own age. The purpose of the present book of Daniel is therefore most clearly recognizable in chapters 8—12 and the revisions just mentioned. Here, veiled by the alienating cloak of a message that apparently looks to the far distant future, we hear the urgent question asked by the apocalyptist from the anguish of his own age. Confronted with the hiddenness of God, he does not ask, "Why this suffering?" but rather, "How long (עַד מָתַי 'ad mātai) will it be" until the terrors seen in the vision are past and the wonderful new age is present (8:13; 12:6)? The cry of the apocalyptist suffering agony because the sanctuary has been laid waste emerges with particular clarity in the great penitential prayer of Daniel 9, which some scholars have erroneously wished to set aside as a later addition. The cry "Make your face shine upon your desolate sanctuary . . . lend your ear and hear, open your eyes and look upon our desolation and upon the city that bears your name" (9:17–18) appears from the context to refer to the destruction of the city in 587, but in reality has in mind the desecration of the sanctuary in the year 168.

This "how long?" is more than the amorphous outcry of a sufferer screaming his agony. It is the cry of someone aware that a turning point has been promised. Daniel 9 shows how the apocalyptist pleads for elucidation of the words of Scripture and inquires after the hour when the seventy years of desolation predicted by Jeremiah (Jer. 25:11–12; 29:10) will be at an end. When the historical prediction in Daniel 11 states that the warrior king, alarmed by rumors (cf. Isa. 37:7), will set forth from conquered Egypt, pitch his pavilion "between the sea and the holy hill, the fairest of all hills [i. e., Zion]," and there perish with no one to help him (11:44–45), it is not hard to recognize the fulfillment of Isaiah's prophecy against the Assyrians together with its reflection in the defeat of Gog, according to which the enemy will perish "upon my mountains" (Isa. 14:25), "the mountains of Israel." (Ezek. 39:17) The "end" is the end determined long ago by God. Thus within the account of the wars in Daniel, which never strays outside the framework of secular history, we find repeated references to the time of the "end" determined by God but not yet reached (11:27, 35). The words of the angel to Daniel cite "the end of years" (11:6), "the end of times" (11:13), "the time of the end" (11:40). The message of Amos, referring in its original context to Israel alone, "The end has come" (8:2), taken up in Ezekiel 7 as the theme for a detailed description of the "Day of Yahweh," returns here extended so as to apply to the history of the "powers" throughout the entire world. The apocalyptist draws his knowledge of the coming "end" from the preaching of the earlier prophets.

But for Daniel, just as for the prototypes of apocalyptic preaching sketched above, the "end" also means a turning point, the beginning of a new age in which the will of God for his people and his world will be realized. The stone that shatters the statue representing the four empires (2:34) becomes a great rock filling the whole earth (2:35). The sovereignty that is taken in judgment from the four beasts, especially the defiant eleventh horn of the fourth beast, is to be given for all time to the "people of the saints of the Most High," represented in the vision by the figure of one resembling a son of man (7:13–14). According to 8:14, the sanctuary will emerge victorious (צִדְק *niṣdaq*). Two series of three formulas each are used in 9:24 to depict the end of the old era and the coming of the new: transgression will be finished, sin brought to an end, and iniquity atoned for; everlasting salvation (צֶדֶק *ṣedeq*) will be brought in, prophet and (prophetic) vision will be sealed, and the most holy place (i. e., the Temple) will be anointed (reconsecrated). In 12:1–3, however, the new event that takes place at the deliverance of the people, more specifically, "every one who is written in the book [of life]," transcends the possibilities of earthly life: "Many of those who sleep in the dust of the earth will wake, some to everlasting life, and some to the reproach of eternal abhorrence. The wise leaders (מַשְׂכִּלִים *maśkîlîm*) shall shine like the bright vault of heaven, and those who have guided the people in the true path shall be like the stars for ever and ever."

The catchwords "old" and "new" used by Deutero-Isaiah to contrast his message of incipient salvation with what was past (see above, p. 217) are not employed here. That the turning point will bring something totally new is, however, the unmistakable message of apocalyptic revelation. As 9:24 puts it, what is new is the "sealing of the prophetic vision." There is a reference in 11:14 to the "establishment [= fulfillment] of a [prophetic] vision" in events taking place just before the end, in the days of Antiochus III (223–187) and Ptolemy V Epiphanes (203–181), although it is unclear what prophecy is referred to.

The first triad of statements in 8:25 might be taken as meaning that when the old gives way to the new only the injustice and wickedness caused by the warrior king will be removed. That this reading does not take account of the full import of these statements is shown by the fact that the period just before the turning point can be referred to twice in brief as a "(time of) wrath" (זַעַם za'am; 8:19; 11:36). This refers to the wrath of God against God's own people. This element cannot be missed in 9:4–19, the prayer of Daniel, which is in content a single great confession of sin made by Daniel on behalf of his people. The time of wrath is brought about by the sin of Israel, for which atonement must be made in order that the new era may dawn (כפר עָוֹן kappēr 'āwôn; 9:24). Using a term borrowed from Isaiah 10:23 and 28:22, the apocalyptist maintains that both the present success of the blasphemous king (11:36) and his final defeat (9:26–27) are based on God's "decree."

This observation raises the question whether it is appropriate, in the Old Testament apocalypticism of Daniel, to speak of a dualism and the irruption of a new eon understood only as the antithesis of the old. The "old" that must pass away is not simply conceived as contrary to God's purpose and contrasted as a whole to the new that is coming. Under the old order, God gave to Nebuchadnezzar "kingdom and power and glory and majesty" (2:37; 5:18) and even delivered into his power the Davidic king and the vessels from the Temple (1:2). Here God's wrath blazes forth against the sins of his people. But here also prophets are endowed with vision to see the coming end of the old order, as in Jeremiah's prediction of the seventy years, revealed to the apocalyptist to mean weeks of years. All of this forbids any simple dualistic system of two eons.

The concrete "calculations" of the apocalyptist are also grounded in this earlier preaching. However one seeks to account chronologically for the seven and especially the subsequent sixty-two weeks of years (9:25), it is clear in any case that the half week during which the cult of Yahweh is inhibited at Jerusalem furnishes the concrete basis for calculating the week of years that leads up to the "end." (9:27) These are no superhistorical speculations, but specific calculations of the end on the basis of concrete history in the light of earlier prophetic promises (Hanhart). The calculation of a "time and times and half a time" (7:25) also rests on this same basis, the words of the prophets being interpreted with reference to specific disasters. The 2,300 evenings and mornings of 8:14 and the 1,290 (12:11) and 1,335 days (12:12) are probably calculated as minor extensions on the same basis. In these calculations the apocalyptist is not acting as a "historian" describing a series of historical events in which the narrow history of Israel and Nebuchadnezzar is followed by the universal history of the world empire and finally by the "eternal kingdom, in which the humanity of mankind will achieve its true reality" (Koch, 28). The apocalyptist is rather the man who, in the hour of deepest crisis, hears the prophetic promises and on the basis of them awaits the "Day of Yahweh" that is both an end point and a turning point.

In this context we can also consider the attitude of the apocalyptist to "wisdom," in which von Rad claimed to see the mother of apocalytpicism. Later apocalyptic speculation, after the close of the Maccabean period of persecution, when the blood of the martyrs flowed in the streets, incorporated in its description of the coming age of God a considerable amount of wisdom material concerning the world and the heavens; cf. for example the book of Enoch. It is also true that the problem of the right time for something plays an important role in Old Testament wisdom and then in Sirach. But this does not strike the real nerve of the apocalypticism that erupts in the age of persecution. Its fundamental focus is an awareness, alien to wisdom literature, of the imminent final crisis of the world and its powers as predicted by the prophets and a firm faith in their promises in the depths of despair. The question "how long?" is not primarily a question looking for general information on the sequence of the ages; it is the question of how God's "righteous (צדק *ṣedeq*) will" can be revealed in the history of the nations, based on faith in the prophetic word, which cannot prove false. This understanding also explains the משכלים *maśkîlîm,* frequently cited as star witnesses for the notion that wisdom was the schoolmistress of apocalypticism. In the prayer of Daniel (9:13), the verb השכיל *hiśkîl* means to heed the truth (אמת *'ĕmet*) of God; in 9:25 in particular it means to heed the "end" and the turning point promised in God's prophetic word. Daniel 11:33 speaks of the martyrdom of those who instructed many of the people in patient obedience; 11:35 indicates that even they did not escape being put to the test, but had to be refined in the fire. Of these "teachers" who guided many in the true path (מצדיקי הרבים *maṣdîqê harabbîm*), 12:3 goes on to say that after the great turning point they will shine like the stars of heaven. These men, from whose circle the apocalyptic instruction of the book of Daniel probably derives, call people's attention to the "end," thus proclaiming God's faithfulness in his word of promise, which they call on the people to obey. They have gone to school with the prophets, and their message is not that of worldly wisdom (von der Osten-Sacken).

We must also consider the actual content of what the apocalyptist says about the coming new era. The statement in Daniel 2, which may even antedate the crisis of the age of Alexander, provides no circumstantial details about the stone that destroys the statue representing the earth's kingdoms and then fills the whole world. We must be content with seeing in this stone something "not made by human hands." God's intervention shapes the new era after the end of the world's empires. During the period of oppression under the Maccabees, the most urgent aspect in the fulfillment of God's promise becomes God's new affirmation of his desecrated sanctuary, which once more "emerges victorious" (נצדק *niṣdaq;* 8:14) when the Most Holy Place is once more "anointed [= consecrated]." (9:24) Daniel 7:27 goes on to say explicitly that "the people of the saints of the Most High" will be given "kingly power and sovereignty and the greatness of all the kingdoms under heaven." *Pace* Noth and following Hanhart, it is this "yes" of God to his people that is probably meant when they are referred to briefly as "the saints of the Most High" (7:18, 22, 25). It may appear surprising that nothing more is made of this "sovereignty," which, unlike the earthly kingdoms represented in the form of beasts, is represented by "one like a son of man" appearing in the clouds. It is obviously meant to be sufficient that in this transfer of sovereignty to the people of God, the God of heaven, whose sovereignty is glorified in quite similar terms in the first half of the book (4:31; 6:27), emerges victorious in his merciful love for his earthly people. Whether the representation of the "saints of the Most High" through one "like a son of man" is meant to have messianic overtones beyond the meaning just described remains in doubt. The interpretation of the vision does not say a single word along these lines. It is certainly impossible to miss the antithesis of a figure like a human being above and figures of beasts below.

But the final revelation in Daniel 10—12 does not return to what has been said of the "saints of the Most High." Instead, 12:2 speaks of the awakening of many who sleep in the dust of the earth. There is no suggestion here of any general resurrection of the dead. It does not go as far as Isaiah 25:8, which speaks of the elimination of death. What we are dealing with here is a partial victory over the power of death. Breaching the fate of death was already suggested in Job 19:25 (see p. 164) and Psalm 73:24 (p. 165) as an audaciously grasped boundary possibility. In both passages a devout individual on the verge of despair clung quite personally to the promise he had received from Yahweh. During the persecutions under Antiochus IV, on the contrary, it was the life of the community that was at risk. Martyrs remained faithful to the death (Dan. 11:32*b*, 33; 2 Macc. 6:18—7:41); those who were faithless betrayed the covenant (11:32*a*). Over them all the will of God to maintain his covenant endures—over the faithful, who will be awakened to eternal life, and over the faithless, unable to escape God even in death, who will be awakened to eternal abhorrence. Daniel 12:1-3 does not look beyond this concrete situation of the time of persecution. The unprecedented statement is not developed in detail in either direction; it is not generalized to be a universal principle. It can be clearly seen in both Daniel 7—9 and in Daniel 12 that the apocalyptist is not moving toward a universalism that would make meaningless the election of his people, who received their promise and their law in the covenant (ברית *bĕrît;* 9:4, 27[unclear]; 11:22, 28, 30, 32). The abolition of the sovereignty of the nations, even though some are granted a limited lifetime (without sovereignty) (7:12), makes room for the sovereignty of the people of God, in whom God's will achieves its purpose.

This brings us to the question of what God requires in the view of the apocalyptist. If the interpretation of apocaltypticism as determinism were correct, there would be no place for free obedience. Now we have unquestionably seen that by the book's own statement all the events of the coming age, the succession of empires and the coming wars of the kings, even the coming apostasy and the obedience of the faithful have been predicted by divine revelation. The "end" has been "determined" to the point of chronological calculation (9:26–27; 11:36). To conclude, however, that this fact leaves people with nothing more than the possibility of mute waiting for what is to come would be to misunderstand what Daniel is saying. It is probably not by accident that side by side with the apocalyptic passages we find the legends depicting the faithfulness of Daniel and his friends (chapters 3 and 6) and the introduction, which describes how Daniel obeys the dietary laws of Israel even at the foreign court. It would also be a misunderstanding of the faithfulness and apostasy mentioned in 11:32–33 if the element of responsible decision for or against faithfulness were eliminated. How else could one understand the testing and refining mentioned in 11:34? With all his faith in the firm governance of history by God, who, faithful to the prophetic vision already proclaimed (9:24b), has determined the time of the "end" and the events leading up to it, the apocalyptist calls for concrete obedience to the instructions given the people of God, and extols those who can patiently await the determined end (12:12). No knowledge of the divinely determined chronology can invalidate this appeal. The range of specific instructions for those actually living under the oppression of foreign hegemony may have shrunk drastically in comparison to the instructions given to a politically independent Israel in the law and the prophets; obedience may be able to express itself only in a resistance that is prepared to suffer; but the call for this obedience is as loud as ever. For the apocalyptist, too, God's gift and God's commandment constitute an indissoluble whole.

Schmidt, Johann Michael. *Die jüdische Apokalyptik: Die Geschichte ihrer Erforschung von den Anfängen bis zu den Textfunden von Qumran* (with bibliography). Neukirchen: Neukirchener Verlag, 1969.—Vielhauer, Philipp. "Die Apokalyptik." In *Neutestamentliche Apokryphen,* vol. 2, pp. 408–421. Edited by Edgar Hennecke and Wilhelm Schneemelcher. Tübingen: Mohr, 1964. English: "Apocalyptic." in *New Testament Apocrypha,* vol. 2, pp. 581–600. Edited by Edgar Hennecke and Wilhelm Schneemelcher. Translated by A. J. B. Higgins. Translation edited by R. McL. Wilson. Philadelphia: Westminster, 1963.—Plöger, Otto. *Theokratie und Eschatologie.* 3d ed. Wissenschaftliche Monographien zum Alten und Neuen Testament, vol. 2. Neukirchen: Neukirchener Verlag, 1968. English: *Theocracy and Eschatology.* Translated by S. Rudman. Richmond: John Knox, 1968.—Gese, Hartmut. "Anfang und Ende der Apokalyptik, dargestellt am Sacharjabuch." *Zeitschrift für Theologie und Kirche* 70 (1973):20–49. Reprinted in his *Vom Sinai zum Zion.* Beiträge zur evangelischen Theologie, vol. 64. Munich: Kaiser, 1974.—Jeremias, Christian. *Die Nachtgesichte des Sacharja: Untersuchungen zu ihrer Stellung im Zusammenhang der Visionsberichte im Alten Testament und zu ihrem Bildmaterial.* Forschungen zur Religion und Literatur des Alten und Neuen Testaments, vol. 117. Göttingen: Vandenhoeck & Ruprecht, 1977.—Lutz, Hanns-Martin. *Jahwe, Jerusalem und die Völker: zur Vorgeschichte von Sach 12,1–8 und*

14,1-4. Wissenschaftliche Monographien zum Alten und Neuen Testament, vol. 27. Neukir chen: Neukirchener Verlag, 1968.—Rowley, Harold Henry. *The Relevance of Apocalyptic.* 3d ed. New York: Association, 1964.—Russell, David Sime. *The Method and Message of Jewish Apocalyptic.* The Old Testament Library. Philadelphia: Westminster, 1964.—Baumgartner, Walter. "Zu den vier Reichen von Daniel." *Theologische Zeitschrift* 1 (1945): 17-22.—Rowley, Harold Henry. *Darius the Mede and the Four World Empires in the Book of Daniel.* 1935. Reprint. Cardiff: University of Wales Press, 1959.—Eissfeldt, Otto. *Taautos und Sanchunjaton.* Sitzungsberichte der Deutschen Akademie der Wissenschaften zu Berlin; Klasse für Sprachen, Literatur und Kunst, 1952, no. 1. Berlin: Akademie-Verlag, 1952. See especially pp. 37-38.—Colpe, C. " ὁ υἱὸς τοῦ ἀνθρώπου ." In *Theologisches Wörterbuch zum Neuen Testament,* vol. 8, cols. 403-481, especially 408-425. Edited by Gerhard Kittel and Gerhard Friedrich. Stuttgart: Kohlhammer, 1969. English: " ὁ υἱὸς τοῦ ἀνθρώπου." In *Theological Dictionary of the New Testament,* vol. 8, pp. 400-477, esp. 406-423. Translated by G. W. Bromiley. Grand Rapids, Mich.: Eerdmans, 1972.—Hanhart, Robert. "Kriterien geschichtlicher Wahrheit in der Makkabäerzeit." In his *Drei Studien zum Judentum,* pp. 7-22. Theologische Existenz heute, new series, vol. 140. Munich: Kaiser, 1967.—Koch, Klaus. "Spätisraelitisches Geschichtsdenken am Beispiel des Buches Daniel." *Historische Zeitschrift* 193/1 (1961):1-32.—Von Rad, Gerhard. *Weisheit in Israel.* Neukirchen: Neukirchener Verlag, 1970. English: *Wisdom in Israel.* Nashville: Abingdon, 1972. See especially the excursus: "The Divine Determination of Times," pp. 263-283, continuing the section on Daniel and apocalyptic in his *Old Testament Theology,* vol. 2.—Von der Osten-Sacken, Peter. *Die Apokalyptik in ihrem Verhältnis zu Prophetie und Weisheit.* Theologische Existenz heute, new series vol. 157. Munich: Kaiser, 1969.—Noth, Martin. "Die Heiligen des Höchsten." In *Interpretationes ad Vetus Testamentum pertinentes* (Festschrift Sigmund Mowinckel), pp. 146-161. Edited by Arvid Kapelrud. Oslo: Land og Kirke, 1955. Reprinted in his *Gesammelte Studien zum Alten Testament,* pp. 274-290. Theologische Bücherei, vol. 6. Munich: Kaiser, 1957. English: "The Holy Ones of the Most High." In his *The Laws in the Pentateuch and Other Studies,* pp. 215-228. Translated by D. R. Ap-Thomas. Edinburgh: Oliver & Boyd, 1966.—Hanhart, Robert. "Die Heiligen des Höchsten." In *Hebräische Wortforschung* (Festschrift Walter Baumgartner), pp. 90-101. Supplements to Vetus Testamentum, vol. 16. Leiden: Brill, 1967.

§23 The Openness of the Old Testament Message

Our presentation of "Old Testament theology" has been based on the fact that Israel, whose canonical scriptures are preserved in the Old Testament, has always been aware of being the "people of Yahweh." This awareness pervades the words of the Old Testament from the early mention of the "troops of Yahweh" in the Song of Deborah (Judg. 5:11, 13) to the late talk of the "people of the saints of the Most High" in Daniel 7:27. At the same time, Israel knows its God as the free Lord, not chosen by Israel, who has freely made himself Israel's God and has proved himself to be Israel's Lord through his guidance in history. In the course of time it became increasingly clear that such guidance through the ages not only could be described in retrospect but could also be looked forward to in hope. Prophecy had focused its attention primarily on Israel; apocalypticism finally expanded its horizon to include the entire world of the nations as the context within which Israel's destiny would be fulfilled.

Even though the Old Testament later had its limits fixed as the canon comprising the "law and the prophets," it remains a book with an open message in that it looks forward to further guidance by the "shepherd of Israel." With all its obscurities and enigmas that cannot be explained, the message cannot be considered final. "Yahwism and future expectation" (Preuss) consequently go hand in hand.

But prophecy teaches us to see the openness of the Old Testament in a more profound sense. Our discussion has attempted to make it clear that Yahweh's "instruction" created a profound internal tension for Israel. On the one hand, this instruction took concrete form in Yahweh's gracious guidance, his protection against enemies in time of trouble, his blessings, proceeding especially from the place of his presence. It gave Israel deliverers and counselors, enabling Israel to see a divine charisma in their work. At the same time, however, it also took the form of a demanding law, expecting Israel's assent and obedience and threatening disobedience with death. The great prophets accompanied Israel along a road that ultimately led to the depths of judgment.

All this was revealed not only through intellectual reflection on God and his people, but through the events of a historical process that were accompanied by the message of the prophetic word. The primal history of P used mythological material to raise the question, with respect to all humanity, whether God would have anything further to do with a world gone "violent." In like fashion, in the full concrete experience of the history that befell "the two houses of Israel" in the Assyrian and Neo-Babylonian periods, the words of the prophets raised the question that was incomparably more direct for Israel: did the "people of Yahweh" have any claim to life in the eyes of their God? In the context of these events Israel learned that the wrath of its God, who kept watch over his word as the "Holy One of Israel" and a "jealous" God, could become a mortal danger to Israel itself, and that the words of the prophets gave the lie to any boast of Israel's own claim to life or even any appeal to the promises made to the fathers (Ezek. 22:24), so that it lay before its enemies as Yahweh's people utterly destitute, naked, resembling dry bones in its death (Ezek. 37:1ff.).

But in the depths of this well-deserved death there was proclaimed to Israel the renewed favor of its God. This, too, was proclaimed not only in the words and promises of the prophets, but in a historical restoration that gave new life to Israel, albeit in a historically altered form, politically insignificant.

At this very point, however, there remained a great unrealized "excess" that insisted once more on expectation of a future of abundant fulfillment. It has been suggested that the great postexilic historical schemata exhibit a sense of this "excess." P makes his entire historical narrative lead up to the sacred worship in which Yahweh vouchsafes his total presence and the sacrificial system with the atoning ceremonies on the great Day of Atonement at the place where the glory of the divine radiance is present. The text of the narrative looks back to the initial events of the Mosaic period; but the account has also been read as the expression of an expectation of a great future. And when the Chronicler, in his retelling of the story of David and Solomon, speaks in such exalted terms of the promise to the house of David and describes the throne of the Davidic dynasty as the throne of the "kingship of Yahweh," we are once more dealing with an unmistakable "excess." The narrative of past events once more turns into a narrative that seeks to keep hope alive for something yet to come.

At the same time, we also find concrete efforts to keep the commandments of the law. We saw in Ezekiel how this attempt to live a life of obedience to the law was made under the aegis of the great expectation that Yahweh would perform an act of redemption on behalf of Israel. This hope cannot be sidetracked through postexilic observance of the commandments. The sense of "rejoicing in the law" (Kraus) that makes itself heard here probably still draws its vitality from these sources. But does this really settle the question of obedience to the law, in view of all that is still to be?

Throughout the documents of the Old Testament, the people of Yahweh are constantly depicted not only as a people awaiting beneficent guidance and deliverance from outward enemies, but as a people that in a deeper sense awaits its own "righteousness," the final end of God's wrath over Israel's sin and its concomitant salvation and redemption. We still hear this expectation in Daniel 9.

The Old Testament expression of this expectation cannot be reduced to a single formula. According to Hebrews 1:1, God "spoke in former times in fragmentary and varied fashion *(polymerôs kaì polytrópôs)* to the fathers." We can see in the Old Testament the excess implied in awaiting total righteousness, the "new covenant," the new heart, the true king of righteousness (Zech. 9:9–10), the true servant of God who bears the sin of many, the gift of the spirit of God to all the people. In all of this, in those very passages where the Old Testament is concerned with its central events, with true yearning for the presence of its God, and with concrete experience of the "righteousness of God," it remains in its message a book of expectation, a book that is open to the future.

Preuss, Horst Dietrich. *Jahweglaube und Zukunftserwartung.* Beiträge zur Wissenschaft vom Alten und Neuen Testament, 5th series, vol. 7. Stuttgart: Kohlhammer, 1968.—Zimmerli, Walther. "Die Bedeutung der grossen Schriftprophetie für das alttestamentliche Reden von Gott." In *Studies in the Religion of Ancient Israel,* pp. 48–64. Supplements to Vetus Testamentum, vol. 23. Leiden: Brill, 1972.—Kraus, Hans-Joachim. "Freude an Gottes Gesetz." *Evangelische Theologie* 10 (1950/51):337-351.

General Index

Index of Hebrew Words

Index of Bible Passages

Index